Sources of Industrial Leadership

Studies of Seven Industries

Edited by

DAVID C. MOWERY
University of California, Berkeley
RICHARD R. NELSON
Columbia University

658.514
S724

PUBLISHED BY THE PRESS SYNDICATE OF THE UNIVERSITY OF CAMBRIDGE
The Pitt Building, Trumpington Street, Cambridge, United Kingdom

CAMBRIDGE UNIVERSITY PRESS
The Edinburgh Building, Cambridge CB2 2RU, UK http://www.cup.cam.ac.uk
40 West 20th Street, New York, NY 10011-4211, USA http://www.cup.org
10 Stamford Road, Oakleigh, Melbourne 3166, Australia
Ruiz de Alarcón 13, 28014 Madrid, Spain

© David C. Mowery and Richard R. Nelson 1999

This book is in copyright. Subject to statutory exception
and to the provisions of relevant collective licensing agreements,
no reproduction of any part may take place without
the written permission of Cambridge University Press.

First published 1999

Printed in the United States of America

Typeface Times Roman 10/12 pt. *System* QuarkXPress [BTS]

A catalog record for this book is available from the British Library.

Library of Congress Cataloging-in-Publication Data

Sources of industrial leadership : studies of seven industries /
edited by David C. Mowery, Richard R. Nelson.

p. cm.

Nine original essays arising from a project supported by the
Center for Economic Policy Research at Stanford University . . . [et
al.].

Includes bibliographical references and index.

ISBN 0-521-64254-X. – ISBN 0-521-64520-4 (pbk.)

1. Technological innovations – Management. 2. Industries –
Technological innovations – Case studies. 3. Comparative advantage
(International trade) I. Mowery, David C. II. Nelson, Richard R.
HD45.S627 1999
658.5′ 14 – dc21 98–44552
CIP

ISBN 0 521 64254 X hardback
ISBN 0 521 64520 4 paperback

Contents

University Libraries
Carnegie Mellon University
Pittsburgh, PA 15213-3890

Acknowledgments

The planning for this research project began in 1992, and the first meeting of the group of chapter authors and other participants was held in January 1993 at Stanford University. Subsequent meetings took place in Milan, Italy; Cambridge, Massachusetts; and on Cape Cod, Massachusetts. The lengthy and intensive discussions at these meetings contributed immeasurably to the quality of the chapters published in this volume, and we are indebted to the participants in those meetings who did not contribute chapters: Giovanni Dosi, Martin Fransman, Peter Murmann, Steven Klepper, Sidney Winter, Keith Pavitt, Robert Merges, Ulrike Schaede, and David Teece. We are especially indebted to Professor Richard Rosenbloom of the Harvard Business School, who played a central role in the origins of this project and made major contributions throughout the discussions and meetings that produced this volume. Support for this project was provided by the Center for Economic Policy Research at Stanford University; the Institute for Management, Innovation and Organization at the Haas School of Business, U.C. Berkeley; IBM Italy; Columbia University; the Harvard Business School; the Alfred P. Sloan Foundation; the U.S. Air Force Office of Scientific Research; and the Andrew Mellon Foundation.

Contributors

Professor Ashish Arora
Heinz School of Public Policy and Management
Carnegie Mellon University

Professor Timothy Bresnahan
Economics Department
Stanford University

Professor Annetine Gelijns
International Center for Health Outcomes & Innovation Research
Columbia University

Professor Rebecca Henderson
Sloan School of Management
Massachusetts Institute of Technology

Dr. Ralph Landau
Center for Economic Policy Research
Stanford University

Professor Richard N. Langlois
Department of Economics
University of Connecticut

Professor Franco Malerba
University of Brescia and CESPRI
Bocconi University

Professor Roberto Mazzoleni
Department of Economics and Geography
Hofstra University

Professor David C. Mowery
Haas School of Business
University of California, Berkeley

Professor Richard R. Nelson
School of International & Public Affairs
Columbia University

Professor Luigi Orsenigo
Department of Economics
Bocconi University

Professor Gary Pisano
Harvard Business School
Harvard University

Professor Nathan Rosenberg
Economics Department
Stanford University

Dr. W. E. Steinmueller
Science Policy Research Unit
University of Sussex

CHAPTER 1

Introduction

DAVID C. MOWERY AND
RICHARD R. NELSON

I. Defining Industrial Leadership

This volume contains studies of the evolution of seven industries, exploring the development of each in the United States, Japan, and Western Europe. The industries are machine tools, organic chemical products, pharmaceutical biotechnology, medical devices, computers, semiconductors, and software. Each industry study compares the development of these industries in the different countries and considers the factors that explain cross-national and cross-industry differences. Together, we hope that these studies will shed light on the sources of industrial leadership, a concept we discuss next.

The choice of these seven industries was motivated by our concern to cover an array of diverse industries in which technological innovation plays an important role. Several of these industries, such as semiconductors and computers, trace their birth to the opening of a major new technology in the postwar period. Technological advance in some of these industries, particularly organic chemical products and semiconductors, has had profound impacts on the products and processes of a wide range of downstream industries. In turn, the technology employed in some of these industries, such as machine tools and computers, has been powerfully influenced by upstream innovation.

At one time or another in the history of virtually all of these industries, firms located in one country or a small number of countries developed superior product or process technologies, ways of organizing production, or marketing strategies that gave them significant advantages over firms based in other countries. The identity of leading firms sometimes changed, occasionally more than once, during the development of several of these industries. In some cases this shift in the locus of firm leadership involved a shift of leadership among different nations, but in others, shifts in firm leadership produced new leading firms of the same nationality as the old leaders. Each industry study attempts to identify the factors that led to the emergence of national leadership, and the reasons behind the shifts that occurred.

We have adopted the term *industrial leadership* to denote our focus on industries in which being ahead of one's competitors in product or process technology, or in production and marketing, gives firms an advantage in world markets. As such, we are concerned with the translation of technological expertise into commercial success, rather than solely with technological innovation per se.

We prefer this term, rather than "comparative advantage," because industrial leadership explicitly denotes performance in industries where technological sophistication and innovative performance are key factors. Other analyses of business history and strategy use the term *competitive advantage* for this purpose, but most of these studies focus on factors internal to the firm. The term *industrial leadership* prevents any presumption as to whether industrial leadership is determined by strengths that firms build for themselves, by their national environment, or by something in between (e.g., regional factors or institutions or other factors that are specific to an industry).

The industry studies in this volume have much in common with some earlier work in which cross-national differences in technology, management, and competitive performance in a particular industry have been the central focus (see, e.g., Beer, 1959, on dyestuffs, or Malerba, 1985, on semiconductors). Such studies often have explored national differences in competitive performance. But most of these previous studies focus on an individual industry or a small number of industries, and thus shed little light on differences in the sources of industrial leadership across industries and historical eras. This issue is the central concern of this volume.

We believe that this volume is unique in (1) considering the evolution of a number of technology-intensive industries in different countries and attempting to explain the factors behind national differences; (2) exploring a number of different explanations of the sources of industrial leadership; and (3) being open to the possibility, indeed the likelihood, that these explanations differ from industry to industry and from era to era.

The approach taken in these studies would seem a useful one for addressing questions of interest to scholars, managers, and policymakers. Examples of such questions include the following:

1 How secure is the U.S. lead in computers or biotechnology?
2 Can Western Europe catch up to the United States and Japan in electronics?
3 Does Japan need to strengthen significantly her university research system in order to keep at the forefront of electronics, or to catch up in pharmaceuticals?

4 What role does competition policy play in the development and maintenance of industrial leadership?

In addition to their intrinsic interest, these kinds of questions are at the heart of debates over strategic trade policy and active industrial policy. We believe that the issues in this debate need clarification and hope that detailed studies of the factors behind the patterns of industrial leadership of the sort we present here can contribute to such a clarification.

II. Summaries of the Industry Studies

Each of the industry histories is a complex story. In this section, we briefly summarize each industry study. Rather than attempting to summarize the detailed analysis of subsequent chapters, we wish here simply to convey an idea of the phenomena addressed in each study.

Firms specializing in the design, production, and sale of machine tools began to emerge in the first decades of the 19th century. Through the middle of the 19th century, British firms were in the forefront of machine tool technology. After that time, the rise of mass production in the United States contributed to the emergence of a significant American machine tool industry. By the early 20th century, U.S. firms had moved into the position of leadership in the design and production of machine tools that they held through World War II. In the late 1950s and early 1960s, numerically controlled machine tools were introduced as a result of R&D programs originally sponsored by the U.S. Department of Defense. By the mid-1970s, numerical control had become standard in a wide range of machine tool types, and Japanese companies had displaced U.S. firms as leaders in many parts of the industry. Our study focuses on the loss by U.S. firms of industrial leadership during the era of numerical control.

British firms also dominated the production of chemicals during the first half of the 19th century, during which the industry relied on craft experience rather than formal science. Dramatic advances in scientific understanding during the last half of the 19th century, however, made it possible to design and produce dyestuffs and, later, synthetic fibers and pharmaceuticals. By the end of the 19th century, German and Swiss firms were the leaders in the organic chemical products industry, leaving British firms far behind. During the period between World Wars I and II, American firms developed significant capabilities in organic chemical products, based on their exploitation of an entirely new feedstock – petroleum. Their development of petroleum-based processes for the production of organic chemical products enabled American firms to establish a strong position in global production and innovation after World War II, one that was shared with firms in Germany and Great Britain. The 1970s and 1980s saw the erosion of American leadership and the spread of the industry to many corners of the world.

German and Swiss producers of fine chemicals (notably, dyestuffs) moved into pharmaceuticals in the late 19th century and largely dominated this industry until the 1930s. Following World War II, American pharmaceuticals firms, none of whom was based in the chemicals industry, and some British firms (including the leading British chemicals firm) joined the German and Swiss as leading innovators and exporters. The chapter on this industry focuses on the effects of new biotechnology-based techniques for drug discovery, development, and production on both incumbent and new pharmaceuticals firms. These new techniques challenged the drug development practices of established pharmaceuticals firms in the United States, Great Britain, Japan, and other Western European nations.

The medical diagnostic devices industry traces its origins to the early 20th century and the development of X-ray imaging technologies. Our study of this industry deals mainly with the period after World War II and concentrates on electronics-based diagnostic medical devices. The study reveals that American, European, and Japanese firms are strong in different parts of the industry. Companies' reputations for producing high-quality equipment, their mastery of complex marketing and regulatory environments, and their connections with the relevant user communities became more important during this period.

The computer industry, the semiconductor industry, and the software industry all were born after World War II and grew up together. American firms soon came to dominate all three industries. By 1980, however, Japanese firms had become strong competitors in portions of the semiconductor industry (i.e., dynamic random-access memories [DRAMs]). Since the late 1980s, however, Japanese firms have been challenged by South Korean firms in these product areas, and U.S. firms have exploited long-standing strengths in product innovation to reestablish dominance of the overall semiconductor industry. Japanese and Taiwanese computer firms also have developed considerable strength in certain niches, such as laptop computers and computer components. Nevertheless, American firms retain a leading position in most types of computers. And throughout the history of the computer software industry, American firms have dominated global markets in packaged software.

III. Perspectives on the Sources of Industrial Leadership

Explaining these different patterns of industrial leadership was the central challenge taken on by the authors of the industry chapters. Although previous research does not adequately come to grips with many of the issues addressed here, this work does provide some relevant arguments and empirical findings. In particular, this earlier work identifies a set of questions, in the form of alternative propositions, that were prominent in all of the industry studies.

The broad questions that guided our work and discussion can be divided roughly into four groups. One was concerned with the factors behind industrial leadership. A second explored the locus of leadership, be it the nation-state, individual firms, or intermediate structures, such as the region or industry-specific institutions. A third set of questions was concerned with the dynamics of industrial leadership and the evolution of industry structure. Finally there were questions about the roles of public policy in the establishment and maintenance of national industrial strength. In our later discussion of these questions, we note supportive empirical evidence from the following chapters, but more detailed discussion of these issues is found in the individual industry studies and in our concluding chapter.

A. Critical Factors Behind Industrial Leadership

Resources. From the beginnings of modern economic analysis, economists have seen the sources of comparative advantage as residing, at least in part, in differences across countries in the availability of the inputs needed in different lines of economic activity. Economists such as David Ricardo, writing in an era when agriculture dominated economic activity, stressed such matters as climate and land quality. As manufacturing became increasingly important, analysis of the sources of comparative advantage shifted to focus on the quality and price of inputs into manufacturing. Both British and Continental economists understood that the skills of its domestic labor force helped explain British dominance of many areas of manufacturing in the mid-19th century. A number of economic historians have identified the availability of university-trained research chemists as an important factor in German firms' ascendancy in dyestuffs in the late 19th century (see, e.g., Beer, 1959).

The general theoretical propositions put forth by economists about the contributions of differences in broadly defined factor endowments (such as the prices of "capital" and "labor") to comparative advantage require considerable refinement to explain the development of the industries covered in this volume. Factor endowments do appear to be important in many of these industries, but these endowments typically include factors (e.g., abundant deposits of petroleum, chemical engineers, public expenditures on industry-specific R&D) that are highly specific to individual industries. In particular, industry-specific labor skills play a major role in the shifting locus of industrial leadership in a number of our cases.

Institutions. Although the quality and prices of factors of production always have been a part of the economists' theory of industrial leadership, institutions also have played a role. The availability in Germany of university-trained chemists rested on a domestic university system that by the middle of the 19th century was the world's strongest in the training of physical scientists. Recent explanations for the rise of Japanese firms in the production of automobiles and consumer electronics have stressed firm organization, interfirm linkages, and Japanese labor and financial institutions (Aoki, 1990; Womack et al., 1991). The U.S. domestic venture capital industry undoubtedly has contributed to U.S. leadership in semiconductors, computer software, and pharmaceutical biotechnology.

As these examples indicate, the distinctions between analyses of industrial leadership that focus on resource endowments and analyses that focus on national institutional differences are blurry and often reflect different perspectives on the same phenomena. Thus the factors singled out in the "resource-based" analyses, such as an abundant supply of highly skilled labor or risk capital, are identified in the institutional discussions as effective universities or financial systems.

Markets. Much of the institutional analysis is concerned with the characteristics of national or regional markets for inputs and outputs. A considerable body of work argues that suppliers and their customers within a nation, region, or some other form of network tend to work with each other and thereby strengthen their capabilities.

Some of this work (Porter, 1990; Lundvall, 1992) argues that intensive interaction with demanding, knowledgeable customers and users improves the innovative and competitive performance of their suppliers. Another important factor in the development of industries characterized by high fixed costs (e.g., high R&D costs) is the scale of domestic market demand, which may enable producers to achieve lower unit costs and thereby provide an "export platform" (see, e.g., Krugman, 1987). This phenomenon has been cited in analyses of postwar Japanese protection of domestic markets for semiconductors or computers and forms the basis for criticism of the postwar policies in many Western European nations that favored domestic "national champions" in such areas as defense and telecommunications.

The influence of international differences in the profile of market demand on industry evolution is highlighted by our cross-industry, cross-national framework. Virtually all accounts of the rise to dominance of the American semiconductor and computer industries, for example, emphasize the procurement and R&D policies of the U.S. Department of Defense. As we noted earlier, the particularities of national markets had a profound effect on the development of machine tools in different countries. The inventive efforts of medical device producers in some cases were influenced by the diseases prominent in the producers' countries. Our industry chapters detail these and many other examples.

Technology. Simple Heckscher–Ohlin trade theory assumes that technology is the same in all firms in all countries, but empirically oriented economists long have understood that firms and national complexes of firms differ in their access to and command over technology. Product cycle theory (Vernon, 1966; Posner, 1961) postulates that firms focus their innovative efforts on products that meet the profile of consumer demand in their domestic market. Trade theory also stresses the advantages to "first movers" in the commercialization of technological advances, in part because of the nonconvexities produced by high fixed costs.

Given the nature of the industries in our study, it is hardly surprising that differences in the technological capabilities of firms and national groups of firms figure prominently. But in explaining industrial leadership, differences in technology may be hard to distinguish from differences in resource availabilities (such as highly trained research workers), or institutions (a strong university system), or a domestic market for advanced products that is largely closed to foreign imports.

B. The Locus of Industrial Leadership

As we noted earlier, the industries included in this study display considerable variation in the locus of industrial leadership and differ in the frequency of shifts in such leadership. In this section, we consider alternative explanations for the persistence of industrial leadership at the level of the firm, the nation-state, or some intermediate unit of analysis (e.g., the region).

The Nation-State. Economists traditionally have viewed comparative advantage as defined by features of the nation-state. Thus, Ricardo focused on major differences in soil and climate between England and Portugal. Most theories that focus on institutional differences presume that such differences are international, not intranational or regional in scope. Both product cycle theory, which we will consider shortly, and the new trade theory see the technological possibilities available to firms as essentially defined by their national environment. "Reserved markets," i.e., domestic markets that are protected against foreign competition by tariff or nontariff barriers, are another example of a national, rather than a firm-level, influence.

Most theories of national comparative advantage assume that the discretionary behavior of firms or differences among national firms in their competitive or technological capabilities account for little. Given national factor availabilities and institutions, firms that are in the right industry succeed, and firms that are in the wrong industry do poorly or fail. As we note later, this assumption often but not always is belied by history.

Firms. These presumptions, of course, contrast with the view that the principal determinants of competitive performance are the firm's strategy and structure, to use Alfred Chandler's (1962) terms, which are based on investments in R&D, production, marketing, and management (see Teece, 1993). In the simplest and starkest version of the firm-based explanation, differences in national conditions, be they factor availabilities or institutions, disappear from view. Thus, the Womack et al. study (1991) of the automotive industry emphasizes firm-level differences, and the authors argue that American firms could attain the performance of Japanese firms by emulating their product-development, manufacturing, and labor policies.

More complex versions of this theory incorporate factors external to the firm, blending national and firm-level influences into their explanation. For example, Chandler (1990) recognizes that the large scale of the American market during the late 19th and early 20th centuries meant that U.S. firms operated in a domestic market that differed fundamentally from that faced by British firms. Scholars like Aoki (1990) stress that broader Japanese institutions – especially those associated with finance and employment – sustain and support the particular managerial and organizational characteristics of Japanese firms. Nevertheless, all of these authors argue that there is considerable room for discretionary behavior of firm managers, whose decisions influence competitive performance and, ultimately, industrial leadership.

Regions, Networks, and Sectoral Support Systems. Still other theories identify the locus of industrial advantage in structures that are larger than the individual firm, but smaller than the nation-state. Alfred Marshall (1948, originally published 1890) identified the complex of institutional structures associated with the "industrial district" as an important factor behind British preeminence in textiles. The industrial district of Marshall, Krugman (1991), Harrison (1992), Piore and Sabel (1984), or Saxenian (1994) includes a collection of firms that compete with each other for customers, but that also cooperate in certain ways, for example, in establishing standards and in collectively supporting institutions that train specialized labor. The district also contains firms that provide specialized or custom inputs and machinery, as well as those providing various financial and brokerage functions.

Most "industrial district" theories argue that a region defines a network, but networks do not always require geographical proximity. For example, the widespread links between 19th-century German chemical companies and German university chemists often connected a professor with his former students – no regional connection necessarily existed. Similarly, important links between university researchers and U.S. biotechnology firms are not always regionally focused (Audretsch and Stephan, 1996). The connections, rather than geographical proximity, are the focus of attention in various studies of the alliances between new biotechnology firms and established pharmaceutical companies that have been involved in R&D and commercialization of several new pharmaceuticals (see Powell et al., 1996). The networks of firm connections that extend from Stanford and MIT include not only firms in Silicon Valley in California, and on Route 128 near Boston, but also firms in Europe and Japan.

We argue that these networks, whether regional or not, influence the emergence of what we call sectoral innovation systems. In addition to the firms in the industry, and their suppliers and customers, such sectoral innovation systems often include the following: specialized labor markets and training institutions; specialized financial intermediaries; professional and industry associations; close links with certain university departments and schools; specialized regulatory structures and other bodies of law tailored to the industry; and government support programs. These sectoral innovation systems differ across industries, but also frequently are very different from country to country for a given sector (see Carlsson, 1989; 1997).

Government policy has influenced the development of many of these industries through its support (intentional or otherwise) for the creation and growth of sectoral innovation systems, structures that include industry-specific networks of institutions, regulatory policies, and R&D infrastructure. The R&D and procurement programs of the U.S. Defense Department contributed powerfully to the entry of new firms into the semiconductor industry, the growth of university–industry research linkages in the computer and electronics industries, and the creation of the academic discipline of computer science. The extramural research support of the U.S. National Institutes of Health helped create competitive firms and strengthened links between academic and industrial researchers in biotechnology. Japan's Ministry of International Trade and Industry provided support of a rather different sort, which incorporated lower levels of public R&D spending, for Japanese firms in the electronics and computer industries.

In view of the globalization and the significant cross-border flows of technological knowledge that are apparent in several of the industries analyzed in this volume, the continuing importance of national or sectoral innovation systems may surprise some readers. Yet these industry studies strongly support the continuing importance of such systems, without denying the realities of increased international interdependence in virtually all of these industries.

C. Dynamics

Although economists often express their theories of comparative advantage in static terms, many of the key variables in those theories, such as resources, institutions, or technologies, change over time. A number of theories examine changes in the nature of a technology, in firm and industry structure, and in supporting institutions as a technology matures. These theories in turn yield several different views of the dynamics of industrial leadership that are germane to our industry studies.

Technology Life Cycle Theory. One group of theories suggest a systematic pattern of change in a technology, an industry, or both as the technology evolves from novelty to maturity. Abernathy and Utterback (1978) are the names most frequently associated with the theory that states that the early days of a technology are characterized by many competing variants. As technological progress proceeds, however, a dominant design emerges, and the focus of technological effort shifts from product design to production process, and production becomes increasingly capital and scale intensive.

Mueller and Tilton (1969) and more recently Klepper and Grady (1990), Utterback (1994), and Klepper (1996) argue that the maturation of a technology is associated with changes in industry structure. When the technology is young and in flux, both entry and exit of firms are high. The maturation of the technology is associated with increasing capital intensity in the industry's production technology, raising entry barriers, increasing average firm size, and producing an oligopolistic industry structure. Some of these accounts argue that increased industry concentration is associated with the rise of a dominant design; others (e.g., Klepper, 1996) do not assert such a link.

Few of these scholars concern themselves with the evolution of firms' vertical and horizontal structure as a technology and an industry mature. In one of the few systematic efforts to address this phenomenon, Stigler (1951) proposed that increases in the size of the industry and in the scale of its markets would result in higher levels of firm-level specialization, with specialty input and equipment firms supplying inputs that formerly were produced in-house. But Chandler argues that economies of scale and scope go together; manufacturing firms historically have broadened their product lines and absorbed a greater range of activities formerly conducted though market channels as they mature. Langlois and Robertson (1995) recently have developed another theory of the determinants of vertical integration, which focuses on whether systems designers and producers develop their own components or buy these on the market. They propose that rapid innovation by independent component suppliers may force systems producers to disintegrate vertically.

One can find some elements consistent with each of these theories in virtually all of our industry histories. But no single pattern fits all of our cases, and there are elements in all of the histories that fit none of these theories. There are two major reasons for the lack of closer correspondence between these industry histories and this group of theories. First, most of these theories are applicable to a narrowly defined product line or market segment, rather than to the broad industries examined in this volume, most of which are populated by firms producing a wide range of products and serving many different types of markets. In addition, the theories discussed focus on a single "life cycle" that is specific to a given product or technology. But all of the industry studies in this volume examine multiple technological generations over longer periods of historical development.

Punctuated Equilibrium. Another recent body of work is concerned with what happens when the technologies or markets that have been the basis for an industry change significantly, a development that happened at least once in all of our industry histories (see, e.g., Tushman and Anderson, 1986; Henderson and Clark, 1990; Christensen and

Rosenbloom, 1994). These analyses argue that firms that were strong in the earlier regime have considerable difficulty in adapting to the new, often fail, and are replaced by new firms.

There are instances of such episodes in a number of our studies, and they occasionally change the locus of industrial leadership. But our studies also cite instances in which established firms hung on in the face of significant changes in the underlying technologies. Indeed, the creative destruction of established firms and their replacement with new ones seem to be largely American phenomena; they have occurred less frequently in postwar Europe and Japan in these industries.

The Dynamics of Comparative Advantage. Two broad theories consider the interaction of technological and industry dynamics in the changing locus of comparative advantage. The two theories point in different directions.

What has come to be called the new trade theory (Krugman, 1987) stresses dynamic increasing returns in terms reminiscent of the analysis of Klepper and other scholars. This theory suggests that successful early entrants into an industry may establish an advantage that latecomers are unable to offset. These "first-mover" advantages are rooted in fixed investments or a head start down a learning curve and are specific to an industry or a firm.

A second group of theories of dynamic comparative advantage predate the Abernathy–Utterback analysis of technology life cycles. This body of theory, developed initially by Posner (1961), Vernon (1966), and Hufbauer (1966), argues that high-income countries generally pioneer in new technology, particularly new product technology, for two reasons. One is that these countries tend to be rich in scientists and engineers, and that abundance supports higher levels of industry R&D investment and a comparative advantage in "new technologies." High-income domestic markets also tend to demand higher-quality goods, forcing firms headquartered in these nations to innovate. New products created for the home market find markets abroad.

In Posner–Vernon product cycle theory, however, few "first-mover advantages" endure for the firms in the high-income economies. Outflows of technology through foreign investment and other channels erode the competitive advantages of firms in the (formerly) high-income "home" economy; this process is especially important in products for which technological change has assumed an incremental character and rate. As a product technology matures, comparative advantage relies more heavily on low factor costs. For these specific products, lower-wage economies may become more competitive production sites.

Elements of both of these theories of dynamic comparative advantage are supported by the chapters in this volume, although neither conceptual framework in its entirety fits the facts of all of our industries. First-mover advantages, based on firm-specific, industry-specific, or national institutional factors, are important in many of these industries and often endure for surprisingly lengthy periods. At the same time, however, cross-national interactions among firms within a single industry contribute to the erosion of these advantages at the firm or industry level. The "product cycle" models developed by Vernon and Posner, despite their rejection in recent years (by Vernon, among others, in 1979), direct one's attention to an important source of industrial leadership, the interactions between domestic firms and their users. Nevertheless, the focus of both sets of theories on products, rather than industries, limits their relevance to the focus of this volume. Moreover, neither theoretical framework treats adequately the interaction of industrial and institutional factors in supporting or undermining industrial leadership.

IV. The Roles of Government Policies

To a considerable extent the debate about industrial policy proceeds as if the issues and the arguments are new. In fact, today's debate sounds much like an echo of many earlier ones.

Modern economic thought traces its roots to debates about industrial policy. Adam Smith's *Wealth of Nations* argued the merits of the "invisible hand" and attacked the mercantilist philosophy that portrayed trade as a zero-sum game, in which one nation benefited at the expense of others. Although the mercantilists advocated subsidies for domestic industries and restrictions on imports or the export of bullion, Smith cast doubt on the ability and the incentives of public officials to plan and direct economic life. At the same time, however, Smith recognized a significant if selective role for government in providing the necessary economic infrastructure (for example, Smith was a strong supporter of the 18th-century British Navigation Acts, because of the support they provided for an important "dual-use" technology, British shipbuilding and naval strength – see Earle, 1995).

Smith's arguments, or an oversimplified version of them, gained a following in Great Britain, and later in the United States, but they did not completely carry the day. In the late 18th century, the United States was still a backward country in manufacturing, relative to the United Kingdom, and Alexander Hamilton's *Report on Manufactures* argued for significant public support through the aggressive building of infrastructure and tariff protection. In the middle of the 19th century, Frederick List argued that Germany could hope to overcome Great Britain's large lead in manufacturing only through policies that involved large government investments in infrastructure, and protection. Although Japan was hindered by treaty from overtly protecting its manufacturing industry, the Japanese government played a significant role in encouraging and supporting the development of certain key manufacturing industries in the days after the Meiji Restoration, and after World War I it had a major role in inducing the development of heavy industry in Japan. The post–World War II Japanese resurgence, from the early 1950s to the early 1970s, occurred in an environment of widespread protection of domestic industry. More recently, South Korean heavy manufacturing firms have grown up in a protected domestic market.

Throughout the post–World War II period, Western Europe has been divided on the merits of an active industrial policy. By and large France has supported active industrial policies. British governments were mildly activist through much of the postwar period, and the relatively conservative stance on these matters of the Blair government is a legacy of the Thatcher government that came to power in 1980. The German government has been relatively conservative in its industrial policies. Within Western Europe as a whole, however, a number of regional programs have been launched by the European Commission to help European "high-tech" industries.

Until the end of World War II, the U.S. position on government help for industry was mixed. With the notable exception of the 19th-century railroads and agriculture, direct subsidies were rarely politically feasible. On the other hand, certain industries, like aviation, received disguised subsidies. Investing in public infrastructure was politically popular at the state and federal levels of government. The massive growth of postwar federal support for university research has clear antecedents in earlier decisions to support the establishment of land grant universities, to subsidize indirectly the development of the railroads, to invest in canals, and to support aviation. And until after World War II the United States scarcely was a staunch advocate of free trade.

During the 1980s, a new debate over industrial policy in the United States was triggered by change in the economic environment. A number of events contributed to this new debate, including slower economic growth after the early 1970s, the achievement by European nations and Japan of levels of productivity and technological sophistication very close to those of the United States, and, especially, the surge of Japanese competition in automobiles and electronics after the late 1970s. The renewed economic vigor of the U.S. economy since 1993 has tempered this debate, but many of the protagonists and issues continue to figure prominently in policy discussions. Moreover, the broad language of this debate is uncannily reminiscent of the debate between Adam Smith and the mercantilists over two hundred years ago.

The American debate about active industrial policy since 1980 seems in many ways different from earlier domestic debates on this topic, perhaps because it developed in the aftermath of a quarter century during which American firms dominated major fields of manufacturing to such an extent that the question of targeted government support never arose. During this period, few citizens, policymakers, or scholars analyzed the lengthy historical record detailing the extent and nature of previous U.S. industrial support policies, lending a certain lack of realism to the proponents of extensive intervention or complete laissez-faire.

This recent U.S. debate has been quite polarized. Contemporary advocates of government support for particular "strategic" industries argue that this support will help these industries gain an advantage on world markets, or, if that is not possible, at least to preserve a strong industry at home. Many of these analysts argue that overall economic and political strength is enhanced by industry-level competitive strength in areas where technological advance is rapid, and that there are major dangers in letting the nation become dependent upon foreigners for the products of these industries.

The most vociferous critics of this view argue that comparative advantage grows naturally out of a nation's base of resources and institutions, and that governments are best advised to avoid activist or "targeted" policies of support. In their view, such policies are largely doomed to frustration, or if "successful" will have a considerable net economic cost. These skeptics note that governments are in a poor position to outperform private markets in the identification of profitable economic or technological opportunities. They also argue that if one nation pursues such policies, others will follow, making all of the world's consumers worse off.

We believe that careful consideration of the industry histories contained in this volume can make this debate more informed, more nuanced, less polarized – indeed, this is a central motive for this volume.

V. The Organization of the Volume

The preceding discussion highlights some of the important themes and issues addressed in subsequent chapters. The collection begins with three studies of different branches of the electronics industry that emerged in the post-1945 era: semiconductors, computer hardware, and computer software. We begin with these because they represent industries whose technologies are truly pervasive and "general-purpose" in nature. Indeed, the postwar evolution of technology and industrial leadership in the other four industries examined in this collection has been powerfully influenced by the growth of these three industries. The next two chapters deal with two much older industries – machine tools and chemicals. As we noted earlier, the histories of these two industries exhibit very different patterns of change in industrial leadership. The next two chapters are concerned with two health-care-related industries: pharmaceuticals and medical devices. Pharmaceuticals is a relatively mature industrial sector that has undergone truly transformative technical change in the past two decades as a result of the biotechnology revolution. Medical devices also have witnessed dramatic technical advances that rely more heavily on the "import" of advances in electronics, computing, and materials from other sectors. Yet the long-term development of industry structure in these two industries is quite similar. Our final chapter seeks to compare the very different patterns of industrial leadership in these seven industries and suggests some possible answers to the questions and issues posed in this chapter.

References

Abernathy, W. and Utterback, J. "Patterns of Industrial Innovation," *Technology Review*, 1978, pp. 41–47.

Aoki, M. "Towards an Economic Model of the Japanese Firm," *The Journal of Economic Literature*, March 1990.

Audretsch, D.B. and Stephan, P.E. "Company-Scientist Locational Links: The Case of Biotechnology," *American Economic Review* 86, 1996, pp. 641–652.

Beer, J. *The Emergence of the German Dye Industry*, University of Illinois Press, Urbana, 1959.

Carlsson, B. *Industrial Dynamics: Technological, Organizational, and Structural Changes in Industries and Firms*, Boston, Kluwer Academic Publishers, 1989.

Carlsson, B., ed. *Technological Systems and Industrial Dynamics*, Boston, Kluwer Academic Publishers, 1997.

Chandler, A. *Strategy and Structure: Chapters in the History of American Industrial Enterprise*, Cambridge, MA, MIT Press, 1962.

Chandler, A. *Scale and Scope: The Dynamics of Industrial Capitalism*, Cambridge, MA, Harvard University Press, 1990.

Christensen, C. and Rosenbloom, R. "Explaining the Attacker's Advantage: Technological Paradigms, Organizational Dynamics and the Value Network," *Industrial and Corporate Change*, 1994, pp. 655–685.

Earle, E.M. "Adam Smith, Alexander Hamilton, Friedrich List: The Economic Foundations of Military Power," in P. Paret, ed., *Makers of Modern Strategy from Machiavelli to the Nuclear Age*, Princeton, NJ, Princeton University Press, 1995.

Harrison, B. "Industrial Districts: New Wine in Old Bottles," *Regional Studies,* 1992, pp. 69–83.

Henderson, R. and Clark, N. "Architectural Innovation: The Reconfiguring of Existing Technologies and the Failure of Established Firms," *Administrative Sciences Quarterly*, 1990, pp. 9–30.

Hufbauer, G.R. *Synthetic Materials and the Theory of International Trade*, Cambridge, MA, Harvard University Press, 1966.

Klepper, S. "Entry, Exit, Growth, and Innovation Over the Product Cycle," *American Economic Review*, 1996, pp. 562–583.

Klepper, S. and Graddy, E. "The Evolution of New Industries and the Determinants of Market Structure," *The Rand Journal of Economics*, 1990.

Krugman, P. *Geography and Trade,* Cambridge, MA, MIT Press, 1991.

Krugman, P., ed. *Strategic Trade Policy and the New International Economics*, Cambridge, MA, MIT Press, 1987.

Langlois, R. and Robertson, P. *Firms, Markets, and Economic Change*, New York, Routledge, 1995.

Lundvall, B.A., ed. "National Systems of Innovation," *Towards a Theory of Innovation and Interactive Learning*, London, Pinter, 1992.

Malerba, F. *The Semiconductor Business*, Madison, University of Wisconsin Press, 1985.

Marshall, A. *Principles of Economics*, 8th ed., New York, Macmillan, 1948.

Mueller, D. and Tilton, J. "Research and Development as Barriers to Entry," *Canadian Journal of Economics*, 1969.

Piore, M. and Sabel, C. *The Second Industrial Divide*, New York, Basic Books, 1984.

Porter, M. *The Competitive Advantage of Nations*, New York, The Free Press, 1990.

Posner, M.V. "International Trade and Technical Change," *Oxford Economic Papers*, Oct. 1961.

Powell, W., Koput, K., and Smith-Doerr, L. "Interorganizational Collaboration and the Locus of Innovation: Networks of Learning in Biotechnology," *Administrative Sciences Quarterly*, 1996, pp. 116–145.

Saxenian, AnnaLee. *Regional Advantage: Culture and Competition in Silicon Valley and Route 128*, Cambridge, MA, Harvard University Press, 1994.

Stigler, G. "The Division of Labor Is Limited by the Extent of the Market," *Journal of Political Economy*, 1951, pp. 185–193.

Teece, D. "Perspectives on Alfred Chandler's Scale and Scope," *Journal of Economic Literature*, March 1993, pp. 199–225.

Tushman, M. and Anderson, D. "Technological Discontinuities and Organizational Environments," *Administrative Sciences Quarterly*, 1986.

Utterback, J. *Mastering the Dynamics of Innovation*, Boston, MA, Harvard University Press, 1994.

Vernon, R. "International Investment and International Trade in the Product Cycle," *Quarterly Journal of Economics*, 1966.

Vernon, R. "The Product Cycle Hypothysis in a New International Environment," *Oxford Bulletin of Economics and Statistics*, 1979, pp. 255–267.

Womack, J., Jones, D., and Roos, D. *The Machine That Changed the World*, New York, Rawson Press, 1991.

CHAPTER 2

The Evolution of Competitive Advantage in the Worldwide Semiconductor Industry, 1947–1996

RICHARD N. LANGLOIS AND
W. EDWARD STEINMUELLER

Introduction

In the half century of its existence, the business of semiconductor manufacture has come to capture the popular imagination as few others have. Starting with only the most common of raw materials – silicon and aluminum – this industry constructs complex electronic systems performing functions that were science fiction only a few decades ago. Even so, the volume of literature on this industry would no doubt have been smaller if the technological and scientific leadership of the United States in that industry had not come under challenge by the emergence of international competition.

The decline of the global market share of American semiconductor producers in the mid-1980s suggested to many that the days of American dominance of science-based industries might be numbered. Although there is little evidence that international competitors had in mind the annihilation of the American industry, many nonetheless read the situation in terms familiar from the Cold War. The loss of American leadership in the semiconductor industry would be the first domino in a cascading fall of downstream electronic-systems industries.[1] Looking through the other end of this same telescope, America's foreign competitors asked the parallel question: How could one possibly succeed in *building* electronic-systems industries without developing a robust semiconductor industry of one's own?

The authors would like to thank the Consortium for Competitiveness and Cooperation for making this transatlantic collaboration possible and for providing a rich dialogue during several project meetings. We would also like to thank the editors, David Mowery and Richard Nelson, for particularly helpful comments. Much of Steinmueller's work on this project was accomplished while he was Professor of the Economics of Technological Change at the Maastricht Economic Research Institute on Innovation and Technology (MERIT) at University of Maastricht, The Netherlands.

[1] Among the more hysterical versions of this thesis are Ferguson (1985) and Forester (1993). The latter, indeed, is testimony to the inertia of intellectual fashion, as the bulk of its assertions and predictions had already been falsified by the time the book was published. By contrast, Ferguson had essentially recanted his earlier views by that time (Ferguson and Morris, 1993).

The voluminous literature generated from the rise of foreign – especially Japanese – competition in semiconductors seemed to have one dominant theme: the United States must not merely learn from but closely imitate Japan. Most analysts assured us, implicitly or explicitly, that Japanese success reflected inherent superiorities in industrial structure and state policy, superiorities of a widely applicable and lasting kind. In its strongest form, the lesson from Japan was read in terms of the inevitable eclipse of the structures of entrepreneurial capitalism by some form of systematic planning, usually of the corporatist or state-corporatist variety.[2] A weaker variant simply indicted the American semiconductor industry and its domestic suppliers for excessive "fragmentation" and vertical disintegration. Writers like Ferguson (1988) and Florida and Kenney (1990) suggested that American faith in industrial districts like Silicon Valley had been misplaced and that only imitating the Japanese *keiretsu* structure would improve the performance of the American industry. This view was echoed by the prestigious MIT Commission on Industrial Productivity, which declared in 1989 that "the traditional structure and institutions of the U.S. industry appear to be inappropriate for meeting the challenge of the much stronger and better-organized Japanese competition" (MIT Commission, 1989, vol. 2, p. 20). The commission pronounced the American merchant semiconductor industry "too fragmented" and called for consolidation and rationalization.

This chapter offers a different, and perhaps even iconoclastic, explanation for the rise, decline, and resurrection of the American semiconductor industry. We argue that industrial leadership is a history-dependent process in which success rests upon the fit between exogenous (or quasi-exogenous) factors and the structures of knowledge, organization, and capability inherited from the past.[3] There is no one "optimal" industrial structure or policy regime independent of time and circumstance. In our story, Japanese success in the 1980s – like American leadership early on and like the renewed American success today – is a matter not of universal and time-invariant superiorities but of a complex of contingent factors and circumstances. There are certainly lessons from the Japanese success. But those lessons must be read carefully and in the proper context.

[2] Corporatism, the coordination of control by an oligarchy of industrial interests, is the underlying hypothesis in Fallows (1994); state corporatism, corporatism under state direction, is the fundamental position of Johnson (1982). All of the studies that view Japanese industrial structure in terms of strongly unified purpose and relatively smooth coordination make the implicit argument that this structure for control is, or tends to be, inherently superior to the more divided and contentious structures prevailing in the United States.

[3] This theme is developed in greater detail and generality in Langlois and Robertson (1995), especially chapters 6 and 7.

Our perspective is informed by the view that competitive advantage ultimately resides in the industrial capabilities of the firms in an industry, even if those capabilities are conditioned on and affected by various background institutions and policies.[4] The significance of economic capabilities – what G. B. Richardson (1972), who coined the term, defined as the "knowledge, experience and skills" of the enterprise – is that they are most often hard to learn; tacit; unpredictable in the rate and direction of their acquisition; and often very difficult to abandon or forget.[5] It is precisely these characteristics of capabilities that make it very difficult for companies in this industry to relocate to positions of advantage when circumstances change. Because the better part of these capabilities evolve from the interactions between semiconductor firms and their customers and from the division of labor within the semiconductor industry, history matters.

Our story is thus one in which background conditions and starting points are as significant as corporate strategy and government policy. Corporate strategies, we will see, are often constrained by circumstance, and government policies often have effects very different from those intended. One centerpiece of our account is the prominent role we give to the extent and structure of end-use demand – a largely exogenous factor – in shaping the fortunes of companies and national industries.

Not surprisingly, we use history to convey our arguments. In what follows, we chronicle in order three major episodes of regional competitive advantage: the early rise of American industry, the challenge posed by Japanese firms in the late 1970s and 1980s, and the recent resurgence of American industry, coupled with the rise of new East Asian producers and growing internationalization. We close with a brief perspective on this history.

I. America's Rise to Dominance

The Invention of the Transistor

The invention of the transistor by Bardeen, Brattain, and Shockley at the Bell Telephone Laboratories after World War II is an oft-told story (Braun and Macdonald, 1978; Morris, 1990; Nelson, 1962). It was an innovation made possible by modern physics and intimately connected to basic research. Interestingly, however, the research was carried out not

[4] Such background institutions and policies are what Nelson (1993) and Lundvall (1992) call "national systems of innovation."

[5] On the notion of capabilities see also Nelson and Winter (1982).

in universities but in one of America's premier corporate research laboratories.[6]

Even though the initial transistors were relatively primitive devices, their potential as a major invention was widely appreciated. AT&T sought and received patents for the first working transistor design, raising the prospect that the company would eventually be able to influence the entire spectrum of electronic industries. Despite this, AT&T immediately undertook a policy of broad public disclosure of the enabling technologies for producing transistors, announced widespread licensing of both original and subsequent transistor patents, and encouraged site visits to interested parties to assure the transfer of the technology to those interested in pursuing the development of the invention (Tilton, 1971, pp. 75–76; Braun and Macdonald, 1978, pp. 54–55).

AT&T had long pursued a policy of cross-licensing agreements, which allowed it to gain from the inventive efforts of others. Although AT&T had developed the transistor and begun using it early in telephone devices and circuits, it was still an extremely immature technology. By allowing access to the transistor, AT&T was betting, in effect, that the spillover benefits to telephony from tapping the capabilities of others would outweigh the forgone revenues of proprietary development (McHugh, 1949; Bello, 1953; Braun and Macdonald, 1978, p. 54; Levin, 1982, pp. 76–77). An AT&T vice president put it this way: "We realized that if this thing [the transistor] was as big as we thought, we couldn't keep it to ourselves and we couldn't make all the technical contributions. It was to our interest to spread it around. If you cast your bread on the water, sometimes it comes back angel food cake."[7] The consequence of this action was thus to create a large cohort of entrants intent on finding ways to commercialize the new technology (Mowery and Steinmueller, 1994). Few industries can claim such an early widespread diffusion of their core technology, which in this case generated intense rivalry to develop competitive advantage by leading in the improvement of the breakthrough innovation.

For the incumbent electronic-component producers, the vacuum-tube firms, the transistor was in large measure a competence-destroying innovation.[8] These firms nonetheless quickly saw the value of the device. At least in part, this was because the transistor remained undeveloped and

[6] It will be a minor theme in this essay – albeit a theme articulated importantly by omission – that universities have played only an indirect role in the development of the semiconductor industry.

[7] Quotation attributed to Jack Morton, in "The Improbable Years," *Electronics* 41: 81 (February 19, 1968), quoted in Tilton (1971, pp. 75–76).

[8] A competence-destroying innovation is one that renders obsolete an organization's existing knowledge and capabilities (Tushman and Anderson, 1986).

even experimental, and much of the transistor work in the vacuum-tube firms took place in large R&D facilities not unlike Bell Labs. Moreover, although these firms produced vacuum tubes, they were diversified systems companies rather than specialists in tube production. Thus, although the transistor was competence destroying for the firm's vacuum-tube operations, it was competence enhancing for the firm as a whole. Nonetheless, as we will see, the near-term future in semiconductors did not belong to the established players but to smaller, newer, more-focused enterprises. Many of these benefited from personnel who left Bell Labs to pursue the development of the transistor elsewhere, establishing a pattern of personnel defection and spin-off that continues today in the United States.

For example, William Shockley left Bell Labs in the early 1950s for the San Francisco peninsula, where he founded Shockley Semiconductor Laboratories. Although his enterprise was never a commercial success, eight of Shockley's team defected in 1957 to found the semiconductor division of Fairchild Camera and Instrument Corporation, an organization of seminal importance in the industry. Largely through the efforts of Jean Hoerni, one of the eight defectors, Fairchild developed the planar process, a technology that allowed large-scale batch production of transistors. Almost immediately, Hoerni's colleague and fellow defector Robert Noyce would extend the planar process to the fabrication of multi-transistor devices – integrated circuits (ICs). The advantages of the planar process for transistor production were overwhelming and recognized immediately throughout the industry (Sparkes, 1973, p. 8). By 1968, Noyce and others had left Fairchild to found the next generation of semiconductor firms. As Saxenian (1994) and others have argued, the localization of many of these firms on the San Franciso peninsula created the kind of industrial district discussed by Alfred Marshall (1961), generating a self-reinforcing system of external economies.

The Role of Demand. The market for semiconductors began with the U.S. military, and it was the Cold War that nurtured this industry in its infancy. Although the transistor provided a practical means to make portable hearing aids and radios, its primary value during its early years lay in military systems, where performance rather than cost is often the deciding factor in adopting new technology.[9] Moreover, the nature of military – and later computer – demand affected the technological trajectory of development in the American industry. Because of its tractabil-

[9] Indeed, Bell's haste in announcing the transistor was motivated at least in part by a desire to preempt any thought the military might have of classifying the technology (Levin, 1982, p. 58).

ity, germanium was the material of choice for transistors destined for consumer markets, where cost considerations dominated, and, as we will see, both Europe and Japan concentrated on this type of transistor early on. The silicon transistor, perfected by Gordon Teal (1976) at Texas Instruments (TI), was more expensive, but the stability of its electrical properties over a wider range of temperatures made it superior for military and space applications. Silicon also proved superior in digital switching applications, where speed was of importance.

Military demand for semiconductors provided several "spillovers" from the development of military devices to civilian applications. Much of this spillover was simply the consequence of accumulating a substantial practical knowledge base about transistor production using the continued revenue flow from military procurement.[10] Without this indirect research finance, American firms would likely have developed the technology at a pace and in directions similar to those of companies in Japan and Europe during this period. But military performance requirements in the United States stimulated the development of transistors with grown rather than contact junctions and encouraged the rapid ascendancy in the United States of silicon over germanium transistors. As Table 2.1 indicates, the unit production of germanium transistors outpaced that of silicon transistors through 1965. Throughout this period, production volumes increased and prices declined with greater experience. In 1957, three years after its first commercial production, the silicon transistor was still an expensive specialty item, the most important uses of which were military applications. The rapid price decline thereafter – much sharper than had been the case for germanium (see Table 2.1) – reflects the production advantages of the planar process for silicon.[11]

There can be little doubt of the importance of military and space demand for the pace and direction of technological change and cost reduction in this early period of the industry's development. Between 1955 and 1958, government procurement absorbed between 36 and 39 percent of industry output, a share that shot up to 45 and 48 percent in 1959–1960.[12] After a 1960 peak in which government demand was $258

[10] Between 1955 and 1959, the prices of transistors for the military market remained four times greater (despite price reductions in both categories of demand) than those for the civilian market (Kleiman, 1966, p. 81).

[11] The physical characteristics of germanium made it unsuitable to the planar process.

[12] The share includes devices produced for the Department of Defense, the Atomic Energy Commission, the Central Intelligence Agency, the Federal Aviation Administration, and NASA (Levin, 1982, p. 60). The share of the consumption in the years 1952–1954, for which no data are available, was similar to that in the peak year, 1960, or about 50 percent of the market (Kraus, 1971, p. 91).

Table 2.1. *U.S. Sales of Germanium and Silicon Transistors (Nominal $)*

	Germanium		*Silicon*	
	Units (M)	Average Value ($)	Units (M)	Average Value ($)
1957	27.7	1.85	1.0	17.81
1958	45.0	1.79	2.1	15.57
1959	77.5	1.96	4.8	14.53
1960	119.1	1.70	8.8	11.27
1961	177.9	1.14	13.0	7.48
1962	213.7	0.82	26.6	4.39
1963	249.4	0.69	50.6	2.65
1964	288.8	0.57	118.1	1.46
1965	333.6	0.50	274.5	0.86

Source: EIA (1974, p. 87).

million, however, government expenditures began to be outstripped by commercial demand for semiconductors. Although the level of government expenditures between 1960 and 1977 fell below $200 million in only two years,[13] the government share of the market in the latter half of the period fluctuated between 8 and 12 percent.

Commercial semiconductor markets began to develop in the late 1950s. Table 2.2 indicates that by 1963 the computer industry had already generated substantial demand for semiconductors.[14] In that year, computer demand roughly equaled the entire consumer-electronics market for transistors. Despite the origins of the transistor in the communica-

[13] The years were 1964 and 1971.

[14] This table reflects a methodology different from the one Levin (1982) used to determine the share of government consumption of semiconductor output. Dodson (1966) focused exclusively on transistors, a measure that raises the estimated average price of a semiconductor sold to the government. It is also likely that he underestimated the total transistor market, which would shift the shares of various demand segments. According to the Business Defense Service Agency, at that time a unit of the Department of Commerce, the value of transistor shipments in 1963 was $311.7 million or about $60 million (25 percent) greater than Dodson's figure. Despite these limitations, Dodson's is the best available study of the structure of final demand for this period.

Table 2.2. *Value of U.S. Transistors by End-Use, 1963*

Military		***Industrial***		***Consumer***	
Space	33.0	Computers	41.6	Car radios	20.6
Aircraft	22.8	Communications	16.0	Portable radios	12.6
Missiles	20.3	Test and measuring	11.7	Organs and hearing aids	7.3
Communications	16.8	Controls	11.5		
Surface systems	10.8	Other	11.5	Television	0.3
Strategic systems	8.8				
Other	6.7				
Total:	**119.2**		**92.3**		**40.8**
Percent:	**47.2**		**36.6**		**16.2**

Source: Dodson (1966, pp. 95–97).

tions industry, civilian demand for transistors in communications was lower than that for military communications.[15]

The Role of American Government Policy. Procurement demand was arguably the most important – and the most salutary – aspect of government policy toward the semiconductor industry in this period. But it was by no means the only aspect. The military provided direct support both for R&D and for production as well as indirect support through military systems contractors.[16] Military efforts to improve the uptake of semiconductor technology continued throughout the 1950s.[17] Table 2.3 presents some estimates of direct government expenditures for R&D and production refinement. According to a Defense Department report, the military also funded R&D indirectly through its defense systems contractors, to the tune of $13.9 million in 1958 and $16.2 million in 1959,

[15] The U.S. consumer market for transistors was dominated by portable radio applications. Non-portable radios continued to be produced with vacuum tubes.

[16] Examples include R&D contracts to Bell (Levin, 1982, p. 67) and Army Signal Corps R&D and pilot manufacturing line contracts with Western Electric, GE, Raytheon, RCA, and Sylvania (Kraus, 1971).

[17] In that same year, the Signal Corps committed $14 million to fund "production refinement" at 12 firms and proceeded to spend a total of about $50 million on support for production engineering measures (PEM) between 1952 and 1964.

Table 2.3. *Estimated U.S. Government Direct Funding for R&D and Production Refinement, 1955–1961*

	1955	1956	1957	1958	1959	1960	1961	Totals
Research and development	3.2	4.1	3.8	4.0	6.3	6.8	11.0	**39.3**
Production refinement								
Transistors	2.7	14.0	0.0	1.9	1.0	0.0	1.7	**21.3**
Diodes and rectifiers	2.2	0.8	0.5	0.2	0.0	1.1	0.8	**5.6**
Total	**8.1**	**18.9**	**4.3**	**6.1**	**7.3**	**7.9**	**13.5**	**66.1**

Source: U.S. Department of Commerce (1961, p. 13, Table 8).

for example. The same report claims that government-sponsored R&D (both direct and indirect) accounted for about a quarter of all semiconductor R&D in those years (Tilton, 1971, p. 93).

These R&D and production-development activities were not as effective in pushing the industry along as were the fact and extent of government demand itself. All the major breakthroughs in transistors were developed privately with the military market (among others) in mind. Despite the $5 million in government R&D on silicon transistors, it was private work at Texas Instruments that yielded results (Teal, 1976). And the planar process, developed privately with the military market in view, rendered obsolete most of the production lines that the military had helped fund (Sparkes, 1973, p. 8).

The government tended to favor R&D contracts with established suppliers, notably the vacuum-tube firms. In 1959, for example, Western Electric and eight established vacuum-tube firms received 78 percent of the government's R&D funding despite accounting for only half of private R&D activity in the industry and only 37 percent of semiconductor sales (see Table 2.4). By contrast, the military was far less biased toward established firms in its role as buyer: in the same year, new firms accounted for 63 percent of all semiconductor sales, but 69 percent of sales to the military (Tilton, 1971, p. 91). The pragmatic policy of awarding work to those firms that could meet supply requirements was particularly important for encouraging new entry, both in the transistor era and in the subsequent development of the integrated circuit.

Competitors in the Wings: European and Japanese Developments. Especially outside the United States, it is common to hear the role of the

Table 2.4. *R&D Funding and Sales in the United States, 1959, by Type of Firm*

	Government R&D funds		Company R&D funds		Semiconductor sales	
Type of firm	*$ million*	*Percent*	*$ million*	*Percent*	*$ million*	*Percent*
"Old" firms	12.7	78	27.2	50	149.5	37
New firms	3.5	22	26.8	50	252.1	63
Total	16.2	100	54.0	100	401.6	100

Note: "Old" firms are Western Electric and eight vacuum-tube firms.
Source: Tilton (1971).

American military in the early semiconductor industry described as an implicit industrial policy accounting for much of America's rise to dominance in the industry, especially with respect to Europe. And there is certainly no disputing the importance of military demand for the growth of the American industry. On the other hand, however, European firms remained competitive in the market for germanium transistors through at least 1964. As we saw, the germanium transistor remained viable in Europe later into the 1960s because of the characteristics of that continent's end-use markets for transistors[18] (Malerba, 1985, pp. 75–80, 88–89). Table 2.5 suggests the relative sizes of the American, Japanese, and European industries in this period.

The incentive for European firms to keep pace with American developments was limited by several factors – the dominance of European consumer over computer markets, the persistence of larger vertically integrated systems firms who viewed transistors as a necessary input into electronic system products rather than as an end product (Malerba, 1985); and the effective closure of the market for American military and space contracts because of the military's "Buy American" policy and similar policies at NASA (Skole, 1968). European firms concentrated on indigenous European markets for consumer products and industrial applications and were not crowded out by American competitors. Neither international trade nor foreign direct investment was a major factor in this period (Tilton, 1971, p. 44).

[18] In Europe, the other distinctive competence was in semiconductor power devices, including the silicon rectifier. Unfortunately for European producers, there were few technological spillovers from the silicon rectifier to other silicon semiconductor products.

Table 2.5. *Production and Consumption of Semiconductors by Country, Selected Years*

Country	Consumption (1956)	Production (1958)	Consumption (1960)	Production (1961)
United States	80	236	560	607
Japan	5	19	54	78
W. Germany	3	10	25	30
Great Britain	2	8	28	35
France	2	8	27	32

Note: $ million (nominal).
Source: Malerba (1985).

The follower strategy of European firms meant that their competitiveness hinged on the ability to adopt advances developed elsewhere. And the R&D capabilities of large European firms initially provided the "absorptive capacity" to follow closely new developments.[19] Significantly, the European firms tended to license technology almost exclusively from those American firms whom they most resembled and almost not at all from the American merchant houses (Malerba, 1985, p. 65). Without a large local military and computer market, integrated electronic system companies prevailed in Europe, resulting in the eventual dependence of these companies on foreign suppliers in the silicon transistor and integrated circuit eras.

Although the early origins of the Japanese semiconductor industry are broadly similar to those of the European, a few significant differences were to prove crucial in explaining the distinctive path of Japanese development in later periods. As in Europe, the principal producers of transistors in the 1950s and 1960s were diversified electronic system companies, including firms that had previously produced vacuum tubes, rather than companies that were principally specialized in semiconductor production. And, as in Europe, the main end-use for transistors in Japan in this period was consumer products rather than the military.

Unlike their European and American counterparts, Japanese firms engaged in – and the Japanese government subsidized – virtually no basic research during this period. The R&D they did undertake was geared

[19] To use the terminology of Cohen and Levinthal (1990).

toward what Kodama (1995, p. 24) picturesquely describes as the "digestion" of foreign technology. The absence of a domestic scientific base forced Japanese companies to adopt a critical and wide-ranging search for new ideas from all sources. This practice was reinforced by Japanese trade policy. Like Europe, Japan responded to American competitive advantage with high tariffs; in addition, Japan imposed quotas and registration requirements (Tyson and Yoffie, 1993, p. 37). In contrast to European governments, moreover, the Japanese government essentially forbade foreign direct investment, thus allowing American firms to tap the Japanese market only through direct export or licensing and technology sales to Japanese firms.[20]

With this combination of policies, Japan was able to achieve a net export surplus in semiconductors from 1956 to 1968.[21] Fundamentally, this strong export position was a consequence of specialization. In 1963, Japanese system output was only $1.2 billion compared to $5.7 billion in Europe and $14 billion in the United States.[22] But Japanese companies developed the transistor as a commodity component for the rapidly growing transistor-radio market, an export market that Japan was able to retain despite much larger rivals in foreign markets.[23] This specialization became a disadvantage, however, as silicon began to replace germanium as the material of choice for transistors. Beginning in 1961, Japanese imports of transistors expanded at a 45 percent annual growth rate, eventually overtaking exports in 1968.

Japanese government policy toward the electronics industry focused on financing export expansion as well as attempting to channel foreign technology toward companies that were most likely to use it productively, a strategy reinforcing the position of incumbents that only a few companies, notably Sony, were able to bypass. The position of incumbents was also reinforced by the fact that Nippon Telephone and Telegraph

[20] Japanese companies have typically supplied some 90 percent of the Japanese semiconductor market, whereas American firms – through imports or foreign direct investment – have supplied between 50 and 70 percent of the European market (Tyson and Yoffie, 1993, p. 34).

[21] Computed from Tilton (1971, p. 45). After 1968, Japan experienced a net import balance for eight years (Dosi, 1984, p. 255), or until nearly the beginning of the period of the Japanese challenge to U.S. dominance discussed later.

[22] The size of the Japanese final electronics production market is from Tilton (1971); that for Europe and the United States is from Sciberras (1977, p. 49). Sciberras cites a Texas Instruments estimate reported by Carrell (1968), an article Tilton (1971) also cites.

[23] The evidence for this is somewhat circumstantial. In 1957 and 1958, Tilton (1971) estimates, transistor radios absorbed two-thirds of Japanese transistor production, a share that fell moderately on an annual basis until it reached one-third in 1964 (p. 157). The years 1957 and 1958 are also the years in which Japan achieved its large net export position in transistors, whereas from 1965 export growth is essentially nil for four years (Dosi, 1984, p. 255).

(NTT), the state telephone monopoly, pursued a policy of buying only from four principal suppliers.[24] The Japanese government also sought increased concentration in the domestic computer industry – without much success. In 1970 there were still six mainframe producers, collectively holding a 50 percent market share in the Japanese domestic market (Fransman, 1990, p. 38). In short, although Japan did pursue industrial policies, it is not clear whether those policies bear direct responsbility for that country's industrial performance in this period. What is clear, however, is that the Japanese electronics industry was able to expand relative to that of the United States and Europe during the 1960s, attaining a level of about $3.25 billion by 1968 compared to Europe's $7.7 billion and America's $24 billion. A central feature of this expansion was that 70 percent of the market for Japanese semiconductor products remained in consumer electronics.

Because the Japanese vacuum-tube firms were much smaller than their American or European counterparts at the beginning of the transistor era, they had less to lose in moving to the new technology. As Tilton (1971, p. 154) notes, rapid growth "also helped create a receptive attitude toward change on the part of the receiving tube producers by reducing the risks associated with new products and new technologies and by increasing costs, in terms of declining market shares, to firms content simply to maintain the status quo." This meant that Japanese systems firms faced many of the same constraints, and adopted many of the same approaches, as the American merchant firms rather than those of the American, or European, systems houses.[25] Moreover, as Michael Porter (1990, pp. 117–122) has pointed out, the large number of actual and potential semiconductor producers in Japan led to a vibrant domestic rivalry that sharpened and focused Japanese firms. As we will see, this is in contrast to the "national champions" approach that was to develop in Europe.

The Integrated-Circuit (IC) Era

In 1958 and 1959, two Americans, Jack Kilby of Texas Instruments and Robert Noyce of Fairchild, were the first to devise practical monolithic circuits. Noyce's approach, based on the planar process that had revolutionized transistor production, was the more immediately practical. After

[24] Fransman (1995) labels this policy "controlled competition." The principal suppliers were NEC, Fujitsu, Hitachi, and Oki.

[25] Unlike European firms, the Japanese firms sought and received licenses from Texas Instruments, Fairchild, and other American merchant firms rather than limiting themselves to arrangements with American systems houses.

struggling over patent claims, the two companies forged a cross-licensing agreement in 1966 that effectively gave them joint claim on the invention. Each company granted licenses to all comers in the range of 2 to 4 percent of IC profits (Reid, 1984, pp. 94–95). This practice reproduced and extended the technology-licensing policies of AT&T, again broadly diffusing the core technological innovation to all entrants.

Incremental technical improvement of the planar process helped set the paradigm or "technological trajectory" for the industry. Improving this process made it possible to increase the number of transistors per IC dramatically over time. Transistor counts per IC increased from 10 to 4,000 in the first decade of the industry's history; from 4,000 to over 500,000 in the second decade; and from 500,000 to 100 million in the third decade.[26] For the first two decades, the 10-million-fold increase in the number of transistors per IC was accompanied by modest increases in the cost of batch processing of a wafer, and almost no change in the average costs of processing the individual IC. This factor alone has been responsible for the enormous cost reduction in electronic circuitry since the birth of the IC and for the production of previously expensive electronic systems on a single IC. Reductions in the cost of components have lowered the cost of electronic systems relative to mechanical ones across a very wide range of applications and have reduced the price of electronic goods relative to all other goods and services in the economy – developments that have led to sustained high growth rates in the electronic systems and semiconductor industries and to changes in industrial structure in both industries.

The Development of the Industry: The Actors. The opportunity created by the IC during the period 1959–1966 produced a wave of new entry into the industry (Wilson et al., 1980, p. 14; Hannan and Freeman, 1989, p. 226). A significant feature of the transition was the disappearance of the vertically integrated American electronics companies that had led in the production of vacuum tubes and that had been able to stay in the race during the discrete semiconductor era. The market shares of those firms declined in the face of new entrants and the growth of relatively specialized manufacturers like TI, Fairchild, and Motorola. As Table 2.6 suggests, by 1965, the vertically integrated system firms had fallen from the top 5 slots in American semiconductor sales, and by 1975 all but RCA had fallen off the top-10 list.

Why did the vertically integrated electronic system firms do so poorly

[26] As size of structures on the silicon crystal is reduced, it has become possible to build denser and more complex arrays of such structures on a crystal of a given size. This is the principal determinant of the increase in transistor count.

Table 2.6. *Leading U.S. Merchant Semiconductor Manufacturers, 1955–1975*

1955	*1960*	*1965*	*1975*
Transistors	***Semiconductors***	***Semiconductors***	***Integrated Circuits***
Hughes	Texas Instruments	Texas Instruments	Texas Instruments
Transitron	Transitron	Motorola	Fairchild
Philco	Philco	Fairchild	National
Sylvania	General Electric	General Instrument	Intel
Texas Instruments	RCA	General Electric	Motorola
General Electric	Motorola	RCA	Rockwell
RCA	Clevite	Sprague	General Instrument
Westinghouse	Fairchild	Philco-Ford	RCA
Motorola	Hughes	Transitron	Signetics (Phillips)
Clevite	Sylvania	Raytheon	American Microsystems

Source: Mackintosh (1978, p. 54).

in this era? Wilson, Ashton, and Egan (1980) point out that the new leaders were either specialized start-ups or multidivisional firms (like TI, Fairchild, and Motorola) in which the semiconductor division dominated overall corporate strategy and in which semiconductor operations absorbed a significant portion of the attention of central management. By contrast, the semiconductor divisions of the integrated system firms were a small part of corporate sales and of corporate strategy, thereby attracting a smaller portion of managerial attention and receiving less autonomy.

This is consistent with the literature of management strategy urging corporations to cultivate their "core competences" and to recognize that deviation from these competences is risky (Teece, 1986; Prahalad and Hamel, 1990). Indeed, recent evidence suggests that specialized competence is important not so much in the core technology itself as in the complementary activities necessary to transform the technology into high-demand products (Christensen and Rosenbloom, 1995). Granstrand, Patel, and Pavitt (1997) argue in general that firms should not try to limit their core competences but rather should strive to widen those competences while retaining focus in complementary and downstream activities. Gambardella and Torrisi (1998) show that electronics firms in the 1980s did better when they narrowed their product focus while expanding their technological competences. Such product specialization is arguably of even greater value when market and technological opportunities are expanding rapidly along a well-defined trajectory (Patel and Pavitt, 1997, p. 153). American merchants in the integrated-circuit era arguably followed this advice: they expanded their technological competence in semiconductor design and fabrication while limiting their product diversification (relative to that of the large system houses) in a way that was shaped by the pattern of end-use demand. As we will see presently, however, the product diversity of American merchants did grow over time, to an extent that was to make them vulnerable to a challenge from even more narrowly focused Japanese firms wielding wide technological capabilities.

The Pattern of Demand. The price advantage of the integrated circuit compared with the transistor assured a relatively rapid diffusion of the new technology. It did not, however, immediately create major shifts in the electronic-system industries. During the first half of the 1960s, the methods for IC manufacturing were still under development and the technical characteristics of the ICs were limited, particularly for use in analog circuits.[27] But the technical capabilities of ICs were ideal for digital circuits, the major customers for which were the military (to which we return later) and the computer industry.

The 1960s was a period of rapid growth for the American computer industry. The leading firm, IBM, had built up its position during the 1950s by relying heavily on outside suppliers. In 1957, IBM had selected TI as its lead supplier, signing an agreement for "exchange of patent licenses, purchasing arrangements, interchange of technical information, and joint development" of semiconductors (Bashe et al., 1986, p. 402). Under this agreement, IBM designed what company biographers describe as the world's first automated transistor production line, which they disassembled in 1959 and shipped to TI (Bashe et al., 1986, pp. 400–402; Pugh et al., 1991, p. 64). By 1960, however, IBM had created its own components division, which geared up to make semiconductors for the phenomenally successful IBM 360 Series, announced in 1964.[28] By the 1970s, IBM's

[27] Analog circuits involve the continuous variation of current or voltage, in contrast to the on-or-off character of digital circuits.

[28] IBM's decision to create internal capabilities in semiconductors and many other components was apparently based on a conscious perception of economies of scope between

dominance in computers had made it the world's largest producer of ICs. Thus the vertical division of labor in the United States became markedly different from, and more diverse than, that in Europe and Japan. Many small, highly specialized merchant firms dealing with relatively autonomous systems companies stood alongside a handful of large, vertically integrated captive producers.[29]

Merchant semiconductor firms faced basically two options. One class of product strategies involved making high-volume standard products, notably memories. Despite IBM's moves to convert from ferrite-core to semiconductor memory, this market continued to be relatively small until 1972. In that year, Intel's 1003 became the best-selling IC in the world, accounting for more than 90 percent of the company's $23.4 million in revenue in that year (Cogan and Burgelman, 1989). The other class of product strategies involved attempting to use the rapidly growing complexity of ICs in the large-scale integration (LSI) period to create differentiated products. For a time, American firms were able to do well with both sets of strategies.

The Role of American Government Policy. The other crucial influence on the American semiconductor industry continued to be the federal government, through its role as both an end-use demander and a supplier of research and development. Because of two technical goals – miniaturization and high reliability – the military was willing to pay the high prices the earliest devices commanded. Military use came to dominate other sources of demand for the early ICs.

Each of the U.S. military services had undertaken a research program in the area of miniaturization aimed at increasing circuit density.[30] In the uncertain world of innovation, there will normally be many different approaches that seemed promising ex ante but appear mistaken – or even silly – ex post. Nonetheless, it remains significant that the technologies pushed by the military were all ex post failures, whereas the successful paradigmatic innovation occurred at the hands of private

component design and computer design. Especially in the era before large-scale integrated circuits, processing speed depended on the integration of component and system, and IBM wished to preserve the ability to adjust both component and system simultaneously instead of responding to autonomous changes in components fabricated – even at low cost – by outside suppliers. Moreover, in a world of centralized mainframe computers, reliability is crucial, and IBM wished to control directly as many determinants of quality as possible (Langlois, 1997).

[29] The other major American captive producer was AT&T. These two American captives also behaved differently than their integrated counterparts overseas in that they generally refrained from selling on the merchant market at all – because of legal constraint in the case of AT&T and of company policy in the case of IBM.

[30] These programs are documented in Kleiman (1966).

companies – Fairchild and TI – whose successful projects had received no government support. The most valuable input from the government may have been its keeping in the air knowledge of the military's fervent desire for miniaturization (Kleiman, 1966, pp. 203–204), an end-use need that was quite abstract and easy to convey. The specific programs themselves were costly not only in direct terms but also in terms of the resources diverted, especially at the companies like RCA and Westinghouse that participated most heavily, a participation that may have contributed to their falling behind in the IC era.[31] Overall, the government, including NASA, spent $32 million on IC R&D between 1959 and 1964, with 70 percent of that coming from the Air Force (Kleiman, 1966, p. 201).

The government also provided much of the early demand for the IC. Along with Westinghouse and RCA, Texas Instruments participated in the *Minuteman II* Program, the first major military use of ICs (Kleiman, 1966, p. 195; Levin, 1982, p. 62). And, while shunning military markets, Fairchild was the major IC vendor to NASA for the *Apollo* Project (Levin, 1982, p. 62). These early purchases hastened American firms down the slopes of their learning curves. And the government insistence on second sourcing sped the diffusion of IC technology. As IC prices fell, however, civilian uses, especially for the computer, quickly came to dominate government procurement (Table 2.7).

European Developments in the IC Era. Much of the technological gap that opened between European and American firms in the period of the integrated circuit was the result of the relative absence of the computer and military demand the United States enjoyed, although there were certainly other factors at work. The European semiconductor producers of the transistor era were mostly large vertically integrated systems firms. These firms naturally specialized – and were successful – in producing transistors to substitute for tubes in consumer and industrial applications. The strong growth in digital IC technology in the United States for computers and military applications was leading to what would become the next generation of components – components for which the capabilities of European firms were less relevant.

Indeed, in the early 1960s, the largest firms, including Philips and Siemens, were reluctant to switch from germanium technology, in which

[31] Kleiman (1966, p. 187) reports, for example, that Westinghouse diverted some 50 professionals to the molecular electronics project. Of course, part of the reason that Westinghouse was willing to take on the project was that its opportunity costs of doing so were much lower than those of leading semiconductor firms like TI or Fairchild (Kleiman, 1966, p. 185).

Table 2.7. *End-Use Shares of Total U.S. Sales of Integrated Circuits and Total Market Value 1962–1978*

Markets	1962	1965	1969	1974	1978
Government	100%	55%	36%	20%	10%
Computer	0	35	44	36	38
Industrial	0	9	16	30	38
Consumer	0	1	4	15	15
Total U.S. domestic shipments (millions)	$4	$79	$413	$1,204	$2,080

Source: Borrus et al. (1983, p. 159).

they were skilled and successful and which was more useful in consumer applications than silicon.[32] These firms were also late to begin IC production, a technology for which they foresaw little demand. And, when they did begin IC production in the late 1960s, it was typically first in linear ICs for internal customers rather than in digital ICs, a field in which they met with little success. Philips, Siemens, and AEG-Telefunken retained strong positions in discrete devices and linear ICs.

Government policy in European countries played a significant role in the comparative lack of demand for digital ICs in the military, computer, and telecommunications sectors. The European computer industry was unable to achieve the output scale of American firms, notably IBM, who often produced in Europe in order to circumvent a 17 percent ad valorem tariff. In telecommunications, a history of national procurement in the larger European markets (France, Germany, Italy, and the United Kingdom) fragmented the market. The absence of significant military demand from Germany and the less-intensive development of avionics for the European military reduced the demand from this sector as well.

The situation in the computer industry is particularly relevant for comparisons with Japan. By the mid-1960s, Britain, France, and Germany had all begun efforts to foster national computer industries (Dosi, 1981, p. 27). As Bresnahan and Malerba (Chapter 3 in this volume) point out, many of those European (and Japanese) policies toward computers were aimed at forestalling IBM with preferential procurement policies as well as outright subventions. By subsidizing national computer makers, who

[32] This paragraph draws on Malerba (1985, pp. 105–124).

were motivated if not constrained to buy from national semiconductor makers, the European computer initiatives thus attempted to create some indigenous demand for logic ICs. Moreover, all three countries initiated R&D programs in computers, some of which spilled over into semiconductors.[33] As Tilton (1971, p. 131) notes, these programs tended to favor a small number of large established firms – to a much greater extent than had American military R&D. Indeed, European government policy in this period encouraged consolidation and rationalization. Especially in Britain and France, which did not initially have "national champions" the size of Philips or Siemens, a wave of mergers took place, in both computers and semiconductors, with government approval and sometimes government instigation. This policy of consolidation had the effect of reducing indigenous competition in the face of penetration by subsidiaries of American firms and generated "champions" that proved unfit to take on the Americans (Tilton, 1971, pp. 131–132).

Japanese Developments in the IC Era. The early development of the Japanese IC industry is one of the few areas of IC industry history that has never received a complete examination.[34] Conflicting accounts of this period by Japanese and American executives were (1) that Japanese firms committed early to IC mass production[35] and (2) that Japanese firms remained dependent on U.S. sources of supply (Okimoto et al., 1984). By 1974, the Japanese output of ICs was valued at ¥125.5 billion, about $560 million at the exchange rate in 1974 (Bank of America 1980, p. 104). This compares with U.S. IC shipments in that year of about $2.1 billion (U.S. Department of Commerce, 1966 et seriatim).

Thus the situation in Japan in this period was in many respects similar to – and perhaps even more dire than – that in Europe. Japan had even less military demand than did Europe, and Japanese firms were even more heavily committed to the production of discrete (especially germanium) devices for consumer applications, in which the Japanese were highly successful and strongly export oriented. The Japanese firms were slow to make the transition to batch-produced silicon devices in the early 1960s, and, when they turned later in the decade to the production of bipolar ICs, they could not compete with Texas Instruments and National Semiconductor. Some Japanese firms accused the Americans of

[33] Several of these programs are described in Dosi (1981, p. 27).

[34] The beginnings of a technical history are contained in Watanabe (1984). Although Watanabe discusses the development of the industry, all of his 87 references (all in the English language) are technical. A more comprehensive business history may be found in Nakagawa (1985).

[35] Watanabe (1984) dates Japanese IC production from the first quarter of 1962.

Table 2.8. *Worldwide Shares of Semiconductor and IC Sales by Region of Producing Company, 1978 and 1989*

	1978		**1989**	
	Semiconductor	IC	Semiconductor	IC
U.S.	59	74	43	45
Japan	28	20	48	47
Europe	13	6	11	7

Source: 1978: Braun and Macdonald (1982, p. 153); 1989: Integrated Circuit Engineering (1990, pp. 1-9 and 3-2).

"dumping" (Okimoto et al., 1984, pp. 14–15). Also, like the Europeans, the Japanese were concerned about the dominance of American computer makers, especially IBM, which held nearly 40 percent of the market during most of the 1960s.

From 1965 to 1972, Japan's policy toward the IC industry was largely focused on market reservation, support for the licensing of foreign technology, and domestic procurement by NTT. The market-reservation policy was largely one of preventing direct foreign investment, which meant that American firms were unable to replicate the pattern of foreign direct investment (FDI) that they had followed in Europe. By the time that this policy was dismantled with a round of liberalization in the mid-1970s, the first opportunity for American firms to repeat their European FDI experience had passed, as Japanese firms were soon to launch their challenge to the U.S. merchant producers.

II. The Japanese Challenge

During the 1970s, the integrated circuit reinforced American dominance of the international market for semiconductors. In the major producing regions, the United States held a two-to-one overall advantage over Japan in market share in semiconductors and a better than three-to-one advantage in integrated circuits (see Table 2.8).[36] A decade later, Japan had over-

[36] The data in Table 2.8 are derived from Integrated Circuit Engineering Corporation (ICE), a U.S. market research firm that defines the "national origin" of semiconductor production as follows: "All figures that describe 'sales or production by geographical headquarters location' include all sales or production by a company regardless of where the

taken the United States in both semiconductor and IC share among the three producing regions, while the European share remained frozen.[37]

The loss of American dominance is striking. How and why did this happen?[38] The answer is to be found in the dynamics of competition between American and Japanese companies in the new generations of IC products introduced beginning in the late 1970s. This competition involved issues of productive efficiency, investment rates and timing, and design strategy. The success of Japanese companies was aided by the nature of end-use markets in Japan, the timing of market developments, and the patterns of investment by American and Japanese companies.

Challenging the Leader: Strategy for Overtaking an Incumbent

The vitality of the American IC industry during its period of dominance was its intense technological competitiveness, supported by its industrial structure. Competition among firms selling to the same customers meant that cooperative technological relationships within the industry were rare, that equipment suppliers were encouraged to offer highly differentiated products, and that the industry had not developed a unified position for lobbying the government. Moreover, because of the peculiar structure of the American industry, the largest producer (IBM) was a customer of both domestic and foreign manufacturers but was not itself a merchant.[39]

product is produced or sold. For example, all of Texas Instruments' semiconductor sales or production, including those from its Japanese and European facilities, would be listed in the North American semiconductor segment" (ICE, 1995, p. 1-1). ICE's data also include captive production volumes, the revenues from nonrecurring engineering costs of developing application-specific integrated circuits, and internal transfers.

[37] Table 2.8 includes the production of American captive producers (primarily IBM), which has often been excluded in other studies The estimated share of American captives in the world total amounted to 10 percent of the total semiconductor and 11 percent of the IC market (ICE, 1990). Excluding them suggests an even more dramatic decline of the U.S. position to 36 percent in semiconductors and 38 percent in ICs, with a 54 percent share for Japanese producers in both markets. Howell, Bartlett, and Davis (1992, p. 9) are among the authors who compare only American merchant companies to Japan. In 1989, they estimate Japanese share of the semiconductor market at 51 percent including other producers (European and Asian) and 38 percent for the United States.

[38] A sample of attempts to answer the question would include Borrus, Millstein, and Zysman (1982); Borrus (1988); Ferguson (1985); Howell, Bartlett, and Davis (1992); Prestowitz (1988); Semiconductor Industry Association (SIA) (1981, 1983); and Tyson (1992).

[39] In another sense, however, the structure of the American semiconductor industry was not peculiar at all. "The coexistence and complementarity of large and small technology-based firms has been a persistent feature of the US in major twentieth century industries" (Wright, 1999, p. 317).

Almost from its origins, the industry had been focused on growth rather than on profit margins. Indeed, the profitability of the industry collectively ran below the average for American manufacturing.[40] The prosperity of the industry was maintained through growth of product markets, a process that required continual investment in physical capacity and in research and development. This meant that American IC companies could not generate large cash reserves from retained earnings; moreover, as these companies were not typically divisions of larger organizations, they could not benefit from intraorganizational transfers of capital. The result was that, during periodic industry downturns, the industry reduced investment spending and laid off workers; in the upturns, the industry delayed in committing to new plant, delay that led to capacity shortages.[41]

In Japanese firms, IC production occurred within a vertically integrated structure similar to that of firms in Europe. But, for a number of reasons, the Japanese firms viewed it as crucial to enter international merchant markets. For one thing, outside customers would help ward off the sorts of internal demands that Malerba (1985) associates with the decline of the European industry. Rather than believing they were on the verge of overtaking American companies, the Japanese saw both their semiconductor and computer industries as relatively weak against IBM and perceived that a key feature of IBM's advantage was technology, specifically its position in ICs (Ferguson and Morris, 1993). The fact that Japanese IC producers were large companies in comparison with their American counterparts gave them the advantage that they were able to mobilize internal capital resources to make investments in the IC industry in a way that U.S. companies could not.

The strategy of the Japanese challenge could therefore be based upon an investment challenge with two elements, investment in capacity and investment in manufacturing quality. This left the problem of identifying which products were vulnerable to a challenge. Hindsight makes it

[40] See Braun and Macdonald (1982, p. 148) for net earnings after tax as a percentage of sales for 1967–1977.

[41] American firms did, of course, have recourse to the arm's-length capital markets. And most economists would see this chronic "undercapitalization" of the industry as a sign that capital markets had "failed." In fact, of course, arm's-length capital markets and the internal capital markets of multidivisional firms are both institutions with pluses and minuses, and neither is sensibly judged against an abstract ideal standard. As we will see, the decentralization and independence of American firms served the industry well in many circumstances, both early and late in our story. But, because of what one might generally view as transaction-cost problems, arm's-length financing may be less adept in smoothing cyclical fluctuations than is internal financing. We include in this venture-capital financing, which is, in any case, typically used for start-up capital rather than for ongoing capitalization of mature businesses.

Table 2.9. *Maximum Market Share in DRAMs by American and Japanese Companies, by Device*

Device	Maximum Market Share (%)	
	United States	Japan
1K	95	5
4K	83	17
16K	59	41
64K	29	71
256K	8	92
1M	4	96
4M	2	98

Source: Dataquest, cited in Methé (1991, p. 69).

obvious that the emerging dynamic random-access memory (DRAM) of the early to mid-1970s was the most attractive market to challenge. At that time, Japanese producers could certainly have concluded that the DRAM market would be suited to the Japanese approach to manufacturing. The potential for the DRAM to become a standardized, mass-produced product had already been demonstrated by Intel's 1003, the 1K DRAM that established the market.

American firms continued to dominate in the early – 1K and 4K – DRAM markets. But an industry recession delayed the American "ramp-up" to the 16K DRAM, which appeared in 1976. Aided by unforeseen production problems among the three leaders, Japanese firms were able to gain a significant share of the 16K market. By mid-1979, 16 companies were producing DRAMs, and Japanese producers accounted for 42 percent of the market (Wilson et al., 1980, pp. 93–94) (see Table 2.9). This was a remarkable development. For the first time, Japanese companies were able to gain a significant foothold in the American market for a leading-edge device. The fact that this was achieved without a significant backlash from the U.S. government or a consolidated response from American IC or system manufacturers signaled that the American market might well be open.

The opportunity opened for Japanese producers in the 16K DRAM market had proved sufficient for them to advance to a position of leadership in the 64K DRAM. Their success relied upon manufacturing advantage and price-cutting. The Japanese fixed early upon a conservative design for their 64K DRAMs, which allowed them simply to scale up existing process technology. By contrast, the American firms insisted on radical new designs and new process technology, which increased development times and start-up problems (Borrus, 1988, p. 144). As a result, Intel, Mostek, and National encountered production difficulties, giving Japanese firms a head start down the experience curve.

Japanese dominance accelerated in the 256K (1982) and 1-megabit (1985) generations (see Table 2.9). The scaleup of 64K DRAM production had caused a very rapid reduction in price, which, combined with the general recession in the U.S. industry in 1985, caused all but two American merchant IC companies to withdraw from DRAM production[42] (Howell et al., 1992, p. 29). In 1990, American market share had fallen to only 2 percent of the new-generation 4-megabit DRAM.[43] (see Table 2.9).

The Role of Demand

As had been the case in the rise of the American semiconductor industry, the pattern of end-use demand was crucial in shaping the bundle of capabilities that Japanese industry possessed – as well as in narrowing and limiting the choices the Japanese firms had open to them. In this case, that end-use demand came largely from consumer electronics and, to a somewhat lesser extent, from telecommunications. Consumer demand helped place the Japanese on a product trajectory – namely, CMOS ICs – that turned out eventually to have much wider applicability.[44] And NTT's demand for high-quality memory chips for telecommunication switching systems helped nudge the industry into a strategy of specialization in high-volume production of DRAMs.

Japan was without a significant military demand that could provide a market to support specialized high-performance devices. Japanese computer manufacturers had attained a moderate success, with 1973 production of ¥472 billion ($2.15 billion). Nonetheless, the consumer

[42] The exceptions were Texas Instruments, which produced in Japan, and Micron Technology, which produced in Idaho.

[43] Again, these figures do not take into account the sizable captive production at IBM and AT&T.

[44] MOS stands for metal-oxide semiconductor, a form of field-effect technology. CMOS stands for "complementary" MOS and NMOS (discussed later) for "negative" MOS.

electronics market of that year was far larger at ¥1,685 billion ($7.66 billion). Consumer electronics accounted for one-half of all electronic equipment production in Japan in 1973, a share that was to remain almost constant throughout the 1970s despite a 50 percent growth in the overall size of production.

The particular consumer product of greatest relevance in the early years was the desktop (and eventually the hand-held) calculator. Although this product may seem mundane, it created a very large demand for ICs: in the early 1970s, nearly 50 percent of the Japanese IC market went for desktop calculators (Watanabe, 1984, p. 1564). Calculators thus provided Japanese firms with a "product driver" that could be used to fund large-scale production of ICs (Borrus, 1988, p. 124). More significantly, perhaps, the calculator market started Japanese firms down the technological trajectory of CMOS production.[45] American firms favored the alternative NMOS technology for the early generations of DRAMs, largely because of its (initially) lower cost and because of conservatism about the technological risks of CMOS. Japanese firms chose to develop expertise in CMOS because its lower power consumption – useful in portable devices – had offsetting benefits in calculators and other consumer applications. But a technological change in the lithography process canceled out the cost advantage of NMOS, and CMOS turned out to have a steeper learning curve. By 1983–1984, the cost of CMOS had fallen below that of NMOS, and CMOS quickly became the clear technological choice for almost all applications. The Americans thus found that much of their previous experience with NMOS had become obsolete and that they lagged behind the Japanese in CMOS.

The Role of Japanese Government Policy

The VLSI Program is the most famous of the efforts made by the Japanese to deepen their technological competence to a level at which it could challenge American dominance. The program sprang from a key goal of Japanese (as of European) industrial policy: to create a mainframe computer industry in competition with, and in imitation of, IBM.

Both NTT and MITI (the Ministry of International Trade and Industry) initiated programs for improving manufacturing capabilities. The NTT project lasted from 1975 to 1981 and was funded on the order of ¥40 billion (about $180 million) (Callon, 1995, p. 37). Several major companies, notably Toshiba and Mitsubishi, who were not traditional suppliers to NTT, were left out, thus allowing MITI in 1976 to create

[45] The remainder of this paragraph follows Ernst and O'Connor (1992, p. 66).

another project in which they could participate.[46] The MITI VLSI Project extended over the period 1976–1980. Total program expenditures are officially given as ¥73.7 billion (about $330 million), of which ¥29.1 billion ($130 million), or some 40 percent, was government subsidy. The two projects were organizationally distinct, although overall oversight of both was technically assigned to MITI. NTT's efforts were conducted at its own laboratories, whereas MITI's VLSI Project was based at a separate facility that combined researchers from participating companies, all of whom continued their own research programs.

In planning the VLSI Project, MITI saw joint organization in a single laboratory as politically valuable and pressed the companies to agree. This feature has attracted great attention and has been emulated in other consortia designs. It was also a feature that, by recent accounts (Fransman, 1990, p. 63; Callon, 1995, p. 57), the companies vehemently opposed. The companies reluctantly accepted MITI's joint laboratory organization as the price of the private research subsidies they really wanted (Fransman, 1990, p. 64). One consequence of the resistance is that only 15–20 percent of the total budget went to the joint laboratories; 80–85 percent went to private research in company laboratories (Fransman, 1990, p. 80).

The technological goal of the VLSI Project was to accelerate Japanese progress in increasing the transistor count in ICs. The initial target was development of techniques for fabricating a 256K device. This goal was hastily bumped up to 1 megabit (1M) when Matsushita, a company with no connection to the project, announced its development of a chip that already met those standards (Sigurdson, 1986, p. 53). Much of the research was focused on high-energy alternatives to the optical lithography techniques then in use[47] (Sigurdson, 1986, p. 83; Fransman, 1995, p. 162; Callon, 1995, p. 119). As it turned out, such techniques have not replaced optical lithography even today – although, as Henderson (1995) has pointed out, the lifespan of optical technology fooled almost everyone.

American Government Policy on the Eve of the Japanese Challenge

Between 1965 and 1984, U.S. government policy may be divided into two periods. As we saw, the first period (1965–1974) was one in which the

[46] Five companies were official participants: NEC, Toshiba, Fujitsu, Hitachi, and Mitsubishi.

[47] Lithography is the "drawing" of the circuit pattern on the wafer, a process somewhat analogous to what a photographic enlarger does in a darkroom. High-energy techniques would use beams of electrons or even x-rays rather than light to draw finer lines.

integrated-circuit industry benefited from the same space and defense programs that had supported the transistor industry's growth. Federal demands for ICs during this period contributed to the rate of cost reduction, producing an externality for commercial markets. By 1974, however, growth in commercial markets for ICs had greatly diminished the ability of procurement to influence the industry: government demand had fallen to 16 percent of industry output (U.S. Department of Commerce, 1979, p. 44). This level was not increased, even with the increases in defense expenditure, in the 1980s.

During the second period, there was only one major defense program directed at the semiconductor industry, the very high speed integrated circuit (VHSIC) program. VHSIC's ambitious goal was to close the gap between military and civilian technology. Although this goal went unmet, the program did improve the capabilities of defense contractors in systems design.[48] During the late 1980s, the strategy of basing military systems on leading-edge commercial components was once again debated in the context of "dual-use" technology, with little effect on practice.

Throughout the period, the industry continued to benefit from American policies governing the re-importation of partially finished goods manufactured offshore and a generally supportive tax treatment of R&D investment. Thus, for approximately a decade (1974–1984), the American industry experienced what was essentially a laissez-faire policy.

European Developments

During the period of the Japanese challenge (1978–1988), European firms adopted policies aimed at staying in the race, including the development of products for consumer electronics, industrial, and automotive applications. The most important initiative in this period was the acquisition of American companies. Table 2.10 shows most of these acquisitions. With the exception of Signetics and Fairchild, the European acquisitions were small specialized companies or minority shares that facilitated technology exchange. Schlumberger's acquisition of Fairchild was spectacularly unsuccessful, leading eventually to the sale of the company to National Semiconductor after the American government threatened to block a proposed sale to Fujitsu.[49] By contrast, Philips's acquisition of Signetics has assisted Europe's largest IC producer in

[48] See Steinmueller (1988a) for further discussion of the VHSIC program and of the problems of attributing a major supportive role in the later period to government – and, specifically, military – procurement policies.

[49] See Steinmueller (1988b) for an account of Fujitsu's offer.

Table 2.10. *European Acquisition of U.S. Semiconductor Companies*

Year	*U.S. Firm*	*European Firm*	*Share Acquired*
1975	Signetics	Philips (NL)	100%
1976	Silconix	Lucas (UK)	24%
1977	Interdesign	Ferranti (UK)	100%
	American Microsystems	Bosch (FRG)	25%
	Litronix	Siemens (FRG)	80%
	Advanced Micro Devices	Siemens (FRG)	20%
1979	Fairchild	Schlumberger (FR)	100%
	Microwave Semiconductor	Siemens (FRG)	100%

Source: Braun and Macdonald (1982, p. 176).

maintaining a relatively strong position, both within Europe and in international markets.

The other developments, less important only because of their limited outcomes, were the European Silicon Structures Initiative (ECU30 million) and the Siemens-Philips Mega-Projekt (DM5 billion). The former program was part of the Eureka Program, which was somewhat effective in upgrading European processing capabilities. The latter program was initially successful, providing Siemens and Philips with a commercial SRAM product. But this position subsequently eroded, and today Europe has a very small share of the international market for SRAMs (European Microelectronics Panel, 1995). Thus, European firm strategy continued to be one of survival through specialization, punctuated by ambitious, but largely unsuccessful, efforts to achieve a technological breakthrough that would propel them to a dominant position in a major semiconductor market.

III. The American Response

An American Resurgence

The year 1985 was the darkest period in American IC industry history, with record layoffs and with Intel, the flagship among American merchants, suffering losses exceeding its book value. Japanese firms had captured the DRAM market almost entirely, and prognostications widely heralded a Japanese move into – and inevitable dominance of – other categories of chip, including the microprocessor (Ferguson, 1985; Reich and Mankin, 1986). But 1985 was actually not the beginning of the end but the beginning of a turnaround. On April 9, 1992, a front-page *New York Times* headline read, "U.S. Chip Makers Stem the Tide in Trade Battles with the Japanese: Predictions of a Trouncing Have Not Panned Out" (Pollack, 1992). During this short period, the United States was able to restore a slight lead in its market share with Japan – a performance we can characterize as a "resurgence" of the American producers. This change of fortunes does not represent a strong reversal in the relative competitive strength of American and Japanese semiconductor producers, an across-the-board restoration of American dominance; Japanese producers remain strong, especially in the product areas in which their competitive position was achieved, notably DRAMs. Rather, the American resurgence reflects a combination of several factors of varying importance:

- A renewed emphasis on manufacturing and some success in improving productivity;
- Organizational innovation and specialization, allowing the American industry to take advantage both of its own structural advantages and of global manufacturing capabilities; and
- A favorable shift in the importance of those products in which American firms have specialized. We view this last factor as the most important of these three.

We examine these factors in turn, reserving the role of American government policy for separate treatment.

Manufacturing Improvements. As we saw, Japanese firms had been nudged by the character of the demand they faced onto the technological trajectory of CMOS – a technology that was to prove superior in cost and performance dimensions in most applications. In 1988, CMOS represented about 40 percent of the value of IC production; by 1994, it was responsible for 80 percent of production value (ICE, 1995). Because American firms had concentrated on NMOS technology, they lagged in converting to CMOS, and that meant that the American companies were engaged in a process of "catch-up" with their Japanese competitors in process technology. This seemed an insurmountable problem, as most American companies feared that DRAM production was the only means of improving or "driving" the state of the art in CMOS technology. In the end, however, this fear proved groundless. American companies were able to make CMOS circuits with sufficient quality, performance, and transistor counts to meet the competition using experience with logic and specialized memory devices such as SRAMs.[50]

What evidence is there that American firms improved their manufacturing productivity significantly? One piece of indirect evidence is that American firms were able to hold their market shares in a number of product segments, including application-specific integrated circuits (ASICs), where American and Japanese companies compete nearly head-to-head.[51] There is also more direct evidence.[52] One of the factors driving the success of Japanese firms in memory products in the early 1980s was the higher quality of the chips they produced. For Japanese chips, defect rates – the fraction of chips that prove to be defective – were probably half to one-tenth the rates for American products. By the second half of that decade, however, American firms had dramatically increased expenditures for quality control, imitating Japanese practices such as total quality management (TQM), greater attention to preventive maintenance, and automated process control and monitoring. By the early 1990s, American manufacturers had probably begun to match the defect levels of their Japanese counterparts. Intel reportedly reduced its defect rate by a factor of 10 (Helm, 1995). There is also evidence that American firms have improved manufacturing yield rates and direct labor productivity since the early 1990s.[53] This represents a closing of the gap, but it doesn't mean that American production facilities (or "fabs") have reached the levels of Japanese or even Taiwanese fabs, in part because American fabs operate at smaller scales on average and cannot take as much advantage of the economies of large production runs.

[50] In part, the claim that the production of DRAMs was necessary as a process driver confused the properties of DRAMs with the fact of volume production. As microprocessors and other nonmemory chips began to be produced in greater volume (because of the growth of the personal computer industry, discussed later), those devices were able to serve as process drivers. Indeed, microprocessor chips are in many ways more complicated than RAMs. They typically require more layers, and that requirement helped give American firms, and their American equipment suppliers, advantage in (among other things) the complex technology of interconnecting levels (Langlois, 1999).

[51] Even here, American firms tend to specialize in the standard-cell approach to ASICs, which is more design-intensive and less manufacturing-intensive than the linear and gate arrays favored by the Japanese. Between 1989 and 1994, however, this specialization diminished somewhat as American firms lost 2 percent of share in standard cells but gained a point in linear and gate arrays (ICE, 1990, 1995).

[52] The remainder of this paragraph follows Macher, Mowery, and Hodges (1998).

[53] According to one study, the yields of American firms increased from 60 percent in 1986 to 84 percent in 1991. The yields of Japanese firms increased over the same period from 75 percent to 93 percent, implying that American firms narrowed the gap in yield rates from 15 percent to 9 percent (US GAO, 1992).

Specialization and Globalization. Nonetheless, the Americans' improved manufacturing capabilities were more than adequate in view of favorable structural changes and demand shifts. The abandonment of the DRAM market by most American firms – including Intel – was a dark cloud with a bright silver lining. When Intel led the world industry in almost all categories, it and many of its American counterparts faced a full plate of product alternatives. With the elimination of mass memory as a viable market, these firms were impelled to specialize and narrow their focus to a smaller subset of choices. As we saw earlier, a relatively narrow product focus coupled with a deepening technological competence can be an extremely successful strategy, as it arguably was in the early days of the industry. It is also, indeed, the strategy that Japanese firms leveraged to success in DRAMs.

The areas in which American firms concentrated can generally be described as higher-margin, design-intensive chips. For such chips, production costs would not be the sole margin of competition; innovation and responsiveness would count for more. And innovation and responsiveness were arguably the strong suits of the "fragmented" American industry. As Nelson and Winter (1977) and others have argued, a decentralized structure permits the trying out of a wider diversity of approaches, leading to rapid trial-and-error learning. And the independence of many firms from larger organizations permits speedier realignment and recombination with suppliers and customers. Building on existing competences in design (especially of logic and specialty circuits) and close ties with the burgeoning American personal computer industry, American firms were able to prosper despite the Japanese edge in manufacturing technology.

Another aspect of specialization that benefited the American industry was the increasing "decoupling" of design from production. Such decoupling is in many respects a natural manifestation of the division of labor in growing markets (Young, 1928); in this case, it was abetted by the development of computerized design tools (Hobday, 1991) and the standardization of manufacturing technology (Macher et al., 1998). On the one hand, this allowed American firms to specialize in design-intensive chips, taking advantage of an American comparative advantage that arguably arises out of the decentralized and "fragmented" structure of that country's industry.[54] On the other hand, it also allowed many

[54] Perhaps surprisingly, the mid-1980s – that dark period for American fortunes – was actually the most fertile period in history for the start-up of new semiconductor firms, by a large margin. Most of these new firms were involved in design-intensive custom devices and ASICs (Angel, 1994, p. 38).

American firms to take advantage of growing production capabilities overseas.

"Globalization" has long been a trend in the semiconductor industry (Langlois et al., 1988), and American firms had long used "offshore" production as a strategy for cost reduction, beginning with outsourcing of assembly and packaging stages.[55] But the decoupling of design from production has enabled American firms to benefit from globalization without investing large amounts of their own money overseas. These "fabless" semiconductor firms are able to contract out production to "silicon foundries" around the world, especially in the Far East.[56] In 1997, the fabless sector generated revenue of almost $8 billion, with industry revenues projected to increase to $18 billion by the year 2000, nearly 6 percent of the total semiconductor market[57]. The Fabless Semiconductor Association – which represents the foundry users – began with 45 members in 1994 and now boasts some 170 members, most of whom are North American (Zajak, 1997; Macher et al., 1998). Aside from the usual benefits of specialization, the fabless-foundry arrangement increases flexibility and response time, as design firms can take advantage of plants already geared up to serve them. The foundries make it possible for chip start-ups to "jump on a freight train moving 150 miles an hour," as one industry executive put it (Engardio et al., 1996). Although the Asian foundries originally lagged integrated firms in production technology, the gap has closed from three years to six months (Zajak, 1997), and three Asian foundries are now operating at the cutting-edge line width of 0.25 micron (LaPedus, 1997b).

[55] The growing internationalization of IC production has led to confusion in the use of official trade statistics. This is not a new phenomenon. Steinmueller (1988a) observed that the attribution of value added between production of finished wafers and final IC devices was a matter of some dispute, since international transfers of ICs during the 1980s followed a very complex pattern: wafers produced in one country would be followed by packaging operations in a second country (often one with different rules of corporate taxation). The packaging operation would be followed by testing operations in the original producing country or yet a third country. Since markets for specific models of partially finished semiconductors are either nonexistent or very thin and controlled by closely related parties, the attribution of value for tax and tariff purposes is neither obvious nor unambiguous.

[56] As we point out later, most of the foundries are in Taiwan and Singapore, with others planned – at least before the recent Asian financial crisis – in such countries as Thailand and China. Israel also boasts a major foundry. Even American firms have gotten into the foundry business: IBM is acting as foundry for Cyrix's line of microprocessors, an association slated to end, however, now that Cyrix has merged with National Semiconductor. Recently, with overcapacity in the DRAM market, Korea is looking to enter the business (LaPedus and Robertson, 1997).

[57] Data from the Fabless Semiconductor Association and Dataquest, cited in Macher, Mowery, and Hodges (1998).

Table 2.11. *Worldwide Merchant Market Product Segments (Percentage)*

	1988	1994
MOS Memory	29	35
MPU and related	17	26
MOS Logic	23	20
Bipolar Logic	11	3
Analog	18	16
Other	2	<1

Source: Integrated Circuit Engineering Corporation (1989, 1995).

Shifts in the Pattern of Demand. Product design has once again become a major determinant of competitive outcomes. This is true not only in the area of custom logic chips and ASICs but – perhaps most importantly – in microprocessor unit (MPU) and related segments, also called the microcomponent segment.[58] Between 1988 and 1994, merchant IC revenues grew by 121 percent, from $41.3 to $91.5 billion. The strong growth in overall revenues has been accompanied by more rapid growth in microprocessor than in memory markets, as illustrated in Table 2.11. This evolution of the product mix in the industry has strongly favored American producers. In the microcomponent portion of the chip market, American companies accounted for 66 percent of world production in 1994, compared with a 29 percent share for Japanese companies.

The importance of the microprocessor segment has meant that a single company, Intel, is responsible for much of the gain of American merchant IC producers. In 1994, Intel accounted for 31 percent of world output in the microcomponent market, led by its strong position in microprocessors. Intel's strategy for recovery, begun in the 1980s, has proved remarkably successful. In the late 1980s, Intel consolidated its intellectual-property position in microprocessors by terminating cross-licensing agreements with other companies and, more importantly, began extending its first-mover advantage over rivals by accelerating the rate of new product introduction. These developments pushed Intel into the position of the largest IC producer in the world, with 1994 sales of $9.85

[58] This segment includes not only microprocessors, but also microcontrollers (less sophisticated microprocessors that are used in embedded applications) and related "support" chips, such as memory controllers, that are necessary to assembling a microprocessor system.

billion, $1 billion more than the second largest producer, NEC. Although Intel dominates the microprocessor market, it is not entirely without competitors; it is significant that its principal competitors are also American firms. Motorola has long produced a rival microprocessor line linked to the Apple computer platform. And, more recently, Cyrix and AMD have mounted a strategy of producing Intel-compatible microprocessors to attack the low-end personal-computer market.

The success of American firms in microprocessors and related chips has been reinforced by trends in end-use demand. In 1989, computer applications took 40 percent of merchant IC sales, followed by consumer and automotive applications at 28 percent.[59] By 1994, the respective shares were 52 percent for computer and 23 percent for consumer and automotive applications. The worldwide changes have led to increasing specialization. North American use of ICs for computer applications soared from 15 to 24 percent of the total value of world merchant sales, while the Japanese IC market for consumer applications fell from 13 to 10 percent of world merchant sales. Thus, in contrast to rough parity (15 versus 13 percent) in 1989, an enormous gap has opened between IC demand for consumer and computer applications in the 1994 markets of Japan and the United States (24 versus 10 percent). Keep in mind that these figures are in terms of revenue, not physical units, and much of the reversal of American fortunes has to do with the high value per component of microprocessors and other design-intensive chips, as against the low value per unit of the mass-produced DRAMs on which Japanese firms long rested their strategies.

Macroeconomic factors have also played a role. In 1985, it took 240 yen to buy a dollar. In late 1992, the exchange rate stood at 127 yen to a dollar. Six months later, it was 106 yen to the dollar, and for most of the past five years the rate has hovered around 100 yen per dollar. Although good news for Japanese consumers and businesses purchasing foreign goods and services, the very rapid increase in the value of the yen was a major shock to Japanese manufacturing companies, including IC producers. The most important long-term result of the strong yen may have been the relative decline in Japanese consumer electronic production.

Economies of scale are key to the success of consumer electronics. Two factors have limited Japan's realization of such economies, although another factor continues to work in Japan's favor. First, the rapid expansion of Korea, China, and the Southeast Asian economies into consumer electronics has divided demand, a trend that is particularly significant

[59] These and succeeding figures in this paragraph are from ICE (1990; 1995).

where margins are small on large-volume low-end products. Second, during the past decade, no major innovation like the videocassette recorder has emerged to create a rapid-growth demand segment.[60] The factor remaining in Japan's favor is the control of mass production of some key components for consumer electronics. Color television picture tubes, specialized ICs, flat panel displays, and laser printing engines are components in the consumer and business-equipment markets for which Japanese firms maintain competitive advantage and in which scale economies are important. But these components are all relatively expensive to produce, especially in an era of dear yen.

This was not the end of the bad news for Japan, however. Between 1989 and 1994, the share of Japanese IC demand for computer and datacom applications fell from 41 to 20 percent of the total worldwide demand for those uses. Meanwhile, the American share of total demand in the computer segment rose from 37 to 46 percent.[61] The change represents a very serious reversal for Japan in the computer market and, again, a movement from a position of rough parity to one of American leadership. Traditional trade theory would discount these changes in downstream markets, assuming that trade flows would adjust to follow international demand. This type of adjustment is not the case, and has never been the case, in the IC industry. Neither the American nor the Japanese market is fully "open" to such adjustments, and imports as a percentage of total demand would be exceptional at 20 percent. Over the past several years, American imports as a share of the Japanese domestic market have hovered around 14 percent; in the American market, which nearly doubled between 1992 and 1994, the share of Japanese imports fell from 21 to 18 percent (ICE, 1995, p. 1-31).

In part, Japanese IC producers (who are also typically computer producers) have been disadvantaged by their failure to develop a vibrant domestic personal computer industry. From a very strong position in the first 15 years of microprocessor developments and the prospect of leadership in personal computer production, Japanese firms have retreated to become producers of specialized computer components and have suffered a marked decline in their international market share. In part, this development reflects the structure of the Japanese computer industry. Because personal computers in Japan are the province of the large vertically integrated systems houses, those firms have – at least until

[60] There are hopes that the digital videodisk (DVD) technology will have this role in the closing years of this decade.

[61] Computed from ICE (1990; 1995). This change is somewhat overstated, since the 1989 figures include data communications as well as computer applications, whereas the 1994 figures include only computer applications.

recently – maintained a strategy of rival incompatible systems (Cottrell, 1995). By contrast, the fragmentation and vertical specialization of the American personal computer industry led to far greater standardization, which allowed both a finer division of labor and the use of a wider network of capabilities (Langlois, 1992). In part, however, the relative decline of Japan in personal computers also reflects the strength of American IC and system producers in accelerating the pace of product innovation. This too may be a by-product of the more fragmented and decentralized – and therefore more nimble – structure of American industry. Moreover, while Japanese computer makers are being pushed by American innovativeness on one side, they are also facing threats to their manufacturing leadership from elsewhere in Asia, and the "sourcing" of many once-strategic components is now more footloose than it had been.

The Rise of Far Eastern Production

Japanese firms were not the only ones who could understand the economics of capacity investment or productivity in manufacturing; they were soon joined by Korean semiconductor producers and by larger American companies who matched Japanese productivity by the simple expedient of establishing Japanese plants. The result is a dilution of the control of capacity investment by Japanese producers, who, even if they could manage to agree on rationing capacity expansion among themselves, could not control the Koreans, who were determined to follow in Japan's footsteps toward the "sunrise" high-technology industry of IC production.

Korean entry was based upon an aggressive investment program and the hiring of American-trained Korean talent.[62] In 1984–1985, Korean companies spent nearly $1.2 billion to enter the market (ICE 1987, p. 2-42), only to arrive at the height of the 1985 recession. Despite this, and because of the long-term perspective of the leading companies, the Koreans emerged from the global recession with relatively modern facilities and a growing share of the market. In 1986 they produced an output of $336 million worth of ICs or about 1.2 percent of the world market (ICE, 1988, pp. 2-24, 1-4). Although relatively small, this was enough to be noticed, since much of Samsung's output was focused on DRAMs. By

[62] "By recruiting heavily among South Korean expatriates at U.S. universities and Silicon Valley chip makers, companies like Samsung Electronics Co. were able to quickly assemble a core of experienced engineers. . . . 'When we have joint meetings with Samsung engineers, they're nearly all [like] Americans,' says one NEC engineer" (Hamilton and Glain, 1995).

Table 2.12. *Worldwide Merchant-Market Sales of DRAMs ($ Million)*

Company	*Country*	*1995*	*1996*
Samsung	Korea	6,462	4,125
NEC	Japan	4,740	3,175
Hitachi	Japan	4,439	2,805
Hyundai	Korea	3,500	2,300
Toshiba	Japan	3,725	2,235
LG Electronics	Korea	3,005	2,005
Texas Instruments	U.S.	3,200	1,600
Micron	U.S.	2,485	1,575
Mitsubishi	Japan	2,215	1,400
Fujitsu	Japan	2,065	1,350

Source: Integrated Circuit Engineering Corporation (1996, 1997).

1993, Korean companies were producing $4.77 billion in ICs, a world market share of 5.2 percent (ICE, 1995, p. 2-46), and Samsung, which produced more than half of this output, became the world's largest memory-chip producer (Hamilton and Glain, 1995). In 1995, three Korean firms were among the top ten producers of DRAMs in the world, selling almost $13 billion worth of ICs (Table 2.12).

In contrast to Korea, Taiwan has developed into a highly diversified producer of semiconductors, with significant and growing capabilities in design as well as in fabrication, both of mass-produced DRAMs and of specialty chips in silicon foundries. The island ranks sixth in the world in the value of integrated-circuit output, having increased production from some $400 million in 1989 to $2.2 billion in 1994. By the year 2000, that figure may rise to $9.4 billion or 5 percent of world output (Dataquest, cited in Marnet, 1996).

The Taiwanese industry has its origins in a porous environment that encouraged foreign direct investment, strategic alliances with foreign firms, and high mobility of engineers, especially to and from the United States (see Table 2.13).[63] Taiwan served for years as an offshore site for American manufacturers, especially in the areas of assembly and packaging. An indigenous semiconductor industry began in the mid-1970s when a quasi-governmental research consortium called the Electronic Research and Service Organization (ERSO) licensed technology from RCA. As it happened, RCA was a leader in CMOS technology; moreover, RCA soon left the industry, leaving ERSO with intellectual-

[63] Much of this paragraph follows Chen and Sewell (1996).

Table 2.13. *The Growth of Semiconductor Design and Fabrication in Taiwan, 1988–1992*

	1988	*1989*	*1990*	*1991*	*1992*
Proportionate value of sector					
Design	7.1	13.9	13.9	14.3	13.7
Mask and fabrication	14.3	19.4	21.4	33.0	37.4
Assembly	78.6	66.7	64.7	52.7	48.9
Total value ($ Million)	1095	1465	1574	1898	2491
Annual growth rate (%)	—	33.8	7.2	20.6	31.2

Source: Chen and Sewell (1996).

property rights to the American firm's technology and a leg up on what would become the dominant technological trajectory (Chen and Sewell, 1996, p. 772). ERSO spun off a number of design houses and a company called UMC to assimilate foreign production technology. Both UMC and ERSO dabbled in DRAMs for the 4K through 64K generations in the early 1980s. It was not until late in that decade, however, that Taiwan gained ground in DRAMs, especially through a joint venture between TI and the Taiwanese computer maker Acer. In 1993, this plant reportedly had the highest yield of any TI DRAM plant in the world, including Miho, Japan (Chen and Sewell, 1996, p. 774).

Perhaps the most significant aspect of the development of the Taiwanese semiconductor industry, however, is its major role in "silicon foundry" production for American fabless semiconductor manufacturers. In the early 1990s, three design houses owned by American-trained Taiwanese integrated backward into fabrication (Chen and Sewell, 1996, p. 774). By 1996, Taiwanese foundries were handling 40 percent of the output of American fabless companies, with firms like Taiwan Semiconductor Manufacturing (TSMC), United Microelectronics, and Winbond Technology producing for American companies like Cirrus Logic, S3, and Trident (Engardio et al., 1996). Most Taiwanese foundries involve joint ventures with American fabless firms (LaPedus, 1997b). Indeed, the Taiwanese industry is in many respects less a competitor with the American industry than it is a symbiotic extension of it.

A number of other Asian nations are beginning to enter the foundry business as a way of entering the broader semiconductor industry. Chartered Semiconductor of Singapore, a partly government owned enterprise, is already a major player, and Malaysia, Thailand, and China all have plans for entry and expansion (Marnet, 1996; LaPedus, 1997a).

How this expansion will be affected by the recent financial crisis in Asia remains to be seen.

The Role of American Government Policy

Trade Policy. American trade policy in the semiconductor arena antedated the period of Japanese ascendancy. For example, it was the threat of American trade sanctions that helped motivate some of the 1970s liberalization of Japanese policies mentioned earlier (Dick, 1995, p. 49). In 1977, American semiconductor firms banded together into the Semiconductor Industry Association (SIA), which was successful in a number of trade initiatives, including the elimination of semiconductor duties in both the United States and Japan[64] (Yoffie, 1988). But American efforts did not acquire bite and urgency until the mid-1980s, when the Japanese takeover of the DRAM market became a dominant fact.[65]

The first salvos were fired on legal ground. In June 1985, the SIA filed a so-called Section 301 complaint with the U.S. Trade Representative, charging that restrictive access to the Japanese market constituted an unfair trade practice. Within weeks, Micron Technology – one of the two remaining American DRAM producers and the only one to produce in the United States – filed a petition with the U.S. Commerce Department charging that Japanese firms were "dumping" 64K DRAMs in the United States. In September 1985, Intel, Advanced Micro Devices (AMD), and National Semiconductor filed a similar complaint, charging dumping in the market for electrically programmable read-only memories (EPROMs).[66] That same month, Micron filed a private antitrust suit against Japanese firms. And, in an unprecedented move, the Commerce Department in December instigated its own investigation of dumping in 256K and 1M DRAMs.

Of the two issues – access to Japanese markets for Americans and "dumping" in American markets by Japanese firms – the latter was the more dramatic and motivating. "Dumping" refers to the practice of

[64] The SIA also lobbied successfully for the Semiconductor Chip Protection Act (SCPA), passed in 1984, which was an attempt to protect intellectual property in chip designs at home and to encourage such protection abroad. Although chip protection was widely desired by the industry, the SCPA has largely proved irrelevant, and almost no cases were filed under it. As Risberg (1990) argues, this is because it is cheaper and faster to protect chip designs by proprietary process technology and first-mover advantages than by litigation.

[65] The following account draws on Dick (1991; 1995), Tyson (1992), and Flamm (1996), the last of which is by far the most detailed and definitive.

[66] EPROMs are "nonvolatile" memory devices in that, unlike DRAMs, they remember information even when the power is turned off.

selling below cost in a foreign market in order to drive indigenous producers out of business, thereby ultimately allowing the dumping firm(s) to raise prices and reap economic rents. This is the international variant of the strategy more generally called predatory pricing. It is controversial among economists whether such a strategy is ever rational (as one may pay the costs without ever reaping the benefits);[67] and it is far from clear in principle let alone in practice whether one can reliably distinguish this strategy from healthy competition. In the case of semiconductors, the problem is compounded by the fact that, because of the prevalence of learning-curve effects, pricing below cost – so-called forward pricing – is in fact the appropriate and desirable policy (Spence, 1981; Dick, 1991). Moreover, this was a policy pioneered in semiconductors not by the Japanese but by Texas Instruments, which used it to good advantage in the 1960s and 1970s.

Given the climate of the times, however, the Commerce Department and the International Trade Commission were favorably disposed to the American petitioners and began to announce penalties for dumping that were to be added like a tariff to the price of Japanese chips sold in the United States. This legal activity catalyzed Japanese producers, notably the market leaders, Hitachi and NEC, to cut back production and raise prices. Meanwhile, ongoing negotiations between the American and Japanese governments were beginning to coalesce into a price-control and output-monitoring scheme formalized as the Semiconductor Trade Agreement (STA), signed in September 1986.

In exchange for superseding the pending legal actions, the STA set up what was effectively a price floor for DRAMs and EPROMs shipped to the United States. The Commerce Department established so-called foreign-market values (FMVs) for each Japanese firm. These firms could undercut rivals so long as their prices did not fall below the relevant FMVs.[68] In order to implement the agreement, MITI was empowered to monitor prices and production of the affected chips as well as to monitor

[67] This is largely because the higher postpredation pricing required to recoup the costs of predation are likely to encourage entry (or reentry). Whether such entry will in fact occur depends on the extent of the cost advantage provided by incumbency. In semiconductors, many have argued, the first-mover advantages that learning effects confer upon incumbents are sufficiently important to raise significant problems of entry, particularly in mass produced product segments. But the entry of Korea, Taiwan, and other countries into the DRAM market suggests that barriers may not in fact have been high enough to make predation a successful strategy.

[68] This was intended to allow low-cost Japanese producers to expand at the expense of high-cost ones and thus to allow the average price of Japanese semiconductors to decline; that, because of the formula used for calculating FMVs, would have the effect of lowering the price floor. Tyson (1992, p. 110) praises this provision on the grounds that it would limit the price increases from the STA and that, by limiting the expansion of high-cost Japanese

seven other categories of device. To do this, the ministry set up a special office that was widely understood to be coordinating as well as monitoring Japanese pricing and production. Another aspect of the STA called for improved access to Japanese markets for American firms, a demand that a "secret" side letter quantified as a 20 percent market share.

The accord functioned smoothly in the main, apart from a rift in 1987 over pricing in third-country markets that led the Reagan administration to impose retaliatory sanctions for a short period. Just before the STA was to expire on July 31, 1991, the two governments negotiated a replacement. Under pressure from American computer manufacturers, who had been hurt by higher chip prices, this accord weakened the provision for price coordination, insisting only that Japanese firms submit data that might be used for dumping claims. Instead, the new accord focused on access to the Japanese market, explicitly mentioning the 20 percent target.[69] This second accord was allowed to run its course and was not renewed in 1996.

What were the effects of the STA and its successor? As Fig. 2.1 suggests, it is extremely clear that prices for DRAMs stabilized by 1986 and began to rise, reaching a peak in 1988–1989. The price of EPROMs followed a similar pattern. Industry officials have claimed that the rents in EPROMs generated by the STA enabled Intel to develop the microprocessor line on which its current success rests[70] – and some have even claimed that many of the largest American companies would have gone bankrupt without those rents (Helm, 1995). Constructing counterfactuals is always a tricky business, however. What is clear is that the price rise in 1988–1989 benefited Japanese DRAM producers at the expense of consumers. One estimate places these "bubble profits" (as they were called in Japan) at $3–4 billion (Flamm, 1996, p. 277).

Can this transfer be laid at the door of the STA? The SIA (1990) has argued that the price increases were the result not of the trade accords themselves but of collusion among Japanese chip producers, a collusion

producers, it would make it easier for low-cost American producers to penetrate the Japanese market. The extent to which competition among Japanese producers mitigated the effects of the STA is doubtful, and it is hard to see how a policy of encouraging cost competition in Japan would *help* American firms enter that market.

[69] The target was reached in the final quarter of 1992 but then fell below it in subsequent periods (Dick, 1995, p. 60). Flamm (1996, p. 279) has suggested that Japanese firms may have consciously chosen to cut back production in the EPROM market in order to increase American market share for political reasons.

[70] Andrew Grove of Intel has also asserted that the pressure the STA exerted on Japan to increase the penetration of American chips led Japanese personal computer makers to adopt Intel microprocessors, which they might not otherwise have done (Siegmann, 1993).

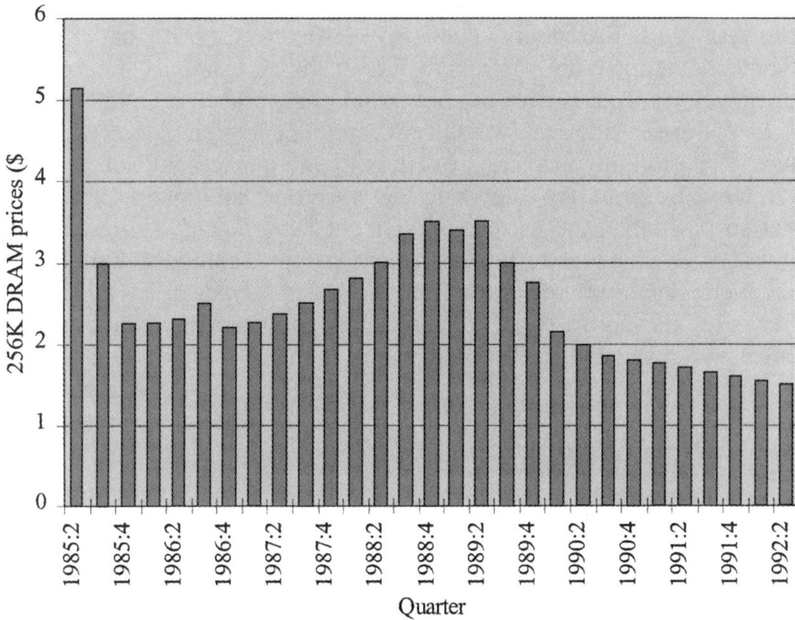

Figure 2.1. Average Selling Prices for 256K DRAMs. *Source:* Dataquest, cited in Tyson (1992, p. 115).

instigated by MITI months before the accord was signed. And it is true that chip prices in 1988–1989 were above the FMV floor, a result of cyclically high demand as well as of output restraint. But economists quickly point out that the STA and the legal actions preceding it were arguably the catalysts to the formation of the cartel, and it was the sanction of the STA that created at MITI a formal mechanism to police and manage that cartel. Indeed, it is a policy irony that, whereas proponents of managed trade typically saw coordination by MITI as one of Japan's unfair advantages, the STA actually strengthened MITI's coordinating role.

As with most complex policy interventions, the STA also had some unintended consequences. Early on, critics – and even some proponents – of managed trade pointed out that Japanese firms were plowing their bubble profits into research and development, which would strengthen those firms for further rounds of competition and the much-feared push into other semiconductor markets (Tyson, 1992, p. 117). Moreover, as Japanese firms are more vertically integrated than American ones, Japanese computer makers would have the advantage of internal transfer prices rather than market prices, giving them an edge over Americans in the computer arena.[71] It is largely this concern, indeed, that led Mowery and Rosenberg (1989, p. 114) to suggest that if "the Semiconductor Trade Agreement thus far is an example of successful 'managed trade,' it is hard to know what might constitute a failure."

In the event, however, the DRAM cartel generated a somewhat different set of unintended consequences – consequences much less happy for Japanese firms. By stabilizing DRAM prices and making that market so profitable, the cartel arrangement kept Japanese firms heavily invested in what was to become a low-margin commodity item. When the high prices attracted entry from Korea and Taiwan, prices and profits began to fall, and the cartel collapsed.[72] By contrast, American firms like Intel were arguably well served in the medium term by their failure in DRAMs, a failure that left them free to pursue high-margin logic and specialty chips that would be in high demand in the burgeoning American personal computer market.

Antitrust Policy and Research Consortia. As we saw, much popular and professional opinion circa 1985 attributed the relative decline of American competitiveness to the inherent inferiorities of American industrial structure relative to that of Japan. Widely touted aspects of the "Japanese model" were research coordination and collaboration in general and the VLSI Project in specific. As a result, much of the American policy response took the form of an attempt to encourage cooperative research – by indirect means as well as by direct subsidy.

On the antitrust front, both Congress and the Antitrust Division of the Justice Department sought to reduce legal obstacles to research cooperation among American firms. In 1984, Congress passed the National Cooperative Research Act, which weakened the brunt of antitrust law when applied to research joint ventures and allowed prospective joint-venture partners to register in advance with the Justice Department and the Federal Trade Commission.[73] For its part, the Reagan Justice

[71] In fact, this possibility didn't materialize, partly because the cartel was short-lived and partly because the structural disadvantages of the Japanese computer makers far outweighed any advantages from cheaper DRAMs.

[72] In this case, the new entrants also faced trade pressure form the Americans. In 1992, Micron filed an antidumping case against three Korean firms, which resulted in penalties as high as 87 percent. In 1993, however, a Korean proposal for an accord patterned on the STA fell through, and the Commerce Department abruptly lowered the duties it had imposed (Dick, 1995, pp. 61–62).

[73] Specifically, the law weakened potential claims to actual damages rather than the treble damages allowed in other antitrust judgments; specified a rule-of-reason requirement rather than a per se rule, thus forcing courts to take into account the efficiency benefits of the venture; and required unsuccessful plaintiffs to pay court costs if the court

Department put in place new antitrust guidelines that recognized international market structure as a factor in the evaluation of horizontal mergers (White, 1985).

But the most significant instance of research collaboration in the 1980s was the formation of an industry consortium with substantial government funding.[74] In 1987, the Defense Science Board, a committee advisory to the American Department of Defense, issued dire warnings that the decline of the American semiconductor industry would have serious repercussions for national defense. The committee proposed a manufacturing facility to be jointly owned by industry and government. In the same year, a committee of the SIA representing 14 major semiconductor manufacturers issued a proposal for a research consortium to be funded by equal private and federal contributions. By the end of the year, the Defense Department agreed to fund such a consortium, with the 14 firms uniting as the founding members of the Semiconductor Manufacturing Technology Consortium (Sematech). The organization was funded at a yearly level of $100 million from federal sources and $100 million from dues assessed to members.[75]

Sematech set up shop in Austin, Texas, staffed importantly by personnel on secondment from the member companies. The goal was to develop cutting-edge production technology of use to consortium firms. By 1989, a large-scale semiconductor fabrication facility had been completed at Sematech headquarters in record time. Largely because of problems of appropriability and proprietary information, however, the Sematech members were unable to agree on an appropriate research program for

declared their suit against a research joint venture to have been "frivolous, unreasonable, without foundation, or in bad faith" (White, 1985, pp. 43–44). It is not clear, however, to what extent the changes allayed the fears of industry or even reduced the level of antitrust scrutiny to which research joint ventures were subject (Grossman and Shapiro, 1986, p. 319).

[74] This account of the formation and goals of Sematech follows Grindley, Mowery, and Silverman (1994). Sematech was not the only consortium founded in this period. The Microelectronics and Computer Corporation (MCC), founded in 1982, is a for-profit organization whose members include some semiconductor firms and whose research agenda includes semiconductor technology, especially packaging (Gibson and Rogers, 1994; Thorpe, 1995). Also predating Sematech, the Semiconductor Research Corporation (SRC) is a consortium funded by private firms, by the Defense Department, and, recently, by Sematech. It concentrates on more basic research at universities. Lately, the Fabless Semiconductor Association has begun sponsoring cooperative efforts by its members (Macher et al., 1998).

[75] The original founding members of Sematech were Advanced Micro Devices (AMD), AT&T, Digital Equipment, Harris, Hewlett-Packard, Intel, IBM, LSI Logic, Micron, Motorola, National Semiconductor, NCR, Rockwell International, and Texas Instruments. Harris left the organization in 1992; LSI and Micron left in 1993. The dues required of each member amount to 1 percent of semiconductor sales revenue, with a minimum of $1 million and a maximum of $15 million.

the facility (Grindley et al., 1994, p. 730). As a result, Sematech quickly reoriented its mission away from developing cutting-edge process technology for and with member companies toward improving the capabilities of the American semiconductor-equipment industry and strengthening cooperation between those firms and the semiconductor manufacturers they serve.[76] This involved "contract R&D" with equipment suppliers, as well as programs to coordinate and set standards, in many cases through the offices of an organization called SEMI/SEMATECH that was set up at Sematech in 1987 to represent equipment makers.

The formation of Sematech is coincident with the turnaround of American fortunes in semiconductors, but few are willing to jump to the conclusion that Sematech somehow *caused* this resurgence. For one thing, the resurgence was already under way before Sematech had produced much in the way of research results. Moreover, it is clear that the factors outlined – the changing pattern of end-use demand, the appreciation of the yen, and the STA – must have primary place in an explanation of renewed American success. This is not to say, however, that Sematech has not proved useful to American industry, even if the mechanisms by which it contributed are hard to pin down (Grindley et al., 1994). Informal studies typically find that member companies are pleased with their association with the consortium[77] (Link et al., 1996). Irwin and Klenow (1996) found that Sematech probably increased the productivity of American R&D by reducing duplication, even if this meant a reduction in private R&D spending of some $300 million per year. And Link, Teece, and Finan (1996, p. 739) found not only that direct benefits to member companies exceeded costs but that "the benefits to member companies from research management and research integration, as well as the indirect benefits from spillovers, were more important than the tangible direct benefits flowing from research results." As in the case of the Japanese VLSI Project (Flamm, 1996, p. 103), then, the ultimate virtue of Sematech may lie not so much in the research it produced as in its role in reducing the transaction costs of research dissemination and in fostering closer "vertical" collaboration and coordination between manufacturers and equipment suppliers.

[76] In 1989, only $30 million of Sematech's budget went into projects with equipment makers; by 1991, that figure was $130 million (Burrows, 1992); see also Link, Teece, and Finan (1996, pp. 743–744). Even more than semiconductor manufacturers, semiconductor equipment suppliers had been accused of "excessive vertical disintegration" (Stowsky, 1989, p. 243). On this industry generally see Langlois (1999).

[77] This presumably excludes the three firms that left the consortium, apparently over a disagreement with Sematech's redirection of attention toward equipment suppliers and away from direct R&D on cutting-edge fabrication (Irwin and Klenow, 1996, p. 327).

The Role of Japanese Government Policy

American concerns about the bilateral trade balance with Japan, especially with regard to semiconductor issues, emerged exactly when major changes were under way in the Japanese telecommunications and computer industries. In the telecommunications industry, NTT was to be privatized, providing deficit relief for the Japanese government and restructuring the Japanese telecommunication industry with the aim of accelerating progress toward the "information society." An incidental effect of these developments was to heighten competition among NTT's suppliers, who were also Japan's leading IC producers. These developments began in the mid-1980s and were complicated by the worldwide 1985 recession in the semiconductor industry. The effects of the recession were severe for the Japanese IC producers, in both semiconductors and electronic systems, creating losses of $3 billion, a development that may have contributed to the willingness of Japanese producers to agree to the Semiconductor Trade Accord.

The other major development of the 1980s was a reorientation of Japanese industrial policy away from support for current technology in the IC industry toward breakthroughs in advanced IC design and the computer industry. Japan's Future Electronic Device Project was organized within a larger program of research on new materials and had a very forward-looking agenda, including research on three-dimensional devices; on ICs for extreme environmental conditions (terminated in 1985); and on biochips (begun in 1986), which aimed at a complete paradigm shift in IC fabrication "to practical electronic devices using proteins."[78] Not surprisingly, none of these projects has had a significant commercial effect.

Support for the computer industry came in the form of the Fifth Generation Project,[79] which was based upon the premise that artificial intelligence was on the verge of commercialization with applications in natural language processing, speech recognition, and other domains. The project was to enable Japan to forge ahead in the computer industry, eclipsing both American system and component companies.[80] Although American industry took the Fifth Generation project more seriously than the Future Electronics Device project, it too proved to be an overly

[78] Fransman (1990) outlines this agenda; the statement quoted is from Karube (1986).

[79] Fransman (1990) provides a detailed case study of the Fifth Generation Project, highlighting major disagreements about its direction as well as chronicling some of the technological difficulties in reaching its goals.

[80] Feigenbaum (1983), an expert in artificial intelligence, argued strongly that without an American response, the entire American information and communication technology industry was in peril.

ambitious effort at "forging ahead" of the United States, and, although the Japanese computer industry did succeed in making significant inroads in IBM's market position during the 1980s, the basis for this progress can be found in incremental improvements in manufacturing competencies rather than breakthrough technologies. Moreover, it became clear in the 1990s that chasing IBM was no longer a desirable goal in a world of open, modular, microprocessor-based computer systems. Many of the problems of the Japanese systems producers who, partly at the behest of the Japanese government, chased the holy grail of competitiveness in mainframe production mirror the problems that beset IBM itself early in this decade (Ferguson and Morris, 1993). Japanese companies generally, and NEC (the domestic market leader) in particular, failed to seize hold of the personal computer, a development that, as we saw, had major implications for the development of IC components.

Europe

The growing role of downstream markets in determining the success of semiconductor firms is further supported by the experience of European producers during the past 10 years. Although European companies have played only a peripheral role in the contest for competitive dominance between American and Japanese producers and the rise of the Koreans as major commodity producers, the European industry has been able to maintain its market share and strengthen its base by reinforcing its capabilities in linear ICs, including those involved in connecting analog and digital circuits. The strong position of European producers in consumer electronics at home and, through direct investments in the United States, in export markets has supported these developments. In addition to consumer electronics, European IC producers have developed the telecommunications and automotive sectors.[81]

During the last decade, European semiconductor research has continued to receive substantial public support, much of which has been channeled through the JESSI Program. This support has contributed to European producers' "staying in the race" by moving to smaller dimensions in IC fabrication. The current goals of JESSI to produce "chip sets" for advanced communication applications, especially for the digital

[81] Europe is the world's largest automobile market, and European producers, despite a less-concentrated industrial structure than that of either the United States or Japan, dominate the European market. This dominance receives some help from protectionist measures in several countries, including Italy, where Japanese imports are severely limited.

communications protocol called asynchronous transfer mode (ATM), are closer to the market and therefore riskier. Of particular note are SGS-Thomson's relative rise as a "merchant" semiconductor company and the continued strength of Philips and Siemens, both of which are also system producers.

Summary

The American resurgence has been largely the result of the industry's ability to improve manufacturing and at the same time – and more importantly – to achieve a dominant position in the fastest-growing segment of the industry during a sustained period of growth. The resurgence is thus based upon both productivity improvements and innovation and reflects the success of American companies, and American industrial structure, in meeting the Japanese challenge. The resurgence has been strengthened by important changes in the structure of electronic system production in Japan and the United States, changes that have led to higher revenues for American IC producers. Intel in particular has benefited enormously from these structural changes, surging to a strong position as the world's leading IC producer from its near-bankruptcy a decade ago.

These structural changes, as well as evidence that the gap in productivity is closing, suggest that American firms will continue to be strong through the opening years of the next century, assuming that the American computer industry remains strong. Stronger demand for the products of the Japanese consumer-electronics industry would increase Japan's share of the world IC market, perhaps pushing Japan slightly ahead of the United States again. But the world has changed. The situation in which the United States and Japan were roughly at parity in the computer industry, with Japan having an additional edge from consumer electronics, has become one in which the two economies are increasingly specialized, the United States in computer-related systems and Japan in consumer-related systems. This structure of demand will support differentiation in domestic production that will reinforce the respective IC segments over time.

Concluding Perspective

At the risk of oversimplification, we can organize our conclusions in terms of three related themes: the importance of end-use demand, the effect of industrial strategy and structure, and the role of government policy.

End-Use Demand

The pattern of end-use demand for semiconductors has always had a distinctly regional character. And the source of that demand has had an important – maybe even dominant – role in shaping the fortunes of regional industries.

American firms benefited early on from military demand, when performance mattered more than price. This demand called forth technological innovations in silicon technology that proved widely applicable to nonmilitary markets and provided the American innovators with early-learning advantages. As military demand tapered off in relative terms, the American computer industry provided an alternative outlet that gave domestic semiconductor firms a specialty in digital devices and later in logic ICs. The Japanese challenge was also driven in many respects by the sources of demand facing Japanese producers. The advantages of CMOS in consumer applications – including, initially, electronic calculators – gave those firms critical experience in what would prove to be the dominant general-purpose technology. At the same time, NTT's demand for memory chips – and for high-quality chips in general – helped focus the Japanese industry into a strategy of specialization in DRAMs fueled by advantages in mass production. Most recently, American firms have benefited from their de facto specialization in design-intensive logic chips (including microprocessors) at a time when the (largely American) personal-computer industry is burgeoning and the (largely Japanese) consumer-electronics sector is declining. European firms have done best when they focused on indigenous sources of demand, which have tended to be more in consumer, industrial, and automotive sectors; they have done worst when, often at the behest of their governments, they have tried to compete against American or Japanese strengths.

Strategy and Structure

From the very beginning, the American semiconductor industry possessed a diverse industrial structure that relied far more heavily than does Japan's or Europe's on relatively small, highly focused firms, often grouped geographically and partaking of what Alfred Marshall (1961) described as external economies. This structure arose out of the open intellectual-property environments that attended the invention of the transistor and of the IC; the innovation-driven character of early military and computer demand; and the American institutions of spin-off and venture capital. Universities played a comparatively small – or at any rate indirect – role in this process.[82]

A decentralized structure served the American industry well during decades of world leadership. But once the maturity of business and technology began to stress and unfocus the competence of the leading American firms, that "fragmented" structure proved vulnerable to a focused attack by Japanese firms specialized in the mass production of high-volume devices. Japanese industrial structure proved effective in this challenge, as the more vertically and horizontally integrated firms could take advantage of internal capital markets and corporate competences in a capital-intensive and process-oriented business. Contrary to the dominant opinion a decade ago, however, this Japanese structure is not obviously superior for all forms of competition under all circumstances. In losing ground to the Japanese in high-volume production, American firms were forced to specialize and refocus. And the "fragmented" American system has responded well in both technological and organizational innovation in this new regime.

Government Policy

We conclude from history that government involvement has played a major role in the evolution of this industry, but that government intervention in the form of industrial and technological policy has had a more equivocal role, one in which success is far better remembered than failure.

American firms benefited greatly from the role of the American military in the early years. But it was the military's role as demander of semiconductors rather than its role as funder of R&D that proved crucial. Japanese firms did gain from the R&D subsidies of the VLSI program, even if the real benefits of that program may have lain in the coordination and collaboration, especially between equipment suppliers and manufacturers, it effected. And purchasing by NTT may have played a role analogous to that played for American firms by military demand. In general, however, we share the view of Porter (1990) that vibrant

[82] The original invention of the transistor came out of a large corporate lab, and most important developments thereafter were driven by semiconductor firms. Saxenian (1994, pp. 41–42) and others have argued that universities like Stanford and Berkeley played a symbiotic role in the development of the Silicon Valley industrial district that bred much of the American semiconductor industry. But a close reading suggests that the importance of those universities lay less in basic research than in their own entrepreneurship and in their training of scientists and engineers for industry, a process that had already been set in motion by defense spending on space and military programs after World War II (Saxenian, 1994, pp. 21–24).

domestic competition among firms in Japan had far more to do with building technological competences than did any coordination from MITI or other government agencies. The 1986 trade accords may have given some American firms breathing space at a crucial time, but they also created some unintended effects, especially for Japan: by cartelizing and making profitable the DRAM market, the STA focused Japanese attention on what would become, with Korean entry, a low-margin commodity market. Sematech may have helped American firms in much the same way that the VLSI Project helped Japanese firms – by increasing coordination and collaboration between equipment suppliers and manufacturers. In the end, however, favorable demand shifts, specialization, and industrial structure probably had more to do with the American resurgence than did government policy. Europe has little to show for decades of government subsidy except survival. And European and Japanese programs to spur a mainframe computer industry both arguably misdirected the attention of domestic semiconductor firms away from their core competences.

If there is a positive entry in the ledger of government involvement, it may lie in the role of government in providing a credible signal and commitment to guide the domestic industry's strategic decisions. The prospect of early military demand in the United States played this role. So, arguably, did the VLSI Project and related policies in Japan, which created a common understanding and expectation about the path of strategy and technological development. Examined individually, the American policy initiatives of the mid-1980s – notably the STA and Sematech – may have fallen short of expectations. Nonetheless, the cumulative effects of the government's expressed willingness to act on the industry's behalf, in spite of political costs and potentially troubling precedents, is arguably a factor in its own right shaping the expectations of both American and Japanese IC producers as well as those of the IC producers of other nations.

Bibliography

Angel, David P. 1994. *Restructuring for Innovation: The Remaking of the U.S. Semiconductor Industry.* New York: Guilford Press.

Bank of America Asia, Ltd. 1980. *The Japanese Semiconductor Industry: 1980.* Hong Kong.

Bashe, Charles J., Lyle R. Johnson, John H. Palmer, and Emerson W. Pugh. 1986. *IBM's Early Computers.* Cambridge, Massachusetts: MIT Press.

Bello, Francis. 1953. "The Year of the Transistor," *Fortune*, March.

Borrus, Michael G. 1988. *Competing for Control: America's Stake in Microelectronics.* Cambridge, Massachusetts: Ballinger.

Borrus, Michael G., James E. Millstein, and John Zysman. 1982. *U.S.–Japanese Competition in the Semiconductor Industry: A Study in International Trade and Technological Development*. Berkeley, California: Institute of International Studies.

Borrus, Michael G., James E. Millstein, and John Zysman. 1983. "Trade and Development in the Semiconductor Industry: Japanese Challenge and American Response," in John Zysman and Laura Tyson, eds., *American Industry in International Competition: Government Policies and Corporate Strategies*. Ithaca, New York: Cornell University Press.

Braun, Ernest, and Stuart Macdonald. 1978. *Revolution in Miniature*. Cambridge: Cambridge University Press. (Second edition, 1982.)

Burrows, Peter. 1992. "Bill Spencer Struggles to Reform Sematech," *Electronic Business* 18(8): 57–62.

Callon, Scott. 1995. *Divided Sun: MITI and the Breakdown of Japanese High Tech Industrial Policy, 1975–1993*. Stanford, California: Stanford University Press.

Carrell, Stewart. 1968. "International Report on Microelectronics," in Morton E. Goldberg, ed., *Impact of Microelectronics. II: Proceedings of the Second Conference on the Impact of Microelectronics*. Chicago: Electronic Industries Association and IIT Research Institute.

Chen, Cheng-Fen, and Graham Sewell. 1996. "Strategies for Technological Development in South Korea and Taiwan: The Case of Semiconductors," *Research Policy* 25(5): 759–783.

Cogan, George W., and Robert A. Burgelman. 1989. "Intel Corporation (A): The DRAM Decision," Stanford Business School Case II-10, reprinted in Robert A. Burgelman, Modesto A. Maidique, and Steven C. Wheelwright, *Strategic Management of Technology and Innovation*. Chicago: Irwin. (Second edition, 1996.)

Cohen, Wesley M., and Daniel A. Levinthal. 1990. "Absorptive Capacity: A New Perspective on Learning and Innovation," *Administrative Science Quarterly* 35: 128–152.

Christensen, Clayton M., and Richard S. Rosenbloom. 1995. "Explaining the Attacker's Advantage: Technological Paradigms, Organizational Dynamics, and the Value Network," *Research Policy* 24(2): 233–257.

Cottrell, Tom. 1995. "Japanese Microcomputer Software: Standards Compatibility and Competitiveness," in David C. Mowery, ed., *The International Computer Software Industry: A Comparative Study of Industrial Evolution and Structure*. New York: Oxford University Press.

Dick, Andrew R. 1991. "Learning by Doing and Dumping in the Semiconductor Industry," *Journal of Law and Economics* 34: 133–159.

Dick, Andrew R. 1995. *Industrial Policy and Semiconductors: Missing the Target*. Washington, D.C.: AEI Press.

Dodson, Edward Ney. 1966. *Component Product Flows in the Electronics Industry*. Ph.D. Dissertation, Stanford University.

Dosi, Giovanni. 1981. *Technical Change and Survival: Europe's Semiconductor Industry*. Sussex: Sussex European Research Center.

Dosi, Giovanni. 1984. *Technical Change and Industrial Transformation*. New York: St. Martin's Press.

Electronic Industries Association. 1974. *Electronic Market Data Book*. Washington, D.C.: EIA.

Engardio, Pete, Margaret Dawson, and Robert D. Hof. 1996. "Taiwan's High-Tech Race," *Business Week*, May 6, p. 22.

Ernst, Dieter, and David O'Connor. 1992. *Competing in the Electronics Industry: the Experience of Newly Industrialising Economies*. Paris: OECD.

European Microelectronics Panel. 1995. *Report*, January 18.

Fallows, James M. 1994. *Looking at the Sun: The Rise of the New East Asian Economic and Political System*. New York: Pantheon Books.

Feigenbaum, Edward A. 1983. *The Fifth Generation*. New York: Addison Wesley.

Ferguson, Charles H. 1985. "American Microelectronics in Decline: Evidence, Analysis, and Alternatives," VLSI Memo No. 85–284, Microsystems Research Center, Massachusetts Institute of Technology.

Ferguson, Charles H. 1988. "From the People Who Brought You Voodoo Economics," *Harvard Business Review* 88: 55–62.

Ferguson, Charles H., and Charles R. Morris. 1993. *Computer Wars: How the West Can Win in a Post-IBM World*. New York: Times Books.

Flamm, Kenneth. 1996. *Mismanaged Trade? Strategic Policy and the Semiconductor Industry*. Washington, D.C.: Brookings Institution Press.

Florida, Richard, and Martin Kenney. 1990. *The Breakthrough Illusion*. New York: Basic Books.

Forester, Tom. 1993. *Silicon Samurai*. Oxford: Basil Blackwell.

Fransman, Martin. 1990. *The Market and Beyond: Information Technology in Japan*. Cambridge: Cambridge University Press.

Fransman, Martin. 1995. *Japan's Computer and Communications Industry: The Evolution of Industrial Giants and Global Competitiveness*. Oxford: Oxford University Press.

Gambardella, Alfonso, and Salvatore Torrisi. 1998. "Does Technological Convergence Imply Convergence in Markets? Evidence from the Electronics Industry," *Research Policy*, 27(5): 447–465.

Gibson, David V., and Everett M. Rogers. 1994. *R&D Collaboration on Trial: The Microelectronics and Computer Technology Corporation*. Boston: Harvard Business School Press.

Golding, Anthony M. 1971. *Semiconductor Industry in Britain and the United States: A Case Study in Innovation, Growth, and the Diffusion of Technology*. Ph.D. Dissertation, University of Sussex.

Granstrand, Ove, Pari Patel, and Keith Pavitt. 1997. "Multi-Technology Corporations: Why They Have 'Distributed' Rather Than 'Distinctive Core' Competencies," *California Management Review* 39(4): 8–25.

Grindley, Peter, David C. Mowery, and Brian Silverman. 1994. "Sematech and Collaborative Research Lessons in the Design of High-Technology Consortia," *Journal of Policy Analysis and Management* 13(4): 723–758.

Grossman, Gene M., and Carl Shapiro. 1986. "Research Joint Ventures: An Antitrust Analysis," *Journal of Law, Economics, and Organization* 2(2): 315–337.

Hamilton, David P., and Steve Glain. 1995. "Silicon Duel: Koreans Move to Grab Memory-Chip Market from the Japanese," *The Wall Street Journal*, March 14, p. A1.

Hannan, Michael T., and John Freeman. 1989. *Organizational Ecology*. Cambridge, Massachusetts: Harvard University Press.

Helm, Leslie. 1995. "In the Chips," *The Los Angeles Times*, March 5, p. D1.

Henderson, Rebecca M. 1995. "Of Life Cycles Real and Imaginary: The Unexpectedly Long Old Age of Optical Lithography," *Research Policy* 24: 631–643.

Hobday, Michael. 1991. "Semiconductor Technology and the Newly Industrializing Countries: The Diffusion of ASICs (Application Specific Integrated Circuits)," *World Development* 19(4): 375–397.

Howell, Thomas R., Brent Bartlett, and Warren Davis. 1992. *Creating Advantage: Semiconductors and Government Industrial Policy in the 1990s*, Cupertino, California, and Washington, D.C.: Semiconductor Industry Association and Dewey Ballantine.

Howell, Thomas R., William A. Noellert, Janet H. MacLoughlin, and Alan W. Wolff. 1988. *The Microelectronics Race: The Impact of Government Policy on International Competition*. Boulder, Colorado: Westview Press.

Integrated Circuit Engineering Corporation (ICE). Various years. *Status of the Integrated Circuit Industry*. Scottsdale, Arizona: ICE.

Irwin, Douglas A., and Peter J. Klenow. 1996. "High-Tech R&D Subsidies: Estimating the Effects of Sematech," *Journal of International Economics* 40(3–4): 323–344.

Johnson, Chalmers. 1982. *MITI and the Japanese Miracle: The Growth of Industrial Policy, 1925-1975*. Stanford, California: Stanford University Press.

Karube, I. 1986. "Trends in Bioelectronics Research," *Science and Technology in Japan* 5(19).

Kleiman, Herbert S. 1966. *The Integrated Circuit: A Case Study of Product Innovation in the Electronics Industry*. DBA Dissertation, George Washington University.

Kodama, Fumio. 1995. *Emerging Patterns of Innovation: Sources of Japan's Technological Edge*. Boston: Harvard Business School Press.

Kraus, Jerome. 1971. *An Economic Study of the U.S. Semiconductor Industry*, Ph.D. Dissertation, New School for Social Research.

Langlois, Richard N. 1992. "External Economies and Economic Progress: The Case of the Microcomputer Industry," *Business History Review* 66(1): 1–50.

Langlois, Richard N. 1997. "Cognition and Capabilities: Opportunities Seized and Missed in the History of the Computer Industry," in Raghu Garud, Praveen Nayyar, and Zur Shapira, eds., *Technological Innovation: Oversights and Foresights*. New York: Cambridge University Press.

Langlois, Richard N. 1999. "Capabilities and Vertical Disintegration in Process

Technology: The Case of Semiconductor Fabrication Equipment." in Nicolai J. Foss and Paul L. Robertson, eds., *Resources, Technology, and Strategy*. London: Routledge. Also circulated as Working Paper 92-10, Consortium on Competitiveness and Cooperation, University of California, Berkeley, November 1992.

Langlois, Richard N., Thomas A. Pugel, Carmela S. Haklisch, Richard R. Nelson, and William G. Egelhoff. 1988. *Microelectronics: An Industry in Transition*. London: Unwin Hyman.

Langlois, Richard N., and Paul L. Robertson. 1995. *Firms, Markets, and Economic Change: A Dynamic Theory of Business Institutions*. London: Routledge.

LaPedus, Mark. 1997a. "Companies Flock to IC-Foundry Scene – Attracted by Strong Growth, Startups Face Some Big Obstacles," *Electronic Buyers' News*, June 16.

LaPedus, Mark. 1997b. "Three Asian Firms Pushing on 0.25 Micron," *Electronic Buyers' News*, June 30.

LaPedus, Mark, and Jack Robertson. 1997. "New Kid on Foundry Block: Korea," *Electronic Buyers' News*, March 31.

Levin, Richard C. 1982. "The Semiconductor Industry," in Richard R. Nelson, ed., *Government and Technical Progress: A Cross-Industry Analysis*. New York: Pergamon Press.

Link, Albert N., David J. Teece, and William F. Finan. 1996. "Estimating the Benefits from Collaboration: The Case of SEMATECH," *Review of Industrial Organization* 11(5): 737–751.

Lundvall, Bengt-Åke, ed. 1992. *National Systems of Innovation: Toward a Theory of Innovation and Interactive Learning*. New York: St. Martin's Press.

McHugh, K.S. 1949. "Bell System Patents and Patent Licensing," *Bell Telephone Magazine*, January, pp. 1–4.

Macher, Jeffrey, David C. Mowery, and David Hodges. 1998. "Performance and Innovation in the U.S. Semiconductor Industry, 1980–1996," in Ralph Landau and David C. Mowery, eds., *Explaining America's Industrial Resurgence*. Washington, D.C.: National Academy Press.

Mackintosh, I.M. 1978. "Large-Scale Integration: Intercontinental Aspects," *IEEE Spectrum* 15(6): 51–56.

Malerba, Franco. 1985. *The Semiconductor Business: The Economics of Rapid Growth and Decline*. Madison: University of Wisconsin Press.

Marnet, Oliver. 1996. "Managed Trade and Barking up the Wrong Trees," *Asia Times*, May 21, p. 9.

Marshall, Alfred. 1961. *Principles of Economics*. Ninth (variorum) Edition, vol. I. London: Macmillan.

Methé, David T. 1991. *Technological Competition in Global Industries: Marketing and Planning Strategies for American Industry*. Westport, Connecticut: Quorum Books.

MIT Commission on Industrial Productivity. 1989. *Working Papers of the Commission on Industrial Productivity*. Cambridge, Massachusetts: MIT Press. (Two volumes.)

Morris, Peter R. 1990. *A History of the World Semiconductor Industry*. London: Peter Peregrinus on behalf of the Institution of Electrical Engineers.

Mowery, David C., and Nathan Rosenberg. 1989. "New Developments in US Technology Policy: Implications for Competitiveness and International Trade Policy," *California Management Review* 32(1): 107–124.

Mowery, David C., and W. Edward Steinmueller. 1994. "Prospects for Entry by Developing Countries into the Global Integrated Circuit Industry: Lessons from the United States, Japan, and the NIEs, 1955–1990," in D.C. Mowery, *Science and Technology Policy in Interdependent Economies*. Boston: Kluwer Academic Publishers.

Nakagawa, Yasuzo. 1985. *Semiconductor Developments in Japan*. Tokyo: Diamond Publishing.

National Advisory Committee on Semiconductors. 1992. *Annual Report*. Washington, D.C.: NACS.

Nelson, Richard R. 1962. "The Link between Science and Invention: The Case of the Transistor," in Richard R. Nelson, ed., *The Rate and Direction of Inventive Activity*. Princeton, New Jersey: Princeton University Press.

Nelson, Richard R., ed. 1993. *National Innovation Systems: A Comparative Analysis*. New York: Oxford University Press.

Nelson, Richard R., and Sidney G. Winter. 1977. "In Search of Useful Theory of Innovation," *Research Policy* 5: 36–76.

Nelson, Richard R., and Sidney G. Winter. 1982. *An Evolutionary Theory of Economic Change*. Cambridge, Massachusetts: Harvard University Press.

Okimoto, Daniel I., Takuo Sugano, and Franklin B. Weinstein. 1984. *Competitive Edge: The Semiconductor Industry in the U.S. and Japan*. Stanford, California: Stanford University Press.

Patel, Pari, and Keith Pavitt. 1997. "The Technological Competencies of the World's Largest Firms: Complex and Path-Dependent, but Not Much Variety," *Research Policy* 26: 141–156.

Pearson, Jamie Parker, ed. 1992. *Digital at Work: Snapshots from the First Thirty-Five Years*. Burlington, Massachusetts: Digital Press.

Pollack, Andrew. 1992. "U.S. Chip Makers Stem the Tide in Trade Battles with Japanese," *The New York Times*, April 9, p. A1.

Porter, Michael E. 1990. *The Competitive Advantage of Nations*. New York: The Free Press.

Prahalad, C. K., and Gary Hamel. 1990. "The Core Competence of the Corporation," *Harvard Business Review*, May-June, pp. 79–91.

Prestowitz, Clyde V. 1988. *Trading Places: How We Allowed Japan to Take the Lead*, New York: Basic Books.

Procassini, Andrew A. 1995. *Competitors in Alliance: Industrial Associations, Global Rivalries and Business-Government Relations*. Westport, Connecticut: Quorum Books.

Pugh, Emerson W., Lyle R. Johnson, and John H. Palmer. 1991. *IBM's 360 and Early 370 Systems*. Cambridge, Massachusetts: MIT Press.

Reich, Robert B., and Eric Mankin. 1986. "Joint Ventures with Japan Give Away Our Future," *Harvard Business Review*, March–April, pp. 78–86.

Reid, T.R. 1984. *The Chip: How Two Americans Invented the Microchip and Launched a Revolution*. New York: Simon & Schuster.

Richardson, G.B. 1972. "The Organisation of Industry," *Economic Journal* 82: 883–896.

Risberg, R.L. 1990. "Five Years Without Infringement Litigation under the Semiconductor Chip Protection Act: Unmasking the Specter of Chip Piracy in an Era of Diverse and Incompatible Process Technologies," *Wisconsin Law Review*, No. 1, pp. 241–277.

Saxenian, Anna Lee. 1994. *Regional Advantage: Culture and Competition in Silicon Valley and Route 128*. Cambridge, Massachusetts: Harvard University Press.

Sciberras, Edmond. 1977. *Multinational Electronics Companies and National Economic Policies*. Greenwich, Connecticut: JAI Press.

Semiconductor Industry Association. 1981. *The International Microelectronic Challenge*, Cupertino, California: SIA.

Semiconductor Industry Association. 1983. *The Effects of Government Targeting on World Semiconductor Competition*. Cupertino, California: SIA.

Semiconductor Industry Association. 1990. *A Deal Is a Deal: Four Years of Experience under the US-Japan Semiconductor Agreement. Fourth Annual Report to the President*. Washington: SIA.

Siegmann, Ken. 1993. "An American Tale of Semi-Success: How American Chip Companies Regained Lead," *The San Francisco Chronicle*, December 20.

Sigurdson, Jon. 1986. Industry and State Partnership in Japan: The Very Large Scale Integrated Circuits (VLSI) Project. Discussion Paper No. 168, Research Policy Institute, University of Lund, Sweden.

Skole, Robert. 1968. "Government Electronics: Federal Outlets Tough for Foreigners," *Electronics* 41: 119–124.

Sparkes, J.J. 1973. "The First Decade of Transistor Development," *Radio and Electronic Engineering* 43: 8–9.

Spence, A. Michael. 1981. "The Learning Curve and Competition," *Bell Journal of Economics* 12(1): 49–70.

Steinmueller, W. Edward. 1987. *Microeconomics and Microelectronics: Studies in the Economics of Integrated Circuit Technology*. Unpublished Ph.D. Dissertation, Stanford University.

Steinmueller, W. Edward. 1988a. "Industry Structure and Government Policies in the U.S. and Japanese Integrated-Circuit Industries," in John B. Shoven, ed., *Government Policy Towards Industry in the United States and Japan*. New York: Cambridge University Press.

Steinmueller, W. Edward. 1988b. "International Joint Ventures in the Integrated Circuit Industry" in David C. Mowery, ed., *International Collaborative Ventures in U.S. Manufacturing*. Cambridge, Massachusetts: Ballinger.

Stowsky, Jay S. 1989. "Weak Links, Strong Bonds: U.S.-Japanese Competition in Semiconductor Production Equipment," in Chalmers Johnson, Laura Tyson, and John Zysman, eds., *Politics and Productivity: The Real Story of Why Japan Works*. Cambridge, Massachusetts: Ballinger.

Teal, Gordon K. 1976. "Single Crystals of Ge and Si Basic to the Transistor and Integrated Circuit," *IEEE Transactions on Electron Devices* ED-23: July, pp. 621–639.

Teece, David J. 1986. "Profiting from Technological Innovation: Implications for Integration, Collaboration, Licensing, and Public Policy," *Research Policy* 15: 285–305.

Thorpe, Helen. 1995. "Is MCC Obsolete?" *Texas Monthly* 23(1): 118.

Tilton, John E. 1971. *International Diffusion of Technology: The Case of Semiconductors*. Washington, D.C.: Brookings Institution.

Tushman, Michael L., and Philip Anderson. 1986. "Technological Discontinuities and Organizational Environments," *Administrative Science Quarterly* 31: 439–465.

Tyson, Laura D'Andrea. 1992. *Who's Bashing Whom? Trade Conflict in High Technology Industries*. Washington, D.C.: Institute for International Economics, November.

Tyson, Laura D'Andrea, and David B. Yoffie. 1993. "Semiconductors: From Manipulated to Managed Trade," in David B. Yoffie, ed., *Beyond Free Trade: Firms, Governments, and Global Competition*. Boston: Harvard Business School Press.

U.S. Department of Commerce. 1961. *Semiconductors: U.S. Production and Trade*. Business and Defense Services Administration. Washington, D.C.: Government Printing Office.

U.S. Department of Commerce. 1966 *et seriatim*. Bureau of the Census, Current Industrial Reports: Selected Electronic and Associated Products, Including Telephone and Telegraph Apparatus, Washington, D.C.: Government Printing Office. (Available years include 1966–1988.)

U.S. Department of Commerce. Industry and Trade Administration, Office of Producer Goods. 1979. "A Report on the Integrated Circuit Industry," Washington, D.C.: Government Printing Office, September.

U.S. General Accounting Office. 1992. *Federal Research: Sematech's Technological Progress and Proposed R&D Program*. Washington, D.C.: U.S. GAO.

Watanabe, Makoto. 1984. "Semiconductor Industry in Japan – Past and Present," *IEEE Transactions on Electron Devices* ED31(11): 1562–1570.

White, Lawrence J. 1985. "Clearing the Legal Path to Cooperative Research," *Technology Review* 88(5): 39–44.

Wilson, Robert W., Peter K. Ashton, and Thomas P. Egan. 1980. *Innovation, Competition, and Government Policy in the Semiconductor Industry*. Lexington, Massachusetts: D.C. Heath.

Wright, Gavin. 1999. "Can a Nation Learn? American Technology as a Network Phenomenon," in Naomi R. Lamoreaux, Daniel M.G. Raff, and Peter Temin, eds., *Learning by Doing in Markets, Firms, and Countries*. Chicago:

University of Chicago Press, pp. 295–326.

Yoffie, David B. 1988. "Creating Political Advantage," *Harvard Business Review* 3: 55–62.

Young, Allyn A. 1928. "Increasing Returns and Economic Progress," *Economic Journal* 38: 523–542.

Zajak, Andrew. 1997. "The High Cost of Shrinking Chips: As Factory Costs Skyrocket, Can Silicon Valley Keep Pace?" *The San Francisco Examiner*, December 14, p. B5.

CHAPTER 3

Industrial Dynamics and the Evolution of Firms' and Nations' Competitive Capabilities in the World Computer Industry

TIMOTHY F. BRESNAHAN AND FRANCO MALERBA

I. The Major Issues

The evolution of the computer industry over the long term illustrates many of the broad themes addressed by this book. In particular, it highlights the coevolution of technology, market structure, and institutions and addresses the sources of international competitive advantage. Since its inception in the early 1950s, the computer industry has been characterized by rapid and sustained technical change, continuous product innovation punctuated by a few major breakthroughs, creation of new uses for computers and new markets, and coexistence between established actors and new entrepreneurial firms. And since the beginning of the industry, one country – the United States – has been the world technological and competitive leader.

From these observations drawn from the history of the world computer industry, some questions emerge. A first set of questions refer to the *relationship between radical change and competition among incumbents and new firms*. How is it that old and new firms coexisted during the history of the computer industry? Is there a link between radical innovations' opening up new markets and the competition between old and new actors? A second set of questions relate to the *specific relationship among technological change, market structure, and institutions* during the history of the industry. Was there a unique type of coevolutionary process during the whole history of the industry? Or was there more than one coevolutionary process? In either case, why? A final set

We would like to thank Salvatore Torrisi for sharing with us his knowledge about the UK industry; Simona Heidemperger, Lu-Leng Chua, and Victoria Danilchouk for much assistance; and Richard Rosenbloom, Giovanni Dosi, Martin Fransman, Steve Klepper, Sidney Winter, Peter Murmann, and particularly David Mowery and Richard Nelson for useful comments and suggestions. We thank the Italian CNR and the Sloan Foundation for research support.

of questions relate to the *persistence of international technological and competitive advantages of one country* during the whole history of the industry. Why was the United States, and not other countries, able to profit from the opportunities to become world technological and competitive leader? How was the United States able to persist in that role? This chapter is going to try to answer these questions using a historical and analytical perspective.

A first look at the major features of the computer industry identifies some aspects that are going to be relevant for the analysis presented in this chapter. First, computer hardware has advanced very rapidly in price/performance measures, fueled by rapid advances in the underlying electronic components as well as in computers themselves.[1] A wide variety of hardware categories has emerged: large and powerful computers such as mainframes, intermediate classes such as minicomputers and workstations, and classes with less expensive products such as personal computers. Technical progress has made the largest computers much more powerful, the smallest more affordable, and has increased choice and variety in between. Computer hardware was once supplied by a few pioneering firms; now there are hundreds of suppliers. The impact of performance increases and price decreases, together with dramatic improvements in complementary technologies such as software, storage devices, and telecommunications, and with considerable innovations and learning by using by customers, has been to build a multibillion-dollar worldwide industry.

Second, widespread adoption of computers in business and among consumers has contributed to this ongoing growth. Three very different kinds of *demand* are important here. First there are the *buyers of large computers for business data processing*. These demanders are professionalized computer specialists in large organizations.[2] These sites have absorbed dramatic increases in computer power. Thus, although mainframe computing sites number only in the tens of thousands, their total market size is very large. A second kind of demand is that for "*individual productivity applications*" on personal computers (PCs). This is a

[1] For an extensive review of measurement studies of computer price/performance ratios, including extensive discussion of alternative definitions of "performance," see Gordon (1989). By any definition of price/performance, 20–25 percent improvements have been sustained over four decades. For a key class of electronic components, semiconductors, see Chapter 2 in this volume by Langlois and Steinmueller, and Malerba (1985).

[2] They have close bilateral working relationships with the most important vendors. The computer business systems are complex pieces of computer software, entailing an equally complex innovation process. In the industrialized countries, most of the sites doing this kind of computing have been in operation for decades. A process of learning by using, plus ever cheaper large computers, has led to considerable replacement and upgrading of facilities.

newer body of applications, first reaching measurable commercial importance about 15 years ago. Most use depends on mass-market software, such as word processing or spreadsheet programs.[3] This market has seen much growth in two ways: by replacement and upgrading and by diffusion, as more and more (especially) white-collar workers have seen their work at least partially computerized. In this segment, individual customers tend to buy hardware and software from a wide variety of vendors in arm's-length, market relationships. Unit sales of successful products run to the millions. Individual demanders are small, however, so that through the late 1980s the market sizes for the first two types of computing were roughly equal. The third demand is composed of *scientific, engineering, and other technical computation*. Served by supercomputers, by minicomputers, and later by workstations, factories, universities, laboratories, and design centers do a tremendous volume of arithmetic.[4] In total, technical computing market size is roughly as large as each of the two kinds of commercial computing described.

This variety in demand has permitted the emergence of *different suppliers and markets*. Market segmentation has meant, for much of the history of the industry, that mainframes, minicomputers, and PCs have served distinct kinds of demands. More importantly, demand variety has permitted the emergence of new, entrepreneurial firms in parallel with established ones. Even as the oldest segment, mainframe computers, was consolidating around a dominant firm (IBM) and dominant design in the early 1960s, other firms (notably DEC) were creating the minicomputer segment. Later, other segments such as personal computers, workstations, and superminicomputers would offer yet more entry opportunities.

This observation leads us to our first analytical distinction. We recognized that there have been several segments emerging and growing in the computer industry since mainframes: minicomputers first, personal computers and workstations later. However, in terms of the type of coevolutionary processes, only three industrial dynamics may be identified. The first surrounds the creation and persistence of IBM's leadership in mainframe computing from the late 1940s to the late 1980s. In the second (for minicomputers, workstations, and personal computers) new entrants played a major role and turbulence was initially very high. In the third, different segments converged.

[3] See Chapter 4 in this volume for a detailed treatment of software.

[4] Here the users are technically sophisticated, and the applications have crisp technical goals. Buyer–seller relationships are more like arm's-length markets than close bilateral links.

A. Industry Dynamics 1: Creation and Persistence of IBM's Leadership in Mainframes (Late 1940s to Late 1980s)

For our purposes, *mainframe computers* are systems used for large departmental or company-wide applications.[5] We shall cover mainframes from the very early period, the time before a clear definition of a business computer or a computer company emerged, up to the late 1980s. IBM arose from an early competitive struggle to dominate supply, in the process determining the technologies needed for computing, the marketing capabilities needed to make computers commercially useful, and the management structures that could link technology and its use. Competitors, customers, and even national governments have defined their computer strategies in relationship to IBM. IBM was the manager of both the cumulative and the disruptive/radical parts of technical change. Customers' learning by using and IBM engineers' learning by doing were focused on the same IBM computer architectures. When an established technology aged, IBM was not only its owner but also the innovator of the new.

B. Industry Dynamics 2: Creation of New Market Segments and Entry: Minicomputers, Workstations, and Microcomputers (Late 1950s to Late 1980s)

The second industry dynamics saw the founding and evolution of new computer segments and markets. *Minicomputers* are machines intended for scientific and engineering use; in business applications, they are often used in support roles such as communications controllers. *Microcomputers* (personal computers) are low-price, small systems for individual applications, both in business sites and at home. *Workstations* are used by individual engineers in graphics and computation-intensive applications such as design. In this dynamics, a series of new markets were opened up by entrepreneurial start-up firms. Although there was some sharing of fundamental technical advances, each new segment's founding was characterized by considerable innovation and entry. As a result, the "technologies," as engineers use that term, of different segments were distinct. Those new segment foundings that led to viable

[5] The boundaries of the mainframe segment are not clear. Commercial minicomputers eventually became much like mainframes. We do not treat the development of the commercial minicomputer segment; for our (international comparison) purposes, the commercial minicomputer segment can be thought of as an extension of the mainframe segment.

markets brought computing to new kinds of demanders. Successful firms tended to be specialized. Buyers were departments of firms or individuals. Each of these segments saw some maturation toward a dominant computer design, and toward a dominant model of the appropriate supplying firm for the segment.

C. Industry Dynamics 3: Entry into the Mainframe Market by Networks of Small Computers and Rent-Destroying Challenge to IBM's Leadership (1990s)

The 1990s have seen a third industry dynamics. Reversing the long-standing trends of Industry Dynamics 1 and 2, this era saw competitive convergence of computers of all sizes in the 1990s. Existing types of small computers were networked together and offered to IBM's traditional customers.[6] The new technical and competitive importance of networks of small computers has eroded the earlier market segmentation among mainframe, mini, and micro. After a decade of stable segmentation, the distinct kinds of computers that had evolved in Industry Dynamics 1 and 2 came into direct competition with one another. "Client/server" platforms use computer networking to link user-friendly clients (such as PCs) with powerful servers (bigger PCs, workstations, minicomputers, or mainframes). The computer network consists of clients and servers, quite likely sold by different hardware and software companies, and networking infrastructure, likely sold by yet others. The networked computer became the platform on which large applications could be built. The buyers in this area are a complex mix of individuals, departments, and enterprises. As we write, neither the dominant design for a network of computers nor one for a computer company in this environment is clear.

The three industry dynamics have been characterized by *coevolution* of firms' capabilities, strategies and organizations, technologies, and market structures, and (often) by changing relationships among the industry, public policy, and national institutions. As we will show in more detail later, at the initial stage of each industry dynamics the coevolutionary process was caused by the introduction of a new technology developed by an inventor or a firm. The new technology spurred entry of new or established firms, which added modifications and changes to the original technology. In our three industry dynamics, the new technology addressed a new demand and new types of users or addressed old types of users in a radically new way. This created specific types

[6] See Bresnahan and Greenstein (1999) for an explanation of this reversal.

of user–producer relationships, which led firms to develop new competencies and organizations. Over time, firms developed appropriate competencies, strategies, and organizations more suitable for the new technology. These firms made innovations and fostered the rate of technical change in specific directions. Relatedly, public policy and institutions were relevant at various stages of the evolution of the computer industry: some policies and institutions remained unchanged over time, and others evolved in tune with the specific industry dynamics and changed in various degrees and forms in different countries. As we will show later, however, this coevolution of technology, firms' capabilities, strategies and organizations, industry structure, and public policy and institutions proceeded *differently in each industry dynamics*, with congruence among firms' strategies, industry characteristics, and countries' performance.[7]

A first look at the three industry dynamics shows that the *United States* has been *persistently the innovative and commercial world leader* in the computer industry. In Industry Dynamics 1, IBM emerged as the world leader. IBM, and therefore the United States, retained its leadership despite competitive attacks from individual companies, strategic alliances, and even whole national computer industries such as Japan's. In Industry Dynamics 2, new successful American firms entered emerging market segments while IBM maintained its dominance in mainframes. Finally, in Industry Dynamics 3, the challenge to IBM's leadership came mainly from American firms, as a result of the convergence between mainframes and networks of smaller computers. We examine the different reasons behind American success in each of the three periods. The chapter is organized in the following way: in Sections II to VI we discuss industry coevolution and the international competitive advantages in a comparative way (the United States, Europe, and Japan). In Sections II and III we analyze the birth of the new industry during the late 1940s and early 1950s and the emergence and persistence of IBM world leadership in mainframes for more than four decades. In Sections IV and V we discuss the growth of new market segments (mini- and microcomputers, respectively) and the entry, success, and growth of new American actors who became world leaders. In Section VI we examine the challenge to IBM domination in mainframes by computer networks and other existing American firms. Finally, in Section VII we draw some general conclusions from the analysis.

[7] A segment not treated is workstations. The history of this segment has many of the same elements as the microcomputer history.

II. The Birth of the New Industry: Major Similarities in the United States and Europe

The early period of many pioneering efforts leading to the emergence of a mainframe computer industry was characterized by extreme similarity in the initial conditions and types of entrants between the United States and Europe, with Japan lagging behind. The scientific capabilities of the universities in the United States and Europe and the structure and capabilities of the connected industries – office equipment and the electrical–electronic industry – were very similar.

A. The Major Role Played by Universities Around the World in the Precommercial Period

In the very early years of the industry (1940s) universities in both the United States and Europe were active at the scientific and prototype levels. In the United States, scientists in universities worked in cooperation with the government, which acted both as a source of funds and as a major potential consumer of technology, notably in the military and the Census Bureau. In addition, a few private firms also funded basic research in computers (IBM, for example, supported the development of the Mark I computer of Aiken at Harvard in 1944).

The scientific commitment by various American and European universities to create digital electromechanical computers led to the development of several machines during the 1940s. In the United States, for example, ENIAC, the first digital electromechanical computer, was developed by Eckert and Mauchly in 1946 with the support of the army at the University of Pennsylvania. The military also sponsored Project Whirlwind at MIT, which led to the development of magnetic core memories. European research in computers was at the world scientific frontier during the 1940s. In the United Kingdom, after the development of the Colossus, a computer similar to ENIAC (1945), and ACE (1945), Manchester and Cambridge universities moved to the forefront of research. Manchester University developed the Mark I, the first computer to use a magnetic drum memory (1948), and the Digital Machine (MADM) (1949), while Cambridge University developed the EDSAC (1949). In Germany, Konrad Zuse of Berlin University was very active in this field. During the 1930s, he built a series of electromechanical calculators (Z-1, Z-2, Z-3, and Z-4). The Z-3 was the first to be fully operational; Z-4 was installed in a German V-2 rocket plant and at the end of the Second World War was leased to the Swiss Polytechnic Institute.

In the United States, the origin of the commercial computer industry arose from the move of the two inventors of ENIAC from the university into the business world. In 1946 Eckert and Mauchly established their own firm, the Eckert–Mauchly Corporation, to develop general-purpose commercial computers for scientific as well as business accounting uses. The Eckert–Mauchly enterprise failed, however, also because external finance (particularly venture capital) was limited.[8]

Later on, in the 1950s, the role of universities expanded to include participation in the development of technologies that would be used in government projects or embedded in existing firms' products.[9]

B. Three Types of Entrants Around the World

Mainframes were the first commercial products developed and sold in the computer industry during the 1950s. They made extensive use of magnetic drum memories and, later on, of transistors. Early computers' functionality focused on scientific uses, then expanded to business uses such as accounting. The first mainframe producers maintained links with universities and continued to have government (military) support. They also opened up extensive linkages with business firms, who became major users of computers.

The success of IBM's model of a computer company, characterized by a Chandlerian three-pronged investment in technology, marketing, and management, is now very familiar. We should remember, however, that this model was not obvious to market participants in the early period.

Three distinct types of entrants entered the industry: office equipment producers, electronics firms, and new firms. Among office equipment firms, the most prominent were IBM, Remington Rand (later Sperry Rand), Burroughs, NCR (which later bought CRC), Olivetti, Bull, and BTM (an IBM distribution partner). Among electronics firms were General Electric, Honeywell, RCA, Siemens, Standard Electrik Lorenz, Telefunken, GEC, and Ferranti. New firms were less important competitively; they included CDC, SDS, ERA, CRC, Eckert–Mauchly, Nixdorf, and Zuse. All three types of entrants were in both the United States and Europe.

At this stage, Japanese firms did not have an important commercial presence in computing (Flamm, 1987). By the late 1950s, however, there

[8] Some (albeit insignificant) financial support came from firms such as Prudential, Nielson, and Northrop Aircraft. These financial sources were not sufficient, and in 1950 the Eckert–Mauchly Corporation was acquired by Remington Rand.

[9] See Organization for Economic Cooperation and Development (1966) and Flamm (1988) for a description of the American and European efforts.

were several Japanese technology initiatives under way. What was to be the largest "Japanese" computer company for some time, IBM Japan, was engaged in protracted negotiations with Japanese government agencies. These negotiations resulted in substantial technology transfer, including favorable licensing of IBM products to the Japanese industry (Anchordoguy, 1989).

In Japan, entry occurred later than in the United States or Europe. Heavy electric equipment firms (Toshiba, Mitsubishi) entered alongside consumer electronics firms (Matsushita, NEC, and Hitachi) that had capabilities in both areas. Japanese regulatory treatment of telecommunications permitted NTT an active role, encouraging its suppliers of communications equipment, notably Oki Electric and Fujitsu, to enter as well. No Japanese business equipment firms (like IBM or BTM) entered. Thus, Japanese entry differed in being later and purely electronically based.

The three types of entrants reflect the specific technological and market features of the new worldwide industry. Computers were a new electronics good, which attracted several existing electronics producers already active in other electronics fields. Similarly, some of the first applications of computers were in business, attracting firms with established connections to business data processing. Interestingly enough, the tension between technology-based and market-oriented firm organizations and competencies would reappear throughout the history of the industry (Davidow, 1986).

Despite the early enthusiasm, there remained fundamental uncertainty on the technological development of the industry, the range of applications, and the potential size of the future market (Rosenberg, 1994). The nature of commercial use of computing and the potential size of the market were unclear. Similarly, the appropriate "business model" and strategy for a computer company were not known. In particular, it was not well established whether the primary usages for computers would be in making calculations or in processing data. Neither was it certain whether the largest demand segments would be military, scientific/engineering, commercial, or other. These uncertainties meant that the most important directions for technical progress, such as the relative importance of calculation speed versus storage access, were unclear. They also meant that the nature of buyer/seller relationships and of commercialization efforts was unsettled.[10]

During the 1950s, the three types of entrants – office equipment

[10] See Katz and Phillips (1982) and Usselman (1993) for a discussion of this uncertainty with particular regard to how it impacted different firms in the industry.

producers, electronic firms, and new firms – had distinct capabilities and distinct strategies, which were similar in Europe and the United States for each group of entrants. The electronics-based firms faced the challenge of either building or acquiring a business-equipment marketing capability – including a substantial field sales force – or finding a way to succeed without it.[11] Many found the potential profitability attractive enough to overcome this barrier.[12] Firms with business equipment capabilities quickly recognized the need to add technological ones. Some, like Remington Rand and National Cash Register (which bought CRC), attempted to obtain these capabilities by acquisition. Internal development of technical capability was the more common strategy, undertaken by IBM and Burroughs in the United States and by Olivetti and BTM in Europe.[13]

To succeed, start-ups such as CDS, SDS, DEC, or Eckert–Mauchly would need to develop both technical and marketing capabilities. Many start-ups focused on the more technical side, producing computers only for specialized uses. Firms of any type would need remarkable financial resources because neither the technical nor the marketing capability could be built without considerable capital.

In Europe, some firms focused on niche strategies: Nixdorf, Zuse, Telefunken, and so on. From the beginning, Nixdorf had the goal of producing small computers for specific uses. In 1952, Heinz Nixdorf founded the Labor fur Impulstechnik (which only in 1968 changed its name to Nixdorf). Nixdorf developed the first vacuum tube calculator for accounting for RWE and then built several computers for Bull and Wanderer. By this route, a capable computer firm in the small-user niche was built.

Among office equipment firms, a major tension arose between the established mechanical and electromechanical core competencies and the emerging electronic ones. For example, the office machinery producer Olivetti entered the field of electromechanical calculators in 1949 by creating (with Bull) a commercialization company for the distribution of Bull's tabulating machinery. In the early 1950s, it started doing R&D on electronic computers in various locations in Italy and the

[11] One class of technically capable potential entrants, telephone companies, did not enter. In the United States, AT&T's entry was blocked by an antitrust consent decree.

[12] Siemens, for example, decided on full-scale entry in 1954, focusing on mainframes for commercial and scientific uses. At the end of the 1950s it produced the first 2002 computer. It must be noted that during the 1950s Siemens contacted IBM for cooperation in computers. Actual cooperation, however, was limited to the supply of readers of punched card and magnetic tape machinery and did not include mainframes (Malerba, 1985).

[13] For a discussion of BTM and Ferranti, see Freeman (1965), Malerba (1985), and Usselman (1993).

United States. Conflicts between the dominant mechanical competence and culture of Olivetti and those of the emerging electronic technology arose from the beginning. The new Electronic Division and the new factory that was going to produce the first electronic calculator, the ELEA 9003 (developed in 1959), were located near Milan, far away from the central headquarters in Ivrea in order to be isolated from the prevailing mechanical culture.

C. American Government Encouragement of (Domestic) Industry Development

Substantial government backing for the early U.S. computer industry offered advantages to firms in the United States. There is little support, however, for the view that the U. S. government "bought success" for IBM and no support whatsoever for a "strategic trade policy" view of U.S. government actions.

Some of the purely technical capabilities needed to build computers were backed by federal, especially military, research funding. Technologies such as transistors and core memories were developed in laboratories – AT&T's and MIT's – before the semiconductor industry took off in the mid-1950s. Some of these developments were heavily dependent on federal money (Flamm, 1987). Further, many early U.S. computer systems were themselves directly supported by federal research funds. In this manner, the army supported ENIAC; the navy and air force supported Project Whirlwind at MIT; the Census Bureau supported UNIVAC; and so on.[14] Further, it was clear that the military was going to purchase many computers from domestic suppliers. At a broad, general level this environment worked to the advantage of IBM. Government support of technical capability development meant that IBM's existing marketing capability could be integrated into full Chandlerian three-pronged investment more effectively. Indeed, many of the technical developments for defense computing were commercially useful. Ultimately, the Defense Calculator became the IBM 701; much of SAGE was valuable in SABRE; and so on. Similarly, reduction in uncertainty and increases in general technical knowledge obtained from defense computers may have been valuable commercially.

Yet this "dual-use" or "spillover" story was not, in fact, an important factor in IBM's success. The U.S. government actions were far removed from intentional strategic trade policy aimed at creating a national

[14] Flamm (1987, chapter 3) tabulates military research support in detail.

champion: IBM. Defense Department agencies supported the development of a domestic computer industry.[15] National defense goals, however, could easily have been met by a largely technical computer industry, with marketing capabilities focused on defense procurement procedures. Indeed, defense support for computer systems development at IBM (including the Naval Ordnance Research Computer [NORC]) and for the 701 Defense Calculator (which was financed by IBM but presold to defense customers) was a small fraction of total IBM effort. Furthermore, government funding at Eckert–Mauchly Computer Corporation and Engineering Research Associates, both purchased by Remington Rand, was actually intended to put IBM at a competitive disadvantage.[16] The Defense Department, however, did act like a well-funded demander with a real need for computer-based weapons systems and let the supplying industry structure emerge in the marketplace.[17]

Another branch of the same government, the U.S. Department of Justice, worked actively to prevent the emergence of IBM as the computer industry's dominant firm. In particular, the U.S. Department of Justice was systematically against IBM's strategy of strengthening marketing and technical capabilities within the same firm. It therefore worked directly against government support of the three-pronged investment. In two antitrust lawsuits, the U.S. Department of Justice sought to characterize IBM's marketing capability as anticompetitive.[18]

The legislative branch was also anti-IBM, tilting procurement policy against the company. Here the issue was more political, having to do with spreading out government procurement funds to states where IBM was not as important an employer as other system companies.[19] Besides,

[15] Soviet production of nuclear arms led to very considerable investment in antiaircraft defenses, whose C^3I (command, control, communication, and intelligence) part – realized in the 1960s in the SAGE system – was heavily computer based.

[16] The IBM-eye view of early developments was that they constituted "Government Funded Competition." Only because of this threat did IBM reverse its standing policy against federal research collaborations, using navy money to design the NORC (Pugh, 1995).

[17] Indeed, Usselman offers a very interesting argument that U.S. procurement policy favored IBM only because it took this form (Usselman, 1993). IBM would not likely have been chosen as the national champion in the critical early phases, nor would a "supply side" procurement policy have led to the development of the IBM commercialization capabilities.

[18] The 1956 consent decree between IBM and the government had, among other provisions, stark limitations on IBM's use of "service bureaus" as a sales device. The second antitrust lawsuit, brought in 1965 and contested for over a decade, viewed IBM's service, sales, and support efforts as anticompetitive lock-in devices.

[19] There is an active debate on whether government agencies were able to evade the law and procure IBM as they saw fit, see Greenstein (1995). There is no debate about the anti-IBM policy itself.

IBM did not initially understand the power of a single computer architecture that could serve both military and business clients and did not expect its federal support to provide spillouts to its commercial data-processing business. In the critical early stages, IBM had separate development efforts and built separate capabilities to pursue new military/scientific customers and to supply its traditional business/commercial customers because it conceived these two lines of business as distinct.[20] It therefore appeared to believe that electronics offered good opportunities for both commercial and governmental business.[21]

Only ex post was it clear that the industry was one in which technology was general-purpose. Spillouts from one use to another eventually proved to be significant but were not anticipated at the time.[22]

In conclusion, government policy was only accidentally favorable to the creation of IBM as a worldwide leader. Parts of the government opposed IBM's most critical investments. The supportive parts of the government were pursuing their own policy goals and were not following any type of strategic trade policy. No one, not even IBM, saw the implications of the positive role of government support for business applications.

III. The Rise and Persistence of IBM World Dominance in Mainframes

In the late 1950s and early 1960s, IBM became the world leader in mainframes, and it remained so for 30 years. IBM was able to be highly innovative in mainframes, addressing the demand from big or medium size users, government, and universities. Three stages can be identified: the rise to worldwide leadership through a high commitment to Chandlerian three-pronged investment, the consolidation of leadership through innovation in a modular product line (IBM System 360), and the continuation of its dominance through waves of highly successful products (IBM System 370, and so on).

[20] See Usselman (1993) on the distinction between IBM's facilities at Poughkeepsie and those at Endicott.

[21] See Pugh (1995) for a discussion of IBM initiatives to shift its existing tab-card-based commercial data processing to electronic form. Katz and Phillips (1982) also discuss IBM's early understanding of commercial as well as defense applications.

[22] Indeed, spillouts to IBM's commercial business from its defense business were important. See Katz and Phillips (1982) or Flamm (1988) for an accounting of some very important technical developments that first appeared in defense sector products.

A. The Generation of IBM World Leadership: The Role of the Three-Pronged Investments

In the 1950s and early 1960s, IBM introduced highly successful families of computers such as the 701 (1952), 650 (1954), and 1401 (1960).[23] Each of these new families involved considerable development of new computing technology, not only processing power but also peripherals. Moving from defense calculation to business data processing, IBM supported business systems very effectively at customers' sites and built capability to address customer wants and needs. This combination of technical drive and customer focus was difficult to achieve, requiring new management structures. IBM's success sprang from its major R&D investments and, more generally, Chandlerian three-pronged investment in managerial capabilities, technology, and marketing.[24] IBM rapidly became the world market leader because of its continuous R&D effort in developing new products, coupled with advanced manufacturing capabilities, excellent marketing competence, and management structures that kept technology and market aligned.

Though much of the attention of the early computer industry was on technical calculations for military and scientific purposes, commercially oriented companies like IBM and Remington Rand were quick to move toward business uses. This movement was not simple, however. Within IBM management, there was wide resistance to building a general-purpose computer on the grounds that demand was limited. In the very early 1950s, creation of a computer such as the 701 would call for a large financial commitment and much R&D. This was to be a stored-program computer, able to use the binary number system instead of the decimal, and would be preassembled by IBM for rapid setup (and later rapid upgrades) at the customer's site. All of these features called for new, and expensive, technological and production capabilities. The resistance was overcome by IBM's new leader, Thomas Watson, Jr., and IBM's 701 quickly overtook Remington Rand's Univac, the leading computer at the time. The 701's combination of advanced technology and customer-aware features like rapid setup was well matched to IBM's strong marketing presence (already established by tabulating card machines) in business data processing.

The resistance within IBM continued with the IBM 650 Magnetic Drum Calculator, which was to become "the Model T of computers" (Cuthbert Hurd).[25] Many IBM managers thought that the computer's

[23] This section draws heavily on Fisher et al. (1983).

[24] See Usselman (1993) and Sobel (1986). [25] Interview, Winter 1995.

rental price, over $1,000/month, would limit demand too sharply to cover the large development costs. IBM was making progress on a broad technical front: the 650 had 1,000 10-digit words of memory, and vastly improved diagnostics, for example. Optional features made it more suitable for calculation or accounting. Accounting reports called for developments in a wide variety of peripherals, including printers, magnetic tape storage devices, and magnetic disk drives. IBM could offer customers an integrated solution, as a result of progress on the computer and a variety of peripherals. After being pushed forward into the marketplace, the 650 became the most successful computer of the 1950s, with about 1,800 units shipped.

Integration and wide technical progress continued to be important throughout the decade. The IBM 1401 was, indeed, much faster and more reliable than the previous-generation 650. Perhaps more important for its use as an accounting machine was the breadth of peripherals. It could use both punch cards and magnetic tape and worked with the simultaneously introduced 1403 chain printer. Sales of this machine were approximately one-quarter of sales of all stored-program electronic computers.

On the marketing side as well, IBM pushed ahead. The company made an early and expensive commitment to field service and support, and to customer education. This took place in an era of widespread ignorance about the potential uses of computers. This marketing commitment was not only domestic. IBM succeeded in dominating the European as well as the Japanese mainframe markets. In Europe, IBM's superiority in products and customer assistance was coupled with a local presence on the main markets. For example, IBM UK and IBM Germany tried very hard (and succeeded to a large extent) to be considered, respectively, a British and a German company. In Japan, IBM Japan was for a long time first in revenues among "Japanese" computer companies. The strategy reflected powerful marketing forces. IBM used the "IBM World Trade" model, making itself as local a company as possible. This meant involving nationals in almost all roles, including senior management. The point of this localization was to ensure that relationship selling efforts worked.[26] The scope of IBM's investment was global, with worldwide exploitation of scale economies in designing and building computers linked to a local marketing organization.

IBM certainly did make major mistakes. The STRETCH committee, an effort to advance its technical capabilities and to build a high-speed

[26] In the mid-1980s, IBM Japan was replaced by IBM Asia/Pacific, a less Japanese entity led by expatriate U.S. citizens.

computer, turned out to be a commercial failure. IBM learned valuable technical lessons from STRETCH, but revenues from the new high-speed computer failed to cover development costs.[27]

The computer business in its early phases had a competitive environment under tremendous increasing returns to scale. All of marketing, technology, demand, and a company business model were still to be invented. Since the first two were quite expensive and the last two very unpredictable, investments were highly uncertain. From a company perspective, IBM pushed forward with very expensive investments in technology, marketing, and management, thereby putting tremendous pressure on rivals' capabilities. As a consequence a very concentrated structure with a single dominant firm emerged.

B. The Consolidation of IBM World Leadership: IBM System 360

By the early 1960s, the main technical features of a commercially useful computer were clear and many of these features were already embodied in products. Important problems remained, however, notably incompatibilities between computers in different families. The final stages in this evolution were the introduction and implementation of the completely modular, compatible computer family. This was the IBM System 360. This product line, and the organization that improved and sold it, became the dominant industry model.

Incompatibilities between different computers forced up costs and created delays in using companies. In the early 1960s, computers were designed to be used either for commercial or for scientific uses, not for both. A user who wanted to run both applications needed two separate machines, support staffs that understood two different bodies of technical knowledge, and so on. In addition, IBM's machines themselves were not compatible across the broad family of processors: a program running on one processor could not be used on another. Users whose needs grew over time could exhaust the capacity of their existing computer and be required to reprogram for the next larger model.

IBM's System 360 was designed to solve these user problems. It was, however, neither an easy decision to make nor a straightforward technical feat. Technically, compatibility over a wide range of sizes and uses of computers changed the design process. Designers could not optimize for specific purposes, but instead needed to be coordinated in the

[27] Some of these technologies were quite important, including transistors, a parallel architecture, and manufacturing processes needed to integrate many different components.

production of general-purpose components that could be specialized. Such coordination raised costs and slowed the invention process. IBM appointed a task force called the SPREAD committee to develop and supervise the project. Developing the new machine required such a big commitment that the venture came to be popularly known as a "bet the company" initiative. IBM employed virtually all its financial, technological, and human capital. Overall, it devoted a larger percentage of its revenue than it (or any of its competitors) had ever spent on any project.

The decision itself was difficult. Designing a new family of computers meant that there would be future compatibility but implied incompatibility in the present. IBM executives responsible for the 1401, for example, argued that competitive pressures forced an investment in improved 1401s.[28] The decision also meant abandoning investments in products under development, even successful ones.[29] The IBM decision to end the proliferation of product lines and put resources into a single development effort was risky and expensive. More importantly, it showed that the management control structures needed for the three-pronged strategy were in place.

The 360 made existing machines obsolete. Even though it was not directly compatible with the existing processors, users found switching irresistible because of the tremendous benefits of the new system.[30] Among the many distinguishing features of the 360 was price/performance superiority not only over IBM's own computers but over the systems of all its competitors. The success of the 360 was immediate and gigantic: more than a thousand orders were made in the first month after announcement, and many more thousands followed.

The introduction of the IBM System 360 drastically changed the structure of IBM and of the overall computer industry. With System 360 the standardization of components and software allowed the exploitation of economies of scale in component production and the consequent upstream vertical integration of computer firms, the supply of a broad line of compatible computers, and the introduction of modularity and incremental modifications in computer design. From a company perspective, this event indicated recognition, after some early confusion, of

[28] Honeywell's introduction of the H-200 computer was followed by 196 instances of lost IBM 1401 sales in the next eight weeks. At that time, the chairman of SPREAD was also head of the General Products Division, responsible for the 1401. The argument for further 1401 investment lost to the new System 360 concept despite such powerful opposition.

[29] The almost finished 8000 project was labeled a "wrong" approach despite the enormous financial resources already devoted to it and was discontinued.

[30] The irony is that to put its customers in a position where they would not need to switch computer families for over 25 years, IBM had to induce them to switch at the beginning.

the importance of scale and scope economies in computer design and commercialization. From an industry perspective, the event was even more important. Success of this strategy at IBM defined a level of innovation and commercialization capability to which other firms, worldwide, were going to be compared by customers.

C. Continued Innovation by the Dominant Firm: The IBM System 370

The 1970s saw continued dominance by IBM of the mainframe segment. IBM introduced a new family of computers, the System 370. These computers represented considerable technical advance, much of it competence-destroying with respect to IBM's own capabilities. As with the System 360, IBM was prepared to give up the rents on existing product lines and on the technologies embodied in them. Backward compatibility of the System 370 helped to preserve IBM's position, for customers did not see much destruction of their own computer-using competencies. They could and did continue to use IBM machines predominantly.

D. Strategies and Evolution of the Losers to IBM Around the Globe

In the era of the IBM System 370, the scope of geographic product markets was once again worldwide. IBM was setting the standard in two senses. First, competitive products needed to respond to IBM price/performance, software availability, and service and support levels. Second, a critical technology choice was whether to establish an IBM-compatible product line or to attempt a separate, incompatible platform. The IBM-compatible strategy would involve development of expensive R&D and manufacturing facilities. IBM kept these costs high for rivals, pushing the technical frontier with repeated own-competence destroying innovations. The 1970 unbundling of IBM hardware and system software, under pressure from U.S. antitrust authorities, made the IBM-compatible strategy easier in the System 370 era. Yet rivals found themselves followers of IBM, producing specific components for some customers but never gaining control of the system/370 architecture. The IBM-incompatible strategy was even more expensive, for it involved departures from IBM complementary software and support infrastructure. To pursue the IBM-incompatible strategy, a competitor would need substantial marketing expenditures for a field sales and service force, software, and so on, as well as technical capabilities comparable to the leader's. Firms also faced marketing choices: would they compete for mainstream large-company data center customers or find smaller market niches?

Facing IBM success, American, European, and Japanese firms adopted variants of these follower strategies. In the following pages, we show how a strategy of direct competition with IBM using a competing platform failed, but how niche strategies and IBM-compatibility strategies permitted survival without threatening IBM dominance.

Head to Head Confrontation with IBM: Always a Losing Strategy

Some rivals introduced a competing platform, trying to replicate the IBM three-pronged investments. This expensive strategy involved the development of a number of computers, each compatible with the others, and development or encouragement of correspondingly compatible peripherals, software, and end-user knowledge. Effective competition by this method involved building two very distinct assets. One was technological: the capability to design and manufacture computers and close technological complements. The other was marketing: the ability to help customers turn computer technology into useful solutions. Such attempts failed all around the world because the electric and electronics companies were not able to develop effective marketing capabilities, and business equipment companies were not able to move the capabilities of the company fully into electronics and to bet completely on the electronic technologies.

This tension between business equipment companies' existing core competencies and electronic technologies is well illustrated by the case of Olivetti. Olivetti's increasing commitment to mechanical office equipment technologies, particularly after the purchase of Underwood in 1959, drained a massive amount of resources and did not allow commitment of considerable resources to mainframes. Consequently, Olivetti decided to focus on mechanical technologies and traditional office equipment products rather than on electronics and mainframes and sold its Electronic Division to GE (later sold to Honeywell) in 1964 (Malerba, 1985).

Compatibility with IBM: A Losing Strategy in the 1960s Becomes a Survival Strategy in the 1970s

Another strategy available to competitor companies in these circumstances was the acceptance of the IBM System 360 platform standard and the sale of IBM-compatible computers. A related strategy was building IBM-compatible peripherals such as storage devices, taken up by plug-compatible manufacturers (PCMs).

Most of the initial attempts to introduce IBM-compatible computers failed. For example, RCA built completely IBM-compatible computers, the Spectra Series.[31] RCA's initial marketing plan was built around availability and superior technical features at the time of IBM order backlogs. Reliability problems and other technical difficulties plagued the Spectra through the System 360 era. Though RCA's effort was profitable for a period, the operations were never really large and were ultimately sold to Univac.

RCA's failure also involved its collaborative partners around the world. In 1964 Siemens, after realizing that its new 3003 Series was already obsolete, started a collaboration with RCA, which was developing the new Spectra 70 series. RCA gave Siemens a license and technical assistance for the Spectra 70 series, which was shipped as the Siemens 4004 in 1965. In the meantime, the IBM System 360 was overtaking the European as well as American markets. For Siemens, the collaboration with RCA proved initially successful at the commercial level: during the 1960s and early 1970s, Siemens increased its market shares (in Germany from 5 percent in 1965 to 16 percent in 1972). This was also due to the introduction of a line of smaller processors (302, 304, 305) and the acquisition of Zuse (1966). Later on, however, RCA's withdrawal from computer production (1971) left Siemens without a partner with advanced technological capabilities.

In the 1970s, with the unbundling decision, the compatibility strategy became more successful. It was pursued by a group of American, European, and Japanese companies, often related through agreements of various types. In particular, the IBM-compatibility strategy of Amdahl, Fujitsu, and Hitachi was successful for a long time in the world market. Amdahl, founded by an ex-IBM designer, was in the IBM-compatible business from the beginning. It had considerable success as a market follower. Japanese firms, which had been investing through domestic consortia in computer technologies, began to make IBM-compatible exports. International linkages were important here. Hitachi had a partnership with RCA and had learned much about the IBM-compatible business from that experience. Fujitsu was lending money to Amdahl from 1972 and later acquired an ownership stake. In an era of IBM dominance of world markets, only Japanese and Japanese-cooperating sellers succeeded in becoming effective followers through the IBM-compatible strategy.

After an initial period, these new compatible entrants made IBM-compatible computers less expensive. This transferred some profits from

[31] Another example was Honeywell's earlier offer of IBM 1401-compatible machines, unfortunately introduced at the time of the System 360 rollout.

IBM to customers. However, control of the System 370 architecture, the operating system, and other key software components, as well as the world dominant market share in mainframe computers remained with IBM.

Unbundling by IBM and monitoring by American antitrust authorities also made peripheral sales by PCMs somewhat easier. The same forces also made third-party leasing and other financing more widely available. This had the effect of lowering returns to IBM. Makers of compatible computers and peripherals limited IBM's market power and its ability to price discriminate. However, it is difficult to conclude that any of this direct, compatible competition had any immediate impact on industry evolution. IBM retained control of the mainframe architecture and IBM's profitability was not destroyed. Actually, its broader competitive effect was to enhance the attractiveness of the IBM platform to customers.

Niche Strategy: Always a Survival Strategy

Another strategy was to avoid head-to-head competition with IBM entirely, seeking out a body of customers not served by the 360 platform. Three kinds of niches emerged: specialized commercial market niches, governments, and protected domestic markets for the non-U.S. producers.

Market Niches. In the United States, the most successful versions of this strategy were "niche" efforts. CDC was very successful with scientific users. NCR found industry-specific niches, notably with smaller computers, in retail trade and banking. In Europe, unlike mainframe suppliers such as Standard Electrik Lorenz and Telefunken, which exited the computer market, some firms decided to enter the market for midrange systems (comparable with IBM's Systems S/32, S/34, S/36, and later AS400). For example, during the 1960s and the 1970s in Germany several firms, such as Nixdorf, Konstanz, Triumph Adler, Kienzle, Dietz, and Krantz, started to produce midrange systems. These systems were all proprietary, focused on sector-specific applications and with specific software. These companies (particularly Nixdorf) experienced major success until the 1980s. The introduction and diffusion of microcomputers and the emergence of standard bundles led to the rapid disappearance of these firms (see the later discussion on the crisis of Nixdorf).

Government Niches. A very important niche was procurement by the government, for both military and civilian uses. In the United States, procurement policy, under pressure from Congressman Jack Brooks's government operations subcommittee, was anti-IBM in intention and effect. Honeywell and Univac took advantage of this and had much more success in the niche market of federal government computer purchases than in the broader commercial computer market. In the other countries, every government protected its weak domestic firms from IBM by use of procurement policy.

Niches by Leading Domestic Customers. In addition, large "domestic" customers had close relations with large "domestic" mainframe producers and would buy "domestic." A buy-German or buy-French attitude among large firms and large institutions was present during the 1960s. In Japan, large Japanese buyers, whether the government or NTT, were influenced to buy Japanese computers. Throughout the 1960s, import market share in Japan fell steadily as Japanese firms' capabilities grew.[32]

E. Coevolution in Europe: The Decline of the Industry and the Role of European National Champions Policies as Exit Barriers

Faced by the mounting competitive challenge from IBM, European producers declined in competitiveness. As previously mentioned, they either did not invest enough in R&D or did not have advanced manufacturing and marketing competencies. Some of them (particularly old office equipment producers such as Olivetti) continued to have difficulties in absorbing the new electronic technology and culture and did not want to abandon mechanical or electromechanical technologies. Other had major productive and coordination problems. For example, ICL inherited two incompatible mainframe product lines, one from ITC and the other from English Electric, and kept them incompatible during the first part of the 1970s, while developing a third (incompatible) line. All three were also IBM-incompatible. The severe crisis faced in the late 1970s and early 1980s led ICL to move to IBM-compatible strategies, reduce its R&D expenditure on mainframes, and increase it on other computer types, while focusing on specific markets: defense, retailing, and financial services. Specialization in these vertical markets still characterizes ICL.

[32] Above and beyond the IBM patents, most Japanese firms sought overseas partners. Oki Electric had Sperry as a partner from 1963; Hitachi, RCA from 1961; Toshiba, GE from 1964; Mitsubishi, TRW from 1962; NEC, Honeywell from 1962. Matsushita never had an overseas partner but had negotiated with Philips before exiting the computer business in 1964. The important exception was Fujitsu, which had no foreign partner at this stage.

Moreover, in their search for international alliances, some European firms chose "big losers" in the technological and commercial race. We have already mentioned Siemens's links with RCA. Also during the 1970s the main European mainframe producers continued to foster their links with foreign firms, without much success: Siemens with Fujitsu, ICL with Fujitsu, and CII with Honeywell. During the 1980s ICL set up a cooperative arrangement with Fujitsu (in which Fujitsu supplied components and semiconductor design tools, while mainframe architecture, design, and software were developed by ICL). In 1991 Fujitsu acquired 80 percent of ICL. Fujitsu, however, did not decrease ICL's R&D expenditures and let ICL follow quite autonomous marketing strategies in Europe. Siemens continued to follow a strategy of international alliances with key producers in mainframes. After the failures of the alliance with RCA and the UNIDATA experience, Siemens's search for a partner led the company to a cooperative alliance with Fujitsu (1977) by selling Fujitsu's large mainframes under Siemens's label. Moreover, Siemens founded Comparex with BASF (which was already marketing Hitachi's computers in Europe) for the production of IBM-compatible computers. Whereas cooperation with Fujitsu continues at the present time, Siemens's involvement in Comparex was strongly reduced by 1988.

In Europe, public policies represented a major exit barrier from mainframe production for "national champions" such as Siemens, CII, and ICL. First, governments intervened by supporting directly or indirectly the mergers between unsuccessful companies in order to create national champions. For example, in 1968 ICL was formed from the merger of International Computers and Tabulators (ICT) (already incorporating the computer operations of BTM, Ferranti, General Electric Powers, and EMI) and English Electric Computers (EEC) (already incorporating the computer operations of Elliot Automation, English Electric, Leo Computers, and Marconi). In the same period in France CSF/CGE and SEA of the Schneider Group merged to form CII. Second, increasingly large programs of support were launched in the various countries. The French Plan Calculs (1967–1971 and 1971–1975), the British Advanced Computer Technology Project (1969), the German First and Second Data Processing Programs (respectively in 1967–1969 and 1969–1970) channeled a large part of public policy support to CII, ICL, and Siemens, respectively (Malerba, 1985). Third, governments protected national champions' markets through public procurement. For example, in 1969 ICL received 94 percent of central government orders for computers and benefited from official government exhortations to "buy from British firms wherever reasonably possible" (Torrisi, 1995).

There was even an attempt to increase the size of IBM competitors through a pan-European company. Siemens, CII, and Philips formed the UNIDATA joint venture. Because of conflicts among the partners and struggle over the control of the joint venture, real cooperation never took off and the joint venture ended in 1975.

In spite of their niche strategies and the national champions policies, market shares of European firms remained quite low. For example, in France in 1972 IBM controlled 58 percent of the installed base, while CII, Siemens, and Philips claimed 12 percent and Honeywell and Bull 18 percent. In 1980 IBM still had 52 percent of the installed base of computers in France, while CII–Honeywell–Bull controlled 31 percent. In the United Kingdom ICL's market share declined from 41 percent in 1968 to 31 percent in 1985.

The effect of protection by individual European governments was to keep an uncompetitive European computer industry alive and sheltered from destruction by IBM. These barriers to exit, however, did not lead European firms to launch major policies and investments able to increase their innovativeness and competitiveness internationally.

F. Coevolution in Japan: Catching Up in the 1960s

Japanese firms, and government policy in that country, behaved very differently. In the early 1960s the Japanese computer industry also lagged behind IBM. In Japan, this situation led to consortia. With help from government procurement policies and large organizations like the telephone company NTT, firms met with considerable success selling computers within Japan. This was not the case in the overseas markets. As a result the country continued to be a net importer of computers. One of the first consortia was the FONTAC project.[33] Planned as an IBM 1401-killer, this 1962–1964 project was late to market, as its completion coincided with the next generation (System 360) announcement from IBM. Both government and private firms participated in the project.

The second half of the 1960s saw a concerted Japanese attempt to catch up in computer technology. Technology initiatives were not pointed at the turbulent, unclear, and unstandardized early computer market. Instead, the establishment of broadly compatible platforms in the System 360 had made the importance of scale, standardization, and compatibility clear. Japanese companies' technical initiative was coordinated by MITI in the "Super High-Performance Computer Project."

[33] See Anchordoguy (1989) and Fransman (1995).

The project had the goal of building specifically Japanese technical capabilities in hardware and software. With IBM patents (extracted as a condition of IBM presence in Japan) and a budget, the Ministry of International Trade and Industry had the resources to encourage cooperation. Six computer firms participated, in order to achieve more rapid time to market and sought quickly commercializable machines. MITI favored a higher technological standard (Anchordoguy, 1989).

In addition to government sponsored R&D, other Japanese institutions supported this early development. From 1968, NTT was active as a buyer of computers and as a coordinator of computer company developments of systems, such as the DIPS-1 System. In particular, NTT supported computer development by three major producers (Fujitsu, Hitachi, and NEC), which were also major telecommunications equipment suppliers.[34] Government subsidized low-interest loans to rent Japanese computers through the Japan Electronic Computer Corporation and encouraged many users to select Japanese brand computers (Anchordoguy, 1989). Other users, with both national and private commercial goals, were encouraged to make this selection as well.

The effect of these early initiatives was to build a very substantial technological capability within some Japanese firms, partially catching up to IBM. This, plus market advantage in the home Japanese market, led to substantial import substitution. Japanese vendors' share of the Japanese computer market grew steadily over the 1960s, reaching almost 60 percent (Anchordoguy, 1989). After IBM's introduction of System/370 this share, however, was substantially reduced, to about 50 percent.

Market success of Japanese vendors was weaker for computer software than for hardware. The creation of the Japan Software Company, a joint venture of the Industrial Bank of Japan, NEC, Fujitsu, and Hitachi, had considerable government subsidy. The firm was not able to ship such key products as the "common language" that would let applications run on any Japanese computer. It was dissolved in 1972.

At the time of the worldwide transition from System/360 to System/370, Japan had built strong but not yet world-competitive computer hardware competencies. Incomplete protection from external competition such as from IBM and no protection from domestic competition among Japanese producers had spurred firms' development efforts. Note that both MITI and NTT avoided European-style "national champion" policies. Each worked with a number of companies that protected only one firm and de facto created a barrier to exit in that

[34] See Fransman (1990) on Japanese developments, especially NTT's role.

single firm. Japanese policies, on the contrary, worked with a number of companies, supporting their cooperation in some technologies, but keeping them in competition. The presence of both cooperation and competition has been a major reason for the moderate success of Japanese policies compared to the failure of European ones.

G. Japanese Advantages Consolidated in the 1970s

Over time, changes in the computer market played to Japanese firms' strengths. When IBM unbundled operating system software from computer hardware, Japanese companies' ability to build strong hardware competencies increased in importance, and their software weakness became less important (because of the opportunity to sell hardware alone).

During the IBM System/370 era, Japanese firms held a large share of the domestic market through government, NTT, and *keiretsu* customer connections. But they lagged in both hardware and software technologies. In the late 1970s two integrated circuit joint ventures were launched by several Japanese computer firms, one sponsored by NTT, the other by MITI. These projects were focused on the creation of a Japanese hardware engineering and manufacturing capability for very large scale integration (VLSI). The scope was ambitious, including manufacturing equipment for integrated circuit devices, integrated circuits, and computer hardware. Separate initiatives dealt with the problem of computer software. In this period software initiatives met with little success. As a result major attempts to establish an integrated computer systems company, with both hardware and key software, plus worldwide service, sales, and support systems, were largely unsuccessful, as measured by world market standards.

The hardware initiatives, by contrast, brought some Japanese firms to the worldwide competitive level. This was reflected in domestic and export markets. Domestically, Fujitsu passed IBM Japan in sales in 1979; by 1982, Fujitsu had 22 percent of the market compared to IBM's 20 percent. NEC and Hitachi were not far behind, with 17 percent and 15 percent, respectively. By the early 1980s, Japan became a net exporter of computer equipment. The exports were largely IBM-compatible mainframes.

As the 1970s ended, the Japanese were by far the most effective followers of IBM. Traditional national competencies, such as relationship selling at home and efficient volume manufacturing for export, were being well exploited.

The next round of consortia technology development efforts was more ambitious. The goal was establishment of a computer architecture independent of IBM.[35] This would take Japanese competencies into direct head-to-head competition with IBM, of the form seen earlier to be very difficult. Accordingly, Japanese efforts involved an attempt not merely to catch up but to leapfrog IBM technologically.

This effort played out in the Fifth Generation Computer Project and in the Supercomputer Project. Again, these were multicompany government- or NTT-sponsored collaborative research efforts. The Supercomputer Project, begun in 1981 with nearly a decade-long time horizon, was a hardware technology-capability project. Involving nine large Japanese computer firms in a variety of subprojects, it attempted (inter alia) to push forward integrated circuit technology in breakthrough areas such as gallium arsenide instead of silicon. Though that and other technology-capability goals were clear, the exact design concept for a future supercomputer was left unresolved. Over the same period, the Fifth Generation Computer Project had more of a computer system development flavor. Its goal was an artificial-intelligence-based thinking machine.[36]

These collaborative research efforts have led to much discussion of "Japan, Inc." It is worth stressing the breadth of Japanese mainframe computer companies' activities in this period. Although these long-term collaborative development projects were part of their activities, they were by far not the most important part. Matching product capabilities with IBM, with Amdahl, and with one another meant that there was plenty of ordinary technological competition. Once again, the appropriate view of "Japan, Inc." includes both some coordination by the government and considerable independence and competition among firms.[37]

The Japanese "leapfrogging" attempts and Japanese firms' technology development efforts again had mixed success. Some of the longer-term technology initiatives, such as gallium arsenide chips and artificial intelligence software, turned out to be far less fruitful directions than anticipated. Yet the overall effort led to the development of more fully realized three-pronged investments – of a Japanese form – by the late 1980s.

[35] The 1982 secret-stealing incident, in which Hitachi was caught attempting to buy IBM trade secrets from a consultant, was often cited as proof of the importance of these efforts.

[36] The SIGMA project, to build Japanese Unix computers and workstations, had a shorter payback span, had equal IBM independence, but still depended on international standards.

[37] Some observers doubt the efficacy of the central coordination. See Callon (1994) for the view that the consortia largely pursued the firms' separate goals, rather than uniting them in a government-led way.

Many observers saw this development as a very real threat to IBM's dominance. Others saw less of a threat.[38]

The Japanese initiatives never had a real market test and so offer little hard evidence resolving the debate about the effectiveness of public/private consortia at this more ambitious level. At the end of the 1980s, the Japanese efforts were coming to fruition. At the same time, the first industry dynamics was coming to an end. The era of IBM dominance of large-systems computing did end, but it was not the Japanese threat that ended it. Instead, it was competition from networked small computers that attacked the large mainframes. To see the origins of that threat, we now move backward in time and examine the second entrepreneurial industry dynamics.

IV. Industry Dynamics 2: Entrepreneurship and Entry in Minicomputers[39]

The second industry dynamics, that of the founding and evolution of new firms, new markets, and new technological capabilities, went forward in parallel with the first. It saw, however, radically different coevolutionary processes. We now return to the early 1960s to follow this very distinct coevolution.

A. Minicomputers: The Sources of American Competitive Advantage Change

The introduction of the first real time interactive general-purpose minicomputer, the PDP8 by DEC in 1965, opened up new types of demand for computers in research laboratories and manufacturing plants (the monitoring and control of industrial processes). In addition, computers were used for technical problem solving activities and focused on specific applications.

In the early 1960s the availability of new types of semiconductor components – integrated circuits – greatly facilitated the introduction of

[38] See Ferguson and Morris (1993) and Anchordoguy (1989) as well as Sobel (1986) for the view that it was a real threat. Ferguson and Anchordoguy are particularly interested in the government policy issues. Since IBM's strengths were integrative, they argue, could not a whole country coordinate the three-pronged investments if it had the right policies? But see Callon (1994) for the view that MITI did not coordinate. Also, see Fransman (1995) for the view that MITI did coordinate but suffered from "vision failure." Although MITI has been quite effective in catching-up programs in mainframes through cooperative programs, it has been unsuccessful in the perception of developments alternative to mainframes (such as computer networks) or in the creation of radically new technologies.

[39] As we mentioned earlier, we will not discuss the dynamics of workstations.

minicomputers. Integrated circuits were smaller and more integrated than transistors (the basic semiconductor component used in mainframes during the 1950s). They were entire circuits on a silicon chip. They formed the basic semiconductor components used in minicomputers.

The appropriate seller marketing model for small business and scientific minicomputers was built on the fact that the relevant buyers were technically fluent.[40] The features of computers that mattered to buyers in these segments could be described quickly in objective, technical language. Institutions for direct communication among buyers about products sprang up. These had a strong engineering fraternity flavor but played some of the same roles as the sales force in the commercial segments. No extensive software support was provided by minicomputer producers, so new intermediate actors emerged between the minicomputer producers and the customers: system houses and value added retailers.

B. High Entry Rates and Rapid Firm Growth in the American Industry

Minicomputers had a major effect on the structure of the American industry. A large number of new specialized minicomputer firms entered the field. DEC, the largest (with about one-third of minicomputer sales over many years), was an entrepreneurial start-up with roots at MIT's Lincoln Laboratory. Other new firms included CCC, Microdata, General Automation, and Computer Automation. Because of the importance of minicomputers in scientific instrumentation, many instrument firms, including Hewlett-Packard, Varian, Perkin-Elmer, and Gould, entered the minicomputer market.[41]

Existing computer firms entered minicomputers late and with mixed success: IBM had a "small mainframe" marketing strategy, not much blessed in the marketplace, whereas Honeywell (another instruments and controls company) did well. The last source of new minicomputer companies were spin-offs. Data General was formed by entrepreneurs leaving DEC; Prime Computer, by executives from Honeywell; Tandem (which might be classified as either a minicomputer or mainframe firm), by an HP marketing executive. Thus, in the early period (through roughly 1975) of the minicomputer market the sources of entrants were different than those in the mainframe market.

[40] This contrasts with the mainframe marketing model, with its extensive field sales forces, customer support and service, and relationships with senior financial or operations executives in customer companies.

[41] Although all of these were entrepreneurial companies, they had been founded to make instruments, not computers.

C. Limited Entry and Slow Firm Growth in Europe and Japan

In Europe, few new minicomputer firms entered the industry, and for several reasons. First, American producers had a first mover advantage and rapidly entered the European market. Second, similarly to American mainframe producers, established European mainframe producers did not move or moved too late and unsuccessfully into minicomputers. Third, limited spin-off from universities took place. Fourth, lack of venture capital impaired the financial support for new ventures. Fifth, the protectionist measures used by the European governments for mainframes (such as public procurement) could not be extended to a market formed by small and medium enterprises and research laboratories.

As previously mentioned, during this period in Germany several producers thrived in the market for midrange systems for specific applications. The case of Nixdorf is highly illustrative of this phenomenon. In 1965, Nixdorf introduced the Universal Computer 820, a small computer with a cash register based on semiconductors. Later, it developed several sector-specific software solutions that targeted small and medium-size firms, mainly for banks and retailing ([POS] and cash registers) and followed a strategy of direct distribution. For its 8870 family (1973), Nixdorf developed the software Comet, which proved to be a major success. During the 1970s, however, the first weaknesses emerged: there was no integration or modularity among the various product lines, internal technology development was limited, and product quality was low.

Japanese efforts in the minicomputer business have been largely unsuccessful. The government-sponsored SIGMA project of the 1980s, for example, which sought to develop a UNIX-based workstation platform for application software development, did not achieve market success.

V. Industry Dynamics 2: The Sources of American Competitive Advantage Persist in Microcomputers

The early 1970s saw the invention of a new technology at the component level, the microprocessor, which permitted the development of smaller and later more user-friendly computers to satisfy the needs of new types of demand: family, hobby, educational, and small business uses. These "microcomputers" or "personal computers" were far less powerful but also far cheaper than the machines discussed so far. This spread computing power through organizations (beyond centralized MIS), leading to the creation of many new applications.

A. High Entry Rates and Rapid Firm Growth in the American Industry

In the United States, the market developed first on the basis of hobbyist demand, with suppliers typically adopting the marketing model of minicomputer producers. In the late 1970s, there were two main de facto standards for personal computers, CP/M and the Apple II. Although the CP/M operating system was itself the proprietary product of Digital Research, it was available on dozens of different brands of computers, most running the Intel 8080 or the competitive nearly compatible Zilog Z80 microprocessor. In these circumstances, the market was quite open to entry. Most CP/M computer firms were entrepreneurial start-ups. Even an English expatriate, Adam Osborne, was able to found an American start-up firm. Osborne Computer's strategy of portability was for some time very successful as the firm had a leading CP/M role. The Apple II system had a proprietary architecture and operating system but was, like CP/M, an open one. Software developers could rely on the Apple or CP/M environment to provide a stable platform for applications or utilities development. A large number of independent software companies came into being, again overwhelmingly entrepreneurial in origin.

Some software products were exceedingly successful and affected the overall demand for microcomputers and the development of the marketplace. Of these, the most important example is VISICALC, a spreadsheet program. Developed by entrepreneurs when they were students, VISICALC provided a strong motivation for accounting or similar number-crunching workers to acquire microcomputers for direct use in work. Market forces transformed the hobbyist personal computer into the business personal computer.

Entrants resembled those in minicomputers. They consisted largely of established electronics (but not computer) firms and de novo entrants: They may also be divided into specialized computer firms (such as Apple, Commodore, Tandy, and Compaq) and clones.

B. The Reaction of IBM

Established mainframe and minicomputer producers had a demand perception lag compared to new personal computer producers. When IBM decided to move in, it did so through external linkages with competent firms: Microsoft for operating system software and Intel for microprocessors. The IBM PC was an advance over CP/M and the Apple II. More importantly, it was a product of long-established IBM rather than an entrepreneurial start-up. Other experienced electronics companies entered in the early 1980s as well. DEC and HP made PCs that were IBM-compatible to varying degrees; ultimately the power of the PC standard in the marketplace compelled them to be fully compatible. AT&T also entered with an IBM PC work-alike. These entry efforts by minicomputer and telephone firms were not linked to any direct marketing connection of the firms' existing product lines. Rather they were attempts to use general electronics design, manufacturing, and marketing capabilities in a growing new area. Mainframe sellers also entered the PC marketplace, notably Wang, Burroughs, and Honeywell. Their machines can best be understood from a marketing perspective: as a courtesy to existing large-computer customers, the firms offered the new small computers as well.

C. Competing Approaches in PCs and the Emergence of the PC Platform

There were other initiatives technically comparable to the IBM PC in the sense that they used 16-bit rather than the previously standard 8-bit microprocessors. Apple, by then an established company, introduced the Apple III. This system, which is much more PC-like than Macintosh-like, generated considerable early enthusiasm in the marketplace. Apple had great difficulties, however, building reliable Apple III systems. Another initiative also had elements of standards continuity: CPM/86. The "86" label here means that the operating system ran on an Intel 8086 microprocessor: it was a 16-bit system with some multiprocessing capabilities. Other entrepreneurial start-ups had, for some time, success in the 16-bit world: consider, for example, Cromemco (a start-up named after a college dormitory).

As extensively documented by Langlois (1990), the potential for many 16-bit initiatives was swept away by the IBM PC standard. This product was both architecturally open and affiliated with the IBM brand name. Only Apple's third effort at more advanced personal computing, the Macintosh (technically very different from Apple III and much cheaper than the little-demanded Lisa system it replaced), was successful in the marketplace. Macintosh enjoyed very substantial product differentiation advantages. Though it was designed as "the computer for the rest of us," that is, as a machine that would have a broad mass market of unsophisticated users, the Macintosh succeeded initially as a niche product for users (such as marketing departments running desktop publishing software) who valued its graphical capabilities.

D. Firms' Strategies in the PC Platform World

The shift from entrepreneurial company supply to an IBM branded supply reflected the changing nature of demand and was widely bemoaned. The relevant chapter of Freiberger (1984) calls this era "The Arrival of the Suits," that is, the replacement of technologists with businessmen as the suppliers of personal computers.

IBM's decision to open the PC architecture traded off future competition for present speed in reaching the market and the standard-setting benefits of openness. Future competition was going to come from other manufacturers of PCs themselves. For a period, however, neither other brand-name PCs from other electronics producers nor "clones" from start-ups were an effective source of competition for IBM.

The Branded Clone Strategy

New successful strategies emerged during the second half of the 1980s. The branded clone is one. After 1986 and the move of Compaq into branded competition, entrepreneurial start-ups began to compete with IBM on a more effective basis: firms with strong technical bases such as ALR and AST were, like Compaq, able to shift to having a brand presence. Entry with specific marketing or distribution advantages, such as that of Dell, was another route. Many overseas firms followed this same path. ACER, for example, first built technical competence in Taiwan as a producer of "clone" computers, often with other firms' brand names on them. Only later did ACER attempt to build its own export brand name. The extent and pace of this increase in competition in the PC segment were difficult to foresee at the outset, if only because the size and growth of the segment, which drew much of the entry, were significantly larger than anticipated.

Competition from Complementary Technologies

Perhaps a more important source of competition, and certainly unanticipated at the time IBM chose the open architecture, were makers of complementary PC components. In particular, the technological leadership determining the direction of technical advance of the PC came to be divided among three groups:

1 Makers of computers, of which IBM was the largest and most influential

2 Intel, maker of the microprocessors in the PCs[42]
3 Microsoft, maker of the operating system for PCs[43]

Divided technical leadership reduced IBM's ability to steer the direction of PC technical change in relation to broader strategic goals.[44]

Despite competition from the other technological leaders and from other PC computer manufacturers that limited IBM's market power as a PC firm, the PC platform was an effective competitor against other ways of supporting first "individual productivity" applications and later small business and small department multiperson applications. The market, not any individual firm, determined most of the rate and direction of technical change in the platform. The market had on its side great economies of scale, not only in the production of individual components, but also in the (external) economies arising from network externalities (Langlois, 1992). In all computer markets seen to date, success for a platform meant levering up suppliers' efforts through customers' complementary investments. In personal computers, this took a new form. Instead of tight bilateral marketing relationships between a platform vendor and the customers, external economies flew through the compatibility of independent software vendors' (ISVs) products with a platform and with the pool of knowledge of how to use the platform and its software. Literally millions of users collectively participated in these external economies, each having only a weak direct link to suppliers. The aggregate strength of the leverage for the platform was at least as large here as in the mainframe case.

E. European Industry: Limited Entry and Survival Only in Niches

In personal computers the success of European firms has been limited for reasons similar to the ones discussed for minicomputers. American microcomputer producers had a first mover advantage and rapidly entered the European market, whereas established European mainframe producers moved late and unsuccessfully into microcomputers. Moreover, outside the United Kingdom the lack of venture capital and the low spin-off from universities limited the rate of European entry.

[42] Competition from licensed clones of Intel chips, such as AMD, was largely irrelevant to the determination of the technical direction of the platform. Competition from almost-clones, such as the NEC V-series, was important in some local markets but never as influential as the Z80 had been earlier on.

[43] Again, competition from other forms that were licensed to make versions of the operating system, such as IBM, was largely irrelevant in terms of Microsoft's role in setting technical direction.

[44] As IBM's failure to establish MCA or OS/2 clearly shows.

The entry of American microcomputer producers in Europe eliminated all the German firms that had entered midrange systems during the 1960s and 1970s. Nixdorf is a case in point. The introduction of personal computers substituted midrange systems in several applications. In addition, Nixdorf's proprietary systems contrasted with open systems or IBM-compatible strategies of several PC producers. Moreover, some of the weaknesses of Nixdorf (already discussed) became more relevant during the 1980s: a late attempt to enter the PC market, a presence in too many vertical markets (cash registers, banks, manufacturing, EDP centers, and communications) with too limited internal technological competencies and high reliance on external technology, and a limited renewal of the most successful products.

The main European mainframe producers, such as Siemens and ICL, entered the PC market late and have not been highly successful. Siemens entered personal computer production in 1985; only in 1987 did ICL (after the unsuccessful development and production of CPM and CDOS small and medium systems during the first part of the 1980s) decide to move to MS-DOS by developing MS-DOS PCs in collaboration with ACER. Both Siemens and ICL undertook acquisition processes in order to strengthen their competencies in PCs and in related fields (software and communications). In 1989 Siemens bought Rolm from IBM, and in 1990 it acquired ailing Nixdorf. In 1991, ICL-Fujitsu acquired Nokia Data System Division.

As in the minicomputer case, few new entries into the microcomputer market were European start-ups. The United Kingdom represents an exception (Torrisi, 1995). Here the presence of Cambridge University, Cambridge Science Park, technical societies such as the Cambridge Computer Club, and high rates of spin-off from established British computer producers and foreign-owned firms produced many new firms (such as Amstrad, Acorn, Sinclair, Cambridge Computers, Apricot, and Psion) in the markets for personal computers, home computers, school computers, and palm-top computers.

Niche strategies have been followed by most new European entrants (Torrisi, 1995). Amstrad represents a case of successful diversification from consumer electronics into low-price products (Thomas, 1990). In 1984, Amstrad, a consumer electronics firm founded in 1968, entered the personal computer business by introducing manufacturing, marketing, and sales techniques that were popular in consumer electronics. Amstrad followed a very aggressive export strategy and targeted the European market by offering low-price, advanced design systems with standard components. Recently, Amstrad's strategy of low-price products with low R&D and lack of a dealer network faced difficulties with the entries of clone producers and of high-quality–low-cost producers such as Atari and Compaq. Psion is an example of innovative entry by a scientist. Unlike Amstrad, Psion was founded by a scientist from Imperial College in London. After developing software games for home computers, the firm introduced the first hand-held computer, the Organizer, in 1984. The firm grew internationally by specializing in hand-held portable computers and software for the home, professional, and retail markets. Psion was able to develop advanced competencies in design, engineering, logistics, and manufacturing. It used direct marketing, sales forces, and retail channels. Psion is now pursuing integration of hand-held computers and radio communications. Finally, Acorn represents a case of rapid identification of a growth area in a protected niche market. Acorn was established in 1982 as a consequence of the launch of BBC's new educational programs and the Department of Education's decision to start information technology (IT) diffusion programs in the national school system. After a period of success, the increasing competition in the home computer market led to a period of crisis for Acorn, which was then acquired by Olivetti. Later on, Acorn developed a new RISC microprocessor for personal computers.

Only one major office equipment producer successfully entered the standard PC market: Olivetti. In the Olivetti case, however, this entry into PCs represented a reentry into the computer industry. After its exit from mainframes in the mid-1960s, Olivetti's electronic competencies did not disappear completely with the sale of its Electronic Division to General Electric. In 1965, the small group of electronic researchers who remained in Olivetti developed a desktop electronic calculator (Programma 101) for business and technical applications. The P101 was innovative because it had a low price ($1,000), was programmable, and did not require specialized personnel. The P101 did not use integrated circuits, but instead automatically assembled ad hoc logic components; it had such a tremendous commercial success that Hewlett Packard paid royalties to Olivetti for the development of its HP 9100, very similar to the P101. The P101 remained an isolated case in the stream of Olivetti mechanical desktop calculators of the 1960s. Actually, in 1968, a new advanced mechanical calculator, Logos 27, was introduced by Olivetti, replacing the P101 (Torrisi, 1996). As a result of the collapse of the mechanical and electromechanical office machinery market of the 1970s, Olivetti reentered the computer industry in 1978. The advantage of not being a mainframe producer (and of having some internal electronics competencies) produced a successful entry into microcomputers. After having produced the first electronic typewriter (1978), Olivetti moved to automatic teller machines and photocopiers, and finally to personal computers. In 1983, it introduced the M24. In order to support and strengthen its entry into microcomputers during the 1980s, Olivetti followed a strategy of international alliances and opened up a wide range of cooperative agreements. Two major agreements with AT&T and DEC were later on terminated.

In this period, traditional European policies could not be effectively used in an attempt to maintain unsuccessful producers in the market, as they were in mainframes. National champions policies in fact proved quite ineffective as barriers to exit, because demand was controllable only to a very limited extent by public procurement and domestic supply could not easily be sheltered by protectionist measures.

F. Japanese Industry: Limited Entry in a Fragmented Domestic Market

The Japanese PC industry was characterized by Japanese firms' efforts focused on the local market in a time of worldwide standards. As a result, Japanese PC hardware exports were small and PC software exports near zero. In 1992, PC domestic shipments were roughly two million units, exports roughly one million. Many of the exports were based on manufacturing and design capabilities for complex electronic artifacts, such as the Toshiba notebooks and laptops.

In early 1995 the Japanese PC market had not yet adopted the IBM/Microsoft/Intel PC standard. A NEC almost-world-standard design had the largest market share. In the early 1990s, NEC held a very large share of the Japanese PC market (53 percent in 1992) (Dataquest in Fransman, 1995, p. 270). The reasons for this success are several: NEC developed its PC in a decentralized way, kept its core competencies in-house, used new marketing channels (such as Bit-Inns and Microcomputer Shops), developed new advanced PC software applications, and pushed compatibility across products such as NEC PC-8000 and NEC PC-9800. Being also a major telecommunication and semiconductor producer, in the process of PC development NEC was favored by the in-house lack of a dominant mainframe culture (see Fransman, 1995, for a detailed description of NEC's involvement in PCs). Based on almost-Intel microprocessors, and an almost–IBM PC architecture, these computers neither gained much connection to worldwide external economies nor obtained the production scale economies of the standard PC. A strong competitor, possibly because it was more graphical and thus more linguistically flexible, has been Apple Japan.[45]

[45] The Open Architecture Group, which includes Toshiba and Fujitsu, has been attempting to establish the worldwide PC standard in Japanese.

Another very interesting contender for the Japanese market standard during the 1980s was TRON. A collaborative effort, neither government- nor NTT-sponsored, TRON was intended to be an all-Japanese microcomputer system. From a new microprocessor through to a Japanese-character set (*kanji*) user interface, TRON would permit complete separation from the world market.

Language differences, and specific market conditions, mattered. For the evolution of the Japanese industry until the 32-bit era, PCs could only accommodate kanji in very clumsy ways. Also, a separate software market did not develop in Japan. The domination of the mainframe market by Fujitsu, Hitachi, and NEC led to the development of customized software, which then hampered the development of standard package software. Even microcomputers were marketed in Japan the way mainframes were in most other places: they came with bundled software, or specific application software written for the individual user site.

Whatever the origins, the effect was a fragmented, specifically Japanese domestic market (Cottrell, 1994). Software and hardware producers in Japan faced little competition from international computers. But with a domestic market substantially smaller than the world market, the Japanese industry was unable to participate in worldwide scale economies and substantial external economies associated with microcomputers.

VI. Computer Systems and Networks: The Sources of American Advantages Change Again

The 1990s saw three linked changes in computer industry structure and the workings of competition. The process of vertical disintegration, which had been historically confined to making each new market segment less integrated than the last, spread to all the segments. The locus of rent generation shifted downstream to software and applications developments. Computer hardware itself became more of a commodity. Finally, there was a change in the competition facing mainframes and commercial minicomputers. Smaller computers could be networked together in "client/server" or related configurations. These new networked architectures meant that the types of users previously served by large computers might now be served by the networks of smaller computers.

A. Open Platforms Connectivities and Complementarities

During the 1980s, computing platforms with open interfaces, such as the IBM/Intel/MS-DOS PC and Unix workstations, became important and took on their own industry dynamics. They allowed interchangeability, connectivity, and interoperability in hardware and system software. Local Area Network (LAN) standards for connecting PCs also began to emerge; though less than fully open, they were far more open than earlier vendor-specific networking interfaces. All this was based on the vast scale of the PC market. Parallel movements in Unix/workstation computers and in Internet networking standards took place in universities and scientific communities.

Open interface standards and specialized technology firms were mutually reinforcing. Standard bundles allowed new software firms to compete in the system software market or in the application software market (which could be packaged or custom) without producing hardware. Entrants would offer whole new systems by fully developing and producing hardware and software (hardware manufacturers), by integrating different parts of the system for specific applications (systems integrators), or by offering specialized software for specific applications.

In a context of standard bundles and application software, the key dimension for successful innovation became the ability to use complementarities by linking technology, users, and applications. It must be noted that application solutions, custom software, and software services required a knowledge base for innovation different from hardware production: an in-depth understanding of end-uses of information systems in terms of horizontal applications (such as spreadsheet or word processing), vertical applications (such as software for banks, transport, and so on), and specific user applications (custom software). Therefore, in order to be successful in applications, firms had to understand market needs, identify the relevant dimensions of specific market applications, target their products to those dimensions, and interact with users on a continuous basis.

Growth in the new client/server architectures changed the linkages between a successful computer product and technology sellers. Now, computer systems development would involve at least the choice of computers as clients and other computers as servers plus software and networking technology to integrate them. Integration services, not unlike traditional systems development services in mainframe use, would be needed as well. Unbundling of clients from servers meant that market forces could have a stronger effect. The existence of de facto market standards in the standalone small computer markets for microcomputers and workstations meant that most new system developments would take advantage of the considerable technical advances in Intel/IBM/Microsoft-based microcomputers or Apple computers (a smaller number of systems used Unix-based clients). Similarly, the unbundled client meant that de facto standard software for microcomputers could be part of large-systems development. The ease of use and familiarity of small computer systems were developed in the market for individual productivity applications and now were redeployed in the market for multiuser departmental or company-wide applications.

Unbundled from the client and the related software, the large computer that formerly defined the computer system became a "server." Servers were rated by technological functionality in performing a variety of "service" tasks: the "file server," "database server," and "application server." As a consequence, the traditional marketing strengths of large-system vendors like IBM were devalued. Close relationships with customers became of little use in selling a standard product.

Computer industry structure underwent, and is still undergoing at this writing, a dramatic shift. The shift has been large enough for some participants and observers to talk of an "old computer industry" as distinct from a "new computer industry." The two are different along a wide variety of dimensions: firm organization, industry structure, technical base, and key technologies for defining the direction of the industry. Roughly speaking, success has shifted from a model with vertically integrated firms closely linked to their customers selling integrated products as "solutions" and called "computer" companies because they made computer systems. Success has shifted to a model of specialized technology-selling firms, with customers (or their system integrators, consultants, or outsourcers) that put together their own systems from components, and "computer" companies that do not make any hardware. These changes have been accomplished with a huge turnover in the rankings of successful firms.

Consequently, a process of vertical disintegration has taken place in the industry. In addition to vertically integrated producers in hardware, system software, and application software, such as Apple and IBM, specialized firms emerged. Given the complexity of the knowledge base required for innovative activities and the heterogeneity of competencies, cooperation among firms and networking strategies became quite widespread by providing complementary and specialized expertise regarding computer hardware or basic operating software, features of specific applications, characteristics of market niches, or user requirements.

As yet, no universally accepted standards for networking computers into client/server architectures have emerged. Firms with client standards as their competitive advantage (Microsoft), others with strong server positions (Oracle, IBM), and yet others with networking competencies (Novell, IBM again) compete to influence the de facto standards setting process. Once again, we see entry of a wide variety of organizational forms with a wide variety of competencies. In the pursuit of the same rents we predict the shakeout with little fear of future contradiction.

B. The United States: Success from Complementarities, Knowledge Externalities, and Variety in Experimentation

Country advantages remained in the United States in this third dynamics, but for new reasons. As we have seen before, in mainframes one world leader emerged. American advantages coincided with IBM advantages. In mini- and microcomputers, on the contrary, entry conditions and an environment conducive to rapid growth of new firms were at the base of American advantages. For networked computing, the sources of American advantages shifted again. Networked computer systems were highly complex and rich in opportunities in all their various components and dimensions. No single firm could innovate in all parts and subsystems. Open platforms and standard bundles permitted compatibility and connectivity among various artifacts introduced by the specialized firms in the various layers, as well as system integration by some firms or even by users. The new specialized entrants were of various types: spin-offs from established computer firms funded by some venture capitalists (technological competence driven), science-based firms established by university scientists and funded by some venture capitalists, new firms with market or marketing competencies.

The presence of strong complementarities and local knowledge externalities gave major international advantages to the United States or, more precisely, to Silicon Valley, which had several firms at the frontier in each market layer. Intense formal and informal communication and high personnel mobility (together with the high entry and growth rates already present in the mini and micro period) allowed firms located in the United States (particularly in Silicon Valley) to be exposed early on to new experiments, knowledge, and technologies. These firms could rapidly take this new knowledge into account in their new artifacts. Relatedly, they could feed their new developments to the other producers in the same or in other layers and to system integrators. Therefore, positive feedback and knowledge increasing returns among producers within and across vertical layers were being created. This mutual positive feedback gave American firms major innovative advantages over competitors located in other areas.

Some American established computer producers (such as IBM) had to reorganize themselves into application oriented groups. Others had a less successful transition. Honeywell was acquired by Bull and pulled out of the general-purpose mainframe market. CDC experienced major difficulties. Burroughs and Univac merged to become Unisys. The combined company, however, soon exited the computer business, leaving behind the former marketing organization, which became a systems integration firm.

C. *Europe: Survival in Niches*

Europe did not have firms active at the frontier in several of the layers of the new computer industry as the United States did. As a consequence, local knowledge externalities and positive feedback did not take place. Therefore, entry of European firms has been mainly related to niches in system integration (Malerba, 1992) and custom software (Malerba and Torrisi, 1996). Cap Gemini Sogeti has been the most successful firm in this realm. In hardware and system software standard bundles, as well as in software package applications, new as well as established American firms continued to be market leaders. Among European producers, only SAP and Software AG have been successful.

In order to survive in the new industry, large established European computer firms tied themselves up with key microprocessor producers. Bull acquired Honeywell, teamed up with IBM by using its RISC microprocessors, and increased its commitment to Unix. Siemens followed a strategy of internal growth and acquisition (Nixdorf) and joined IBM's Power PC initiative. Finally, ICL, acquired by Fujitsu, increased its links with Sun (RISC architecture).

In addition, all the main European computer producers moved into vertical markets and applications: Siemens-Nixdorf in banking, public institutions, universities, hospitals, and infrastructure; ICL in distribution. After an unsuccessful attempt to team up with DEC (Alpha processors), Olivetti exited from the PC business in 1997 and focused on software and system integration in banking, office information systems, and distribution. In addition, it entered the mobile phones market forcefully.

The internal market program of the European Commission (EC), through the dismantling of trade barriers, the harmonization of technical norms, and the setting of European standards, has attempted to create a homogeneous market, therefore increasing the incentives for entry and growth of successful European producers in niches not already occupied by American producers. Also, European R&D cooperative policies such as Esprit and Eureka have proved somewhat successful in developing

European standards, fostering additional communication and interaction among domestic producers, and teaming up (private) resources for entry in new advanced and expensive technologies. As in the Japanese case, the evidence on the effects of these European cooperative policies on the successful development of new products (Malerba, 1992) is controversial.

D. Japan

Japanese computer firms found many of their earlier competencies greatly devalued by computer systems and networks. Large system development based on large Japanese-sourced computers and with one-off software development for individual sites, however well done, was vulnerable to competitive pressure from much more widely sold hardware and system software platforms and more flexible development environments. A Japan-only PC standard began to look much less attractive as worldwide PC standard bundles started to advance rapidly. Although some firms prospered in specific markets (Toshiba in laptop computers, Canon in printer engines, and so on), the traditional giants had great difficulties. Mitsubishi exited the mainframe business. Fujitsu sought to invest in multimedia, often through overseas subsidiaries, and became a Sun reseller. NEC saw declining shares even in the Japanese PC market and considered conforming itself to the worldwide standard.

VII. Conclusions

The analysis of the long-term evolution of the computer industry in the three major advanced areas (United States, Europe, and Japan) has highlighted several general points.

First, until the 1990s, competitive technical change was not a destroyer of competencies, but demand opening and competence widening. Second, each industry dynamics had a separate coevolutionary process and was characterized by a different model of the firm. Third, the United States, Europe, and Japan exhibited different forms of supply, which were due to competitive, institutional, and other country-specific features. Fourth, despite separate coevolutionary processes, shifting sources, and locations of comparative advantages, American world leadership persisted. Finally, public policy differed according to the country and the market segment. All these points will be discussed in more detail in the next pages.

A. Competitive Technical Change Was Not Competence Destroying, but Demand Opening and Competence Widening

A look at the role of technological change in the overall evolution of the computer industry shows that, until the recent competitive convergence of mainframes with networked computing, competitive technical change has only rarely destroyed the competencies of the main established leaders within a certain industry segment. In the early mainframe period, entry was mainly by established electronics and office equipment producers. The founding of new demand segments, such as mini and micro, did not destroy the existing capabilities of established mainframe producers in the mainframe market segment. Rather, it was *demand opening and competence widening*: it opened new demand segments with different types of competences and firm organizations, different customers, a different user–producer relationship, and the entry of new firms.

Later on, however, competitive convergence meant a convergence on the same type of demand and competence destroying technical change. In fact, the emergence of competitive networked computers using client/server architectures challenged the large-systems competencies of established firms (for a more detailed discussion, see Bresnahan and Greenstein, 1995).

Within each segment, technological competencies were routinely destroyed by the technological and market leader. IBM continually advanced mainframes and DEC minis in ways that devalued not only specific old machines but the technical basis of whole product families. In the PC market, Intel and Microsoft routinely made own strategic competence destroying investments, as did Apple. Even when radically new semiconductor components were invented, the industry leader in a market segment was able to adopt and introduce them into new computer families in that segment. Thus in mainframes IBM was effectively able to adopt integrated circuits in the 1960s and microprocessors in the 1970s.

B. Each Industry Dynamic Had a Separate Coevolutionary Process

In each of the three coevolutionary processes, a new technology and a new demand have brought entrants into the industry, thus affecting industry structure. Entrants have in turn introduced innovations, modifications, and changes to the original technology. By opening up a new demand (new types of users), the new technology has created new user–producer relationships and has affected firms' competencies, strategies, and organization.

However, in each specific market segment a distinct coevolutionary process took place. In *mainframes*, coevolution has been characterized by rapid technological change in favor of processing power and data flow speed. Large systems required user–producer relationships, the centralized organization of users' information systems, and extensive sales and services efforts by large vendors. Internal finance supported the activities of the large established firms. Market structure was concentrated and suppliers were vertically integrated. A dominant design (IBM/360) emerged in the growth phase of the segment and a market leader (IBM) dominated the industry early on, with a coordinating role over the whole platform and an ability to steer the direction of technical change. The role of universities was relevant as a seeding role only in the early period and declined later. U.S. government policy played a role in early support for technological exploration and as a major buyer of early computers. Later, as governments in other countries did, it opposed the market leader by antitrust policy or anti-IBM procurement.

In *minicomputers* and *microcomputers*, coevolution has been characterized by a type of technological change that developed dedicated applications in the case of minicomputers or systems with increased ease of use and a lower price/performance ratio in the case of microcomputers. The relationship with customers required much less post-sales effort, maintenance, and service, either because the user was already technically advanced (minicomputers) or because the system was easy to use (microcomputers). The structure of the market has been characterized by high entry early on and then by increasing concentration in platforms in both minicomputers and microcomputers. A major difference existed, however, between the mini and micro segments. Niche leaders emerged in specific dedicated applications for minicomputers, whereas the main microcomputer platforms have been general-purpose with competitive supply of commodity hardware. Concentration emerged at the key component level-operating system. Venture capital has played a major role in affecting firms' entry and growth. In this coevolutionary process, the form of government policies (so important in mainframes) did not play a major role, whereas more general policies favoring education and skill development helped microcomputer diffusion.

Finally, in *computer networks*, a stable market structure has not yet emerged at this writing. Connectivity and compatibility have led to modular, open, and multifirm client/server platforms. Technical change is following a variety of directions with an upsurge in the number of potential technologies associated with the relevant platforms. In this situation, interdependencies and network externalities have increased. The structure of the industry has thus been characterized by highly heterogeneous firms in terms of size and specialization, active in various platform components and connected by standard interfaces to firms in other segments. Firms have a wide variety of mechanisms for commercializing their products. There is widespread speculation that one or a few of the firms controlling key interfaces for connecting modular products will come to dominate networked computing, but no single firm has so far been able to govern change and coordinate platform standards. Public policy again plays a role limited to infrastructure and skills.[46]

C. The Appropriate Model of the Firm Was Different in Each Coevolution

In each coevolutionary process, a different appropriate model of the firm emerged, with its own competencies, organization, and strategy (Bresnahan and Greenstein, 1995). *Mainframes* were produced and integrated by the same firm and used in a centralized organization by the MIS department. In this context, a Chandlerian integrated firm became quite successful. This firm was active in the development, manufacturing, marketing, and distribution of large systems and produced some of the components in-house. Market success was related to major and continuous R&D efforts and investments in management, production, and marketing. User–producer relationships were relevant in establishing competitive advantages, because computer firms supplied systems that solved users' problems, had close interactions with the MIS department of large users, and offered assistance and post-sales services. Large integrated firms controlled and coordinated system development, even in the presence of modularity, because they could control key interfaces. Compatibility across products and over subsequent product families allowed the persistence of existing standards and lock-in of the existing customer base. In *minicomputers*, firms spent less on sales, marketing, and support. Systems were characterized by simple programmable processors and were used for specific tasks; end-users (engineers, scientists, technicians) were technically sophisticated, in most cases developing their own applications. In addition, there was no need to develop compatibility across systems for different uses (much less between minicomputers and mainframes). In *microcomputers*, firms specialized in components that were part of the platform competed with other specialized firms and did not control buyers' acceptance of the platform nor

[46] Antitrust actions against the potential dominant firm Microsoft have been toothless.

of the standard. In fact, microcomputer platforms involved several disintegrated firms' developing parts of the platform connected by interface standards. Even the IBM PC platform became the IBM/Microsoft/Intel platform, in which innovation was decentralized. Control over the direction of technical progress of the platform by a single firm became very difficult (even by IBM, the sponsoring firm [Bresnahan and Greenstein, 1995]). Distribution took place through retail outlets and other decentralized distribution channels.

With divided technical leadership, the potential competition among component suppliers reinforces existing standards. Flexibility in design is limited because unilateral changes by specific component vendors have to be compatible with the standard. Changing component standards is quite difficult because it requires the coordination of several firms. These features of microcomputers continued in the *computer networks* period, in which modularity and connectedness have increased "local" developments and local feedbacks. This favored the vertically disintegrated firm active in components and parts of the platform and contributed to the slow emergence of a dominant platform for client/server computing in the present.

As a consequence, the decline of the centralized vertically integrated large firm in the 1990s is not due to a decline in competencies. Rather, it is due to changing market conditions, from a single-firm platform to a multifirm platform, with no single firm able to coordinate efforts and compatibility within the platform (Bresnahan and Greenstein, 1995).

Within the evolution of each market segment, there has been a partial convergence to a single firm organizational model, punctuated by the introduction of competing organizational models, which slowed convergence. For example, in mainframes after the rise of IBM to world leadership, Amdahl, Hitachi, and Fujitsu developed a successful imitation strategy. In PCs, after Apple and IBM became industry leaders, there were both "clones" and entrepreneurial branded PC firms, such as Compaq. Please note also that these new strategies were successful because they matched firms' capabilities with demand, technological, and competitive conditions. In some cases, similar strategies were introduced by other firms but came "too early." In mainframes, RCA earlier attempted the same strategy as Amdahl but failed. HP and AT&T anticipated Compaq but did not have great success.

D. Countries Exhibited Different Forms of Supply

During each industry dynamics in each major geographical area, the form of supply was greatly affected by competitive, institutional, and other country-specific features. Unlike in the United States, the evolution of the mainframe computer industry in *Europe* has been highly influenced by public policy protecting national champions, therefore limiting the exit of unsuccessful producers and perpetuating a concentrated market structure characterized by a national champion and by IBM. In Europe, mini- and microcomputer industrial evolution has been characterized by limited entry of new producers and lack of venture capital, with American entrants dominating the European market and a few established mainframe producers competing unsuccessfully with them. Finally, in the convergence of mainframes and client/servers, the lack of advanced competitiveness (together with limited entry) in most of computer components impeded the workings of local network externalities and interdependencies, thus generating a market structure again dominated by American firms. In *Japan*, the evolution of the computer industry has always been characterized by a market structure in which few large vertically integrated Japanese computer firms have entered and dominated each of the new segments, and by a public policy that has supported some competition among Japanese producers together with cooperative research efforts at the technological frontier.

E. American World Leadership Persisted Despite Shifting Sources and Locations of Competitive Advantages

The striking feature of the computer industry is that despite technological discontinuities and three different industrial dynamics, countries' international advantages and disadvantages persisted over a long period. Over four decades, the United States has always been at the technological frontier and the world commercial leader. However, the United States has shifted its competitive advantages over time, whereas other countries have not been able to match these advantages. What is at the base of this persistent technological and competitive leadership?

Some factors favoring American competitiveness *persisted over time*. First, the large size and rapid growth of the American market have been unmatched elsewhere. Rapid growth is related to rapid diffusion of new types of computers in the appropriate population of adopters. It is also related to education in computer technologies and a highly skilled labor force in information technology. Second, venture capital facilitated the entry of new innovative firms and the funding of a variety of new initiatives in the United States, in minis and micros as well as in workstations and computer networks. Finally, U.S. universities have always been a source of entrepreneurship and have been highly receptive to the launching of new scientific fields and academic curricula.

Other sources of American competitive advantages have been *changing over time*. In *mainframes*, the major sources of American advantages were linked *to a single firm's advantages*. IBM presented a unique commitment to R&D policies and to the Chandlerian three-pronged investments in management, production, and marketing. No other firm in the world has been able to match IBM's capabilities and investments. In *mini- and microcomputers*, U.S. advantages were related to the favorable entry and growth conditions for new firms in new market segments and the development of open multifirm platforms that created local knowledge externalities. In *computer networks*, U.S. advantages were related to the presence of local knowledge externalities and strong complementarities between various components of the open multifirm standard platform.

Some of these advantages were *transmitted from segment to segment*. For example, the success of venture capital in supporting minicomputers (as well as microelectronics ventures) led to the availability of abundant venture capital in microcomputers and computer networks. Moreover, some of the entrepreneurs spurring entry in microcomputers and later in computer networks came from established firms active in minicomputers (and microcomputers later).

The geographic location of the competencies supporting American success has several times shifted within that large country. In mainframes, American advantages were related to the areas of IBM location of R&D and production, centered in New York but widely dispersed. For minicomputers, the sources of competitive advantages were mainly centered in the eastern part of the United States, with important exceptions like, western entrant Hewlett Packard. In microcomputing and even more so in computer networks, we have seen a regional shift from areas in the eastern United States (such as Route 128) to the central and western regions (such as Silicon Valley). This implies the need to consider carefully the unit of analysis of competitive advantages: the division/department, the firm, the region, or the country (see Saxenian, 1994, for more detail).

F. Universities Played Specific Roles During the History of the Industry

Universities played two roles in the computer industry. First, very early in its development, they were generators of scientific knowledge and prototypes in several advanced countries. At the beginning of the industry, universities were the locus of the first big university-led projects and relevant sources of scientific as well as technological knowledge. Second, in the United States they played a role as sources of scientific knowledge and entrepreneurship in minicomputers and microcomputers. The role of MIT in innovation and entrepreneurship in minicomputers and of Stanford and the University of Texas in microcomputers and workstations has been relevant. Only Cambridge in the United Kingdom has played a similar (albeit more reduced) role in Europe.

G. Public Policy Differed According to the Country and the Market Segment

In *mainframes*, public policy has been of a *top-down, mission-oriented type*. It has been quite different in the United States, Europe, and Japan. Early American military policies (and to a lesser extent those of the United Kingdom) supported early exploration and opening windows to different technological alternatives. In addition, nonmilitary procurement fostered competition through buying from multiple sources. As we have documented earlier, the American military and government pursued goals driven by military–government needs, but also helped the technological and commercial development of the industry. As we have shown in this chapter, however, these policies were not at the base of the success of IBM. In *Europe*, there has been major involvement of various governments in the support of national champions in an attempt to create strong competitors to IBM. These policies (research subsidies and public procurement) were not successful, because they did not foster competition in the domestic market and were protective of a single (laggard) firm. Moreover at the time of their launch, IBM was already in a dominant position in the various European countries and the national champions had already accumulated technological and commercial lags. De facto these policies created a barrier to exit for unsuccessful producers. In *Japan*, on the other hand, public policy has been successful in the catching-up process with IBM, because (contrary to the European experience) it nurtured multiple competitors, coordinated imitation of IBM through coerced licensing, and sponsored collaborative research. As we have seen, the failure of Japanese policy has been related to a market shift, not to policy as such.

Please note that *antitrust policy* played two different roles. First, it played an anti-IBM role both in the United States and in Europe. In the United States, IBM had to unbundle mainframe hardware from software and was forced to handle Amdahl and the PCMs more gently. In Europe, antitrust policies have been very attentive to IBM as well. Second, antitrust policy had a competition increasing role only in the United States. In fact, in Europe competition policy was highly tolerant of the domestic national champions.

On the contrary, in *microcomputers and computer networks*, public policy has been focused mainly on *infrastructure, education, and standards*. Direct or indirect support for the creation of favorable conditions, such as an advanced infrastructure or the creation of skills, has proved quite successful in enlarging the size and fostering the growth of the market, increasing communication and interaction, and assisting entrepreneurship (Malerba, 1992).

Two final comments on policy relate to the dynamic setting in which these policies are launched and take place. First, the discussion of the computer industry clearly shows us that public policy has to be "adapted" and tuned to the specific stage and market segment that have been selected for intervention. For example, apart from their relative success or failure in various countries, government policies for mainframes could not be used for minis, microcomputers, or computer networks. Second, imitation policies aim at a moving target. Think of catching-up policies; in situations of rapid technical change, such policies should not focus only on the established world leader and the winning technology. The policy target itself may be displaced by a new world leader or by a shift in the relevant technology or market. This is the case of the successful catching up by Japan in mainframes during the 1980s, which, however, was confronted by a major shift in technology and market at the moment of the catching up. In this sense, public policies should be flexible and sensitive and keep open windows on a wide range of technologies and market developments.

Bibliography

Anchordoguy, Marie (1989), *Computers Inc.: Japan's Challenge to IBM*, Cambridge, Mass., Harvard University Press.

Bresnahan, Timothy and Shane Greenstein (1999), "Technological Competition and the Structure of the Computer Industry," *Journal of Industrial Economics*, v47, n1, pp 1–40.

Bresnahan, Timothy and Shane Greenstein (1995), The Competitive Crash in Large-Scale Commercial Computing," in Ralph Landau, Nathan Rosenberg and Timothy Taylor, eds. *Growth & Development: The Economics of the 21st Century*, Stanford, Calif., Stanford University Press.

Brock, Gerald W. (1975), *The U.S. Computer Industry: A Study in Market Power*, Cambridge, Mass., Ballinger Publishing Co.

Callon, Scott (1994), *Divided Sun: MITI and the Breakdown of Japanese High-Tech Industry Policy*, Stanford, Calif., Stanford University Press.

Campbell-Kelly, Martin (1989), *ICL: A Business and Technical History*, New York, Oxford University Press.

Chandler, Alfred (1977), *The Visible Hand: The Managerial Revolution in American Business*, Cambridge, Mass., Belknap Press.

Cortada, James (1993), *Before the Computer: IBM NCR, Burroughs, and Remington Rand and the Industry They Created, 1965–1956*, Princeton, N.J, Princeton University Press.

Cottrell, Tom (1994), "Fragmented Standards and the Development of Japan's Microcomputer Software Industry," *Research Policy*, v23, n2, pp 143–174.

Davidow, William H. (1986), *Marketing High Technology: An Insider's View*, New York, Free Press; London, Collier Macmillian.

Ferguson, Charles (1990), "Computers and the Coming of the U.S. Keiretsu," *Harvard Business Review*, v68, n4, pp 55–70.

Ferguson, Charles and Charles Morris (1993), *Computer Wars: How the West Can Win in a Post-IBM World*, New York, Times Books, Random House.

Fisher, Franklin, James McKie, and Richard Mancke (1983), *IBM and the U.S. Data Processing Industry: An Economic History*, New York, Praeger.

Flamm, Kenneth (1987), *Targeting the Computer: Government Support and International Competition*, Washington D.C., The Brookings Institution.

Flamm, Kenneth (1988), *Creating the Computer: Government, Industry and High Technology*, Washington D.C., The Brookings Institution.

Fransman, Martin (1990), *The Market and Beyond: Cooperation and Competition in Information Technology Development in the Japanese System*, Cambridge, England, and New York, Cambridge University Press.

Fransman, Martin (1995), *Japan's Computer and Communication Industry*, Oxford, Oxford University Press.

Freiberger, Paul (1984), *Fire in the Valley: The Making of the Personal Computer*, Berkeley, Calif., Osborne/McGraw-Hill.

Freeman, Christopher (1965), "Research and Development in Electronic Capital Goods," *National Institute, Economic Review,* n34, pp 40–97.

Gordon, Robert J. (1989), "The Postwar Evolution of Computer Prices," in Dale W. Jorgenson and Ralph Landau, eds., *Technology and Capital Formation*, Cambridge, Mass., MIT Press.

Greenstein, Shane M. (1995), Sole-Sourcing versus Competitive Bidding: U.S. Government Agencies' (Procedural) Choices for Mainframe Computer Procurement," *Journal of Industrial Economics*.

Hendry, John (1990), *Innovating for Failure: Government Policy and the Early British Computer Industry*, Cambridge, Mass., MIT Press.

Jublin, J. and J.-M. Quatrepoint (1976) *French Ordinateurs: de l'affaire Bull à l'assassinat du plan Calcul*, Paris, Alain Moreau.

Katz, Barbara and Almarin Phillips (1982), "The Computer Industry," in Richard R. Nelson, ed., *Government and Technical Progress: A Cross-Industry Analysis*, Elmsford, N.Y., Pergamon Press.

Kelly, T. (1987), *The British Computer Industry. Crisis and Development*, London, Croom Helm.

Langlois, Richard (1990), "Creating External Capabilities: Innovation and Vertical Disintegration in the Microcomputer Industry," *Business and Economic History*, v19, pp 93–102.

Langlois, Richard (1992), "External Economics and Economic Progress; the case of the Microcomputer Industry," *Business History Review,* v66, n1, pp 1–50, Spring.

Langlois, Richard (1995), "Cognition and Capabilities: Opportunities Seized and Missed in the History of the Computer Industry" in R. Garud et al., eds., *Technological Entrepreneurship: Oversights and Foresights*, New York, Cambridge University Press.

Malerba, Franco (1985), *The Semiconductor Business*, Madison, University of Wisconsin Press.

Malerba, Franco (1992), "The Organization of the Innovative Process," in N. Rosenberg, R. Landau, and D. Mowery, eds., *Technology and the Wealth of Nations*, Stanford, Calif., Stanford University Press.

Malerba, Franco and Salvatore Torrisi (1995), "The Dynamics of Market Structure and Innovation in the Western European Software Industry," in D. Mowery, ed., *The International Computer Software Industry: a Comparative Study of Industry Evolution and Structure*, Oxford, Oxford University Press.

Nelson, Richard (1992), *U.S. Technological Leadership: Where Did It Come From and Where Did It Go?* Ann Arbor, University of Michigan Press.

Nelson, Richard (1993), *National Innovation Systems: A Comparative Analysis*, New York, Oxford University Press.

Norberg, Arthur (1993), "New Engineering Companies and the Evolution of the United States Computer Industry," *Business and Economic History*, v22, n1, pp 181–193.

Organization for Economic Cooperation and Development (1966), "Gap in Technology–Electronic Computers," Paris.

Pugh, Emerson (1995), *Building IBM: Shaping an Industry and Its Technology*, Cambridge, Mass., MIT Press.

Rosenberg, Nathan (1996), "Uncertainty and Technological Change," in Jeffrey Fuhrer, C. Little, and Jane Sneddon, eds., *Technology and Growth: Conference Proceedings*, Boston, Federal Reserve Bank.

Saxenian, AnnaLee (1994), *Regional Advantage: Culture and Competition in Silicon Valley and Route 128*, Cambridge, Mass., Harvard University Press.

Sobel, Robert (1986), *IBM vs Japan: The Struggle for the Future*, New York, Stein & Day.

Thomas, D. (1990), *Alan Sugar: The Amstrad Story*, London, Century.

Torrisi, Salvatore (1995), *The UK Computer Industry*, Milan, Bocconi University, mimeo.

Torrisi, Salvatore (1996), "Discontinuità e credibilità delle strategie di ingresso nell'Informatica" in C. Bussolati, F. Malerba, and S. Torrisi ed., *L'evoluzione delle industrie ad alta tecnologia in Italia*, Bologna, Il Mulino.

Usselman, Steven W. (1996), "IBM and Its Imitators: Organizational Capabilities and the Emergence of the International Computer Industry," in David E.H. Edgerton, ed., *Industrial Research and Innovation in Business*, Cheltenham, U.K., Elgar.

CHAPTER 4

The Computer Software Industry

DAVID C. MOWERY

I. Introduction

Computer software is the stored, machine-readable code that instructs a computer to carry out specific tasks. There are three broad classes of software: (1) operating systems, which control the internal operations of a computer, including network controllers and compilers (also known as "system-level" software); (2) applications tools, which support the development of applications in such areas as computer-aided software engineering and databases; and (3) applications solutions, which enable a computer to perform specific tasks needed by the end-user (as opposed to tasks that manage the computer's internal operations), such as accounting and word processing.[1] All three of these types of software can be provided in either "standard" or "custom" form.

This chapter examines the development of the software industries of the United States, Japan, and Western Europe. I focus on "traded software," i.e., software produced for sale (often by specialized, independent vendors), in contrast to software produced by computer users, or "embedded" software that is incorporated in other products, such as measurement instruments or automobile fuel control systems. Although U.S. firms have dominated the traded software industry from its beginnings, there has been considerable turnover among the leading U.S. software firms – in other words, this industry historically has been characterized by competitive strength at the level of the nation, rather than the firm (in the language of the Introduction, "comparative" advantage appears to be more enduring than "competitive" advantage).

Research for this chapter was supported by the Alfred P. Sloan Foundation and the U.S. Air Force Office of Scientific Research. Earlier drafts benefited from comments from Richard Nelson, Tim Bresnahan, and Anita McGahan.

[1] "Tools" are "programs used to generate applications to retrieve, organize, manage, and manipulate data" (IDC, 1993, p. 65); they include database programs, programmer tools, and computer-aided software engineering products in this category. "Applications" include "programs designed to solve specific problems inherent across all industries or in a particular industry or business function," e.g., standard office tools, such as word processing and spreadsheet software, as well as applications specific to a given industry, such as banking or finance. The last category, "system-level software," includes operating systems and software controlling network operations.

The very existence of the software industry, and the emergence of independent vendors of software that are not divisions of computer manufacturing firms, also reflect tendencies toward increased vertical specialization that have characterized the development of the broader electronics industry complex (semiconductors, computers, and hardware) in the United States and other industrial economies.

II. The Structure of the International Software Market: An Overview

Although software has been produced for computers since the early 1950s, users and computer manufacturers dominated its manufacture through the late 1960s. Both groups retain important roles in software production, but the period since 1978 has witnessed the rapid growth of firms specializing in the production of traded software. Estimates of industry output suggest that software produced for sale in Japan, Western Europe, and the United States amounted to $90 billion in 1994 (U.S. International Trade Commission, 1995). U.S. firms dominate the global software market, especially desktop computer software, the most rapidly growing market segment.

This chapter focuses on traded software, but a great deal of software is developed by computer users for internal use, rather than for commercial sale.[2] Much of the custom operating system and applications software for large mainframe computers, for example, is provided by computer service bureaus as part of contracts that cover both computer services (e.g., operating a complex mainframe or network installation) and software. Determining the boundaries between "computer services" and "computer software," even in the traded software sector, often is impossible, since customized software frequently is sold in conjunction with computer services. In addition, statistical surveys of the industry differ in their definitions of the activities that are included in "computer services."[3]

Data on the current domestic consumption of custom and packaged software, computer services, and related products and services within the United States, Western Europe, and Japan are scarce, and internationally

[2] Moreover, much of the software development activity carried out by users in the manufacturing sector is included in their reported R&D spending, and much of the software development activity of nonmanufacturing user firms may be omitted from public statistics on R&D spending. In addition, the software development activities of independent software firms may not be reported as R&D.

[3] For example, data from the OECD and IDC that are cited elsewhere in this chapter do not always agree on the types of services included under the heading "computer services" and therefore may yield different estimates of the size of the software industry.

Table 4.1. *Domestic Consumption of Software and Computer Services in the United States, Japan, and Western Europe (billions of dollars)*

	packaged software			custom software	processing services
	1985	1992	1994	1985	1985
U.S.	12.60	28.46	35.60	4.17	11.1
Japan	.27	5.96	7.50	2.74	3.77
Western Europe*	5.21	23.85	26.57	4.72	5.33

* "Western Europe" is defined to include the following 17 nations: France, Germany, Italy, United Kingdom, Austria, Belgium, Denmark, Finland, Netherlands, Norway, Spain, Sweden, Switzerland, Ireland, Portugal, Turkey, and Greece.
Source: Estimates of 1985 consumption are from OECD (1989); estimates of 1992 and 1994 consumption are from Internation Data Commission (1993, 1994).

comparable data on these markets are even more difficult to obtain. Since detailed time-series data also are not available on consumption patterns in these three markets, the data discussed in the following section present a "snapshot" of a dynamic industry, some elements of which may have changed since the publication of these data. The data in Table 4.1 are taken from studies by the Organization for Economic Cooperation and Development (OECD) (1985) and the International Data Corporation (IDC, 1993; 1994); they suggest that in 1985, standard software accounted for more than 50% of Western European traded software, more than 70% of the U.S. traded software market, and less than 10% of the Japanese market (see the next section for a more detailed discussion). In recent years, sales of standard software, especially operating systems and applications software, have grown more rapidly than sales of "custom" software in all three regions.

The data in Table 4.1 highlight one of the most striking contrasts among these three markets, the significance of packaged (standard) software in domestic consumption. As of 1985, packaged software accounted for more than 75% of the traded software in the U.S. domestic market, substantially higher than that of Western Europe (54%) and far larger than its 9.4% share of Japan's domestic software consumption. From slightly more than $16 billion in 1985 (in 1992 dollars), the U.S. market for packaged software grew at an average annual rate of slightly more than 10%, to $33.9 billion in 1994 and $46.2 billion in 1996; in late 1997, the U.S. Department of Commerce projected that domestic consumption would exceed $52 billion for that year (U.S. Department of Commerce,

1997, p. 28-4).[4] Although consumption of packaged software has grown rapidly in other industrial economies, foreign markets are smaller than that of the United States. By 1994, the Western European market for packaged software (according to the definitions employed in Table 4.1) was 75% as large as the U.S. market. The Japanese market for packaged software, while still less than one-quarter the size of the U.S. market, also grew rapidly during 1985–1994. Estimated consumption of packaged software in Western Europe in 1996 was $32 billion, and the Japanese packaged software market amounted to $11.4 billion in that year (U.S. Department of Commerce, 1998, p. 28-4).[5]

Tables 4.2 and 4.3 contain additional data on market share and consumption patterns in packaged software for 1992 and 1993 for the product categories defined earlier. Table 4.2 displays market shares of U.S. and non-U.S. firms in the three major regional markets for each of the three classes of packaged software in 1993, revealing the dominance of U.S. firms in the U.S. and foreign packaged software markets. As of that year, U.S. firms' market share in their home market was greater than 80% for all three types of packaged software and exceeded 60% in non-U.S. markets for tools and system-level software. Non-U.S. firms accounted for more than 58% of Western Europe's applications software consumption and more than 64% of the Japanese applications software market in 1993.

The large size of the U.S. packaged software market, as well as the fact that it was the first large industrial-economy market to experience rapid growth, have given the early U.S. entrants in this industry formidable "first-mover" advantages. Nevertheless, these advantages appear to be stronger for operating systems and tools than for applications software.

[4] Measuring the overall size of the U.S. computer software industry is difficult – its relative youth and limited public statistical agency budgets mean that longitudinal data are very scarce. In addition, the complex structure of the software industry complicates the measurement of industry output, even if one ignores problems of definition and quality adjustment. For example, many firms provide both custom software and computer services, making it difficult to separate the share of output accounted for by software alone. Nevertheless, the available data suggest that the packaged software segment of this industry now is growing more rapidly than other product areas. According to the 1997 *U.S. Statistical Abstract*, "computer programming services," which include many firms that produce "custom" software that is developed for specific customers and applications, grew from $22.7 billion in 1990 to $34.8 billion in 1995, a slower rate of growth than that of packaged software (U.S. Bureau of the Census, 1997).

[5] The December 1993 study of world packaged software markets by the International Data Corporation noted that "custom software, produced by consultants and system integrators, constitutes a greater percentage of the software market in all regions of the world except the United States" (IDC, 1993, p. 7). Since a larger share of domestically consumed custom software in Japan is supplied in "bundled" form, as part of hardware, by computer producers, most data on Japanese domestic consumption of software probably underestimate the size of this software market.

Table 4.2. *Market Shares of U.S. and non-U.S. Firms in Packaged Software, by Region and Product Category, 1993*

US Firms:	Tools	Applications	System-level
consuming region:			
US	83.5%	87.9%	94.3%
W. Europe	74.6	41.3	88.7
Japan	64.7	35.3	73.7
Non-U.S. Firms:	**Tools**	**Applications**	**System-level**
consuming region:			
US	16.5%	12.1%	5.7%
W. Europe	25.3	58.7	11.3
Japan	35.3	64.7	26.3

Source: International Data Corporation (1994).

The differences in U.S. firms' market share among the three classes of packaged software appear to reflect the importance of user–producer linkages in applications, which make much greater demands for "user-friendliness" and adaptation to local operating conditions (e.g., non-English languages and characters) than tools or operating systems. These linkages also account for the importance of domestic firms in supplying custom software to local firms in all three markets (see Malerba and Torrisi, 1996; Baba et al., 1996).

The data in Table 4.2 include traded software produced by independent software vendors (ISVs) and by manufacturers of computer systems, who remain important suppliers of both custom and packaged software in all three regional markets. Table 4.3 contains 1993 market share data for U.S. and non-U.S. ISVs and systems manufacturers in the

Table 4.3. *Share of Worldwide Packaged Software Revenues, by Vendor Category, 1993*

U.S. Independent Software Vendors		48.3%
By consuming region:		
U.S.	61.0%	
W. Europe	39.2	
Japan	30.1	
U.S. Systems Manufacturers		26.7
By consuming region:		
U.S.	27.9	
W. Europe	24.1	
Japan	24.0	
Non-U.S. Independent Software Vendors		20.2
By consuming region:		
U.S.	8.5	
W. Europe	31.2	
Japan	33.0	
Non-U.S. Systems Manufacturers		4.9
By consuming region:		
U.S.	2.6	
W. Europe	5.6	
Japan	12.9	

Source: International Data Corporation (1994).

packaged software markets of Japan, Western Europe, and the United States. United States–based ISVs account for more than 60% of the U.S. packaged software market; when the shares of U.S. and non-U.S. ISVs are combined, the ISV share of the U.S. software market rises to more than 69%. But these data indicate that in 1993 the share of ISVs in the U.S. market was slightly smaller than the market share of U.S. and non-U.S. ISVs in the Western European packaged software market, which amounted to more than 70%. U.S. and non-U.S. ISVs accounted for just over 63% of the far smaller Japanese packaged software market.

U.S. manufacturers of computer systems are the dominant non-ISV suppliers of packaged software, accounting for more than one-quarter of demand in the United States, Western Europe, and Japan. Computer systems manufacturers are most important as suppliers of operating systems software, much of which is installed in their mainframe computers and minicomputers. ISVs accounted for less than 40% of standard operating system revenues in all three markets in 1992. Their share of revenues for standard applications software, however, exceeded 85% in these three markets in 1992 (IDC, 1993).

In 1992, mainframes accounted for more than 31% of global packaged software revenues, minicomputers accounted for 19%, "personal computers" accounted for almost 33%, and Unix-based systems (largely desktop workstations and network servers) accounted for almost 17%. Mainframes accounted for the largest shares of operating system and tool software revenues (respectively, 47.5% and 30.9%) in 1992, and PCs accounted for the largest share of packaged applications software revenues (46.5%). Growth in desktop software sales has continued to outstrip growth in the sales of software in all other market segments since this time.

III. Four Eras in the Growth of the Global Software Industry

The growth of the global computer software industry has been marked by at least four distinct eras, the most recent of which is in its early stages. During the early years of the first era (1945–1965), covering the development and early commercialization of the computer, software as it is currently known did not exist. Even after the development of the concept of a stored program, software was largely custom-developed for individual pieces of equipment. During the 1950s, however, the commercialization and widespread adoption of "standard" computer architectures supported the emergence of software that could operate on more than one type of computer or in more than one computer installation. In the United States, the development of the IBM 650, followed by the even more dominant IBM 360, provided a large market for standard operating systems and application programs. The emergence of a large installed base of a single mainframe architecture occurred first and to the greatest extent in the United States. Nevertheless, most of the software for early mainframe computers was produced by their manufacturers and users.

The second era (1965–1978) witnessed the entry of independent software vendors into the industry. During the late 1960s, producers of mainframe computers began to "unbundle" their software product offerings from their hardware products, separating the pricing and distribution of hardware and software. This development provided opportunities for entry by independent producers of standard and custom operating systems, as well as independent suppliers of applications software for mainframes. Unbundling occurred first in the United States and has progressed further in the United States and Western Europe than in the Japanese software industry.

Although independent suppliers of software began to enter in significant numbers in the early 1970s, computer manufacturers and users remained important sources of both custom and standard software in Japan, Western Europe, and the United States during this period. Some service bureaus that had provided users with operating services and programming solutions began to unbundle their services from their software, providing yet another group of entrants into the independent development and sale of traded software. Sophisticated users of computer systems, especially users of mainframe computers, also developed expertise in the creation of solutions to their applications and operating system needs. A number of leading suppliers of traded software in Japan, Western Europe, and the United States were founded by computer specialists formerly employed by major mainframe users.

During the third era (1978–1993), the development and diffusion of the desktop computer produced explosive growth in the traded software industry. Once again, the United States was the "first mover" in this transformation, and the U.S. market quickly emerged as the largest single one for such packaged software. Rapid adoption of the desktop computer in the United States supported the early emergence of a few "dominant designs" in desktop computer architecture, creating the first mass market for packaged software. The independent vendors that entered the desktop software industry in the United States were largely new to the industry. Few of the major suppliers of desktop software came from the ranks of the leading independent producers of mainframe and minicomputer software, and mainframe and minicomputer ISVs are still minor factors in desktop software.

Rapid diffusion of low-cost desktop computer hardware, combined with the rapid emergence of a few "dominant designs" for this architecture, eroded vertical integration between hardware and software producers and opened up great opportunities for ISVs. Declines in the costs of computing technology have continually expanded the array of potential applications for computers; many of these applications rely on software solutions for their realization. A growing installed base of ever-cheaper computers has been an important source of dynamism and entry into the traded software industry, because the expansion of market niches in applications has outrun the ability of established computer manufacturers and major producers of packaged software to supply them.[6]

The desktop computer software industry has a cost structure that resembles that of the publishing and entertainment industries much more than that of custom software – the returns to a product that is a "hit" are enormous and production costs are extremely low. And as in these other industries, the growth of a mass market for software elevated the importance of formal intellectual property rights, especially copyright and patent protection. A significant contrast between software and the publishing and entertainment industries, however, is the importance of product standards and consumption externalities in the software market. Users in the mass software market often resist switching among operating systems or even well-established applications because of the high costs of learning new skills, as well as their concern over the availability of an abundant library of applications software that complements an operating system. These switching costs typically are higher for the less-skilled users who dominate mass markets for software and support the development of "bandwagons" and the creation through market forces of product standards. As the widespread adoption of desktop computers created a true mass market for software during the 1980s, these de facto product standards in hardware and software became much more important to the commercial fortunes of software producers than was true during the 1960s and 1970s.

The fourth era in the development of the software industry (1994 to the present) has been dominated by the growth of networking among desktop computers, both within enterprises through local area networks linked to a server and among millions of users through the Internet. Networking has opened opportunities for the emergence of new software market segments (for example, the operating system software that is currently installed in desktop computers may reside on the network or the server), the emergence of new "dominant designs,"[7] and potentially, the erosion of currently dominant software firms' positions. Some

[6] Bresnahan and Greenstein (1995) point out that a similar erosion of multiproduct economies of scope appears to have occurred among computer hardware manufacturers with the introduction of the microcomputer.

[7] In early November 1995, Microsoft, the dominant firm in operating systems software for desktop microcomputers, announced its acquisition of Netwise, a leading supplier of networking software. According to Rosane Googin, an analyst quoted in a wire-service report on the acquisition, Microsoft's acquisition of Netwise was based on the recognition that "'the desktop paradigm is breaking down and the network is indeed the computer. . . . The leaders of the stand-alone PC are bowing to the new paradigm,' Googin said. 'Microsoft is the king of the desktop and the desktop has to be connected'" (Reuters, 1995). Microsoft has continued to acquire firms and to develop technologies for network-

network applications that are growing rapidly, such as the Worldwide Web, use software (hypertext markup language [html]) that operates equally effectively on all platforms, rather than being "locked into" a single architecture. As in the previous eras of this industry's development, the growth of network users and applications has been more rapid in the United States than in other industrial economies, and U.S. firms have maintained dominant positions in these markets.

IV. The Emergence and Growth of the Computer Software Industries of the United States, Western Europe, and Japan

As this summary of the industry's development suggests, U.S. dominance in the global software industry has rested in part on the position of the U.S. market as a leader in the large-scale adoption of new computing technologies and applications throughout the brief history of the industry.[8] Much of the hardware whose adoption by U.S. users propelled the growth of demand for software has relied heavily on foreign sources for components, and the computer systems themselves frequently have been manufactured abroad. But because of its tendency to lead other large markets in the adoption of new computing technologies and applications, as well as the dominance of the English language within the global software industry, the United States has consistently served as a "lead market" in the growth of demand for new types of software. In both Western Europe and Japan, a complex combination of forces (some of which reflect industrial evolution, others of which result from government policies) has prevented the emergence of comparably large, homogeneous markets for hardware or software, and as a result the growth of independent software vendors in these regions has been slow.

A. The United States

The United States was one of several nations that made important advances in computer technology in the early postwar period, often with direct funding, procurement contracts, or other forms of encouragement

ing applications. The firm also has entered the development and distribution of content in ventures that seek to exploit the potential convergence of desktop computing and mass entertainment. The firm has entered into an alliance with the NBC television network to form the MSNBC cable channel, and in April 1997, it acquired WebTV, a U.S. firm that has developed technologies that enable television sets to connect to the Internet.

[8] Cottrell (1995) stresses the slow pace of Japanese adoption of desktop computers as an influential factor in the slow emergence of that nation's packaged software industry.

from the military services. The concept of computer software as a distinguishable component of a computer system was effectively born with the advent of the von Neumann architecture for stored-program computers.[9] But even after the von Neumann scheme became dominant in the 1950s, software remained closely bound to hardware.

The development of a U.S. software industry really began only when computers appeared in significant numbers. The most commercially successful machine of the decade, with sales of 1,800 units, was the low-priced IBM 650 (Fisher et al., 1983, p. 17).[10] Widespread adoption of the 650 provided strong incentives for the development of standard software for it. Along with the development by IBM and other major hardware producers of standard languages such as COBOL and FORTRAN, widespread adoption of a single platform contributed to the growth of "internal" software production by large users. But the primary suppliers of the software and services for mainframe computers well into the 1960s were the manufacturers of these machines. In the case of IBM, which leased many of its machines, the costs of software and services were "bundled" with the lease payments. By the late 1950s, however, a number of independent software firms had entered the custom software industry. These firms included the Computer Usage Company and Computer Sciences Corporation, both of which were founded by former IBM employees (Campbell-Kelly, 1995). Many more independent firms entered the mainframe software industry during the 1960s.

Steinmueller (1996) argues that several developments in the 1960s contributed to the development of independent software vendors in the United States during the 1960s. IBM's introduction of the 360 in 1965 provided a single mainframe architecture for users demanding different levels of computing power and created a "migration path" within this architecture for users whose needs for computing power increased (Flamm, 1987). The 360, with a standard operating system that spanned all machines in this product family, increased the size of the installed base of mainframe computers that could use packaged software designed to

[9] The Eckert–Mauchly ENIAC, the first operational electronic computer design, did not rely on software, but was hard-wired to solve a particular set of problems. In 1946, von Neumann began advising the Eckert–Mauchly team, which was working on the development of the EDVAC. This collaboration developed the concept of the stored-program computer: instead of being hard-wired, the EDVAC's instructions were to be stored in memory, facilitating their modification. As we would now say, the computer could be programmed by software rather than hardware. Von Neumann's abstract discussion of the concept (von Neumann, 1945, reprinted in Aspray and Burks, 1987) circulated widely and served as the logical basis for virtually all subsequent computers.

[10] Government procurement played an important role in the introduction of the 650: the projected sale of 50 machines to the federal government (a substantial portion of forecast sales of 250 machines) influenced IBM's decision to initiate the project.

operate specific applications, enhancing the attractiveness of entry by independent software developers. IBM "unbundled" its pricing and supply of software and services in 1968, a decision that was encouraged by the threat of antitrust prosecution,[11] and this action by the dominant manufacturer of hardware (a firm that remains among the leading software suppliers worldwide) provided still greater opportunities for the entry of independent software vendors. Finally, the introduction of the minicomputer in the mid-1960s by firms that typically did not provide bundled software and services opened up another market segment for independent software vendors.

The epochal innovation for the U.S. computer software industry, of course, was the microprocessor, which was subsequently incorporated into the microcomputer. The rapid adoption of the microcomputer within the United States after 1980 created opportunities for entry by independent software vendors. But these entry prospects were made still more attractive by the rapid emergence of "dominant designs" within the U.S. microcomputer market, the IBM PC and the Apple Macintosh architectures.

Both the entry of independent software vendors and the rise to dominance of the IBM PC architecture were linked to IBM's decision to obtain most of the components for its microcomputer from external vendors, including Intel (supplier of the microprocessor) and Microsoft (supplier of the PC operating system, MS-DOS), without forcing them to restrict sales of these components to other producers. The decision to purchase the operating system software from Microsoft was driven by two factors. Development of the IBM PC was undertaken by an autonomous business unit that had insufficient staff or time to undertake in-house development of a family of components or a unique operating system. Equally important, however, was IBM's concern that the PC operate the large number of applications and other programs developed for Microsoft's BASIC operating system. In fact, early IBM PCs contained both the MS-DOS and BASIC operating systems software.[12]

Although these demand conditions favored its growth, the U.S. software industry also rested on a research and personnel infrastructure created by federal investments. Perhaps the most important result

[11] As the U.S. International Trade Commission (1995, p. 2-2) pointed out in its recent study, U.S. government procurement of computer services from independent suppliers aided the growth of a sizable population of such firms by the late 1960s. These firms were among the first entrants into the provision of custom software for mainframe computers after IBM's unbundling of services and software.

[12] This discussion owes a considerable debt to Professor Thomas Cottrell of the University of Calgary; see Cottrell (1995; 1996).

of these investments was the development of a large university-based research complex that provided a steady stream of new ideas, some new products, and a large number of entrepreneurs and engineers eager to participate in this industry. Like postwar defense-related funding of R&D and procurement in semiconductors, federal policy toward the software industry was motivated mainly by national security concerns; nevertheless, federal financial support for a broad-based research infrastructure spawned a vigorous civilian industry.

In contrast to their frequent depiction as organizations that specialize in basic research, U.S. universities were responsible for important advances during the late 1940s and early 1950s in computer architectures and hardware. The federal government's early postwar efforts to develop computer technology relied heavily on university researchers, and the first large-scale computer system development project, the Semi-Automated Ground Environment (SAGE), was managed by MIT's Lincoln Laboratories for the U.S. Air Force during the 1950s. Technological advances and researchers from universities entered the domestic electronics industry, and industry dominated the development of computer hardware after the mid-1950s. Universities remained important, however, in many software advances from the mid-1950s onward. The contributions of U.S. universities to these developments relied on the growth of a new academic discipline, computer science. The creation of this academic field was aided by federal support during the 1950s and 1960s for research, facilities construction, and purchases of the scientific instrument that was indispensable to computer science research, the mainframe computer. The primary sources of this funding were the Defense Department's Advanced Research Projects Agency, a supporter of fundamental research with defense applications, and the National Science Foundation.

Throughout the postwar period, the federal government has accounted for a large share of total U.S. demand for software. Flamm (1987, pp. 122–123) estimated that the federal government was the largest single U.S. customer for traded software in 1982. More recent data on market trends are not available, but the federal government's share of the U.S. market for traded software almost certainly has declined during the past decade. There are few examples of major "standard" operating systems, programming languages, or applications with substantial civilian markets being developed initially for federal agencies.[13] But the development of custom software and services for

[13] In 1981, the Department of Defense announced the development of Ada, a standard software language that was to be mandatory in all DoD procurement programs. The Ada initiative sought to create a standardized software environment that could produce a "vir-

federal purchasers constituted for much of the 1960s and 1970s a rapidly growing industry in the Washington, D.C., region.

Although federal policy contributed to the development of a strong technological and R&D infrastructure for the computer software industry, U.S. government policy also affected the U.S. market's emergence as a "testbed" for new software technologies. The unbundling of software from hardware was hastened by the threat of federal antitrust action against IBM in the late 1960s. Moreover, as was noted earlier, many of the independent vendors who responded to the opportunities created by IBM's "unbundling" policy had been suppliers of computer services to federal government agencies. The more recent growth in network applications and Internet-based software and other products has benefited from another antitrust action – the restructuring and deregulation of the U.S. telecommunications industry that took place in 1984 as a result of the settlement of the federal antitrust suit against AT&T.

Trade policy also played an important role in laying the foundation for the U.S. software industry. The relatively liberal U.S. policy toward imports of computer hardware and components supported rapid declines in price–performance ratios in most areas of computer hardware, and thereby accelerated domestic adoption of the hardware platforms that provided the mass markets for software producers. Western European and Japanese governments' protection of their regional hardware industries has been associated with higher hardware costs and slower rates of domestic adoption, impeding the growth of their domestic software markets.

The future of the U.S. software industry also will be influenced by the federal government's antitrust oversight of such large software firms as Microsoft. Federal antitrust complaints produced modest changes in the firm's policies for licensing and distributing its operating system software in 1994 and blocked Microsoft's acquisition of Intuit, a leading producer of personal financial software in 1995 (Hill and Clark, 1995). Microsoft's distribution of a "browser" software product for the Worldwide Web in 1995 also triggered an antitrust complaint from Netscape, the dominant supplier of Web software. The Netscape complaint, as well as the other federal antitrust actions against Microsoft, seek to prevent the firm from

tuous cycle" similar to that associated with the growth of a "dominant design" in the civilian microcomputer market, where the diffusion of the IBM PC supported growth in the production of low-cost packaged software for a huge variety of applications. But in contrast to COBOL, Ada has been employed to only a limited extent in nondefense systems thus far, partly because it was developed to meet requirements that had few civilian counterparts.

exploiting its dominance of operating system software unfairly to gain a dominant position in other product lines. These concerns have been extended and given weight by the filing of a federal antitrust suit against Microsoft in 1998. The key issues through all of these episodes have not changed – is Microsoft using its dominant position in operating systems software to monopolize emerging, related technologies in areas such as browsers for the Internet, personal-finance applications software, and other products?

As I noted earlier, each of the four eras in this industry's development has been characterized by different dominant technologies, a very different structure of supply, and different dominant firms (especially in the United States). High barriers to entry in one era have not deterred entry and the eventual unseating of previously dominant firms in the next (see Bresnahan, 1998, for a much fuller discussion). Microsoft's current dominance and (in contrast to many software and computer firms that dominated their epochs) the firm's recognition of the opportunities and threats to its dominance posed by the Internet raise the possibility that this firm, unlike previously dominant firms, could make the transition to a new technological "trajectory" in a dominant position. In this case, Microsoft could maintain or expand its market power and reduce the software industry's innovative performance, with negative implications for consumer welfare. There is little doubt that the historical development of the U.S. software industry has benefited from a tough federal antitrust policy, which may have prevented IBM from cementing a dominant position as a supplier of both hardware and software in the late 1960s. The most recent rounds of federal actions against Microsoft are likely to restrain the firm's behavior in day-to-day operations. But the ability of antitrust enforcement to offset the effects of the market-based "bandwagons" in mass markets for desktop software that have underpinned Microsoft's market power is largely untested, as is the ability of Microsoft to maintain that market power in a new and different era of computing.

B. Western Europe

Several Western European nations, including Great Britain and Germany, pioneered in the development of computing technology in the 1940s. Nevertheless, the growth of the Western European software industry has followed a different path from that of the U.S. industry. As I noted earlier, Western European packaged software firms have modest regional market shares in applications and tools but are more competitive with U.S. firms in applications software. Both national governments and the Commission of the European Union have launched ambitious programs of support for the software industry that focus on commercial, rather than defense-related, applications, but these programs thus far appear to have had little effect on the regional software industry.

In Great Britain, computing technology originated in defense-related wartime research and postwar demands for air-defense, cryptology, and nuclear weapons applications. But in contrast to the U.S. situation, the British defense R&D infrastructure failed to support both civilian and defense-related advances in computing technology (Grindley, 1996). The smaller size of British defense-related procurement and R&D programs provided fewer opportunities for entry by new firms and less support for the training of engineers and technicians needed by the commercial software industry. A similar segregation of military from civilian applications may have been present within the postwar French computer industry, although this is less well documented. In general, military R&D and procurement spending had modest or negative effects on the growth of Western Europe's computer software industry.

A second important factor in the development of Western Europe's software industry was the fragmentation of regional markets for computing systems and software that resulted from linguistic differences and the "national champion" strategies of the leading European economies in their computer industries. Motivated by concerns over national security and prestige, these national champion policies granted favorable treatment for defense and nondefense procurement and R&D to a single domestic firm in each of these economies. The resulting balkanization of the Western European market for computer systems, services, and software prevented the emergence of a large installed base of standard-architecture mainframe computers similar to that in the United States. In addition, the noncompetitive environment in which national champions found themselves, as well as their gentle treatment by national governments (compare the U.S. government's threats of antitrust prosecution that influenced IBM's decision to change its pricing and sales practices in software and services), reduced incentives for systems vendors to unbundle their services and software products and stunted the early growth of independent software vendors.

In addition to fragmenting the Western European software market, the national champion strategies that sought to protect and promote national computer hardware producers largely failed in their immediate promotional objective (Bresnahan and Malerba, 1999). The weakness of the Western European hardware industry impeded the development of a strong regional packaged software industry, since U.S. software firms (primarily in operating systems) were able to exploit their proximity to domestic developers of new hardware architectures and to the early users of these new products. U.S. packaged software firms began to penetrate Western European markets in the 1970s, and the strong position of Microsoft and other U.S. producers of packaged operating systems and tools software made it difficult for Western European software firms to compete. The national champion industrial strategies of Western European governments now have been largely supplanted by regional policies. Nonetheless, continuing protection of the Western European information technology hardware industry against imports has slowed the diffusion of advanced workstation and desktop computers, further retarding the development of the large, standardized installed base that might otherwise have aided the growth of the European packaged software industry.[14]

Finally, the extensive interaction between university and industry research, lubricated in many cases by government research funds, that contributed to the rise of the U.S. computer software industry has been lacking in most Western European nations, with the possible exception of Germany (see Malerba and Torrisi, 1996). According to managers in most Western European economies, severe shortages of skilled software developers impede the growth of the software industry (Malerba and Torrisi, 1996). In addition, European universities, especially outside Germany, have not been important sources of new technologies and firms for the Western European software industry. Throughout Western Europe since at least 1980, national and EU programs have sought to strengthen the links between universities and the regional European software industry, so as to expand the supply of skilled software developers and strengthen the R&D infrastructure of the industry. A number of observers argue that these programs have improved the situation, but European universities still occupy a less significant position in training and research within the software industries of their nations than is true of U.S. universities within the U.S. software industry.

[14] Commenting on a 1991 European Union Commission paper on strategies for the regional development of information technology, the *Financial Times* noted that "as IT becomes more deeply-embedded throughout economies, its benefits increasingly accrue from its application rather than from its production. . . . European demand [for advanced IT equipment] is depressed by artificially high prices. Many types of computer equipment and consumer electronics products cost twice as much as in the US – a difference which cannot be explained simply by higher distribution overheads. In some cases, product prices have been increased as a result of EC anti-dumping actions" (1991, p. 16).

C. Japan

The Japanese software industry presents an interesting contrast to those of Western Europe and the United States. Defense-related R&D and procurement have played little or no role in the development of Japan's computer hardware and software industries, and the considerable competitive strengths of Japan's computer hardware industry thus far have not produced a strong packaged computer software industry. Indeed, if anything, the opposite appears to be the case – competition among Japan's mainframe computer manufacturers in desktop systems delayed the emergence of a dominant design within Japan's installed base, reducing the attractiveness of entry into the packaged software industry by independent vendors (Cottrell, 1996). In January 1993, Japan's Ministry of International Trade and Industry designated the software industry a "distressed industry," qualifying software firms for subsidies to cover the costs of employee retraining or transfer (Nakahara, 1993).

Many of the difficulties of Japan's packaged software industry reflect the unusual character of Japan's domestic market for computers. According to Dunn (1994), mainframe computers accounted for 70% of total Japanese domestic expenditures on hardware in 1991, versus 45% of U.S. and Western European hardware investments. Not surprisingly, domestic consumption of software in Japan is more heavily dominated by custom mainframe software than is true of the United States or Western Europe. In contrast to the United States, where new entrants have played major roles in the introduction of minicomputers, workstations, and microcomputers, in Japan producers of mainframe computers dominate domestic sales of minicomputers and desktop systems. Moreover, Japanese mainframe producers also are important suppliers of custom software – the unbundling of software and hardware that occurred in the U.S. computer industry has been less significant. Other independent suppliers of custom software include firms that have "spun off" from major user industries such as steel and banking; in a number of cases, these suppliers retain formal (partial ownership) or informal links with the enterprises from which they emerged (Baba et al., 1996).

The mainframe computer producers' prominent role in desktop computer production and marketing, the demanding requirements of Japanese-language word processing, and protection against imports (through formal and informal means) of the domestic desktop market all contributed to fragmentation in Japan's installed base of desktop computers (Cottrell, 1996). Although the "Wintel" architecture has expanded its share of the Japanese desktop computer market since 1990, this market remains more fragmented among incompatible desktop architectures, and more heavily dominated by producers of mainframe systems, than the markets of the United States or Western Europe. The fragmentation of Japanese desktop computer architectures also reflects the relatively slow domestic diffusion of desktop computers in Japan. Slow diffusion was one result of the control of domestic distribution and marketing of these machines by mainframe producers, who reaped larger profits from sales of mainframes and minicomputers (Cottrell, 1996). Data from Fransman's recent analysis (1995) of Japan's computer industry reveal far lower levels of penetration by personal computers in Japan than in either Western Europe or the United States in the early 1990s. Moreover, Japanese users of personal computers are significantly less likely to operate within local area networks than is true of users in Germany or the United States (see Figs. 4.1 and 4.2). The modest diffusion of network-based computing in Japan represents a significant handicap to entry by Japanese firms into the next wave of innovation in the software industry.

The production of custom software, especially by mainframe vendors, has been organized around large software "factories" (Cusumano, 1991), extending and improving techniques originally developed for large defense-related software projects in the United States. The "factory" model of software development and production stressed high levels of code quality (i.e., few errors in individual lines of code within a program), extensive task decomposition, and reuse of modules of code within large custom programs. The software factory was a rational adaptation to a domestic market dominated by large, complex customized software programs in an environment characterized by shortages of skilled software engineers. The factory approach was developed for the production of large custom programs for mainframe computers and may be useful for the development of embedded software, which is complex, is highly customized for a specific product, and has much more demanding requirements for error-free code than most desktop packaged software. But it appears to be less well suited to the dynamic packaged software market, in which user needs often cannot be specified in detail at the outset of a development project and frequently change during its execution (Dunn, 1994). Outside Japan, many of the constraints on innovation and technical advance imposed by the "productivity bottleneck" in software development have been reduced

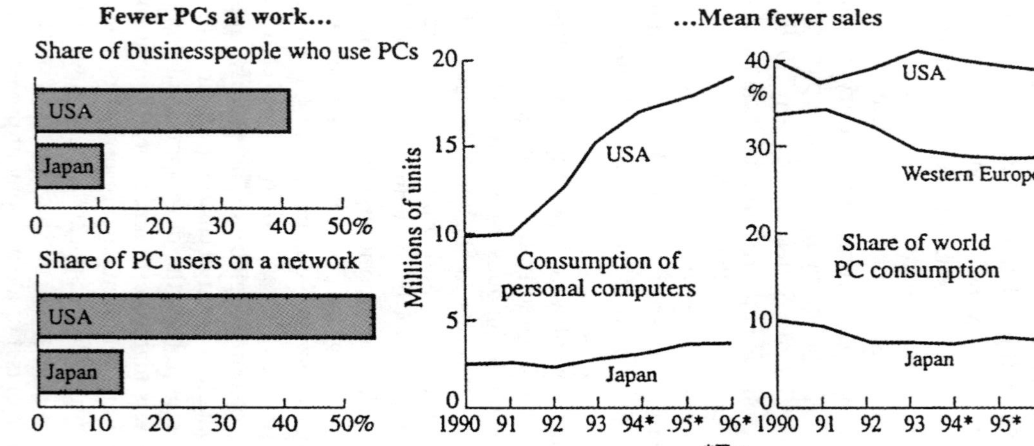

Figure 4.1. The Use of PCs in Japan, the United States, and Europe, 1990–1996. *Source:* NTT. Reprinted with permission of Oxford University Press from M. Fransman, *Japan's Computer and Communications Industry* (New York: Oxford University Press, 1995), p. 176.

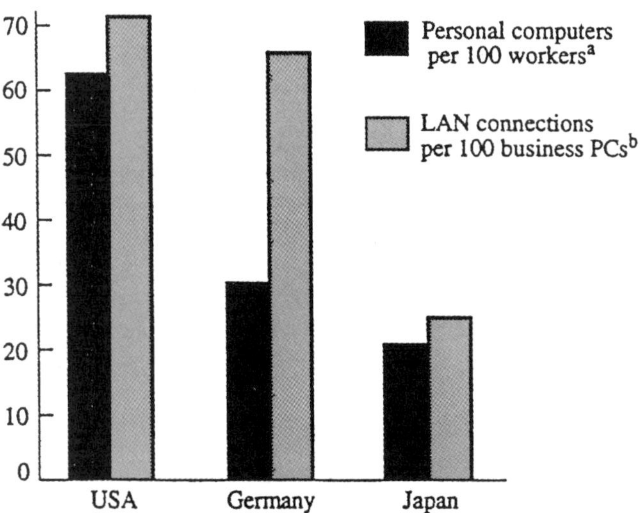

Figure 4.2. The Diffusion of PCs and PC/LAN Connections in Japan, the United States, and Germany, 1993. [a]Based on 1993 employment data; includes home PCs. [b]LAN = local area network. *Source:* International Data Corporation; Merrill Lynch & Co. Reprinted with permission of Oxford University Press from M. Fransman, *Japan's Computer and Communications Industry* (New York: Oxford University Press, 1995), p. 176.

through the development of standard hardware platforms, rather than through the reuse of programming code.[15]

Correctly or incorrectly, Japanese government policies are widely viewed as important factors in the dramatic postwar growth of Japan's microelectronics and computer hardware industries. The record of policy success in these electronics industries, however, is not matched by comparable results in Japan's software industry. The shortage of skilled software engineers in Japan, like that in Western Europe, reflects the slow response of Japan's domestic university system to the demands of the software industry (Baba et al., 1995). Computer science departments have been established in very few Japanese universities, and academic research and training in software engineering lag behind those in U.S. universities. But the failures of Japanese government policy in software extend beyond university-based education and research. MITI's much-touted powers of "administrative guidance," for example, failed to produce a sufficiently dominant, indigenous Japanese architectural to

[15] Developers of complex packaged operating systems software (e.g., Microsoft, as discussed in Smith and Cusumano 1993), now employ many more formal project management techniques, some of which resemble the software factory.

provide greater opportunities for the packaged software industry. The several cooperative R&D projects in information technology that have been partially supported by government funds, such as the "Fifth Generation" computer project and the Sigma project, also have done little to improve the competitiveness of Japan's software industry.

The failure of these projects in software has been attributed by Baba et al. (1996) to the inability of the Japanese cooperative R&D model and MITI's "administrative guidance" to deal effectively with the high levels of technical and market uncertainty that characterize this industry. The ineffectiveness of Japanese government policy in software is indicative of the broader challenges facing Japan's industrial policy as the nation seeks to operate at the frontier of new technologies. The uncertainties that confront government policymakers now are much greater than those characteristic of the situation during much of the 1950s and 1960s, when Japan was a technological borrower and follower, able to learn from the mistakes and successes of other nations.

Japanese government policy also has been slow to address the intellectual property needs of the emergent packaged software industry. Historically, intellectual property protection for software in Japan has been relatively weak, as is compatible with a domestic software industry that is dominated by the production of custom software (see Merges, 1996). But the weak protection of intellectual property has had a chilling effect on the growth of Japanese packaged software, because the profitability of packaged software depends so heavily on strong protection. In addition, the adoption of the "Wintel" architecture within Japan also was delayed by weak intellectual property protection. According to Cottrell (1996), concerns over protection of the MS-DOS operating system software delayed Microsoft's decision to license this product to Japanese desktop computer manufacturers and contributed to the fragmentation of Japanese desktop computer architecture. Although intellectual property protection for software has been strengthened somewhat, both the letter and the enforcement of this protection remain somewhat weaker than is true of the United States.

Still another policy-based obstacle to the growth of a Japanese software industry is the lack of significant deregulation and competition in Japan's telecommunications industry. An important contributor to the development of network-based applications of computer hardware and software in the United States, as was noted earlier, was the restructuring of the U.S. telecommunications industry that began in 1984. In Japan, however, the partial privatization of NTT has not reduced control of the firm by the state, which continues to exercise significant monopoly power over the pricing of leased lines and other network components.

According to the *Economist* (1997, p. 63), leased lines linking company offices in Japan are up to four times as expensive as is the case in the United States.

This interpretation of Japanese weakness in the packaged software industry rejects explanations that rely on failures of "creativity" or "entrepreneurship." Among its other deficiencies, such an explanation ignores the striking success of Japanese producers in game software. Instead, the structure and performance of Japan's software industry reflect a series of rational responses to an unusual domestic market structure that in turn stem from the strength of Japan's mainframe computer producers and the idiosyncratic character of Japanese domestic demand for computer applications.

V. National and Sectoral Innovation Systems in Software

The development of the U.S. and Japanese software industries exhibits some of the same contrasts associated with other postwar high-technology industries in these economies – new firms are very prominent in the U.S. software industry, and established producers (especially mainframe computer manufacturers) remain far more important in Japan. Differences in national financial systems and intellectual property rights regimes clearly underlie much of the U.S.–Japanese contrast. The Western European traded software industry, however, occupies something of a middle ground between the extremes represented by the U.S. and Japanese industries. New entrants have been somewhat less prominent in the Western European software industry than that of the United States, although some, such as SAP, have been very successful. But the weakness of European computer manufacturers has prevented their software subsidiaries from developing strength in domestic markets comparable to that of the Japanese computer vendors' software subsidiaries.

This section discusses a number of factors that underlie the contrasting patterns of development and competitive strength of the U.S., Japanese, and Western European software industries. These include the structure and role of central government policies toward the industry; the relationship between competitive strength in computer hardware and software in the evolution of the software industry; and the importance and characteristics of user–producer relationships in software. Many of these themes are rooted in the contrasting structures of the national innovation systems of the competing economies, while others are more specific to the software industry. The collective influence of these factors seems likely to maintain significant differences in the structure and the likely future path of development among the software industries of these three regions. Indeed, the low physical capital intensity and high human capital intensity associated with this industry have enabled national influences, rather than the industry-specific influences commonly associated with mass-production technologies, to affect the software industry throughout its development.

A. Government Policy: Defense-Related Technology Policies and Software

One important similarity between the software industry and other electronics-based postwar "new industries" is the pervasive role of government in its development. The close links between the computer hardware industry, seen by many postwar governments as an important component of their defense industrial base, and software meant that from its inception, the software industry benefited from defense-related R&D funding and procurement. As in other postwar high-technology industries, the scale and structure of the U.S. Department of Defense's policies differed from those of other industrial governments and seem to have had stronger positive effects on the competitiveness of the U.S. commercial industry. The effects of defense-related R&D and procurement spending in the U.S. software industry were influenced by two characteristics of these expenditures: (1) military demand for software, which accounted for a substantial share of industry revenues, required very different product characteristics from those of commercial software; and (2) defense-related R&D funding supported an extensive academic research enterprise.

These two factors meant that the direct spin-offs associated with defense-related expenditures in software differed from those in other U.S. postwar high-technology industries. There are few examples of commercially successful civilian software products that were derived directly from military development or procurement programs, in contrast to the U.S. semiconductor or commercial aircraft industries of the 1950s. Rather than "embodied" spin-offs, however, the U.S. software industry benefited from defense funding for a large domestic R&D infrastructure and technological advances that could be applied in modified form to civilian products.

Other postwar governments, including those of Great Britain and the Soviet Union, were also concerned with the development of a strong computer industry for national security reasons (often in connection with nuclear weapons programs), but their policies nevertheless failed to create a national research infrastructure that could support innovation in civilian software products. Surprisingly, the defense-oriented "industrial policy" of the postwar U.S. government was more successful in establishing a strong domestic industry than the civilian "strategic technology" programs of other governments. But rather than creating a large flow of defense–civilian technological spin-offs, defense spending aided the growth of the U.S. computer software industry by supporting the establishment and growth of computer science in U.S. universities. In addition, the rapid growth of defense-related markets for software created substantial opportunities for the employment of software engineers and developers, many of whom went on to establish firms or develop products for civilian markets.[16]

B. Government Policy: Intellectual Property Rights

Another important arena for government policy in the software industry is intellectual property rights (see Merges, 1996). The software industry is characterized by high fixed costs and relatively "nonrivalrous" output (i.e., the information-intensive nature of software means that its exploitation by a number of parties does not degrade its quality, in contrast to a piece of grazing land), and strong intellectual property rights may create significant monopoly power (Romer, 1993). On the other hand, the history of the Japanese software industry suggests that weak intellectual property protection can limit the growth of a domestic packaged software industry.

The importance of intellectual property rights in software has increased since 1980, because the growth of mass markets for software has increased the value of property rights in such products. But the effort to define intellectual property rights in software in Japan, the United States, and Western Europe has also begun to press against the limits of existing structures of patent and copyright statute and interpretation. Technological advance in software often has a cumulative character; one generation of product technologies relies on the previous generation, and strong technological complementarities link different software programs. Tight protection of prior generations of

[16] Describing the effects of the Air Force SAGE development project on the pool of skilled software developers in the United States, one veteran of the SAGE project noted that "the chances are reasonably high that on a large data processing job in the 1970s you would find at least one person who had worked with the SAGE system" (Bennington, 1983, p. 351).

art therefore may slow technological advance on a broad front (see Merges and Nelson, 1994). This concern motivated the European Union's recent efforts to define acceptable forms of "reverse engineering" of protected software programs, which produced a policy that is more lenient in its treatment of this practice than is U.S. policy (Merges, 1996).

The software intellectual property rights regimes that have emerged from legislative debates and court battles in Japan, the United States, and Western Europe are partly endogenous. Industry political action and legislator perceptions of national economic interest have produced intellectual property regimes that serve the dominant economic interests within the software industries of each of these areas – in some cases, these are independent software vendors, and in others, they are subsidiaries of computer manufacturers or even users of software. The evolution of intellectual property protection thus is affected by the path of industry development, rather than operating as a strictly exogenous influence on development.

The endogenous character of national or regional intellectual property rights regimes is hardly surprising. But this endogeneity extends to many other institutional components of national innovation systems. Analyses of their evolution and effects on industry must adopt a more nuanced and complex view of causes and effects. Among other things, this endogeneity means that the historical evolution of industries and national innovation systems is a path-dependent process.

C. Government Policy: Competition Policy

Another area of policy that has begun to affect the software industry is competition policy. Postwar U.S. antitrust policy was more stringent that those of Japan or most Western European economies and contributed to the importance of new, small firms in the postwar U.S. semiconductor and computer industries (Mowery, 1995). During the 1980s, U.S. antitrust policy was relaxed significantly, especially in sectors characterized by high R&D intensity and strong foreign competition, and owners of intellectual property rights benefited from a more benign judicial attitude. But Justice Department antitrust scrutiny of the U.S. industry, especially the dominant supplier of packaged software, has increased dramatically since 1993, as has private antitrust litigation. The federal antitrust suit against Microsoft that was filed in 1998 could constrain this firm's behavior and affect the course of technological advance in the software industry, although the effects of antitrust action on the long-term innovative performance of this industry are controversial (see Teece, 1998, and Katz and Shapiro, 1998, for contrasting views on these issues).[17]

Simultaneously, the emergent EU policies toward market power and intellectual property rights seem to be moving somewhat closer to the policies of the U.S. government. Indeed, one of the most novel aspects of the 1994 Microsoft antitrust investigation and settlement was the close coordination between EU and U.S. Justice Department antitrust authorities (Novak, 1994), in a tacit acknowledgment of the growing similarities in their enforcement philosophies. And the EU competition policy authorities expressed concerns in 1997 and 1998 over Microsoft's market power that echoed those of the U.S. Justice Department.

D. The Role of Universities

Government policy has affected the role of universities in the software industry. The legitimation of computer science as an academic discipline in U.S. universities, for example, received a substantial boost from the funding commitments of the Advanced Research Projects Agency and the National Science Foundation during the 1960s.[18] The organizational and disciplinary flexibility of U.S. universities in computer science has not been matched in the other economies examined in this chapter. This difference is important, because university-based computer science research activities have been important sources of the innovations that have spawned new products and firms in the United States. In addition, university-based research has played an important indirect role in the software industry's growth, by training skilled personnel whose movement into industrial employment transfers university research findings to industry. Throughout Western Europe and Japan, shortages of skilled personnel have impeded the development of domestic software industries.

[17] Predicting the outcomes, let alone the effects, of large-scale antitrust actions such as the federal suit against Microsoft also is complicated by the fact that the legal doctrine and enforcement policy underlying antitrust policy in the area of "tying," which is central to the Justice Department's suit against Microsoft, are much less clear than in the case of mergers; as Katz and Shapiro note, "Merger policy is fairly coherent, while policy toward tying is not" (1998, p. 2). Moreover, the unusual economics of software (high fixed costs and consumer benefits of unknown magnitude associated with integrating different products) mean that the effects of even a much more well-defined antitrust policy on tying, should one eventually emerge, are uncertain.

[18] The response of U.S. universities to external expressions of interest (and external sources of research support) in reorganizing their disciplinary departments, creating new departments, or adding new components to existing departments of electrical engineering is not unique to computer software but has ample historical precedent (Rosenberg and Nelson, 1994).

E. Does a Strong Domestic Software Industry Require a Strong Domestic Hardware Industry?

The interaction between national hardware and software industries is an issue whose full complexity can be appreciated only through a comparative analysis of industry development. U.S. dominance of the Western European software industry, for example, has been facilitated by the European computer hardware industry's weakness, especially in desktop computers. A comparison of the U.S. and Western European computer software industries suggests that (especially in packaged software) a strong domestic hardware industry is necessary to support the growth of a strong domestic software industry.

Comparing the U.S. and Japanese software industries, however, requires that this conclusion be qualified. Japan's computer hardware industry is much stronger than that of Western Europe. But Japanese strength in computer hardware has not been translated into strength in traded software. Japan's strength in computer hardware, which has facilitated the development of competing architectures in mainframes, minicomputers, and microcomputers, in fact appears to have retarded the growth of its packaged software industry. As in Western Europe, Japan's domestic software industry is strongest in the development of custom software solutions (by hardware manufacturers or independent firms) that require extensive familiarity with user needs.

The interaction between domestic hardware and software producers that has influenced the contrasting paths of development of the U.S., Japanese, and Western European computer software industries thus appears to vary among segments of both the hardware and software industries. The importance of strong links between hardware and software developers also has changed over time. In the early years of the industry's development, U.S. software producers derived competitive advantages from their links with the dominant global producers of mainframe, minicomputer, and desktop systems. But the importance of these linkages appears to have declined. Nevertheless, the central position of the U.S. market as the "testbed" for developing new applications in such areas as networking and the Internet reflects the enduring importance of user–producer interactions in the software industry. Regardless of the national origin of the hardware on which new software operates, United States–located software firms will have advantages over firms without a presence in this market.

The importance of user–producer links also means that vertical integration of hardware and software production, especially hardware and applications software, is likely to remain the exception rather than the rule in the traded software industry. Developers of many new hardware products that rely on packaged software therefore must develop strategies to attract independent software developers to their architecture, creating "bandwagons" of software developers to exploit network externalities. The competition among Reduced Instruction-Set Computing (RISC) microprocessors used in workstations (Khazam and Mowery, 1996) is a good example of these strategies in action. A more recent example is the intermittent effort of Apple Computer to attract software developers to its operating system and architecture by licensing its operating system to producers of "clones" of the Macintosh computer. By expanding the output and lowering the price of machines using the Macintosh operating system, Apple managers hoped to attract software developers to expand the library of applications software for this architecture. A larger, more current applications library would increase the attractiveness to consumers of Apple's hardware – any losses in market share to "clones," according to this theory, should be recouped through a combination of licensing revenues and growth in the size of the overall market for the computer. Apple senior managers' concern over the firm's loss of market share to its cloners (see Gomes, 1997) nevertheless led the firm to terminate its licensing policy in 1997.

The importance of software-based bandwagons for the commercial prospects of new hardware products increases as one moves from mainframes to microcomputers, reflecting the fact that this last class of hardware is sold to a large market of users who are individually far less sophisticated than operators of mainframe computers. As the number of users of desktop systems expands, the demand for standardized solutions to a broader array of nonstandard applications grows, user "lock-in" to a graphical interface or applications suite is more likely, and extensive libraries of standard software for a specific architecture become more important. These bandwagon effects thus far appear to be more important in microcomputers than in workstations, because workstations have not yet penetrated the mass market of less sophisticated users.

The strategic importance of software bandwagons for hardware commercialization may decline somewhat if software becomes genuinely independent of hardware architectures in desktop and other systems. "Open systems" architectures, which enable an operating system and its related applications to run on any one of a diverse array of hardware platforms, will weaken any need for links between the developers of such hardware and those creating standard software for these systems. The widespread adoption of open systems would reduce the burden on would-be commercializers of new hardware technologies to attract a significant following of software developers. But genuinely "open systems" remain a goal, rather than a reality.

The growth of Web-based network computing might have a similar effect on the interdependence of operating-system and applications software that has enabled Microsoft to use its market power in operating-system software to dominate major applications markets in desktop software. The need for a large library of applications programs to complement desktop operating-system software means that the ultimate success of the Web-based model of desktop computing depends on the ability of its promoters to attract independent developers of applications. Sun Microsystems, a major promoter of network-based computing, has characterized its Java software product as the basis for the creation of applications that can operate in such networks. Bandwagons and consumption externalities thus will continue to play a very important role in the success of new software products, be these operating systems or applications.

F. The Evolving Division of Labor Among Users, Hardware Producers, and Independent Software Vendors

The production of computer software was dominated by users and by producers of computer hardware in the early years of the industry. These suppliers were gradually supplemented by other entities. In Japan, such sophisticated users as steel firms and financial institutions "spun off" firms that became important providers of software and services, while elsewhere, new firms were established to provide these services. The relative importance of different structures of the division of labor contrasts strikingly among the United States, Japan, and Western Europe, but in all three areas, one observes a mix of structures, rather than a single structure for the division of labor in software development and production. Rather than any single approach's (e.g., independent software vendors, in-house production by hardware manufacturers) being dominant, new forms of this division of labor supplement previous structures (Steinmueller, 1996).

This coexistence is attributable in part to the presence of a large installed base of older hardware with specialized applications and operating system software in the United States, Western Europe, and Japan. As Bresnahan and Greenstein (1996) argue, the switching costs associated with abandoning older systems are so high as to impede their replacement. Organizational routines and policies have literally grown up around these systems, and their revision is extraordinarily costly, especially for large "back-office" operations in commercial databases, etc. Differences among nations in the characteristics of their domestic installed base also are likely to support enduring differences in the structure of their domestic software industries, creating country-specific niches for independent software vendors and vertically integrated units of manufacturers.

The importance of user–producer linkages in the software industry, as well as the limited effectiveness thus far of software factories, will limit the growth of offshore production of software (Yourdon, 1992, regards such offshore software production as a threat to U.S. software industry employees). A number of European and U.S. firms have developed substantial software production operations in economies with a large, low-cost technical work force, such as India. Nevertheless, these foreign software development operations are most effective for the creation of the many lines of code needed for large, complex custom programs. Moreover, this structure of production is not well suited to the short development cycles, rapid prototyping, and high responsiveness to user needs that are necessary for packaged software development – proximity to users is essential in this product line. Offshore production of software thus may expand, but it will affect the segments of the software industry that are growing much more slowly than packaged software.

VI. Conclusion

The computer software industry is in many respects an exaggerated version of the other high-technology industries examined in this project. Although it is common to characterize the high-technology sector as one in which intellectual and human capital are at least as important as physical capital, computer software is a special case – physical capital is of little or no importance in the development, production, and distribution of new products. But human capital, especially a pool of skilled software developers, is a critically important competitive asset. On the other hand, the success of computer software products has been critically influenced by their compatibility with the installed base of computer hardware, a major physical capital investment.

A number of technological and market-related trends are likely to influence the future of the software industry and the role of U.S. firms within this industry. The commercial success of an expanding array of new capital goods, ranging from microprocessors to medical instruments, depends on the quality and availability of software for their operation, as the previous discussion of software bandwagons noted. The functions, features, and even the safety of a growing array of products also depend on the quality of the "embedded" software that is rapidly expanding in significance within many complex capital and consumer goods (e.g., automobiles). The growing importance of embedded software may enhance the desirability and competitive advantages associated with the factory approach to software development used by some large Japanese producers of electronic systems. Computer software thus is *sui generis*, but its influence within the innovation processes of other capital-goods and consumer durable industries appears to be growing steadily.

Should genuinely open systems in desktop computing become widespread as a result of the growth in network computing and Web-based software, the competitive significance of the lock-in effects associated with the large installed base of the "Wintel" architectural standard should diminish, and the entry barriers associated with these dominant architectures could decline somewhat. Nevertheless, users of much of the software associated with these platforms will remain locked in by their investments in the skills and techniques needed to operate these applications and operating systems, and the producers of the software will retain a large market. Moreover, consumption externalities and bandwagon effects, such as those observed in the interdependence between operating systems and applications software, will remain important in the competitive dynamics of this industry.

Yet another interesting question concerns the importance of a strong domestic software industry for entry into emerging segments of the consumer and business electronics industries. The long-awaited and much-discussed convergence of telecommunications and computing technologies that has been accelerated through the widespread diffusion of networking technologies now seems likely to support the emergence of some entirely new electronic products for home and business applications. It remains to be seen whether production of the hardware associated with these emerging applications will have to be situated in close proximity with the developers of the necessary operating, applications, and entertainment software.[19]

Regardless of the national identity of the manufacturers of the hardware on which the "next wave" of applications operates, however, it seems a virtual certainty that these applications will appear initially in the United States. In many respects, the role of the U.S. market as the consistent leader in new product introduction and innovation in computer software is consistent with at least some aspects of Vernon's

[19] The unsuccessful efforts of large Japanese producers of consumer electronics to diversify into some forms of entertainment software through acquisitions of U.S. movie studios suggest that common ownership of the software and hardware in these emerging technologies may be very difficult to achieve or to manage once accomplished.

international product cycle model. Multinational production strategies and direct foreign investment in production facilities are of little importance in the software industry, characterized as it is by minimal physical capital requirements for manufacture of its products. Nevertheless, the factors discussed earlier contribute to remarkably enduring and significant international differences in consumption patterns, user–producer interactions, and other characteristics that have strengthened the position of the U.S. market as the site for innovations that subsequently diffuse throughout the industrial economies. Thus far, this pattern has provided first-mover advantages and dominance to U.S. firms in global markets. As long as the United States remains the largest single English-language market for packaged software and retains its status as the "lead adopter" of new desktop and network computing technologies, the product cycle model is likely to retain considerable validity for this industry.

References

Abernathy, W.J., and J.M. Utterback, "Patterns of Industrial Innovation," *Technology Review* 80, 1978, 40–47.

Baba, Y., S. Takai, and Y. Mizuta, "The User-Driven Evolution of the Japanese Software Industry: The Case of Customized Software for Mainframes," in D.C. Mowery, ed., *The International Computer Software Industry: A Comparative Study of Industry Evolution and Structure* (New York: Oxford University Press, 1996).

Benington, H.D., "Production of Large Computer Programs," *Annals of the History of Computing* 5, 1983, 350–361.

Bresnahan, T.F., "New Modes of Competition: Implications for the Future Structure of the Computer Industry," presented at the Stanford Workshop on Intellectual Property and Industry Competitive Standards, Stanford, CA, April 17–18, 1998.

Bresnahan, T., and S. Greenstein, "Technological Competition and the Structure of the Computer Industry," unpublished MS, 1995.

Bresnahan, T.F., and S. Greenstein, "The Competitive Crash in Large-Scale Computing," in R. Landau, T. Taylor, and G. Wright, eds., *The Mosaic of Economic Growth* (Stanford, CA: Stanford University Press, 1996).

Campbell-Kelly, M., "Development and Structure of the International Software Industry, 1950–1990," *Business and Economic History* 24, 1995, 73–110.

Cottrell, T., "Standards and the Arrested Development of Japan's Microcomputer Software Industry," in D.C. Mowery, ed., *The International Computer Software Industry: A Comparative Study of Industry Evolution and Structure* (New York: Oxford University Press, 1996).

Cottrell, T., "Strategy and Survival in the Microcomputer Software Industry,

1981–1986," unpublished Ph.D. dissertation, Haas School of Business, University of California at Berkeley, 1995.

Cusumano, M., *Japan's Software Factories: A Challenge to U.S. Management* (New York: Oxford University Press, 1991).

Cusumano, M., Y. Mylonadis, and R.S. Rosenbloom, "Strategic Maneuvering and Mass-Market Dynamics: The Triumph of Beta over VHS," CCC working paper 90–5, Berkeley, CA, 1990.

Dunn, M.E., "Can Japan Compete? An Analysis of New Product Definition and Development Practices in Japanese Software Firms," unpublished M.A. thesis, Asian Studies, University of California at Berkeley, 1994.

Economist, "Doing It Differently," April 19, 1997, pp. 62–63.

Financial Times, "Europe and Electronics," March 27, 1991, p. 20.

Fisher, F.M., J.W. McKie, and R.B. Mancke, *IBM and the U.S. Data Processing Industry* (New York: Praeger, 1983).

Flamm, K., *Creating the Computer* (Washington, D.C.: Brookings Institution, 1987).

Fransman, M., *Japan's Computer and Communications Industry* (New York: Oxford University Press, 1995).

Freeman, C., *Technology and Economic Performance* (London: Frances Pinter, 1987).

Gomes, L., "For WebTV's Perlman, Microsoft Deal Is Vindication After His Exile at Apple," *Wall Street Journal*, April 9, 1997, p. B6.

Gomes, L., "Apple Moderates Its Position in Talks over Fees with Clone-Making Firms," *Wall Street Journal*, April 10, 1997, p. B16.

Grindley, P., "The Future of the UK Software Industry: Limitations of Independent Production," in D.C. Mowery, ed., *The International Computer Software Industry: A Comparative Study of Industry Evolution and Structure* (New York: Oxford University Press, 1996).

Hill, C.W.L., and G.R. Jones, *Strategic Management: An Integrated Approach*, 3d ed. (Boston: Houghton Mifflin, 1995).

Hill, G., and D. Clark, "In Failed Acquisition of Intuit, Microsoft Sees Challenges Rising," *Wall Street Journal Europe*, May 22, 1995, p. A1.

International Data Corporation, *1993 Worldwide Software Review and Forecast* (Framingham, MA: IDC, 1993).

International Data Corporation, *1994 Worldwide Software Review and Forecast* (Framingham, MA: IDC, 1994).

Katz, M.L., and C. Shapiro, "Antitrust in Software Markets," presented at the Institutional Analysis workshop, Haas School of Business, University of California at Berkeley, April 23, 1998.

Khazam, J., and D.C. Mowery, "Tails That Wag Dogs: The Influence of Software-Based 'Network Externalities' on the Creation of Dominant Designs in RISC Technologies," in D.C. Mowery, ed., *The International Computer Software Industry* (New York: Oxford University Press, 1996).

Lundvall, B.-A., *National Systems of Innovation – Towards a Theory of Innovation and Interactive Learning* (London: Frances Pinter, 1992).

Malerba, F., and S. Torrisi, "The Dynamics of Market Structure and Innovation in the Western European Software Industry," in D.C. Mowery, ed., *The International Computer Software Industry: A Comparative Study of Industry Evolution and Structure* (New York: Oxford University Press, 1996).
Merges, R., "A Comparative Look at Intellectual Property Rights and the Software Industry," in D.C. Mowery, ed., *The International Computer Software Industry: A Comparative Study of Industry Evolution and Structure* (New York: Oxford University Press, 1996).
Merges, R.P., and R.R. Nelson, "On Limiting or Encouraging Rivalry in Technical Progress: The Effect of Patent Scope Decisions," *Journal of Economic Behavior and Organization* 25, 1994, 1–24.
Mowery, D.C., "The Boundaries of the U.S. Firm in R&D," in N. Lamoureaux and D. Rapp, eds., *The Coordination of Economic Activity Within and Among Firms* (Chicago: University of Chicago Press for NBER, 1995).
Mowery, D.C., and Langlois, R., "Spinning Off and Spinning On(?): The Federal Government Role in the Development of the U.S. Computer Software Industry," *Research Policy* 25, 1996, 947–966.
Nakahara, T., "The Industrial Organization and Information Structure of the Software Industry: A U.S.–Japan Comparison," unpublished MS, Center for Economic Policy Research, Stanford University, May 1993.
Nelson, R.R., *National Innovation Systems: A Comparative Analysis* (New York: Oxford University Press, 1993).
Nelson, R.R., and G. Wright, "The Erosion of U.S. Technological Leadership as a Factor in Postwar Economic Convergence," in W.J. Baumol, R.R. Nelson, and E. Wolff, eds., *Convergence of Productivity* (New York: Oxford University Press, 1994).
Novak, V., "Antitrust's Bingaman Talks Tough on Microsoft Case," *Wall Street Journal*, July 19, 1994, p. B1.
OECD (Organization for Economic Cooperation and Development), *Software: An Emerging Industry* (Paris: OECD, 1985).
OECD (Organisation for Economic Cooperation and Development), *The Internationalisation of Software and Computer Services* (Paris: OECD, 1989).
Reuters News Service, "Microsoft, Compaq Snare Computer Networking Firms," November 6, 1995.
Romer, P., "Implementing a National Technology Strategy with Self-Organizing Industry Investment Boards," *Brookings Papers on Economic Activity* #2, 1993, 345–390.
Rosenberg, N., and R.R. Nelson, "American Universities and Technical Advance in Industry," *Research Policy* 24, 1994, 323–348.
Smith, S.A., and M. Cusumano, "Beyond the Software Factory: A Comparison of 'Classic' and PC Software Developers," Sloan School of Management Working Paper #3607-93, M.I.T., 1993.
Steinmueller, W.E., "The U.S. Software Industry: An Analysis and Interpretive History," in D.C. Mowery, ed., *The International Computer Software*

Industry: A Comparative Study of Industry Evolution and Structure (New York: Oxford University Press, 1996).

Swann, P., and J. Gill, *Corporate Vision and Rapid Technological Change* (London: Routledge, 1993).

Teece, D.J., "Profiting from Technological Innovation: Implications for Integration, Collaboration, Licensing, and Public Policy," *Research Policy* 15, 1986, 285–305.

Teece, D.J., "The Meaning of Monopoly: Antitrust Analysis in High Technology Industries," presented at the Institutional Analysis Workshop, Haas School of Business, University of California at Berkeley, April 30, 1998.

U.S. Bureau of the Census, *Statistical Abstract of the United States: 1997* (Washington, D.C.: U.S. Government Printing Office, 1997).

U.S. Department of Commerce, *U.S. Industry and Trade Outlook 1998* (New York: McGraw-Hill, 1998).

U.S. International Trade Commission, *A Competitive Assessment of the U.S. Computer Software Industry* (Washington, DC: U.S. International Trade Commission, 1995).

Vernon, R.S., "The Product Cycle Hypothesis in a New International Environment," *Oxford Bulletin of Economics and Statistics* 41, 1979, 255–267.

Von Hippel, E., "'Sticky Information' and the Locus of Problem Solving: Implications for Innovation," *Management Science* 40, 1994, 429–439.

Von Neumann, J., "First Draft of a Report on the EDVAC," reprinted in W. Aspray and A. Burks, eds., *Papers of John von Neumann on Computing and Computer Theory* (Cambridge, MA: MIT Press, 1987).

Yourdon, E., *The Decline and Fall of the American Programmer* (Englewood Cliffs, NJ: Prentice-Hall, 1992).

CHAPTER 5

Innovation in the Machine Tool Industry: A Historical Perspective on the Dynamics of Comparative Advantage

ROBERTO MAZZOLENI

I. Introduction

The most important features of the evolution of comparative advantage in the machine tool (henceforth MT) industry since World War II have been the decline of the U.S. industry and the rise of the Japanese to the status of leading producing and exporting country. The U.S. industry lost the rank of largest producer that it held since the manufacture of MTs became a specialized business activity in the second half of the nineteenth century. After becoming a net importer of MTs for the first time in 1978 (Fig. 5.1), the U.S. has become dependent on imports for more than 50% of its MT consumption. The counterpart to the decline of the U.S. industry is the growth of the Japanese industry. A small and technologically backward sector until the 1950s, the Japanese industry became the largest producer and exporter during the 1980s (Tables 5.1 and 5.2).

The convergence among industrialized countries during the second postwar period explains only in part the international differences in sectoral growth rates. Instead, the evolution of comparative advantage has been driven fundamentally by the international differences in innovative performance in the development and diffusion of numerical control (NC) technology (Table 5.3). Whereas innovation has been a prominent factor in the activities of MT firms throughout the industry history, its consequences on the pattern of national comparative advantage have been quite limited with the important exception of the sequence of innovations in MT designs by American builders during the second half of the nineteenth century. In that period the U.S. industry acquired the technological and commercial leadership to the detriment of the British. The innovative MT designs developed by American builders provided a key input to the diffusion of the American system of manufacture

I wish to acknowledge the comments provided by Ross Thomson, seminar participants at the Scuola Superiore Sant' Anna (Pisa, Italy), and the participants to the Matrix Project's discussion meetings in Milan, Palo Alto, and Cape Cod. Richard Nelson and David Mowery have provided encouragement and suggestions on many earlier drafts of this chapter. I wish to thank them both wholeheartedly. However, I alone bear the responsibility for the ideas presented in this chapter.

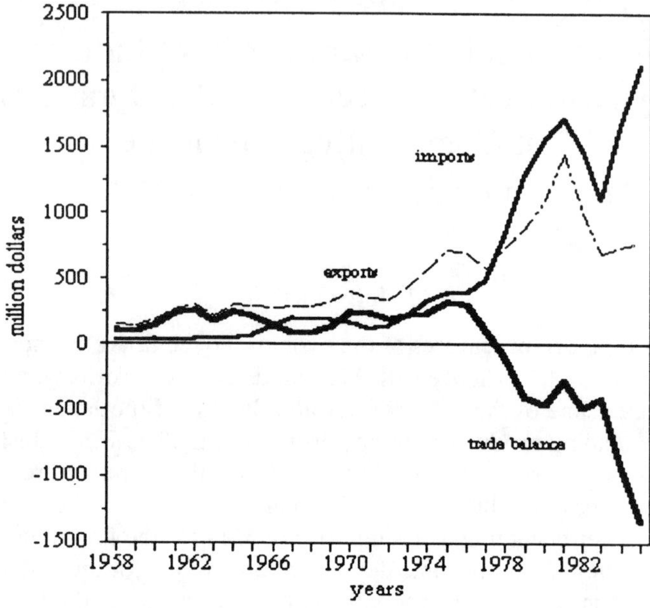

Figure 5.1. U.S. Machine Tool Trade Balance (1958–1985). *Source:* NMTBA, *Economic Handbook*, various issues.

by interchangeable parts, and later of mass-production methods (N. Rosenberg, 1963; Hounshell, 1984; Rolt, 1965).

Since then, the U.S. industry has played a dominant role in the progress of MT technology. NC was no exception. However, in spite of the early lead in the commercialization and users' adoption of numerically controlled MTs (NCMTs), the diffusion of the new technology in the United States faltered between 1965 and 1975. During that period, other national industries undertook the development of NC technology, adapting it to the manufacturing contexts of their customer base and the MT designs in which they specialized. Progress was especially rapid in Japan, where the innovative efforts were directed toward the adaptation of NC to low cost general-purpose NCMTs.[1]

[1] The distinction between general-purpose and special-purpose MTs is somewhat arbitrarily drawn in the literature and different uses of the terminology are quite common. In an attempt to clarify what is otherwise a murky distinction, let me specify that I will refer to a general-purpose (special-purpose) MT as one which is intended for the production of a broad (narrow) dimensional range of metal parts. A partially overlapping distinction can be drawn by reference to the production lot size for which an MT is intended. Ordered by increasing lot size, there are universal machines, automatic production equipment, and single-purpose equipment.

Table 5.1. *National Share of World Exports of Machine Tools (1913–1995)*

Year	Germany	United States	United Kingdom	Japan	Italy	France	Switzerland	Taiwan	S. Korea
1913[a]	48	33	12	-	-	-	-	-	-
1921	30	35	14	-	-	-	-	-	-
1937	48	35	7	-	-	-	5	-	-
1955	24.5	22.7	10.5	0.5	2.6	3.2	10.0	-	-
1965	27.1	16.3	7.3	2.4	5.4[#]	4.5[#]	8.1[#]	-	-
1975[b]	29.9	7.2	6.2	5.3	7.4	5.5	7.5	0.3[d]	-
1980	25.8	5.5	5.9	12.6	7.4	4.5	7.6	1.4[d]	-
1985[c]	20.0	4.7	3.5	22.1	6.4	2.4	8.8	2.2	0.3
1990	23.6	4.8	3.8	18.3	9.1	2.4	12.6	3.0	0.4
1995	22.8	7.6	3.4	25.3	8.6	1.9	9.1	4.5	0.9

[a] Data for the years 1913–1937 reproduced from UNIDO (1984) do not include the exports from Eastern European countries; 1955 and 1965 data are from Collis (1989).

[b] World export data from UNIDO (1984), country data from NMTBA, *Economic Handbook*, various issues.

[c] Data from *American Machinist*, various issues.

[d] Jacobsson (1986).

Author's estimates based on data in UNIDO (1984) and Collis (1989).

Table 5.2. *Distribution of Numerically Controlled Machine Tools Production in Six OECD Countries (Percentage of Value)*

	1975	1980	1983	1990
Japan	23.1	54.2	54.4	45.0
United States	43.8	21.8	16.5	8.6
Germany	11.5	11.7	16.5	31.3
Italy	8.5	6.6	6.2	6.4
United Kingdom	7.8	3.0	3.7	4.0
France	5.3	2.7	2.7	4.7

Source: Data for 1975, 1980, 1985 from ECE (1986); 1990 data elaborated from NMTBA, *Economic Handbook*, 1993–1994.

The distinctive competencies in the design of multifunction MTs, such as turning and machining centers, and their production in large volumes became the basis of the superior performance of the Japanese firms. First mover advantages from learning and scale economies supported the Japanese industry's rise to dominance (Jacobsson, 1986). Why did these advantages accrue to the Japanese firms? The argument presented here is that the different competitiveness of the U.S. and Japanese firms in that segment of the market was not motivated by differences in their access to basic technologies. Rather, it reflected a divergence in the broad directions of innovation in NCMTs' design pursued by the firms in the two countries. Differences in the structure of domestic market demand (Carlsson, 1984; DiFilippo, 1986; Melman, 1983; Noble, 1984; Watanabe, 1983) contributed to steering the innovative efforts in different directions. Yet, the growth of NCMTs' imports from Japan suggests that a sizable potential market for low-cost general-purpose equipment existed in the United States. The U.S. industry's lack of competitiveness in that market segment resulted from a failure to perceive the existence and size of that market and to enact product development and manufacturing strategies necessary to reduce the cost of adoption (Jacobsson, 1986; Mazzoleni, 1997).

The strategic failures of the U.S. control suppliers are particularly noteworthy since their innovation strategies defined the nature of the NC systems available to MT builders who lacked in-house capabilities for NC design and manufacturing. While this pattern of vertical specialization emerged early in every national industry, there were significant differences in the degree of coordination achieved among the innovative strategies of control suppliers and MT firms. Dissatisfied with the NC systems available from specialized suppliers, a growing number of U.S. MT firms developed in-house capabilities in the early 1970s (Sciberras and Payne, 1985). The result was a fragmented market with few possibilities for achieving scale economies. By comparison, Fujitsu-Fanuc, a control supplier, had acquired a dominant market position in Japan focusing its technology development strategy on systems suitable for the low-cost general-purpose equipment in which Japanese firms specialized. The emergence of a de facto standard in the design of NC systems facilitated the conversion of the Japanese MT firms' product lines from conventional to NCMTs designs and allowed Fujitsu-Fanuc to benefit from scale economies and a broad feedback from MT builders and users.

The goal of the chapter is to cast these events in the broader context of the evolution of MT technology and of the relationship between the nature of domestic markets and the product specialization of national

Table 5.3. *Share of NC Machine Tools in Total Machine Tool Production in Various Countries*

year	U.S.[a]	Japan[b]	Germany[c]	U.K.[d]	France[e]	Italy[f]	Taiwan[g]	S. Korea[h]
1964	8.7	-	-	-	-	-	-	-
1965	10.9	-	2	-	-	-	-	-
1966	14.5	1	2	2.5	4	6	-	-
1967	15.2	1.3	5.1	5.3	4.4	6.8	-	-
1968	20.5	2.8	-	7.0	-	-	-	-
1969	17.4	-	-	7.7	-	-	-	-
1970	13.5	6.1	7	7.2	-	-	-	-
1971	14.5	7.5	-	8.7	-	-	-	-
1972	13.4	9.2	-	5.9	-	-	-	-
1973	15.2	11.8	-	6.2	-	-	-	-
1974	17.5	12.2	-	6.3	-	-	-	-
1975	21.0	12.7	-	7.3	11.1	-	-	-
1976	23.0	16.2	-	7.6	12.2	15.2	-	-
1977	20.2	18.7	10	8.2	16.5	-	-	-
1978	20.7	21.7	11	10.7	22.6	10.3	-	-
1979	25.0	32.4	12.1	11.5	22.4	-	-	-
1980	28.5	39.1	14.3	14.5	19.8	-	-	-
1981	29.3	41.0	15.1	18.6	25.7	-	-	4.8
1982	30.1	44.4	23.4	22.3	31	-	-	12.6
1983	34.1	50.6	29.6	25	45.4	-	7	13.3
1984	31.3	55.5	34.2	32	59.9	20	13.4	16.9
1985	30.2	55.4	38.2	32	54.3	-	15.0	21.7
1986	31.8	-	43.9	33	-	-	20.4	-
1987	35.6	-	44.7	35	-	38.9	17.8	-
1988	35.5	59.4	51.7	-	-	38.0	21.9	26.7
1989	36.6	63.6	51.9	-	66.4	41.7	29.7	33.7
1990	40.7	65.4	57.0	-	64.2	38.0	27.6	35.2

[a] Data for 1964–1978 include only NC metal cutting equipment.
Source: NMTBA, *Economic Handbook*, various issues.
[b] Data for 1970–1985 include only NC metal cutting equipment.
Sources: 1966: Collis (1988); 1967–1968: Dai-ichi Kangyo Bank (1970); 1970–1990: MITI and NMTBA, *Economic Handbook*, various issues.

Notes to Table 5.3 (*cont.*)

[c] Data for 1965–1967 and 1970 include only metal cutting equipment.
Sources: 1965–1966 and 1970: Collis (1988); 1967: OECD (1970); 1977–1987: Carlsson (1989); 1988–1990: NMTBA, *Economic Handbook*, various issues.

[d] *Sources:* 1966–1982: shipment data from NMTBA, *Economic Handbook*, various issues; 1983–1987: production data from Carlsson (1989).

[e] Data for 1966–1967 include only metal cutting equipment.
Sources: 1966: Collis (1988); 1967: OECD (1970); 1975–1985: Carlsson (1989); 1989–1990: NMTBA, *Economic Handbook*, various issues.

[f] Only metal cutting equipment. 1987–1990 NC shipments include only lathes, milling machines, and machining centers.
Sources: 1966, 1984: Collis (1988); 1967, 1978: UNIDO (1984); 1984: Ashburn (1986); 1987–1990: NMTBA, *Economic Handbook*, various issues.

[g] *Sources:* 1983–1987: Carlsson (1989); 1988–1990: NMTBA, *Economic Handbook*, various issues.

[h] *Sources:* 1981–1985: Carlsson (1989); 1988–1990: NMTBA, *Economic Handbook*, various issues.

industries. Accordingly, Section II provides a review of the pre–World War II period, focusing on the context in which the U.S. industry rose to dominance in the second half of the nineteenth century and national differences in product specialization emerged. Section III discusses the origins of NC technology and follows the national patterns of its development and diffusion until the 1970s. The focus is primarily on the factors underlying the emergence of Japanese dominance and the poor performance of the U.S. industry. Next (Section IV), the competitive environment of the 1980s and the performance of national industries during that decade are discussed. Section V provides a brief overview of the role of government policies. The chapter concludes with a rejoinder on the relationship between innovation in MT technology and the dynamics of comparative advantage.

II. An Era of American Dominance: The Machine Tool Industry Before World War II

MTs are power-driven equipment used to cut or form metal products. In spite of the relatively small size of the industry output (roughly $40 billion in 1990), MTs play a central role in the production process of many metalworking industries. Innovations in MT design realized by either specialized firms or users themselves contribute significantly to productivity growth and rising product quality in the using sectors. Since MT firms play a crucial role in the diffusion of new metalworking technology, the industry's innovative performance is considered to be of strategic significance for the competitiveness of a country's using sectors (Carlsson and Jacobsson, 1991). In fact, this role has been a distinguishing feature of the industry since its origins, when the design and manufacture of MTs became the purview of specialized firms.

From the late 18th century the use of machine tools became increasingly common, particularly in the United Kingdom, just as the manufacture of iron products expanded. At that time, the development of innovative machine tools was carried out largely by firms which employed them in-house for the manufacture of other products, as it happened at the engineering shop of Henry Maudslay, the most prominent inventor of that time (Rolt, 1965; Roe, 1916). However, a process of vertical specialization had begun whereby the sale of machine tools to other users became a substantial business activity for the shops of British inventors such as James Fox, James Nasmyth, and Joseph Whitworth (Rolt, 1965). Although these and other British builders dominated innovation during the first half of the century, a similar pattern of industry evolution can be observed in the United States since the 1840s.

An important influence on the development of MT designs in the United States arose from the army's interest in the development of guns assembled from interchangeable parts. This interest motivated the contracts awarded by the U.S. government to Eli Whitney and Simeon North in 1798 and 1799, respectively (Roe, 1916). The method of manufacturing by interchangeable parts was then adopted by the government's armories in Springfield and Harper's Ferry, and later by the Colt's Armory in Hartford, Connecticut. The diffusion of the method was accompanied by improvements in machine tool design such as to reduce the amount of hand fitting required for assembling the final product from its constituent parts. The progress of the U.S. machine tool builders in this direction was such that in 1853 the British government contracted with the firm of Robbins & Lawrence in Windsor, Vermont, for the shipment of 157 machine tools to the Enfield Arsenal. The interchangeable parts' system of manufacture began its diffusion in Europe.

Although the method was first conceived as a way to reduce the cost and time for ordnance repair, the new manufacturing system (including the standardization of parts and the division of the manufacturing process into simple operations) later proved to be profitable in old and new industries whose products required accurate fitting of metal components. New MTs capable of greater accuracy and higher rates of metal removal were developed and diffused to the manufacturing of clocks, textile and agricultural machinery, steam engines, railroad equipment, sewing machines, typewriters, bicycles, electrical equipment, and other MTs.

The rise of a specialized industry transformed the institutional mechanisms involved in the diffusion of the new MTs. Earlier, users invented new MTs for their own production needs and profited from them by preventing their diffusion to other firms. The convergence among the needs of firms in various metalworking industries created the opportunity for MT inventors to profit from innovation by promoting the diffusion of their MTs across the spectrum of users. In turn, the MT builders' contacts with a growing variety of using firms provided access to information on the users' needs and innovations in materials and components that could be implemented usefully in the design and manufacture of MTs. Thus, the process of technological convergence led to both the growth of the market for MTs and the emergence of the industry as an important institutional mechanism for the diffusion of innovative manufacturing technology (N. Rosenberg, 1963).

The rapid growth of the U.S. manufacturing industries during the late nineteenth century promoted a distinctive trend in the direction of innovation. Whereas productivity growth was achieved first by adopting general purpose MTs that could be continuously employed in the production of varied metal parts, the growing manufacturing volume of using firms created the conditions for the economic use of specialized machines.[2] By the end of the century, a differentiated market had emerged including the basic designs of general-purpose MTs and a great variety of special-purpose machines for large-scale production. With few exceptions, the segmentation of the product market was mirrored by the industry's horizontal specialization. Absent significant economies of scope, the MT firms specialized in narrow product lines. Further, because of the limited market size the MT industry did not experience the emergence of large managerial corporations typical of other industrial sectors (Wagoner, 1966).

The trend toward the design of special-purpose MTs was reinforced by the growth of the automobile industry beginning in the 1910s (Rolt, 1965; Wagoner, 1966).[3] The pioneers of automobile manufacturing adopted the machinery and manufacturing processes of other sectors;

[2] Greater metal removal capacity was achieved by designing automatic machines, machines that could perform multiple cuts at one time, and special-purpose machines. Typically, these designs traded machining versatility for speed of operation within a narrow class of metal parts. Although specialized by the nature of the metal-cutting operation performed, these MTs were often used by a large variety of industries either as standardized equipment or customized to the demands of individual users.

[3] An example of this trend is the diffusion of the transfer machine, first adopted by the Waltham Watch Co. (Rolt, 1965). It consisted of a series of linked workstations performing a sequence of operations on a workpiece. Greater productivity was gained at the cost of the equipment's extreme specialization, since transfer machines were often single-purpose (i.e., suitable for a single metal part). A degree of flexibility was gained by developing a modular design of the workstations, a trend pioneered by the Cincinnati Milling Machine Co. in 1907.

soon after the turn of the century the industry needs became an independent stimulus to the design of specialized machinery. As early as 1910, the U.S. automobile industry accounted for 25–30% of domestic MT sales. At that time Henry Ford's development of the assembly line made it possible to achieve significant economies at a vastly increased scale of production. This created the need for faster production of metal components and thus a strong demand for automatic machines. This trend continued after the post–World War I depression, when output growth in the industry occurred largely through the growth of plants' production volumes at Ford, General Motors, and later Chrysler.

The faster diffusion of mass-production methods among the U.S. manufacturing industries during the early twentieth century widened the divergence in the direction of progress in MT design pursued by the U.S. and the European firms. Even in countries like Great Britain, Germany, and Switzerland, where progress in the industry had been remarkable, the development of special-purpose equipment for high-volume production lagged behind.[4]

At the turn of the century the British MT industry had undergone a process of renewal. The failure of the industry to maintain the technological leadership acquired early in the century was related to the lagging diffusion of interchangeable parts manufacturing among domestic metalworking industries. By the time these methods spread among new industries (such as the bicycle and sewing machine) toward the end of the century, their production needs were met by equipment produced in-house, imports from the United States, or the products of a new generation of British MT firms (Floud, 1976; Saul, 1967).

In Germany a specialized MT industry formed during the industrialization process of the late nineteenth century, relying extensively

[4] Available data do not permit precise quantification of national differences in the nature of demand. Indirect evidence is provided by differences in the aggregate production and consumption of MTs and by differences in the output level of major using industries. In 1913 the production of metalworking machinery in the United States was $60.3 million (estimates in Robertson, 1966); in Germany it was $49 million (estimates based on data from *American Machinist*, 1914). However, domestic shipments were $44.3 million for the United States and $29.5 for Germany. In 1927, production levels were $175.6 million in the United States and $68 million in Germany, while domestic shipments were, respectively, $150.2 million and $40.3 million (Pilger, 1928). The differences between U.S. and European manufacturing practices and equipment are evident in the automobile industry. European firms typically used less specialized MTs and did not introduce the moving assembly line until after World War I (Landes, 1969; Maxcy and Silberston, 1959; Bardou et al., 1982). Although the automobile industry was the largest consumer of MTs in the European countries, the scale of production at Ford or General Motors dwarfed the largest of the European manufacturers. Compare Ford's output of 2,000,000 units in 1925 with Opel's 43,000 units in 1928 (Sloan, 1965).

on imitation of British and U.S. MTs for the development of product designs (Milward and Saul, 1973). However, by the first decade of the twentieth century, several firms had acquired sophisticated capabilities in the design of general-purpose MTs and special-purpose equipment for the heavy engineering sectors. Although output grew at a formidable pace in that period, the German industry did not experience the process of horizontal specialization that occurred among the U.S. firms, nor did it focus as much on the development of special-purpose MTs (Verein Deutscher Werkzeugmaschinenfabriken, 1991).[5]

The differences in the stage of development of the U.S. and European manufacturing industries and those in the direction of innovation in MT design influenced the patterns of international trade.[6] Based on available accounts, it is likely that the U.S. firms maintained a clear technological advantage over both British and German competitors in the area of special-purpose MTs for mass-production and high-precision jobs. However, foreign trade was dominated by the demand for general-purpose MTs and specialized equipment for the heavy engineering industries. U.S., British, and German firms had achieved comparable design and performance standards in these product lines, so that competition was more intense. Lower prices and active marketing efforts allowed British and especially German firms to gain market shares in industrializing countries in Europe, South America, and Asia.[7] Indeed, in 1910 the German industry had become the world's largest exporter (Pilger, 1928).

[5] The institutional context of the German industry evolution was also quite different from the U.S. case. In particular, the local MT builders' association played an important role in facilitating the sharing of marketing and technical information among firms, establishing solid ties between the industry and the scientific research of the academic community and fostering the industry interests in the formulation of national economic policy (Verein Deutscher Werkzeugmaschinenfabriken, 1991).

[6] However, both U.S. and German firms were involved in the development of new cutting tool materials and electric motors (Rolt, 1965). Although these innovations had phenomenal consequences for MT productivity, their development did not have significant consequences on the relative competitiveness of national industries. In both cases, the innovations originated outside the industry and no significant international differences existed in terms of access to the relevant technologies.

[7] Contemporary analysts argue that the U.S. firms' international competitiveness was hurt by the lack of a consistent export strategy (Carden, 1909; Pilger, 1928; Fraser and Doriot, 1932; Wagoner, 1966). Although the international sales of MT firms were handled typically by independent agents, British and German MT firms were more active than their U.S. competitors soliciting business. Company representatives visited foreign plants to exchange information about new products and manufacturing needs, as well as to assist customers with the implementation of new equipment. These practices were usually neglected by the U.S. firms or adopted only when foreign orders were needed to compensate for the decline in domestic business (Carden, 1909; Wagoner, 1966).

In the aftermath of World War I, the international diffusion of industrial development promoted the emergence of indigenous capabilities in the design and manufacture of MTs. In addition to European countries like France, Italy, and Sweden, this process was slowly unfolding also in Japan, where MT production experienced a sustained growth in response to industry and military demand in the 1930s. Poor quality and limited productive capacity contributed to holding the import dependence at around 50% (Mitsubishi Economic Research Bureau, 1936), but the military needs provided the motivation for policy measures (Machine Tool Industry Act of 1938) aimed at supporting the domestic industry. Fiscal exemptions accompanied the definition of public standards in lathe design in order to facilitate the entry by small machine shops (Asahi, 1939).[8] Although output grew rapidly at the outset of World War II, the Japanese firms still lacked the technical capabilities of firms in the United States and the major producing countries in Europe (Carus and McNichols, 1944).

After World War II the world MT industry was dominated by the U.S. firms. The technological developments that the U.S. users had pioneered since earlier times found increasing diffusion among firms in other countries, and especially Europe. Accordingly, one trend in the postwar development of MT technology focused on the automation of mass-production manufacturing equipment, a trend that came to be known as Detroit automation (Carlsson, 1984) as it was dominated by the model of production typical of the automobile industry. However, the war had given a phenomenal impetus to the development of aircraft-related technology. Ushered by the invention of the jet engine at the end of the war, the growth of military and commercial aviation proceeded at a breathtaking pace and transformed the aircraft industry into one of the largest users of machine tools. With the aircraft industry's rapid growth, its manufacturing needs became a powerful influence on the direction of innovation in machine tool technology.

III. The Development of NC and the Emergence of Japanese Dominance

The area of innovation where the influence of the aircraft industry was greatest consisted of the development of automated systems for controlling the motion of machine tool components with a high degree of

[8] The S-type lathe design was the result of a joint project whose participants included the War Office, the Navy Department, the Department of Commerce and Industry, the Imperial University in Tokyo, and the five largest manufacturers of MTs (Friedman, 1988).

precision.[9] Research in this area led to the development of NC technology at the MIT Servomechanism Laboratory in 1952.

NC automates machining operations on the basis of numerical information stored on program tapes. Early on, the objective of the technical development work sponsored by the U.S. Air Force was to achieve the machinability of complex shapes which were impossible or too costly to produce with existing metal-cutting techniques (Noble, 1984; Reintijes, 1991). Through R&D funds and procurement contracts, the U.S. Air Force directed the development of NC toward sophisticated and costly machine tool applications of great interest for military aircraft manufacturing. The spillovers to other industries with less exacting requirements were far from automatic. A considerable amount of adaptive and innovative work was required in order to expand the range of commercially viable applications.

A wider diffusion of NC technology occurred after the mid-1970s when performance improvements and cost savings achieved thanks to the use of microprocessor-based controls made the adoption of NC technology profitable across the spectrum of manufacturing processes: from small- and medium-batch production to one-of-a-kind and large-batch manufacturing (Ashburn, 1978). The higher productivity that NC afforded to batch production created the conditions for users to adopt or strengthen competitive strategies based on greater product variety and short product cycles, rather than mass-production economies. The timing and sectoral patterns of this shift toward flexible manufacturing strategies differed in important ways across national economic areas as a result of differences in the structure of market demand and in the inherited areas of competitive strength of the national MT industries.

A. The United States

The development of NC tapped the resources of a sophisticated research university. However, transferring the technology from the laboratory to the shop floor proved difficult and its commercialization required MT firms to acquire novel capabilities in the design, manufacturing, and marketing of a radically new product.[10] In fact, the intended military use resulted in a very expensive and complex technology. Although the U.S.

[9] Early technical developments of this kind include tracer controls and the record-playback system developed jointly by General Electric, Giddings & Lewis, and Lockheed in 1948 (Noble, 1984).

[10] The MIT efforts at disseminating information about NC technology were followed by only a handful of projects from firms in the aircraft industry (Glen Martin, Bendix, and Lockheed). These consisted of either in-house projects or ad hoc collaborations with MT firms (Noble, 1984; Reintijes, 1991).

Air Force's procurement policy strengthened the incentives for NC adoption among its contractors, its effects were otherwise limited. The diffusion of the technology to commercial applications was hindered by its high cost, unreliability, and the fact that its implementation required users to change the organization of the manufacturing process. By contrast, its benefits were not altogether apparent outside the context of highly specific metalworking needs such as those of aircraft production. These factors contributed to curb the speed of NCMTs' diffusion outside applications with exacting accuracy and repeatability requirements throughout the 1960s.

During the 1970s it became increasingly clear that the industry's pioneering role in the development of NC had not resulted in the creation of broad first-mover advantages. This failure was connected to the users' weak demand for flexible manufacturing and the MT firms' lack of product development strategies aimed at the needs of the low end of the MT market.

Users' Adoption and the Development of NC Technology. After the conclusion of MIT's NC project, the U.S. Air Force used the instrument of procurement contracts to foster the diffusion of NCMTs. With the rise in the aircraft industry demand during the late 1950s, a growing number of firms entered the development of NC. The early diffusion occurred in high-end applications of the market. Soon though, the spreading interest in NC stimulated several MT builders and control firms to focus on cheaper applications (Fig. 5.2). Simple point-to-point (PTP)[11] or positioning controls were expected to be adequate for a large share of metalworking needs and to provide a significant saving in control system costs (Noble, 1984).

These expectations proved incorrect as during the 1960s the composition of the U.S. market demand shifted toward more complex and expensive application (Fig. 5.3).[12] This shift documents in part the crucial influence of the aircraft industry's demand for NCMTs. A number of surveys and the commentary about the development of the technology from engineers at MT and control system firms provide additional and important insights on the factors underlying the evolution of the U.S. NCMTs' market.

[11] In PTP systems, the tool is disengaged from the metal part when the control signals position the tool or worktable. Continuous path (CP) systems control tool and worktable motions while the tool is cutting.

[12] During the early 1960s, shipments of PTP systems exceeded those of CP controls (both in value and in unit terms). By 1967, however, CP controls accounted for more than 50% of the value of domestic shipments. In 1971 the number of NCMT units equipped with CP control exceeded 50% of domestic unit shipments.

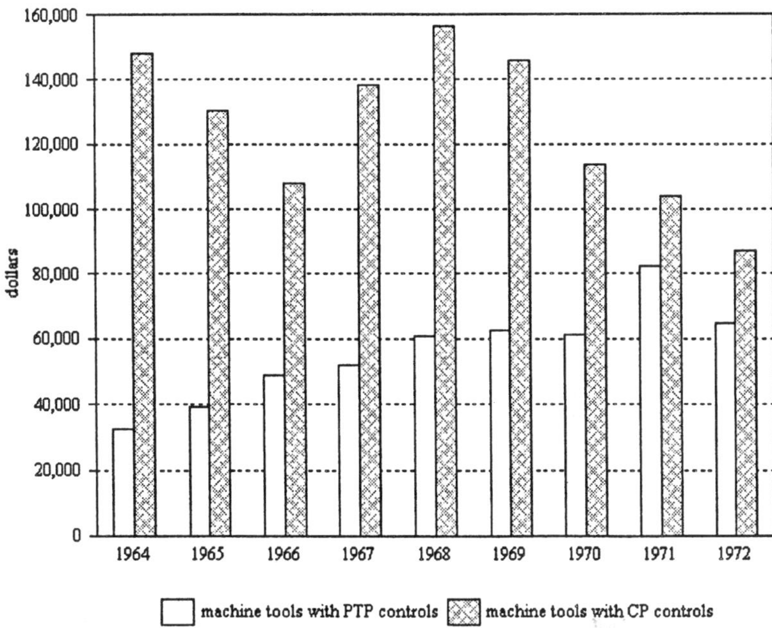

Figure 5.2. Average Price of U.S. Machine Tools Equipped with NC by Type of Control System (1964–1972). *Source: Current Industrial Reports Series MQ-35W* (1965–1973).

One such concerns the mismatch between users' expectations and the state of the technology during the early 1960s. At that time, the complexity and cost of NC systems as well as the poorly accomplished adaptation of MT designs to NC limited the areas of metalworking where NC proved profitable. Yet, several engineers argued that the range of MT types and metalworking plants where NC was implemented likely failed to reflect these limits (Leone, 1967; J. Rosenberg, 1963; Greening, 1971) because of a mismatch between users' expectations and the actual shopfloor performance of NCMTs.[13] As a result, the financial outcomes of adoption were often disappointing.

The information on the profitability of the technology arising from the experience of early adopters can be presumed to have played an

[13] Control vendors rushed to the market with controls that had not been tested in a production setting (Leone, 1967). Further, the lack of appropriate coordination between the design and manufacturing functions of MT and control unit builders caused malfunctions that were haphazardly dealt with ex post or design imperfections that rendered the accuracy of NCMTs inferior to the rated performance of the control system (J. Rosenberg, 1963). As a result, users faced higher average downtime than expected (Sandford, 1970).

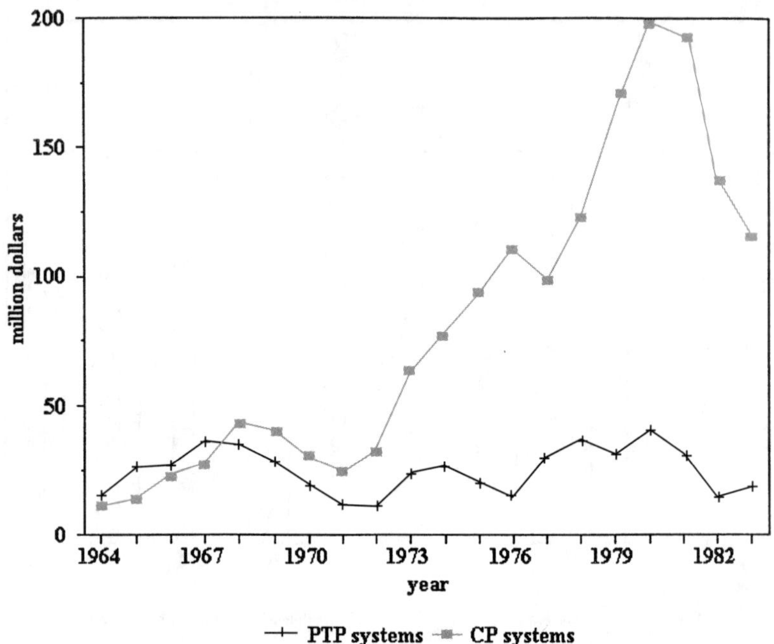

Figure 5.3. U.S. Shipments of NC Units by Type of Control (1964–1983). *Source: Current Industrial Reports Series MQ-35W* (1965–1973) for 1964–1972 data; *Current Industrial Reports Series MA-36A* (1976–1984) for 1975–1983 data; author's estimates for 1973–1974.

important role in fostering the observed shift in the balance of NCMTs' shipments toward more complex applications catering to sophisticated metalworking users.[14] Thus, when much improved and cheaper solid-state components became available throughout the 1960s, the firms in the industry responded to the evolution of market demand in an adaptive fashion, focusing their innovative efforts on the performance of more complex NC systems and paying little attention to the needs of less sophisticated users (Collis, 1988; Hatschek and Schaffer, 1973).

[14] This phenomenon is reflected in the interindustry differences in the rate of adoption. During the years 1954–1963, investment in NC was $278 million. The aircraft industry led among all SIC three-digit industries with $78.8 million, followed by the demand from government, foreign buyers, and educational institutions with $32.2 million. Metalworking machinery was third ($27.6 million), while motor vehicles and equipment invested $18.3 million. Between 1964 and 1968, the aircraft industry purchased an additional 1,718 units, the metalworking machinery group 1,372, the machine shops industry purchased 840, special industrial machinery 677, and the communications equipment industry 672. The federal government purchased at least another 1,404 units, the great majority of which were likely installed at plants in the aircraft industry (U.S. Department of Commerce, 1969).

According to this interpretation, the burden of the explanation for the U.S. firms' failure to perceive a latent demand for low-cost NCMTs is placed on the response of their innovative strategy to the evolving conditions of market demand and technological opportunity. Although the problems encountered by many early (and often poorly informed) adopters of NC may be considered to be typical of all new technologies, one cannot avoid questioning why the U.S. firms' innovative strategies failed to pursue improvements of the technology such as to preempt the rise in MT imports.

Innovative Strategies of the U.S. Machine Tool Firms and Specialized Control Suppliers. The analysis of the U.S. firms' product development strategies cannot be severed from a broader discussion of the evolution of the industry's vertical structure and the conditions of technological opportunity. NC was a radical innovation in MT technology, whose development required capabilities in electronics that were not common among MT firms. Thus, the commercialization of NCMTs raised important issues of business strategy concerning how to cope with the complementarities among the relevant capabilities (Teece, 1986).

Early innovators included large electronics firms and small specialized control equipment suppliers. None among these considered in-house development or acquisition of complementary capabilities in MT design, manufacturing, and marketing. Conversely, toward the end of the 1950s several MT firms entered the development of NC control systems, including a handful of manufacturers with diversified product lines and builders of specialized equipment.[15] In general, these development efforts focused on PTP control systems.

A key consideration in the MT firms' evaluation of the integration strategy was the assessment of their ability to keep pace with technological developments at specialized electronics firms. The risks involved were enhanced by the rapid introduction of new solid-state devices and the shifting pattern of demand from PTP to more complex continuous path (CP) systems during the 1960s. Accordingly, only four MT firms (Cincinnati Milling, Giddings & Lewis, Pratt & Whitney, and Warner & Swasey) continued to make exclusive use of in-house control technology, while specialized suppliers dominated the rest of the market.

The most important benefit of integration was the possibility of enhancing system performance by controlling the technical inter-

[15] At the 1960 Chicago Machine Tool Show, 40 MT firms displayed NC equipment (*American Machinist*, 1960). Of these, 12 companies featured their own NC systems, while the others used the controls of 15 specialized firms. A 1964 buyer's guide includes 196 NCMTs and 75 control system lines from 49 manufacturers (*American Machinist*, 1964).

dependence between control system and MT designs.[16] Among the firms that did not integrate, their relationship with control suppliers did not depart significantly from a pattern of arm's-length contracting. This was largely a consequence of the fact that the MT builders regarded the choice of control units to be the customers' prerogative. Thus, they usually offered several control options on their products, while the control supplier retained responsibility for interfacing, customer training, and maintenance. These practices preserved enough flexibility to meet consumers' demands but had little effect on achieving cost savings through standardization and volume purchases.[17]

The MT builders' heterogeneous response to the make-or-buy decision reflected firm-level differences in the perceived strategic relevance of developing in-house capabilities in the design and manufacture of the controls vis-à-vis the attendant risks. The development of soft-wired controls based on general-purpose minicomputers (later microcomputers or programmable controllers) and specialized application software reduced considerably the technical obstacles to the design and manufacturing of controls. From the late 1960s and throughout the 1970s, competition in the control system business became more intense as a new cohort of specialized firms entered the industry and a growing number of MT firms acquired internal capabilities.[18]

The debate accompanying the trend toward vertical integration (Wilson, 1970; 1972) and some builders' retrospective comments discussed in Sciberras and Payne (1985) suggest that the competitive significance of integration was difficult to assess. In any case, the primary

[16] Areas of interdependence included the coupling of the control circuitry with the servomechanisms driving the spindle or worktable (the latter could be one of several types of AC or DC electric motors and hydraulic motors) and the feed-back loop from MT parts to control system (different measuring elements could be used and applied to different mechanical components of the MT).

[17] This practice was reasonable (if not fully rational) in light of the emergence of proprietary standards in control systems and computer programs for tape preparation during the 1960s. The preparation of part programs required first the use of a NC computer program to produce a generalized instruction format and then the use of a computer program called postprocessor to produce an instruction format specialized to the individual control unit–MT pair. Several public or proprietary NC programs existed for specific computers, while the postprocessors were typically developed by either the MT firms or by the users themselves (Howe, 1969). Repeat buyers of NCMTs were likely to have sunk specific investments in assets, capabilities, and information about particular controls and programming languages. Accordingly, the MT firms' decision to let the customer decide was intendedly rational, given that standardizing on one control type could have meant losing access to a portion of the potential market (Mazzoleni, 1997).

[18] Among the firms that developed soft-wired controls in the early 1970s were Kearney & Trecker (leader in machining centers) and Sundstrand. It is also worth noting that at the same time, MT firms that had an internal capability (including Warner & Swasey and Pratt & Whitney) began to offer other controls.

motivation for integrating was the MT builders' desire to develop innovative NCMT designs without depending on specialized suppliers. The results of this trend were the growth of the captive market for NC systems and the fragmentation of market share.[19]

While the emergent technological opportunities fostered performance improvements and intense market competition in the high end of the market, the development of low-cost controls for basic general-purpose MTs lagged behind.[20] Certainly, an important factor was that the high end of the market proved profitable throughout the late 1960s in part because of large orders from the U.S. Department of Defense. By contrast, in 1971 the Small Business Administration canceled a loan program for investment in NCMTs because of the lack of interest from potential users. Only during the recession of the early 1970s were the control suppliers' development strategies aimed at the latent demand for NCMTs from such users as job shops working for the automobile manufacturers.[21]

The commercial outcomes of these efforts were thwarted early on by the unstable market conditions prevailing during the years 1973–1975. The demand for new equipment did not enter a stable expansion until 1976, when the automobile sector invested heavily in equipment for producing new smaller engines. At that juncture the demand for

[19] The increased competition in the control system business motivated the exit of specialized vendors such as Sperry Vickers and Superior Electric in 1976. However, market concentration remained low. General Electric, the leading supplier during the 1960s and part of the 1970s, experienced a steady decline in its market share to 13% in 1981. Allen-Bradley's share was 16% and General Numeric's 8%. In the same year, Cincinnati Milacron was the largest captive vendor, with a 12% share, followed by Bridgeport with 10% (Fong, 1996). A rough estimate of the MT industry's dependence on specialized suppliers of NC is the ratio of MT firms' expenditure on NC systems and the total value of NC systems shipped by U.S. firms. This ratio declined from about 64% in 1972 to 51% in 1977 and 23% in 1982 (estimates based on data from *Census of Manufactures*, 1972, 1977, 1982, and *Current Industrial Reports Series MA-36A*, 1973, 1978, 1983).

[20] A comparison with the trajectory of technology development pursued in Japan raises an interesting puzzle concerning the limited diffusion of low-cost open-loop controls in the U.S. market. Superior Electric, the U.S. firm that undertook the development of open-loop controls in the mid-1960s, left the industry in 1976 after having incurred significant losses. The firm's difficulties in gaining access to the market were due at least in part to the lack of support from MT firms (Mazzoleni, 1997).

[21] For example, during the second half of the 1960s General Electric's technology development focused on direct numerical control, providing centralized control of multiple MTs. Acquisition costs and poor reliability frustrated this technology's market success. In the early 1970s General Electric (as well as Bendix and Allen-Bradley) directed its development efforts to the low-cost segment of the market. The new product line featured hard-wired controls. General Electric retained this design until the late 1970s, well after it had become evident that soft-wired controls would be the dominant design (Sciberras and Payne, 1985).

NCMTs grew considerably across all sectors (including the job shop industry). Conforming to a traditional pattern, the rising demand strained the domestic industry's productive capacity and increased the share of imports. Domestic builders' backlog of orders grew to almost two years of output and impatient buyers began to turn to standardized imported NCMTs available for prompt delivery from the U.S. distributors. By 1981 imports accounted for 32.7% of domestic consumption of NCMTs.

Although the initial motivation to purchase foreign (mainly Japanese) NCMTs was the short delivery time, U.S. users soon realized that the cost and performance were often superior to those of domestic products. The narrowing or reversal of the technology gap between U.S. and foreign NCMTs occurred in both the area of NC controls and that of MT design.[22] The largest U.S. control firms failed to adopt microprocessor-based soft-wired controls until 1979 (Sciberras and Payne, 1985). The flaws of the U.S. firms' innovative record were particularly conspicuous in the area of low-cost general-purpose equipment such as NC turning and machining centers.

Perhaps even more important is the fact that the U.S. firms failed to anticipate changes in the pattern of competition in the NCMTs. The penchant for manufacturing of customized equipment prevented the U.S. MT firms from achieving scale and standardization economies. It also increased the complexity of managing production and shipment schedules, which turned out to be a liability when the surging demand put pressure on firms' productive capacity. In the mid-1970s the leading Japanese firms began to develop manufacturing capabilities for the large-volume production of limited variations on their basic designs, multifunctional equipment like turning and machining centers.[23] Standardization enabled firms to achieve cost savings and to offer rapid delivery to the users. The diffusion of these kinds of MTs grew at a rapid pace at the end of the decade and it was the main driver of the growth in U.S. imports of NCMTs.

[22] As mentioned, starting in 1976 General Numeric began to sell Fanuc's control systems on the U.S. market; its share of that market was reportedly 8% in 1981 (Fong, 1996). At the 1980 International Machine Tool Show General Numeric controls were displayed on about twice as many MTs as General Electric's or Allen-Bradley's.

[23] Holland (1989) provides evidence of the failure to enact such strategy at Burgmaster, a U.S. firm whose success was built on a turret drill designed in the mid-1950s. Burgmaster's attempt to create a low-price NC turret drill for mass production in the late 1960s was abandoned shortly after its introduction in the U.S. market. Innovative NCMT designs (the horizontal and vertical machining centers) were first introduced in 1976. Interestingly, Yamazaki, a Japanese lathe builder that had been granted a manufacturing license on Burgmaster's NC turret drills, commercialized its machining centers also in 1976 for 50% less than Burgmaster's price.

B. Japan

The emergence of the Japanese dominance in the MT industry occurred during the second half of the 1970s. However, for much of the postwar period the technical advances of Japanese industry drew on technology licensing from European and U.S. firms (Sciberras and Payne, 1985; Fransman, 1986). This transfer of technology was stimulated by the Ministry of International Trade and Industry (MITI) through tariff protection and a ban on foreign direct investment (Machinery Promotion Law of 1956). MITI also organized foreign technology flows through an approval system for companies' licensing agreements (Friedman, 1988).

Against the backdrop of such policy measures, early Japanese efforts in the area of NC development drew on scientific and technological knowledge originating from the MIT ServoLab and U.S. licensors. However, these efforts aimed at adapting licensed technologies to the needs of the domestic market and the product specialization of the local industry.

The Japanese MT output consisted mostly of small general-purpose MTs. Accordingly, NC development was directed toward exploiting its potential advantages for manufacturing flexibility and savings in labor costs, rather than accuracy and repeatability. As the development work proceeded, several Japanese firms acquired distinctive capabilities in the design of general-purpose NCMTs such as lathes and machining centers, and in large-volume production. These capabilities were crucial in supporting the export strategy undertaken by the Japanese firms in the second half of the 1970s.

The most important factors in the Japanese MT industry's success were (a) the rapid accumulation of technical capabilities in the application of NC to the low-cost general-purpose MTs in which the industry was specialized; (b) the responsiveness to changes in demand achieved as a result of the coordination between the dominant control supplier, Fanuc, and the domestic MT builders; (c) the adoption of manufacturing strategies focusing on the large-volume production of relatively standardized MTs in the 1970s.

The Application of NC to Low-Cost General-Purpose Machine Tools. The research on NC began in 1955 at two universities (Tokyo Institute of Technology and Tokyo University), followed by a development project at the Mechanical Engineering Laboratory of MITI, and two collaborative projects from industry involving the electrical equipment firm Fujitsu, in conjunction with two MT builders, Makino and Hitachi Seiki (Fransman, 1986; Friedman, 1988). By then Fujitsu had established a specialized division, Fanuc, devoted to the development of NC and had obtained a controlling patent on an open-loop control system based on the stepping motor in 1959. Although its commercialization began only later, during the early 1960s Fanuc engaged in collaborations with MT firms and in-house projects and pursued a small-scale entry into the MT market in order to accumulate experience with the design and manufacturing.

Fujitsu was followed by other firms such as Oki Electric, Mitsubishi Electric, and Toshiba, which acquired technological licenses from Bendix, General Electric, and Kearney & Trecker during the early 1960s. Progress occurred also in MT design, particularly in the area of machining centers.[24] The number of firms involved in the production of NCMTs or related prototyping activities reached about 60 by the end of the 1960s. The focus of these development efforts was on the application of NC to low-cost machinery, which required that sophisticated performance be traded for cost reductions. These needs were met adequately by the open-loop technology developed by Fujitsu-Fanuc, which in fact dominated the development efforts and the market for controls.[25]

The advances in technology accompanied the growing diffusion of NCMTs. Unit output grew from 39 units in 1965 to 388 in 1968, and 1,451 in 1970. Much of this growth concentrated on NC lathes and machining centers. The former's share of output grew from less than 5% in 1967 to 40% by 1970, with the latter accounting for another 23%. In these product areas a handful of firms upgraded their designs and improved the quality of their manufacturing processes, narrowing the technological gap with the leading U.S. and European firms. Domestic demand was dominated by the automobile and the general machinery industries. Fanuc emerged as the leading supplier of controls with market shares hovering around 90% (Shomura, 1969).

Responsiveness to Changes in Market Demand. The concentration in the control systems' market arguably brought along numerous benefits. The use of Fanuc's controls as standard on the Japanese NCMTs reduced the

[24] Hitachi Seiki realized the first exemplars in 1962 although production was postponed because of insufficient demand. Commercialization of machining centers started again in 1966. In 1968, Makino Milling developed an automatic tool changer different from the design patented by the U.S. firm Kearney & Trecker (*Industrial Japan*, 1969, pp. 65–68).

[25] The rapidly growing technical competences of firms like Fanuc, Oki, Mitsubishi, and Toshiba gained international recognition for the development of direct numerical control systems (Ashburn, 1988). The extent of the advances was sufficient to reorient the technology flows, as Japanese firms began to export licenses. In particular, Fujitsu Fanuc licensed Siemens for the manufacturing and marketing of stepping motors and open-loop controls.

builders' (or users' as the case may be) need to develop a variety of post-processor programs (see note 17). It also promoted the improvement of MT performance by standardizing the characteristics of the drives controlling worktable and spindle motions. The users could also benefit from the reduced cost of maintaining spare parts and of developing basic troubleshooting competencies.

Fanuc's sales volume provided it with the incentive to engage in the development of a modular design that could be easily configured for individual MT applications. This design strategy facilitated production planning and the production of standardized components in large volumes. Yet, the potential benefits of these strategies could not have materialized without a corresponding commitment from the MT builders to standardize equipment designs. Contrary to the U.S. industry, in which customized equipment was actually the more profitable business for many firms, the Japanese firms were specialized in the production of standard general-purpose designs. The transition to production of standardized NC equipment did not require a major change in the manufacturing and marketing practices of the MT firms.

Of course, the emergence of a dominant design supplied by a single firm, Fanuc, exposed MT firms to the hazards of unilateral technological dependence and to the risk of complacency by Fanuc. With respect to the former, it is worth noticing that other firms (including MT builders) maintained or developed internal capabilities in NC technology and that Fanuc did not attempt to enter the MT business directly. With respect to the latter, Fanuc proved to be extraordinarily able to adapt its control system technology and design to emergent users' needs and technological opportunities (Ashburn, 1974; Inaba, 1992).

Indeed, the diffuse interactions with MT builders and users that Fanuc enjoyed by virtue of its quasi-monopoly position provided the company with broad informational feedback to steer the course of its innovative strategy. The information flows were strengthened further by the intracorporate grouping tying MT users and builders.[26] These features of the industry structure proved very important to allow the domestic MT firms to respond in a timely manner to the changes in the focus of investment demand.

The diffusion of NC gained momentum in the early 1970s, when the demand began to reflect ongoing changes in the manufacturing needs of the user industries. The latter's growth prospects began to change in the late 1960s (*Industrial Review of Japan*, 1971, pp. 51–53). The international

[26] Examples include Toyoda Machine Works, Toshiba, Fanuc, and Mitsubishi. Lee (1996) argues that the Japanese users played a very important role in MT innovation, very often through the intracorporate links to MT builders.

competitiveness of firms in the automotive and electrical machinery industries had come to depend increasingly on improved quality, product differentiation, and responsiveness to customer demand. These goals called for measures to achieve productivity growth by enhancing the firms' manufacturing flexibility, rather than by pursuing scale economies. A broad rationalization of production was undertaken, aimed at exploiting the flexibility of manufacturing processes organized through networks of subcontractors. The participation of the small and medium-size firms in the pursuit of those goals constituted the foundation for the widening base of NCMTs' adopters. The onset of these changes strengthened the economic incentives for the MT industry to foster the development and diffusion of NC equipment, while retreating from the production of more basic MTs.

Several firms, including Shin Nippon Koki, Yaskawa, and Toyoda, entered the NC market in the early 1970s, although their success at ousting Fanuc from its leadership position was very limited. Only one large MT firm, Okuma, undertook in-house production of control units. The success of new entrants was curbed by Fanuc's innovative performance and its responsiveness to changing cost conditions and technological opportunities. In particular, Fanuc was the first large control supplier to develop a microprocessor-based system whose benefits ranged from easier programming to simpler design, greater reliability, and lower cost. Although the new computer numerical control (CNC) technology favored the entry of several builders in the production of control units (in-house production accounted for 27.2% in 1976),[27] Fanuc continued to dominate the business with Mitsubishi far back as a runner-up (cumulative production at these two firms was in a ratio of 8 to 1).

The Strategy of Large-Volume Production of Basic Designs. In the MT business, several firms designed their market strategies around the high-volume production of simple MTs, and beginning in the mid-1970s, of CNC lathes and machining centers.[28] These changes were spurred by the

[27] Six of them in 1977, namely, Okuma Machinery Works, Japax Inc., Enshu, Hitachi Seiki, Washino Machine, and Nippei Industry (Fujimoto, 1977).

[28] Yamazaki, a leading firm in the segment of ordinary lathes since the early 1960s, had decidedly moved toward the production of small NC lathes first and NC machining centers later. Operating under licenses from the U.S. firms Strippit and Burgmaster, Yamazaki had become one of the largest MT firms in Japan. In an effort to foster the systematic development of export markets, Yamazaki established its own distribution and servicing network in the United States as early as 1968 (Holland, 1989). Other leading firms (Ikegai, Hitachi Seiki, Okuma, and Makino Milling Machine) also shifted their product focus increasingly toward NCMTs and rationalized their production activities by subcontracting to smaller firms or abandoning altogether the production of conventional designs (JETRO, 1975).

accelerating rationalization of manufacturing activity that followed the rise in energy prices at the end of 1973. During the recession that began in 1975, the industry suffered from severe problems of excess capacity that resulted in bankruptcies and drastic employment reductions. The value of production fell by 36% in 1975 (about 50% in units) and remained stable at that level in 1976. The market segment in which the effects of the recession were less severe was NCMTs, since the investment consisted mainly of equipment upgrades that could reduce the users' manpower needs. The expectation of continuing growth in that market segment induced a number of firms to refocus their product mix on low-cost standard NCMTs for the domestic and export markets. In particular, they targeted the U.S. market, where the growth of domestic investment from 1975 promised to create favorable conditions for foreign firms (Japan External Trade Organization, 1975). Accordingly, the Japanese firms invested in complementary assets such as overseas distribution and service centers, and in a few cases assembly plants.

In 1976, Fanuc and Siemens established a joint venture company in the United States, General Numeric. Yamazaki added a plant for knocked-down assembly to its marketing and aftersale assistance center, first in the United States, and later in Europe. Other firms, including Okuma, Mori Seiki, Makino Milling, Ikegai, and Hitachi Seiki, also established subsidiaries abroad. Still others entered marketing and technological licensing agreements with U.S. or German firms or established manufacturing joint ventures with them (Nagasawa, 1976; Tanaka, 1977). For many of these firms, access to the U.S. users came increasingly through independent distributors, who were eager to meet the demand with foreign equipment given the long lead times required by the U.S. MT builders.

The success of the Japanese firms rested on competitive pricing of standardized general-purpose equipment. High-volume production contributed to cost reductions through scale and learning economies, but also to the Japanese firms' ability to offer attractive delivery terms. As the U.S. firms' backlogs grew to more than a year's production, the Japanese MTs stockpiled at owned or independent distribution centers in the United States were ready to be delivered to impatient buyers. The export ratio for the industry jumped from 16.1% in 1974 to 26.7% in 1975 and 41.8% in 1976. Total exports of metalcutting equipment grew from $207.6 million in 1975 to $942.8 in 1979 and $1,409.2 in 1981. After the recession years, the Japanese demand for MTs increased rapidly particularly because of the investment by small and medium-sized firms. By 1980 64% of domestic investment in NCMTs came from those firms (fewer than 300 employees), up from about 28% in 1970 (Jacobsson, 1986).

C. The European Countries

The effects of the growing competitiveness of the Japanese industry were considerably weaker for the European firms. The apparent reason is that the Japanese firms' export strategy targeted the U.S. market, the world's largest, rather than the European ones. However, this choice had to do with the limited diffusion of NC among European users and the nature of the local industry's capabilities in the areas of NC and conventional MTs.

The development of NCMTs had begun in several European nations, although at different times. France and Great Britain were the pioneers, largely because of the presence of a military aircraft industry. In both countries, the pattern of technology development shared with the U.S. case a strong emphasis on the machining precision afforded by NC. The British case illustrates the consequences on the rate and direction of innovation stemming from the declining competitiveness of domestic users. From the late 1960s and early 1970s, the production of NCMTs has diffused to other European countries, most significantly Germany, Sweden, and Italy. Not until the 1980s did the capabilities of those industries in the area of NC become a significant aspect of their competitive strategies. The export performance of German and Italian firms rested instead on capabilities in specialized MT development honed by their interactions with users. The market focus of these firms delayed the adoption of NC in their product designs until the late 1970s, but also it reduced the competitive threats posed by the technological developments in Japan.

In the United Kingdom the development of NC had begun by the mid-1950s. The presence of a strong military demand, particularly in the aircraft industry, directed innovation toward the realization of sophisticated controls by specialized electronic firms (including Ferranti, Plessey, and GEC). Although this sustained the growth of NCMTs output during the 1960s, the failure to broaden the market constrained growth opportunities in the 1970s. The problems of the British MT industry were, to a significant extent, related to those faced by the domestic automobile industry, the largest user of British MTs, and the engineering industries more generally. The weakness of internal demand provided very tenuous incentives for MT innovation, and the British firms increasingly concentrated on the production of standardized conventional MTs, which was subject to competition from less industrialized countries (UNIDO, 1984).

During the 1970s, the government support of R&D was mainly directed to universities and failed to engage users in the development of commercially successful NCMTs.

The German MT industry had grown to dominate the export markets and had become the world's largest producer in 1970. Although the industry products remained competitive in world markets throughout the decade, the continuing strengths of the German industry relied on distinctive capabilities in the production of special-purpose MTs, such as gear-cutting, grinding, and metal-forming equipment (MIT Commission, 1989; Englmann et al., 1994). The limited diffusion of NC until the mid-1970s reflected the difficulties of developing NC applications for the specialized equipment in which the German firms excelled. Early adopters of NC among MT firms specialized in the production of lathes and procured the controls from outside suppliers, including Siemens (which in fact was licensed to market Fanuc's open-loop controls), AEG (also producing open-loop controls), and Bendix-licensee Bosch. The growth of the internal market for NCMTs accelerated with the introduction of microprocessor-based NC in 1976 (Dreher and Lay, 1992). As internal demand grew, so did imports from Japan. The domestic builders were at a disadvantage in the low-cost market segment because of their inferior design capabilities. Further, as more and more builders of general-purpose MTs attempted the transition to NC, they found insufficient cooperation from Siemens and began turning to Fanuc (Sciberras and Payne, 1985).

A similar pattern emerged in Italy, whose share of world output tripled between 1965 and 1980 (about 6.5%). Its domestic market, dominated by users from the automobile, electrical appliances, office machines, and mechanical engineering industries, consisted of specialized MTs tailored to customers' needs for the most part (Zanfei, 1994). The capabilities developed in the custom engineering of MTs enabled the Italian industry to improve its export performance from the early 1970s. At that time, the diffusion of NC also began to grow as larger (Olivetti) and smaller (CEA, ECS, San Giorgio) electronic firms undertook the development of specialized controls for local MT builders. The fragmentation and limited size of the domestic market did not nurture the emergence of a dominant firm, although specialized makers served market niches. General-purpose MT builders who entered the production of NC equipment in the late 1970s and 1980s were likely to buy controls from foreign firms, like Siemens and Fanuc. However, the growing competitiveness of the Italian MT industry was strongly focused on the export of specialized equipment and was significantly influenced only later by the diffusion of NC.

IV. Innovation, Firm Strategy, and National Competitiveness in the 1980s

The growth of the world market for NCMTs gained momentum during the 1980s as a result of two trends. On the supply side, progress in control technology and MT designs increased the attractiveness of NCMTs relative to conventional equipment across a wider spectrum of machining operations. Features like simplified programming and maintenance, increased reliability, faster metal removal, modular designs, and declining costs made NCMTs a plausible substitute for simple machines like engine lathes as well as for production machines like turret lathes. Besides its applications to stand-alone equipment, CNC was linked with robotics and handling equipment in the development of systemic approaches to automation, such as flexible manufacturing systems (FMS) and cells (FMCs).[29] The improvements in control technology also led to innovations in other component technologies and materials, according to a recurrent pattern in the industry (N. Rosenberg, 1976).

On the demand side, the evolving nature of global competition in large using industries (from automobile to electrical equipment) fostered a gradual transformation of the manufacturing strategies in the metalworking industries. Objectives like inventory reduction, quality control, and shorter product cycles became a common concern for manufacturing establishments across firms in the United States, Europe, and Japan. Notwithstanding the existence and importance of national and sectoral differences in the extent and methods by which these objectives were pursued, it is fair to say that during the 1980s the competitive strategies of U.S., European, and Japanese companies were characterized by an increasing quest for manufacturing flexibility and a movement toward small- and medium-batch production runs. These trends led to a convergence of MT needs toward NC applications.

As discussed in the next subsections, the competitive environment differed across market segments (see the taxonomy in Table 5.4) and important differences emerged in the nature of the firms' strategies and of their distinctive capabilities (Ehrnberg and Jacobsson, 1993). The Japanese firms continued to focus on standardized general-purpose equipment, in which their capabilities were the basis of competitive advantage.

[29] The distinction between FMCs and FMSs is ambiguous. It hinges on the number of MTs linked. By this measure, a FMS includes more than three MTs. Of course, there is no upper limit to the number of MTs. FMSs can be extremely expensive installations, especially when their implementation has a large engineering component. According to Bessant and Haywood (1991), MTs represent on average 35–40% (50–55%) of the total FMS (FMC) cost.

Table 5.4. *Segments of Market for Numerically Controlled Metalworking Equipment*

general purpose stand-alone NCMTs machining centers turning centers	general purpose FMS and FMC systems for rotational parts system for prismatic parts
special purpose stand-alone NCMTs jig-borers gear-cutting laser cutting electro-discharge grinders	special-purpose systems flexible transfer lines FMS using special purpose equipment

Competition in that market segment came predominantly from Taiwanese and South Korean firms. The European firms were more successful at undertaking the application of NC to specialized machining needs (including customized general-purpose and special-purpose equipment, in systemic or stand-alone configuration). The U.S. industry's response to the changing nature of the market was impaired by the appreciation of the dollar until the mid-1980s. While exits from the industry became widespread, the surviving firms concentrated on the high end of the market for specialized applications. Only in the second half of the decade did the trade restrictions imposed by the Reagan administration provide an opportunity for U.S. firms to create a niche in standard low-cost equipment.

A. Standardized CNC Machine Tools: Japan's First-Mover Advantages

As the global market for standard CNC lathes and machining centers continued to grow during the 1980s, the Japanese industry exploited its first-mover advantages. The most successful firms (Okuma, Yamazaki, Mori Seiki, Hitachi Seiki) pursued a strategy of cost leadership, supported by scale economies and investment in complementary assets. Furthermore, their competitive position in the United States, their largest export market, was strengthened by the evolution of the dollar–yen exchange rate. By the mid-1980s, the yearly output of the leading Japanese producers of CNC lathes and machining centers was roughly four and two times larger, respectively, than that of the largest European and U.S. firms (Sciberras and Payne, 1985).[30]

The Japanese firms continued to pursue innovations in their product designs and their manufacturing processes. With respect to the latter, it is notable that the largest Japanese builders adopted FMSs shortly after the conclusion of a cooperative research project sponsored by the MITI in the early 1980s.[31] The new process technology enabled the Japanese firms to provide some degree of standardized customization on their products and to reduce the length of product cycles from about eight years in the late 1970s to three years (Sciberras and Payne,

[30] Jacobsson (1986) estimates economies of scale on the order of a 60% reduction in unit costs as output of CNC lathes grows from 100 units per year to about 1,000.

[31] Started in 1976, this project included participants such as Fanuc, four industrial machinery firms, nine MT builders, and seven electronics firms (Collis, 1988). Although the FMS realized by the project was too complex and sophisticated, the MT builders acquired knowledge that supported the development of simpler systems. These were first installed in-house for the production of NCMTs. Only later they were commercialized to outside firms.

1985), thus raising the hurdles faced by competitors attempting to enter this market segment.

By the mid-1980s, Japanese products accounted for about 50% of the U.S. consumption of CNC turning and machining centers. In the early 1980s, the U.S. industry had already urged the government to adopt protectionist measures that could halt the decline of its share of the domestic market. Export restrictions were agreed to in 1986. Their effects and those of the adverse dynamics of the exchange rate in the second half of the 1980s were mitigated by the direct foreign investment in assembly and manufacturing facilities undertaken by many Japanese builders. An effect of the quotas set in the Voluntary Restraint Agreement (VRA) was to push the Japanese exports toward higher-priced models, a trend that had already been triggered by the increased competition from Taiwanese manufacturers in the more basic product lines.

B. Collapse and Recovery in the U.S. Industry

The U.S. industry collapsed during the first half of the 1980s. During the recession of 1981–1983, domestic shipments fell from about $5 billion to $2 billion. The macroeconomic conditions aggravated the crisis of the U.S. MT industry, as high interest rates and the appreciation of the dollar made it increasingly difficult for the local firms to invest in new process technology or product development. The imports' share of domestic consumption continued to grow, reaching 49.8% in 1986 (59.4% for NCMTs). The difficulties in which the industry was mired led to increasingly open requests for intervention by the government. Although until 1986 no government policy initiatives were specifically geared to the MT industry, legislation passed during the first half of the 1980s attempted to halt what was a broader crisis of the U.S. manufacturing industries.

Two areas of intervention were the reduction of antitrust restrictions to joint research activities by manufacturing firms and the creation of institutional mechanisms to harness the country's research infrastructure to the innovative needs of industry.[32] The significance of these actions with respect to the conduct of MT firms was limited indeed. The relaxation of the antitrust constraint did not remove a binding constraint on cooperative research in the MT industry. To start with, industry

[32] However, in 1980 the U.S. Department of Justice had stated that joint ventures for basic research were exempt from antitrust constraints (U.S. Dept. of Justice, 1990). The National Cooperative Research Act of 1984 extended the range of research activities that could be jointly undertaken without violating the antitrust laws.

concentration was quite low and cooperative efforts would not have triggered antitrust action. Even more important, the extent of R&D cooperation among MT firms was negligible. Much of their R&D activity focused on product development and applied research, and cooperative projects were typically undertaken with using firms. Overall, MT firms were not at all eager to establish the conditions for intraindustry cooperation in technology development and often voiced their lack of interest in the latter (Ashburn, 1984).[33]

Rather, a fraction of the U.S. MT builders asked for trade protection from the allegedly unfair practices of the Japanese firms. These demands culminated in a petition filed in 1982 by Houdaille, a conglomerate controlling several MT firms (Holland, 1989). The following year the National Machine Tool Builders Association filed another petition for industry protection. As mentioned before, these petitions were turned down by the Reagan administration. However, the perceived threat of U.S. protectionist measures led to action by the Japanese competitors.

In 1978 the Japanese MITI established an export cartel setting floor prices in U.S. dollars for MTs to preempt dumping charges. The concern with possible import restrictions in the United States induced several Japanese firms to consider investing in manufacturing facilities there. Following Yamazaki (which established its first U.S. assembly plant in 1974), other Japanese firms, including Hitachi Seiki, Makino Milling, and Okuma, undertook direct investment in U.S. manufacturing facilities during the first half of the 1980s.[34]

Direct investment in the U.S. market was not the only response to the threat of protectionist policies. Many firms were eager to license U.S. firms to manufacture their own product lines for the U.S. market. In fact, finding potential licensees in the U.S. market became increasingly easy. The domestic recession and the declining competitiveness vis-a-vis foreign competitors forced struggling U.S. builders to adapt to the new market conditions. The motivations for acquiring licenses from foreign firms were varied. Some firms aimed at expanding the product

[33] According to the *American Machinist*, the National Machine Tool Builders Association responded very dispassionately to the news that the Department of Justice had cleared of antitrust problems the proposal for a limited partnership among MT firms for cooperative R&D. The chairman of the association at that time pointed out that the U.S. firms were still the technological leaders and their competitive problems were not caused by insufficient R&D (*American Machinist*, 1984, p. 23).

[34] Similar events characterized the control system business in which General Electric lost the leadership to General Numeric (the Fanuc-Siemens joint venture) and focused increasingly on systemic applications. In 1986 GE entered a joint venture with Fanuc for the development, manufacture, sales, and servicing of industrial automation equipment (including CNCs, programmable logic controllers, and factory automation), otherwise abandoning the CNC business.

lines for direct sales to users. Others attempted to avoid drastic reduction in the rate of utilization of productive capacity when funds for new product development were not available (U.S. Department of Commerce, 1984).

The decreasing size of the U.S. MT market and the competition from imports led to the restructuring of the industry. Productive capacity was cut significantly while the industry concentration rose as the largest and more technologically sophisticated firms pursued (through mergers, acquisitions, or internal growth) the creation of global product lines for factory automation.[35]

The short-term effects of the restructuring were hardly sufficient to reverse the declining competitiveness of the industry. As noted, the imports' penetration of the U.S. market peaked at more than 50% in 1986, when the trade deficit had reached $1.5 billion. The number of establishments had dropped from 1,394 in 1982 to 652 in 1987 and employment in the industry decreased by about 25%. The crisis had been particularly severe for small firms. Among the largest builders, the MT divisions of conglomerate firms like Textron and Houdaille were either sold or shut down. Others were forced to concentrate on customized work and high-end products to attract business, or to diversify in new product areas (as in the case of Cincinnati Milacron). Finally in 1986, the industry received the protection it had sought when the Reagan administration negotiated export restrictions from Japan, South Korea, and Taiwan.

The implementation of the VRAs led to an increase in the number of Japanese transplants in the United States, from 16 in 1980 to 34 in 1990. According to Finegold et al. (1994, pp. 121–124), many of these transplants consisted of assembly facilities and warehouses for distribution. Few firms, notably Yamazaki and Okuma, had manufacturing facilities in the United States that might have benefited the domestic firms by demonstrating best-practice production technology and organization. Although these indirect benefits are poorly documented, it is clear that the VRAs induced an upward shift in the unit price of Japanese imports

[35] Large builders of the 1970s like Cross Co., Kearney & Trecker, Bendix Machine Tool Division, and Warner & Swasey had become divisions of Giddings & Lewis by 1991. Cross & Trecker merged in 1978 and acquired Bendix in 1984. Before then, Bendix had acquired Warner & Swasey (grinding machines and turning machines) and entered marketing and manufacturing agreements with a variety of foreign firms. In 1991 Cross & Trecker was acquired by Giddings & Lewis. The newly formed giant continued its strategy of product line diversification by acquiring Fadal Engineering in 1996. Internal growth was predominantly behind Cincinnati Milacron's diversification in robotics, plastic machinery, and cutting tool materials. The robotics division was sold off in the late 1980s. At that time the company undertook a successful product development program, Wolfpack, in the area of turning centers and machining centers.

and thus created the opportunity for U.S. firms like Fadal Engineering and Haas Automation to make inroads in the production of low-cost equipment (Finegold et al., 1994). These firms pursued the same strategy of cost leadership that had favored the success of Japanese and Taiwanese firms.

Another significant trend of the late 1980s was the change in the U.S. firms' export strategy. Traditionally, the U.S. industry had been quite inward-looking while pushing exports only in times of recession in the domestic market. The globalization of the MT market has finally led to a more active approach to foreign markets, and the export share of output has increased consistently since 1985. Besides the traditional European markets, export growth has been considerable in emerging markets, including Mexico, South Korea, Taiwan, and China.

C. *The Case of South Korea and Taiwan*

The growth of the South Korean MT industry was favored by the rising manufacturing output, acquisition of technology through licensing and imitation especially from the Japanese firms, and the government's protectionist policies (Jacobsson, 1986). The government's role was pervasive in the growth of the South Korean industry, which was considered of strategic importance for the economy's development and protected through import restrictions in the area of NCMTs and subsidies to development activities. After developing a national base in the production of simple conventional MTs, Korean firms undertook the development of NCMTs, initially based on Fanuc's control technology and only later on in-house controls.

The growth of the Taiwanese industry did not benefit from government policies and was far less dependent on the growth of internal demand. Production of NCMTs began during the second half of the 1970s and was predominantly directed to the export markets. Even when the domestic investment in NC lathes grew significantly from 1984, much of the domestic demand was met by imports of more advanced designs from abroad. It appears that specific demands from the local users played a limited role in the development of NC lathes by Taiwanese firms. Rather, the MT distributors in the U.S. markets provided the inducements for local firms to specialize in the production of low-cost NC lathes (Jacobsson, 1986). On the other hand, the industry's leading firms could meet these demands thanks to adequate manufacturing capabilities and the low cost of inputs. The design of NCMTs was based largely on either technology licensed from Japanese firms or the imitation of their simplest NCMT designs. Only later did a few firms acquire capabilities in the design and manufacturing of control units, aided by the government's efforts through the Mechanical Industry Research Laboratories (Fransman, 1986).

D. The Market for Specialized CNC Applications: The European Response

The increased competition in the low end of the general-purpose CNC market and its effects on the product policy of the Japanese firms were of some consequence for the product policy of the European industries. From the early 1980s the diffusion of NC in the largest European producing nations had been increasing quickly, especially when the introduction of CNC favored the development of operator interfaces that made shopfloor programming much easier. This development of the control technology was particularly important in countries like Germany and Italy, where the typical domestic users were small and medium-size firms performing subcontract work and characterized by skilled shopfloor personnel.

In Germany, the adoption of new control technology by MT builders and users was also facilitated by access to the results of research performed at the technical universities and by the participation in cooperative R&D projects and the technology transfer programs of the Fraunhofer Institutes. The Federal Ministry of Research and Technology's Production Technology Program provided financial support for these R&D activities under conditions of disclosure of the results (Englmann et al., 1994). The institutional support and the growth of the domestic market allowed several firms in Germany (Deckel, Maho, Gildemeister, Heller) to develop standard CNC MT designs. However, the price cuts that these firms had to implement in the early 1980s in order to compete with Japanese competitors reduced their profit margins. Furthermore, their production volumes remained well below those of the leading Japanese firms.

This fact had at least two important consequences. First, the limited market size did not make possible the emergence of a low-cost supplier of standardized controls. Siemens, the largest domestic supplier, did not pursue such a strategy and focused instead on the industrial controls and factory automation aspects of the industry. Second, the limited volume of output did not provide MT firms with the incentives to invest in productivity-enhancing manufacturing equipment, like flexible manufacturing systems. Available and limited investment funds were commonly allocated to product development (Sciberras and Payne, 1985).

The European firms were more successful in the market for specialized MT applications. This market's fragmentation reflects the differentiated nature of the users' needs and the presence of entry barriers resulting from established supplier–customer relationships. Besides being the source of innovative ideas, user–producer interactions are a fundamental aspect of business transactions as engineering services are bundled with the sale of the equipment. In this double function, user–producer interactions generate locational advantages, reputation effects, and relational investments. These advantages of incumbency buttressed the ability of the firms in Europe and the United States to thwart the penetration of their market segments by the Japanese firms.

The application of CNC to specialized metalcutting equipment by the German, Italian, and Swiss firms often occurred by tailoring controls to the specific characteristics of the MTs and the customers' use environment. This product design practice favored the emergence of small specialized firms willing to customize controls according to builders' specifications as well as hybrid organizational arrangements whereby the MT firms would customize standard controls from outside firms.[36]

The engineering capabilities of German, Italian, and Swedish firms and their knowledge of the users' manufacturing environments became important assets in the development of FMSs. By the beginning of the 1980s, Japanese firms led in the number of FMS installations (see Table 5.5). However, as flexible manufacturing began to diffuse among the U.S. and European firms, local firms entered the fray. In Europe, where market growth was particularly rapid, several firms specialized in the development of systemic applications (Werner und Kolbe and Huller Hille in Germany, Mandelli and Comau in Italy, SMT in Sweden). The market growth was slower in the United States, where large users were more likely to adopt inflexible automation equipment such as transfer lines. Case study evidence suggests also that U.S. users of FMSs did not take full advantage of their flexibility (Table 5.6) and experienced poor system performance because of weaknesses in the preliminary process engineering work (Jaikumar, 1986).

The Japanese industry did not benefit from first-mover advantages in the area of systemic applications. The most important reason is that

[36] Recent studies of the product development process among German firms suggest that the established practices in the design of customized equipment may be responsible for the widespread use of specialized controllers (Ruth, 1996). The configuration of the control systems is ancillary to the design of the MT, a practice that often results in the need for customization of available control systems. The superior product performance enabled the firms to satisfy the customers' expectations, although from several accounts it appears that in the late 1980s the price–performance trade-offs involved led users to believe that the German MTs were overengineered.

Table 5.5. *Cumulative Number of Installations of Flexible Manufacturing Systems in the United States, Japan, and Western Europe*

	U.S.	Japan	Western Europe
1975	8	25	2
1980	28	71	27
1985	90	166	208

Source: Reproduced from Ehrnberg and Jacobsson (1993).

Table 5.6. *Number of Product Variants Processed by FMS in Europe, the United States, and Japan*

	% of installations		
Number of variants	Europe	U.S.	Japan
1-10	34	41	27
11-50	49	22	24
51-100	8	13	20
101+	9	24	29
Total	100	100	100

Source: ECE (1986).

FMSs are mostly customized and require extensive engineering work, interactions with customers, and specific knowledge of users' manufacturing processes. The informational spillovers across applications are quite localized to specific technological and organizational characteristics of the user environment. Furthermore, the development of FMSs requires capabilities not only in MT technology, but also in the integration of MTs, robots, automated guided vehicles, and handling equipment into a sophisticated control system. The variety of the technical capabilities required made it difficult for any one firm to develop distinctive competencies.

Different kinds of firms were able to enter the market, complementing internal with external capabilities according to varied organizational arrangements. Besides firms specialized in system integration, entrants included joint ventures involving control firms (like Fanuc,[37] Mitsubishi, Shin Nippon, Siemens, Allen Bradley, Bosch), MT firms, and users' engineering divisions. The import penetration of the European, Japanese, and U.S. markets was quite low (Table 5.7), and although a large number of firms undertook the development of FMSs, only few firms in Germany (Werner und Kolb and Huller Hille) and Italy (Mandelli) had a strong product focus on systems (Ehrnberg and Jacobsson, 1993).

Already by the second half of the 1980s, the limited growth prospects of the FMSs' market induced several firms in Japan and Europe to undertake the standardization of system design and the development of smaller systems (i.e., FMCs). These require considerably less complex control systems and are likely to have a greater market, including small and midsize firms. In the area of stand-alone equipment too, advances in control performance (such as the introduction of 32-bit controls in 1986–1987) made the users' choice between specialized and standard equipment increasingly sensitive to price considerations. Better performing controls could be used to substitute for customization of the MT, thus altering the price–performance tradeoffs implicit in the choice between specialized and standard MTs. By the late 1980s, a growing share of the European users (in Germany and Italy as well) was turning to the Japanese firms for cheaper products with excellent performance rather than to domestic builders, whose products were perceived as overengineered and costly (Englmann et al., 1994).

[37] In this respect it is interesting to notice that Fanuc established two joint ventures in the U.S. market. Fanuc teamed up with General Motors for the development of robotics systems in 1984, and with General Electric in 1986. Fanuc has also been supplying control hardware to several European firms.

Table 5.7. *Cumulative Shares of Regional Installations of Flexible Manufacturing Systems (until 1988, Percentages)*

		nationality of supplying firm:		
		U.S.	Europe	Japan
nationality of adopting firm:	U.S.	71.13	10.31	18.56
	Europe	2.22	92.61	5.17
	Japan	0	1.71	98.29

Source: Elaboration of data in Ehrnberg and Jacobsson (1993).

V. The Role of Government Policies in the Evolution of the Industry

Although government policies have been of limited overall significance in the creation of national competitive advantages in the MT industry, the historical account suggests several instances of industry-specific national policies that either contributed to the progress of the technology or shaped the organization of the industry's activities.

A. The United States

Important examples of the former can be found in the U.S. government policies. From the beginning of the nineteenth century, the U.S. government provided the economic incentive for developing MTs that could realize the principle of interchangeable parts in the manufacture of rifles and guns. This occurred through procurement contracts to private armories, such as Eli Whitney's, and through the support of innovative efforts at the public armories at Springfield and Harper's Ferry. These policies laid the stage for the development of MT technology that found applicability in other metalworking sectors and that played an important role in the emergence of mass-production methods. The second instance of a "targeted" U.S. government policy influencing the machine tool industry is the support provided by the U.S. Air Force to the development of NC. Even in this case, the technology ultimately diffused to other sectors of the economy and promoted the emergence of the flexible manufacturing methods. However, while the Air Force hastened the development of NC technology, it also contributed to the factors behind the U.S. firms' neglect of the segment of the market demand, which formed the basis for entry in the U.S. market by Japanese producers of low-cost NCMTs.

Another hallmark of the U.S. policy during the 1980s, noted in other chapters in this volume, was the shift from discouragement to active support for (and, in some cases, subsidization of) collaboration among firms in R&D and other business activities. The National Cooperative Research Act of 1984 and the Export Trading Company Act of 1982 both permitted interfirm cooperation, respectively, in R&D and export activities. As was noted earlier, however, the MT industry found it very difficult to develop a strategy for collaborative R&D.

The major R&D collaboration involving MT firms, the National Center for Manufacturing Sciences (NCMS), enlisted the participation of a large number of U.S. MT users, as well as MT producers. The NCMS was formed only after the machine tool firms themselves were unable to agree on a joint R&D program. Similarly, only in 1987 did the NMTBA obtain the certification granting immunity from antitrust prosecution of collaborative export activities among its member firms. The first coalition of firms to use this immunity was formed in Michigan in 1988 (*American Machinist*, Metalworking Trends, October 1988, p. 37), six years after the relevant legislation had been passed.

The effects of both of these programs thus far on the competitive performance of the U.S. MT industry appear to be modest (Finegold et al., 1994). The industry's trade position since the late 1980s has been affected by several factors, ranging from improved exchange rate conditions to trade protection and the restructuring of the U.S. industry and its leading firms. The downsized industry appears to be more competitive in the domestic and foreign markets, but this is much more likely to be a consequence of the innovative efforts and the market strategies pursued by the firms that survived the crisis (like Cincinnati Milacron, Ingersoll Rand, Giddings & Lewis) and those that were born during the 1980s (like Fadal Engineering and Haas Automation).

B. Japan

The Japanese government has implemented a number of policies for the support of its MT industry during the postwar period, largely under the supervision of MITI. During the 1950s and 1960s, these policies restricted MT imports and foreign direct investment in the industry, while encouraging inward technology transfer through licensing and limited joint ventures. During the 1970s, however, MITI's focus had shifted to promoting R&D collaboration among Japanese machine tool firms.

Although direct subsidies for R&D projects in this industry have been modest (Friedman, 1988), MITI and the Japanese Machine Tool Builders Association have sponsored a series of collaborative R&D projects that link firms, government laboratories, and universities (Ito, 1996). There is little evidence on the effects of these projects on the technological or competitive performance of Japanese MT firms.

C. Germany

The policy of the German government toward its domestic MT industry is similar in some important respects to that of the Japanese government, although the German government has not imposed formal restrictions on imports or foreign direct investment in this industry. One important difference between German and Japanese government policy, however, concerns the strength of the relevant public research infrastructure in these nations. In Germany, the Fraunhofer Institutes and the technical universities have long provided a very strong research infrastructure for the nation's engineering industries, including MTs. Accordingly, government policies of assistance for the German MT industry have focused in large part on facilitating access to this infrastructure by German firms, especially smaller enterprises. In addition, of course, this strong domestic R&D infrastructure has also played an important role in training engineers for positions in German MT firms (Englmann et al., 1994).

The effectiveness of these policies, however, is also difficult to assess. Indeed, these policies and the strong sectoral institutions within the German MT industry failed to prevent its decline in the early 1990s.

VI. Conclusions

The recent rise of Japanese firms to market dominance has a historical counterpart in that of the U.S. MT firms in the second half of the nineteenth century. In both cases, the shifts in the national comparative advantage occurred during periods of rapid technical advance conforming to a common pattern, wherein sequences of innovations broadened the applicability of novel design ideas, materials, and components outside the specific domains for which they were intended. Remarkably, both historical episodes are associated with the emergence of new manufacturing paradigms (interchangeable parts' system and flexible manufacturing). This link is an essential element of the explanation proposed here as to why these sequences of innovations had such powerful consequences for the pattern of comparative advantage.

In the presence of diffuse complementarities among the innovative activities of MT producers and users, the flows of information not only between users and producers, but also among producers of different technologies, play a central role in bringing the technological opportunities to bear on the manufacturing needs of users. Localized user–producer interactions, learning spillovers across producers, and national differences in the structure of MT demand contribute to the emergence of international differences in the rate and direction of development of the new technology. From the perspective of individual firms, these differences matter insofar as they foster the acquisition of distinctive capabilities in product design and manufacturing. Given such international differences in the product specialization of firms and their manufacturing practices, their international competitiveness is driven to a significant extent by the relative growth of the demand segments to which their capabilities are geared. In this respect, the international diffusion of alternative manufacturing practices among using firms plays a phenomenally important role.

The historical evidence from the MT industry bears this characterization of the evolution of comparative advantage. In particular, the foregoing analysis indicates that persistent differences existed between the innovative strategies pursued in the area of NCMTs by the U.S. and Japanese firms during the 1960s and 1970s. Although these differences originated from firm-specific factors like technological capabilities and product specialization, their persistence over time calls attention to the learning process underlying the evolution of firms' perceptions of market and technological opportunities. The main proposition here is that such a learning process did not produce a rapid convergence of those perceptions.

The early commercialization efforts in the United States engendered the perception that NC technology was useful only in the context of manufacturing operations with stringent accuracy requirements. The demand from high-end users became the focus of technology development by the leading MT firms and control suppliers. By contrast, the state of the Japanese MT industry directed Fanuc's innovative efforts toward the development of low-cost adaptations of NC technology. This facilitated its adoption by firms specializing in basic general-purpose MTs, and its diffusion among users whose concerns were to realize productivity gains in batch production of metal parts. The flexibility of NC manufacturing became thus the focus of the users' and producers' perceptions.

The evolution of the strategies pursued by different firms reflects the peculiarities of the market environments on which they concentrated and the nature of the feedback generated by their exploration of the market and technological opportunities. The emergence of first-mover advantages outside their market environment was possible only after the convergence in the patterns of demand from users in different countries. The influence of government policies on this process was only secondary. However, policy played a more important role in Europe and the United States once the direction of change in manufacturing technology had become clear and the competitiveness of national industries was threatened.

It is worth emphasizing once again that the first movers were not really the first inventors. In fact, the historical record shows that the sequences of innovations that culminated in the technological convergence of users' demand were set in motion by peculiar needs, such as the need for timely repair of firearms in the battlefield and for machining of integral aircraft wing parts. The technological convergence that followed had little in common with these needs and at best was poorly perceived.

References

American Machinist (1914), Vol. 40, No. 24.

American Machinist (1960), August 22, pp. 191–194.

American Machinist (1964), Special Report No. 559, October 26.

American Machinist (1984), "Limited Partnership for R&D Is Proposed," December, p. 23.

American Machinist, various issues (1986–1996).

Asahi, I. (1939), *The Economic Strength of Japan*, The Hokuseido Press, Tokyo.

Ashburn, A. (1974), "Japan: Faster and More Automatic," *American Machinist*, November 25, pp. 72–74.

Ashburn, A. (1978), "The Changing Role of NC," *American Machinist*, November, p. 5.

Ashburn, A. (1984), "Is There a Place for Joint Research?" *American Machinist*, January, p. 5.

Ashburn, A. (1986), "Japan Widens Machine Tool Gap," *American Machinist*, February, pp. 87–92.

Ashburn, A. (1988), "The Machine Tool Industry: The Crumbling Foundation," in D.A. Hicks (ed.), *Is New Technology Enough? Making and Remaking U.S. Basic Industries*, American Enterprise Institute for Public Policy Research, Washington, DC, pp. 19–85.

Bardou, J.P., J.J. Chanaron, P. Fridenson, and J.M. Laux (1982), *The Automobile Revolution*, The University of North Carolina Press, Chapel Hill, NC.

Bessant, J. and B. Haywood (1991), "Mechatronics and the Machinery Industry," in C. Freeman, M. Sharp, and W. Walker (eds.), *Technology and the Future of Europe: Global Competition in the 1990s*, Pinter, London, pp. 245–260.

Carden, G.L. (1909), *Machine Tool Trade in Germany, France, Switzerland, Italy, and United Kingdom*, Document No. 1498, U.S. House of Representatives, 60th Congress, Government Printing Office, Washington, DC.

Carlsson, B. (1984), "The Development and Use of Machine Tools in Historical Perspective," *Journal of Economic Behavior and Organization*, Vol. 5, pp. 91–114.

Carlsson, B. (1989), "Small-Scale Industry at a Crossroads: U.S. Machine Tools in Global Perspective," *Small Business Economics*, Vol. 1, pp. 245–261.

Carlsson, B. and S. Jacobsson (1991), "What Makes the Automation Industry Strategic?" *Economics of Innovation and New Technology*, Vol. 1, pp. 257–269.

Carus, C.D. and C.L. McNichols (1944), *Japan: Its Resources and Industries*, Harper & Brothers, New York.

Census of Manufactures (1972, 1977, 1982), "Industry Series, Metalworking Machinery and Equipment," U.S. Bureau of the Census, Washington, D.C.: U.S. Government Printing Office.

Collis, D.J. (1988), "The Machine Tool Industry and Industrial Policy, 1955–82," in A.M. Spence and H.A. Hazard (eds.), *International Competitiveness*, Ballinger, Cambridge, MA, pp. 75–114.

Collis, D.J. (1989), *Kingsbury Machine Tool Corporation*, Case Study 9-388-110, Harvard Business School Publishing Division, Boston, MA.

Current Industrial Reports Series MA-36A (1973–1984), "Switchgear, Switchboard Apparatus, Relays and Industrial Controls," U.S. Department of Commerce.

Current Industrial Reports Series MQ-35W (1965–1973), "Metalworking Machinery," U.S. Department of Commerce.

Dai-ichi Kangyo Bank (1970), "Trends in Industries: Machine Tools," *Dai-ichi Kangyo Bank Report*, February.

DiFilippo, A. (1986), *Military Spending and Industrial Decline: A Study of the American Machine Tool Industry*, Greenwood Press, Westport, CT.

Dreher, C. and G. Lay (1992), "Diversity on Firm Level: Different Modes of Usage of NC/CNC Machine Tools in German Mechanical Engineering," *Revue d'Economie Industrielle*, Vol. 59, 1st Quarter, pp. 86–98.

Economic Commission for Europe (1986), *Recent Trends in Flexible Manufacturing*, United Nations, New York.

Ehrnberg, E. and S. Jacobsson (1993), "Technological Discontinuity and Competitive Strategy – Revival Through FMS for the European Machine Tool Industry?" *Technological Forecasting and Social Change*, Vol. 44, pp. 27–48.

Englmann, F.C. et al. (1994), "The German Machine-Tool Industry," Appendix B in D. Finegold (ed.), *The Decline of the U.S. Machine-Tool Industry and Prospects for Its Sustainable Recovery*, Vol. 2. *Appendices*, RAND Critical Technologies Institute, Santa Monica, CA.

Finegold, D. et al. (1994), *The Decline of the U.S. Machine-Tool Industry and Prospects for Its Sustainable Recovery*, Vol. 1, RAND Critical Technologies Institute, Santa Monica, CA.

Floud, R. (1976), *The British Machine Tool Industry 1850–1914*, Cambridge University Press, Cambridge.

Fong, G.R. (1996), *Export Dependence Versus the New Protectionism: Constraints on Trade Policy in the Industrial World*, Garland, New York.

Fransman, M. (1986), "International Competitiveness, Technical Change and the State: The Machine Tool Industry in Taiwan and Japan," *World Development*, Vol. 14, No. 12, pp. 1375–1396.

Fraser, C.E. and G.F. Doriot (1932), *Analyzing Our Industries*, McGraw-Hill, New York.

Friedman, D. (1988), *The Misunderstood Miracle: Industrial Development and Political Change in Japan*, Cornell University Press, Ithaca, NY.

Fujimoto, H. (1977), "Machine Tools Improved with NC Assist," *Business Japan*, November, pp. 59–64.

Greening, J.H. (1971), "Build a 'Master Plan' for NC," *American Machinist*, Special Report No. 648, March 22, pp. 71–78.

Hatschek, R.L. and G. Schaffer (1973), "Stress Profit in NC Operations," *American Machinist*, May 14, p. 80.

Holland, M. (1989), *When the Machine Stopped: A Cautionary Tale from Industrial America*, Harvard Business School Press, Boston, MA.

Hounshell, D.A. (1984), *From the American System to Mass Production, 1800–1932*, The Johns Hopkins University Press, Baltimore.

Howe, R.E. (ed.) (1969), *Introduction to Numerical Control in Manufacturing*, American Society of Tool and Manufacturing Engineers, Dearborn, MI.

Inaba, S. (1992), *Walking the Narrow Path: The FANUC Story*, private publication.

Industrial Japan (1969), "Japan Machine Tool Fair Big Hit; Technical Advances Impress Visitors," January, pp. 65–68.

Industrial Review of Japan (1971), "Machine Tools," p. 51.

Ito, Y. (1996), "Research and Development Activities to Enhance Market Competitiveness of Products in Japanese Machine Tool Industry," in L. Rasmussen and F. Rauner (eds.), *Industrial Cultures and Production*, Springer-Verlag, London.

Jacobsson, S. (1986), *Electronics and Industrial Policy: The Case of Computer Controlled Lathes*, Allen & Unwin, London.

Jaikumar, R. (1986), "Postindustrial Manufacturing," *Harvard Business Review*, November–December, pp. 69–76.

Japan External Trade Organization (1975), "Japan's Future Supply Capacity," *Focus Japan*, February, No. 15.

Landes, D.S. (1969), *The Unbound Prometheus*, Cambridge University Press, Cambridge.

Lee, K.R. (1996), "The Role of User Firms in the Innovation of Machine Tools: The Japanese Case," *Research Policy*, Vol. 25, pp. 491–507.

Leone, W.C. (1967), *Production Automation and Numerical Control*, The Ronald Press Company, New York.

Maxcy, G. and A. Silberston (1959), *The Motor Industry*, Allen & Unwin, London.

Mazzoleni, R. (1997), "Learning and Path-Dependence in the Diffusion of Innovations: Comparative Evidence on Numerically Controlled Machine Tools," *Research Policy*, Vol. 26, pp. 405–428.

Melman, S. (1983), "How the Yankees Lost Their Know-How," *Technology Review*, October, pp. 56–64.

Milward, A.S. and S.B. Saul (1973), *The Economic Development of Continental Europe: 1780–1870*, Rowman & Littlefield, Totowa, NJ.

MIT Commission on Industrial Productivity (1989), *The US Machine Tool Industry and Its Foreign Competitors*, Working Paper.

Mitsubishi Economic Research Bureau (1936), *Japanese Trade and Industry: Present and Future*, MacMillan, London.

Nagasawa, K. (1976), "Makers Stress Need to Maintain Export Ratio at Over 20% as One of Long-Term Strategies," *Industrial Review of Japan*, Machine Tools, pp. 87–88.

National Machine Tool Builders Association, *Economic Handbook of the Machine Tool Industry*, various issues.

Noble, D.F. (1984), *Forces of Production*, Knopf, New York.

OECD (1970), *NC Machine Tools: Their Introduction in the Engineering Industries*.

Pilger, T. (1928), *German Metal-Working Machinery Industry and Trade*, Trade Information Bulletin No. 540, United States Department of Commerce, Bureau of Foreign and Domestic Commerce.

Reintijes, J.F. (1991), *Numerical Control: Making a New Technology*, Oxford University Press, New York.

Roe, J.W. (1916), *English and American Tool Builders*, Yale University Press, New Haven, CT.

Rolt, L.T.C. (1965), *A Short History of Machine Tools*, MIT Press, Cambridge, MA.

Robertson, R.M. (1966), "Changing Production of Metalworking Machinery, 1860–1920," in National Bureau of Economic Research (ed.), *Output, Employment, and Productivity in the United States After 1800*, Columbia University Press, New York, pp. 479–495.

Rosenberg, J. (1963), "Types and Selection of Contouring Systems," in Frank W. Wilson (ed.), *Numerical Control in Manufacturing*, McGraw-Hill, New York, pp. 169–180.

Rosenberg, N. (1963), "Technological Change in the Machine Tool Industry 1840–1910," *Journal of Economic History*, Vol. 23, pp. 414–443.

Rosenberg, N. (1976), *Perspectives on Technology*, Cambridge University Press, Cambridge.

Ruth, K. (1996), "Industrial Cultures and Machine Tool Industries: Competitiveness and Innovation Trajectories," in L. Rasmussen and F. Rauner (eds.), *Industrial Cultures and Production*, Springer-Verlag, London.

Sandford, J.E. (1970), "The Inside Angles on NC Downtime," *Iron Age*, July 2, pp. 52–57.

Saul, S.B. (1967), "The Market and the Development of the Mechanical Engineering Industries in Britain, 1860–1914," *Economic History Review*, Vol. 20, No. 1, pp. 111–130.

Sciberras, E. and B.D. Payne (1985), *Machine Tool Industry: Technical Change and International Competitiveness*, Longman, Harlow, England.

Shomura, K. (1969), "Japan's Growth Industries and Representative Enterprises," *Industrial Japan Quarterly*, January, No. 14, pp. 17–18.

Sloan, A.P., Jr. (1965), *My Years with General Motors*, MacFadden-Bartell Books, New York.

Tanaka, S. (1977), "Makers Suffering from Slow Domestic Sales in 1976 Boosted Export Ratio to over 30%," *Industrial Review of Japan*, Machine Tools, pp. 90–91.

Teece, D.J. (1986), "Profiting from Technological Innovation," *Research Policy*, Vol. 15, No. 6, pp. 285–305.

United Nations Industrial Development Organization (1984), *World Non-Electrical Machinery*, United Nations, New York.

United States Department of Commerce (1969), *Fifteen Years of Numerically Controlled Machine Tools, 1954–1968*, Business and Defense Services Administration, Washington, DC.

United States Department of Commerce (1984), *A Competitive Assessment of the U.S. Manufacturing Automation Equipment Industries*, Office of Industry Assessment, International Trade Administration, Washington, DC.

United States Department of Justice (1990), *Antitrust Guide Concerning Research Joint Ventures*, Antitrust Division, Government Printing Office, Washington, DC.

Verein Deutscher Werkzeugmaschinenfabriken (1991), *Ein Jahrhundert VDW*, Britting Verlag, München, Germany.

Wagoner, H.D. (1966), *The U.S. Machine Tool Industry from 1900 to 1950*, MIT Press, Cambridge, MA.

Watanabe, S. (1983), *Market Structure, Industrial Technology and Technological Development: The Case of the Japanese Electronic-Based NC Machine Tool Industry*, Working Paper WEP2–22/WP111, I.L.O., Geneva.

Wilson, R.A. (1970), "Machine Tool Controls: Whose Business Is It?" *Iron Age*, February 12, pp. 45–46.

Wilson, R.A. (1972), "Value Engineering Brings CNC into Focus," *Iron Age*, May 25, pp. 81–83.

Zanfei, A. (1994), "The Italian Machine Tool Industry," Appendix C in D. Finegold (ed.), *The Decline of the U.S. Machine-Tool Industry and Prospects for Its Sustainable Recovery*, Vol. 2. *Appendices*, RAND Critical Technologies Institute, Santa Monica, CA.

CHAPTER 6

Dynamics of Comparative Advantage in the Chemical Industry

ASHISH ARORA, RALPH LANDAU, AND NATHAN ROSENBERG

I. Introduction

The chemical industry is one the largest manufacturing industries in the world. In 1995, the sales of the U.S. chemical industry amounted to $372 billion, while those of Western Europe taken together amounted to $495 billion and the Japanese chemical industry, $252 billion. In terms of value added, chemicals and allied products account for about 10.4% of U.S. manufacturing output and 1.9% of the U.S. gross domestic product (GDP). Not only is the chemical industry very large, it is also very complex. In fact, the chemical processing industries (CPIs) group has been called the most miscellaneous of industries and the description is apt. The chemicals and allied products group (SIC 28) can be divided into three major subgroups: (1) basic chemicals such as acids, alkalis, salts, and organic chemicals; (2) intermediate chemical products such as synthetic fibers, plastic materials, and colors and pigments; (3) consumer chemical products such as drugs, cosmetics, soaps, as well as paint, fertilizers, and explosives. Even if one excludes closely related sectors such as refining, and paper and pulp, the CPI produce somewhere on the order of 50,000–70,000 products. Many of the products are new, the results of product innovation, but many older products survive, even if their relative importance has declined.

The most important class of chemicals are the organic compounds, which are much more pervasive and varied than the inorganic compounds, such as salt and minerals and products derived from them such as chlorine, bleach, caustic soda, and sulfuric acid. Organic inputs, like oil and natural gas, contain hydrocarbons which form the backbone of final organic chemical outputs. In the first stage of processing, raw materials are refined to produce primary outputs such as benzene and ethylene. Primary outputs like these are the building blocks of the chemical indus-

We are grateful to our colleagues from the Chemical Industry Project, especially Alfonso Gambardella and Peter Murmann, for useful comments and suggestions. We also thank the editors and members of the Matrix Project for helpful comments. The customary disclaimers apply.

try. In subsequent processing, chemicals such as chlorine and oxygen are added to the hydrocarbon backbones to give the compounds certain desired characteristics. In other words, organic products are more closely related to each other through common technologies and inputs than are inorganic chemicals (see Landau, 1995, P. 23; CMA, 1994). The chemical industry in the 1850s, however, was predominantly inorganic. The organic part of the industry consisted of products such as coke-oven by-products, and various products derived from wood and other natural sources. The complex nature of these products and the limited development of organic chemistry limited the production and uses of organic compounds.

The developments which led to the rise of organic compounds as the mainstay of the chemical industry form a key element of the story of shifting dynamic comparative advantage in the chemical industry. Organic chemicals, which will be the focus of much of this chapter, constitute the "high-tech" part of this industry and account for the bulk of the considerable R&D spending in this industry. Virtually all major products (and the bulk of process innovations as well) in chemicals belong to the class of organic chemicals. Synthetic dyestuffs, which powered the rise of the German chemical industry in the 19th century, are organic, as are synthetic fibers, plastics, and pharmaceuticals.

Two other features of the chemical industry are worth noting. First, the industry is highly interdependent; its main customers are other firms, often chemical firms themselves. An estimated 27% of the output of the chemical industry is consumed within the industry and nearly half of the total output is consumed within manufacturing. The figures would be even higher if one excluded pharmaceuticals and accounted for foreign trade. Thus many large firms typically interact with other firms in a variety of markets, as competitors in some markets and as suppliers or customers in other markets. Second, the chemical industry has always had a global character. Not only has foreign trade been an important factor in the evolution of the industry, so have international movements of capital and technology. Needless to say, the extent of globalization has increased over time. In 1994 the book value of direct foreign investments in the United States was $61.3B, compared to $51.6B of U.S. investment in foreign chemical companies. A great deal of international trade consists of intrafirm transactions of such companies. In 1994 U.S. chemical company parents exports amounted to $51.5B, of which over two-thirds went to their foreign affiliates. Likewise, 56% of the U.S. chemical imports were channeled through the U.S. affiliates of foreign companies. International technology flows, which are often related to capital, are also significant. In 1993, U.S. companies received $2.3B in royalties and licensing fees and paid $1.2B (all figures taken from the CMA, 1994). The global character of the industry is even more marked in countries such as Germany and Britain, with much smaller domestic markets than that in the United States.

This chapter analyzes the dynamics of competitive advantage with reference to the chemical industry in four countries – the United States, Germany, Britain, and Japan. The countries have been selected not only because they are among the largest chemical producing countries but also because their experiences illuminate how competitive advantage shifts across nations over time. Section II provides a brief description of the development of the industry. Briefly, sometime around the 1890s, Germany overtook Britain as the leading chemical producing nation. The German chemical industry's rapid growth was based on innovations which exploited the newly emerging breakthroughs in organic chemistry, especially in synthetic dyestuffs and related chemicals. The U.S. chemical industry, although technologically not as sophisticated as the European chemical industries, grew by intensively exploiting its natural resource endowments. During the interwar years, the U.S. chemical industry grew in technological sophistication. The Second World War marks both the peak of U.S. dominance as well as the later period, in which other countries, especially Japan, grew rapidly and closed much of the gap with the United States. Japan is now the second largest chemical producer in the world, but its chemical industry is still not perceived to be as innovative as those of the other three countries. These patterns provide the context within which Section III analyzes the firm and industry level factors that determine competitive advantage. Section IV pulls together some of the main themes and concludes the chapter.

II. Shifting Comparative Advantage and the Development of the Industry

A. 1850–1914

Growth and Composition of Output. In 1850, Britain led in the production of chemicals. It produced mineral acids, especially sulfuric acid, alkali, caustic soda, and bleach. Although systematic comparative data are not available for this period, Table 6.1 gives the output of sulfuric acid, a good proxy for total chemical output. This table shows that, even as late as 1875, Britain produced about seven times as much sulfuric acid

Table 6.1. *Sulfuric Acid Production: 1865–1913, Britain, Germany, and United States (Thousands of Tons per Annum)*

	Germany	Britain	US
1865	na	380	53.6
1870	na	590	93.7
1875	103.5	730	133.9
1880	156	900	379
1885	343	890	535
1895	650.7	770	na
1900	830	1010	940
1904	1300	na	1289
1913	1600	1150	2200

Source: Extracted from Murmann and Landau (1995).

Table 6.2. *Chemical Production, 1913–1993: Selected Countries*

	USA	Britain	Japan	Germany	World
1913	1.53 (16)	1.1 (11)	0.15 (2)	2.4 (24)	10
1927	9.45 (42)	2.3 (10)	0.55 (2)	3.6 (16)	22.5
1938	8 (30)	2.3 (9)	1.5 (6)	5.9 (22)	26.9
1951	71.8 (43)	14.7 (9)	6.5 (4)	9.7 (8)	166
1970	49.2 (29)	7.6 (4.5)	15.3 (9)	13.5 (8)	171
1980	168.3 (23)	31.8 (4.5)	79.2 (11)	59.3 (8)	719
1993	313.5 (25)	49.6 (4)	208 (17)	98.6 (8)	1250

Note: Sales given in billions of reichsmark up to 1938, in billions of deutchmark for 1951, and in billions of U.S. dollars thereafter. Percentage share in total world output given in parentheses.
Source: Eichengreen (1998).

as did Germany, and about six times as much as the United States. It is fair to say that the large domestic demand from industries such as textiles, soap, and glass was a major reason for the British dominance. In turn, the large demand was related to the large domestic market, and the high levels of per capita income in Britain.[1] In 1856, the first synthetic dye (aniline mauve) was discovered by Perkin, and this event is customarily treated as having launched the modern organic chemical industry. Although the organic dyes were first discovered and commercialized in Britain, within 15 years, Germany overtook Britain in the production of organic dyes.

By the 1880s, Germany dominated the organic chemical industry. The leading German chemical firms of today were major players in this rise to dominance. In 1880, German firms accounted for a little less than half the total world output of synthetic dyes. By 1913, the dominance was even more marked (see Table 6.2): Of an estimated world output of 160,000 tons, Germany produced 140,000. Although this share would come down in the aftermath of World War I, German dominance in this sector was extremely long-lived. German production of inorganic chemicals also grew, pulled by the growth in the organic chemical industry and general industrial growth. Even so, Britain remained a significant producer and exporter of coal tar and other organic intermediates such as benzole. Further, in inorganics sectors such as soda ash, caustic, and bleach, Britain remained the leading producer in the world, and a major exporter, till around the eve of World War I. Hardie and Pratt (1966, p. 69) note that in 1913, Britain imported £1.893 million worth of dyestuffs and exported £14.34 million worth of heavy inorganic chemicals. Table 6.2 provides the value of chemicals output for various countries for selected years after 1913. On the eve of the First World War, which is the earliest for which systematic comparative data are available, Germany was the leading producer, followed by the United States, which had also overtaken Britain by this time.

The figures in Table 6.3 should be interpreted with some caution because of changing industry definitions, but the picture they paint is quite unambiguous – the U.S. chemical industry grew strongly after the 1860s, and around the turn of the century, the pace of growth picked up quite rapidly. The United States grew into a major producer of inorganic chemicals, exploiting its rich natural resources, such as abundant and cheap wood, and mineral deposits (Rosenberg, 1972; Nelson and Wright,

[1] The following facts, taken from Landes (1969, p. 225), are illuminating: In 1850, Britain had more cotton spindlage than the United States, Germany, France, Switzerland, and Austria-Hungary combined. Britain also had a third of the world's steam engine capacity.

Table 6.3. *World Exports of Chemicals, 1899–1959, by Country of Origin: Selected Countries and Years (Percentages of World Exports)*

	USA	Britain	Germany[1]	Other W. Europe[2]	Japan	Other	World Exports in billion US $
1899	14.2	19.6	35.0	13.1	0.4	4.2	0.26
1913	11.2	20.0	40.2	13.1	1.0	0.3	0.59
1929	18.1	17.5	30.9	15.3	1.8	0.4	1.04
1937	16.9	16.0	31.6	19.4	3.0	0.3	0.98
1950[1]	34.6	17.9	10.4	20.5	0.8	0.5	2.17
1959	27.4	15.0	20.2	21.1	3.1	0.2	5.48
1993	13.0	5.2	12.7	13.1	13.0	33.4	309.2

[1] West German figures for 1950, 1959, 1993.
[2] Comprises Italy, Belgium-Luxembourg, Netherlands (except in 1899 and 1913), Sweden, and Switzerland.
Source: Eichengreen (1998, Table 2), based on Maizel (1963, p. 302) and Chemical Manufacturer's Association (1994).

1992).[2] It relied upon imported technology for the most part, and important segments, such as dyestuffs, pharmaceuticals, and fine chemicals, owed a great deal to subsidiaries and affiliates of foreign firms, especially German firms (Steen, 1995). However, U.S. industry modified and adapted the imported technology to suit domestic conditions and made a number of improvements. By the end of the 19th century, a number of important innovations were made in areas such as electrochemistry and sulfur, which were American in origin.

The Japanese chemical industry in the 19th century was still quite small, as Table 6.3 clearly shows. Even on the eve of World War I, the Japanese economy accounted for only about 2% of the world output, and even less, 1%, of world exports. In 1900, the Japanese economy was

[2] It is important not to lose sight of the fact that till the Second World War, organic compounds were nowhere near as important as they became after the war. Thus focusing upon dyestuffs alone (as one is sometimes tempted to do) may be misleading in some respects. In 1921, in the United States, inorganic chemicals accounted for a little over half the total value of output of about $444 million. The major organic categories consisted of coal tar products (less than one-fifth) and plastics (less than one-tenth). The natural resource dependence of the chemical industry is further underscored by the fact that products classified as electrochemicals accounted for just under one-eighth of the total output of the chemical industry. One should note that the U.S. chemical industry retained its inorganic character far longer than did the German one.

predominantly agricultural: The shares in industrial output of chemicals, steel, and machinery were 10.7%, 0.4%, and 10%, respectively, while those for textiles and food were about 36% each (Harada, 1995). As one would expect, the Japanese chemical industry in the late 19th century was strongly influenced by the requirements of agriculture and the military. Its major products were relatively simple: soda ash and sulfuric acid, and later, superphosphate, and ammonium sulfate using the Cyanamid and (after World War I) variants of the Haber-Bosch process for the production of synthetic ammonia.

The pattern of international comparative advantage is even more pronounced if one looks at the export performance. As Table 6.3 shows, the German chemical industry was a very successful exporter. Between 1900 and 1913, German exports trebled, reaching a tenth of the total national output of chemicals. In 1913, Germany accounted for 40% of the world exports, while its share in total production was far less, at 24%. The biggest export earners for Germany were synthetic dyestuffs, pharmaceutical and photographic material, fine chemicals, and basic inputs such as potash and sulfate of ammonia. The U.S. industry was largely geared to the domestic market, accounting for 16% of the world output and only 11% of the world exports. By comparison, the British chemical industry accounted for about 20% of the world exports, at a time when it accounted for only 11% of the world output.

Evolution of Industry Structure. In the 1850s the British chemical industry consisted largely of family owned and run firms of fairly modest size. Competition from the Solvay soda process in alkali and from German dyestuff firms prompted exit and consolidation in those two sectors. In alkalis, by the 1880s, the Leblanc soda industry was facing severe financial hardship and had to seek recourse to cartelization and eventually, amalgamation into the United Alkali Company (UAC). Although these measures merely delayed the inevitable, by the early 1900s, a number of larger companies had emerged on the scene.[3] The process of mergers and amalgamation in the dyestuffs sector continued well into the 1920s, in part under pressure from the British government, which was more appreciative of the strategic nature of the industry. The process culminated in 1926, with the formation of Imperial Chemical Industries (ICI), which included the ammonia soda business of Brunner, Mond; the dynamite and fertilizer business of Nobel; the dyestuffs businesses of

[3] United Alkali Company was still large, albeit with an uncertain future. Brunner, Mond, had grown into a very large alkali producer, British Dynamite was a leading explosives manufacturer, and Levinstein, and Read and Holliday were the leading dyestuffs companies.

Table 6.4. *Growth of the Chemical Industry, 1849–1939, United States Chemical Industry*

Year	Number of establishments	Wage earners: '000s	Value of products: $ millions	Value added by manufacture: millions	Employees per establishment	Value added per establishment, in '000s of dollars
1849	170	1.4	5	1.7	8.23	10
1859	299	2	5.4	2.3	6.68	7.69
1869	444	6.1	24.3	9.9	13.73	22.297
1879	649	11.1	44.4	16.5	17.10	25.424
1889	632	17.4	70.7	31.5	27.53	49.842
1899	530	23.5	79.7	34.9	44.33	65.85
1904	572	30.2	121.7	52.6	52.79	91.96
1909	597	35	177.4	79.3	58.62	132.83
1914	633	44.4	221.6	96.2	70.14	151.98
1919	1053	90.4	730.6	367.7	85.84	349.19
1921	981	58.7	502.5	255.1	59.83	260.04
1923	1039	90.1	788.4	387.3	86.71	372.76
1925	996	70	688.6	341.1	70.28	342.47
1927	1028	67.7	746.3	373.7	65.85	363.52
1929	1676	79.1	959.1	508.4	47.19	303.34
1931	1556	61.4	687.4	393.6	39.46	252.96
1933	1367	64.8	582.6	323.5	47.40	236.65
1935	1580	81.5	820.8	430.1	51.58	272.22
1937	1667	97.8	1144.6	605.7	58.66	363.34
1939	1931	89.9	1197.6	667.6	46.55	345.73

Note: The figures include compressed and liquefied gases, explosives, insecticides and fungicides, and wood distillation products. They do not include drugs and medicines. The value of output in this category for 1937 was $335.8 million.
Source: Census of Manufacturing *Chemical Facts and Figures* (1940, 1).

British Dyestuffs; and the Leblanc alkali business of the UAC. The other British chemical firms of some note either were highly specialized (e.g., Laporte in hydrogen peroxide or BOC in air separation) or focused on consumer goods (e.g., Glaxo in drugs and food products, Lever Brothers in soaps and cosmetics, Courtaulds in textiles and later synthetic fibers).

By the 1880s, the German chemical industry was similarly dominated by a few large companies. The big three (BASF, Bayer, and Hoechst) dominated in dyestuffs and organic chemicals, although there were independent pharmaceutical firms (e.g., Boehringer, Schering, Merck) and firms such as Henkel (detergents), Degussa, Dynamit, and Griesham Elektron. Moreover, even though the major firms competed among themselves, there appears to have been a tacit understanding that developed, and the extent of overlap in terms of product lines was limited. The German chemical industry experienced a growing consolidation in the period leading up to the war. Tariff barriers, a favorable legal climate, and macroeconomic instability leading to frequent recessions and overcapacity combined to encourage cartels and syndicates. The more famous of these were in the dyestuffs sector, with BASF, Bayer, and Agfa in one group, and Hoechst, Casella, and Kalle in the other. These cartel arrangements were formalized between 1904 and 1907.

For most of the 19th century, the U.S. chemical industry was characterized by small, geographically localized firms, which largely produced simple inorganic chemicals. Oil companies, explosives and fertilizer firms, and electrochemical firms were larger. As Table 6.4 shows, initially the number of establishments increased with output, but around the turn of the century, growth in production was actually accompanied by a decline in the number of establishments. Development of the U.S. transport infrastructure, and the economic integration that followed, led to a consolidation in a number of sectors. The process of consolidation was accompanied by downward integration into marketing and distribution by a number of chemical firms. Hitherto, chemical firms had largely sold through jobbers. Wishing to insulate themselves from price competition, firms tried to develop brand images for their products, a move that required greater control over marketing and distribution (Arora and Rosenberg, 1998). The implied increase in fixed costs meant that even in growing markets, the number of producers fell. A number of larger firms emerged through this process, the most prominent being Allied Chemicals, Union Carbide, and American Cyanamid.[4] However, the large size and geographical extent of the market, and vigorous antitrust enforcement in the early part of the 20th century prevented anything approaching the European situation. Antitrust pressures are also credited with inducing U.S. firms to invest in technology as a means of growth and diversification.

[4] American Cyanamid, which started as a Wall Street financed fertilizer company, grew by rapidly acquiring a variety of companies in heavy chemicals (Kalbfleisch), engineering (Chemical Engineering Corporation), solvents and industrial chemicals (Selden), dyes (Calco), explosives (Burton), and pharmaceuticals (Lederle). From 1910 to 1916, the share of fertilizers dropped from 100% to 75%. By 1929, American Cyanamid was the fourth largest and the most diversified U.S. chemical company (Haynes, 1947, Vol. IV, p. 46).

The Policy Context. Although the different countries covered here were at different stages of industrialization, and consequently government policies toward the industry differed, the differences do not appear to have mattered a great deal. Britain was richer, but Germany and the United States had more rapidly growing economies. All countries were on a gold standard, which meant that macroeconomic conditions were roughly similar. Britain followed free trade policies for most of this period, while both the United States and Germany provided some measure of tariff protection to their industries. In Japan, earlier treaties prohibiting tariff barriers meant that only the Sino–Japanese War of 1894–1895 and later World War I provided a period of natural protection, and the industry grew rapidly during these periods.

Tariff protection doubtless benefited the protected industries, but its long-term effects appear to be limited.[5] By the 1880s, the German dyestuffs producers were the dominant exporters and had also set up production facilities in a number of other countries. Murmann and Landau (1998) note that as major importers, German chemical producers had little to gain and much to lose from erecting tariff barriers. By the same token, import protection did little for the long-term prospects of the U.S. dyestuffs firms, many of which collapsed soon after tariffs were reduced.[6] Tariff protection after World War I did provide breathing space for companies such as ICI in Britain by bolstering its bargaining position in its negotiations with the dyestuffs and nitrogen cartels dominated by IG Farben. ICI used the opportunity to invest and develop its capabilities in ammonia, organic chemistry, and polymers. On balance, Eichengreen (1998) concludes, there is little evidence that the chemical industry in any of these countries derived a significant long-lasting advantage from the exercise of strategic trade policy.

Chemicals, and especially organic dyestuffs, was and still is in many respects a "high-tech" industry, and intellectual property rights, especially patent rights, have often been crucial. Germany, before its unification in 1871, lacked a uniform patent law. The reforms of the German patent system in 1877 had come at an opportune time for the

[5] British alkali exports to Germany had been hurt when German tariffs were raised in 1879. In 1897, the United States, the single most important market for British exports of soda, increased its duties on soda ash, caustic, and bicarbonate by 50%. British exports declined steeply in response and never quite recovered as Solvay soda producers in the United States expanded capacity (Haber, 1958, p. 216).

[6] In the 1870s, a number of firms entered the industry as a result of a 50 cents plus 35% ad valorem tariff (Haynes, 1947, vol. I, p. 311). But after the tariff was lowered in 1883, to 10% below the average American tariff level in the 19th century, only the established firms, such as Read Holliday, Heller and Merz, and Schoellkopf managed to survive, in part because they were able to produce coal-tar intermediates such as phenol.

German dyestuffs industry and coincided with the establishment of in-house R&D facilities in many of the leading firms (Marsh, 1994). There is some evidence to suggest that the British and French dyestuffs industries suffered because their patent law did not evolve in tune with the requirements of the dyestuffs industry. Travis (1993) documents an important patent litigation in France – the Fuchsine case – in which the French courts provided excessively broad protection to a patent for a red synthetic dye (Fuchsine). The decision effectively prohibited any alternative process innovations for producing the dyestuff in question and is said to have led to the flight of a large section of the French synthetic dyestuffs industry to Switzerland.

Patent litigation also dogged the British dyestuffs industry during the 1860s. Once again, the problem was that the underlying knowledge base was inadequate for effectively delineating the scope of patents, which sometimes tended to be excessively broad (Arora, 1997). The weak examination requirement in Britain is also said to have allowed German firms to assert dyestuffs patents in Britain that had been rejected by the German patent office (Haber, 1958, p. 91). German chemical companies, on the other hand, skillfully and aggressively used the patent system to capitalize on their lead in organic chemistry. Broad process patents were typical, but often the precise composition of the dyestuff was protected through secrecy. Similarly, the Haber-Bosch process for ammonia was protected by a number of patents, but details of the catalyst system were kept secret.[7] On the whole, although patent protection was undoubtedly important, there is little to suggest that such protection differed drastically across countries. As we discuss later, what did differ was the ability of firms to innovate and benefit from patent protection, as the expropriation of German patents after World War I amply demonstrates.

One important difference, whose implications we discuss later, was in institutions of higher education. The German university system had a much stronger science base, particularly in organic chemistry, and appears to have been far more responsive to the industry and its needs than universities in Britain. German universities turned out more capable researchers and, perhaps just as importantly, turned out many more of them. By the 1830s, the German system of higher learning was perhaps the most advanced in the world, thanks in part to a secondary

[7] U.S. companies also used patents once they started their own R&D programs. However, as described later, competition between innovators, the sheer number of different companies that could develop new products and processes, and the even larger number that could invent around and imitate without infringing meant that long-lasting advantage was limited to a few well-known cases.

school system that was stronger than its British counterpart.[8] Germany also pioneered in some ways the concept of the research university, and Liebeg's laboratory in Giessen attracted students from many parts of the world, including a sizable fraction from Britain, in the 1930s and 1940s. German schools, polytechnics, and universities benefited from generous state policies, in marked contrast to the situation in Britain, where science or technology oriented educational institutions often had great difficulty surviving.[9] Undoubtedly, German chemical companies benefited from the ready supply of trained and skilled chemists and engineers and the proximity of many leading chemists. However, as we discuss later, perhaps the crucial differences lie in the ability and willingness of German managers to invest in science and technology, and in commercialization of the fruits of science and technology.

B. World War I and the Interwar Period

Growth and Composition of Output. The cutting off of imports of German organic chemicals and dyestuffs during the First World War provided a significant opportunity for the United States and Britain. Furthermore, during and after the war, there was considerable government support for the industry as its strategic nature was fully appreciated (synthetic ammonia, explosives, poison gas, dyes, pharmaceuticals). In addition to the war-induced dislocations in trade, exports were also curtailed by higher tariffs. After World War I, the British chemical industry also pressed, successfully, for protective tariffs and a variety of measures to restrain German exports. In Britain, tariffs were imposed in the 1920s and protection was further enhanced in 1931. U.S. dyestuffs producers were also sheltered from German imports by tariffs, but only for a relatively brief period after the war.

World War I had provided another opportunity to the chemical industries in Britain and the United States. As a consequence of the war, and then as a part of war reparations, they expropriated German industrial property, including German patents and trademarks. In the United States, some forty-five hundred patents were singled out in consultation with leading domestic firms and made available on a nonexclusive basis.

[8] Prussia, the largest of the pre-unification German states, had instituted compulsory primary education by 1772. Britain waited almost 130 years before doing so. The German secondary school system was also more broad-based (Landau and Murmann, 1998).

[9] The failure of the Royal College of Chemistry to survive after the death of its patron, Prince Albert, and the return to Germany of August Hoffman, its first professor, in 1865 provide a case in point.

These included the valuable patents on the Haber-Bosch process, as well as a number of pharmaceutical patents. Other forms of industrial property, such as the Bayer trademark, were also expropriated, and in Britain, a Hoechst dyestuffs factory was taken over. Even though patent protection is far from the whole story of German dyestuffs success, the German firms felt the loss of the patents keenly. However, the salutary impact on the British and U.S. firms was far more limited. The removal of patent barriers was not enough, absent in-house knowledge and experience, for these firms to compete successfully with German dyestuffs firms. The removal of patent barriers did contribute to the decision to institute in-house R&D programs (Mowery, 1981), as German firms had in the 1880s. Synthetic dyestuffs decreased in importance after World War I, and growth opportunities arose in synthetic polymers – synthetic fibers, synthetic rubbers, and plastics and resins. The investments in R&D, initially inspired by a desire to build technological capability in dyestuffs and high-pressure synthesis, enabled firms such as DuPont and ICI to exploit opportunities in synthetic polymers starting sometime during the 1930s.

The 1920s was generally a period of rapid growth, especially in the United States, where the growth of automobiles and other consumer goods provided a strong stimulus for new products such as plastic resins, antifreeze, cellophane, rayon, in addition to the more traditional intermediate products of the chemical industry. By the 1930s, the larger U.S. firms had become innovators in their own right, with innovations such as neoprene, tetraethyl lead, and antifreeze. Recently available patenting data for the interwar period from Cantwell (1995) illustrate the point. Although one must interpret statistics based on patent counts with caution, the trends displayed by the patents statistics shown in Table 6.5 are interesting. They show that Europe continued to be an important source of chemical technology through the interwar years, but that U.S. technological capabilities in chemicals were growing rapidly as well. During the 1930s, a number of major products were invented, but their full economic impact would only be felt in the post–World War II era. The development of synthetic polymers was probably the most significant. Synthetic polymer based products, virtually unknown before the 1930s, currently account for somewhere between 25% and 35% of the output of the CPI.

During the interwar years, domestic military buildup in both Germany and Japan was significant. The autarchic preferences of military planners proved to be a significant stimulus to the chemical industries in both countries. The industries received trade protection, as well as direct subsidies and other forms of state patronage. In the German case, state

Table 6.5. *Annual Average Percentage Growth in Total US Patents and Patents Granted to European Residents Classified by Selected Field of Technological Activity, Selected Periods*

SECTOR	1890-96 to 1920-24	1920-24 to 1927-29	1927-29 to 1933-39	1920-24 to 1933-39
Inorganic chemicals	*5.20*	*-1.39*	*6.21*	*2.88*
	2.27	7.10	3.12	4.80
Agricultural chemicals	*3.04*	*-4.55*	*9.74*	*3.37*
	4.56	-0.65	12.06	6.42
Photographic chemistry	*4.69*	*4.32*	*13.11*	*9.26*
	3.21	22.22	11.91	16.22
Synthetic resins and fibers	*6.74*	*17.40*	*11.02*	*13.71*
	5.07	21.63	18.68	19.95
Bleaching and dying	*2.64*	*13.08*	*5.70*	*8.80*
	3.54	11.38	5.45	7.95
Pharmaceuticals	*2.88*	*7.93*	*6.78*	*7.27*
	2.07	19.15	2.76	9.49
Rubber and plastic products	*2.52*	*-10.30*	*-0.67*	*-4.91*
	0.65	0.93	6.60	4.13
Coal and petroleum products	*5.82*	*13.38*	*10.94*	*11.98*
	5.46	8.21	11.10	9.85
Telecommunications	*3.73*	*7.47*	*0.61*	*3.49*
	3.44	24.34	3.08	11.73
Office equipment	*9.28*	*-6.77*	*5.16*	*-0.13*
	10.00	3.10	10.92	7.50
Motor vehicles	*5.75*	*-4.24*	*-3.78*	*-3.97*
	10.5	-3.19	-0.91	-1.89
Metallurgical processes	*4.27*	*2.91*	2.52	*2.69*
	3.73	3.38	4.95	4.27
Aircraft	*12.61*	*1.15*	*-2.54*	*-0.98*
	14.33	-1.15	0.45	-0.24
TOTAL (All manufacturing)	***1.95***	***1.74***	***-0.39***	***0.51***
	2.04	**5.02**	**3.24**	**4.00**

Note: The italicized figures represent total patenting; the figures below them represent growth rates of patents granted to European residents.
Source: Cantwell (1995, Tables 3 and 4, pp. 298–299, 302–303).

intervention was a mixed blessing, because it forced the chemical industry to expend large sums of money and manpower in areas such as synthetic rubber and oil from coal. These research projects were technologically successful and sustained the German war effort during World War II but turned out to have very low commercial payoff.

The primary locus of growth in the Japanese chemical industry was in the area of synthetic ammonia fertilizers and inorganic chemicals. As in other countries, the First World War had underlined the strategic nature of the industry and the state provided technical and other assistance to the chemical industry. Japanese firms licensed ammonia technology from European chemical companies, while the state owned Special Nitrogen Research Laboratory (SNRL) carried out research in nitrogen fixation. Even though the indigenously developed technology did not achieve commercial success, the SNRL played an important role in the efficient domestic utilization of the imported technologies (Harada, 1995). During this period the established *Zaibatsu* (large industrial groups, and forerunners of today's *keiretsu*) were generally reluctant to commit significant resources to emerging fields such as chemicals. The opening was exploited by a small group of aggressive entrepreneurs whose efforts centered around electrochemicals. The firms they founded were associated with industrial groups such as Nissan, Nichitsu (Showa Denko), Nisso, and Mori (Hikino et al., 1996).

Consolidation and Concentration in Industry Structure. Consolidation in industry structure was caused by the same underlying forces: increasing fixed costs due to larger production scales, as well as the increasing importance of R&D. Often trade recessions or other such shocks precipitated bouts of consolidation whereby weaker firms would be taken over. In Europe, cartels were legal, and Germany (where cartels were legalized in 1897) even had state sponsored cartels in potash and nitrogenous fertilizers. In the period immediately following the First World War, the German Ministry of Interior found 47 cartels in the chemical industry. Thirteen of these were concerned with inorganics, and two (major ones) with dyestuffs (Haber, 1971, p. 267). In dyestuffs there were numerous agreements involving profit pools. The efforts of the Leblanc alkali producers to cartelize the market by forming the United Alkali Company in Britain in the 1890s are well known. But as Haber points out, United Alkali's chief competitor, Brunner, Mond, the commercializers of the Solvay ammonia soda process in Britain, behaved in a "gentlemanly" fashion toward it. The two companies did not attempt to entice each other's customers and entered into long-term contracts with their customers. In 1927, these companies, along with others, were merged into ICI, which by 1948 is reported to have accounted for somewhere between 30% and 45% of the total British chemical output (Reddaway, 1958). Concentration in Germany had proceeded even more rapidly. IG Farben accounted for over half, and in some cases, over three-quarters of the entire German output of important chemical products. In fact, even though the German chemical industry consisted of more than 3,000 firms, including some rather large firms, IG dominated the German industry. Consolidation in the national chemical industries preceded and facilitated the rise of the international cartels.

Cartels, both national and international, remained an important feature of the industry in Europe till World War II. There were major international cartels, often unstable, in areas such as nitrogen fertilizers, dyestuffs, and dynamite. In fact, the chemical industry during this period has been described as a "gentlemen's club," with most markets dominated by a few large firms. These firms shared markets and, through their control over technology, limited entry of new firms into the industry. The leading U.S. firms, such as Du Pont and Standard Oil, could not, for legal reasons, join these cartels. Instead, they entered into broad technology sharing agreements with firms such as IG Farben and ICI. It is difficult to assess the extent to which these agreements also allowed de facto market sharing, but both firms would later face antitrust challenges to their European pacts. It does appear that these large, multiproduct firms, interacting with each other in a variety of market sharing agreements, tended to behave less aggressively toward each other (see, e.g., Bernheim and Whinston, 1990). Within the United States, a large market and the less tolerant view taken by the antitrust authorities of the exercise of market power provided an opportunity for a number of firms, such as Dow, Hercules (which was spun off by Du Pont as part of an antitrust decree), and Air Products. Many of these firms were closely associated with the rise of petrochemicals, the result of a convergence between oil refining and chemicals.

C. World War II and After

Petrochemicals was in some senses a uniquely American phenomenon. The oil refining industry and the chemical industry, hitherto separate industries, grew closer together in the interwar years. In the United States the move had begun earlier and the early lead and experience of the U.S. industry were to prove a source of technological advantage for a limited period of time. The United States had abundant reserves of oil and natural gas and had a large oil refining industry by the early part of the 20th century. By contrast, Germany and Britain had abundant coal (which the United States had as well) but little oil. In 1940, 71% of world refining capacity was located in North America with only 7% in Western Europe. German supremacy in organic chemicals was based on coal and coke-oven by-products, and initially oil was seen primarily as an energy source. But the relative scarcity of coke-oven by-products in the United States and the relative abundance of natural gas and refinery gases made the latter attractive as inputs. The shift to oil and natural gas based feedstocks was led by Union Carbide and Dow among the chemical companies and by Standard Oil and Shell among the oil companies.[10] It is unlikely that we would make so much of the shift in feedstocks but for the fact that the huge growth in synthetic polymers output depended critically on the tremendous increase in availability, after World War II, of building block chemicals such as ethylene and propylene, and on the concomitant large decreases in their prices.

The United States emerged as the dominant chemical producing nation at the end of World War II. Many German chemical installations had been bombed and damaged.[11] And, as in Britain, the war had taken a heavy toll or the economic infrastructure. However, in both Germany and Britain, the chemical industry rebuilt and grew rapidly. Nonetheless, the division of Germany after the war and the removal of a substantial amount of capacity as reparation had a substantial, if short-lived, impact on German production, which is reflected in Table 6.3. For the years 1938 and 1951, the share of the United States in world production rose from 30% to 43%, while that of West Germany fell to 8% from an earlier German share of 22%. The British industry managed to hold on to its share of world output, while that of the Japanese industry dipped slightly. Between 1950 and 1960, while Germany and Japan recovered, the British share dropped.

The chemical industry in the United States grew rapidly, as the postwar economic expansion provided growing demand for the major product innovations of the 1930s – synthetic fibers, and plastics.[12] While companies such as Du Pont, which had made substantial investments in in-house R&D in the interwar years, relied upon major product innovations for growth, others such as Dow and Union Carbide established themselves as innovative and low-cost producers of a variety of important intermediate inputs. A number of oil companies, most notably Shell, Exxon, Amoco, Arco, and Phillips Petroleum, entered and become major players in basic and intermediate chemicals derived from petroleum feedstocks. The spread of petrochemicals before the Second World War was slow and limited to the United States. Haynes (1947, Vol. V, Chap. 15) notes that between 1921 and 1939, the volume of organic chemicals not derived from coal rose from about 21 million pounds to about 3

[10] The implications of this "convergence" for industrial structure are more fully discussed in Arora and Gambardella (1998).

[11] German patents and other industrial property were expropriated after World War II. The impact, for both Germany and its competitors, was limited because German technology was based on coal chemistry, while the industry was shifting to technologies based on liquid hydrocarbons – oil and natural gas.

[12] See Landau (1998) for a detailed discussion of two major innovations – polyethylene, and purified terephthalic acid for polyester.

billion pounds, while increasing in value from $9.2 million to about $400 million. During the latter year, coal based organic compounds totaled 300 million pounds in weight, and $260 million in value.[13] By 1950, half the total U.S. production (by weight) was based on oil and natural gas, and by 1960 this figure had reached 88%. But the early U.S. dominance was not very long lived as petrochemicals spread to Western Europe and Japan. The rise of petrochemicals was swift in Western Europe after the Second World War. In Britain, only 7% of the chemical production (by weight) was based on oil in 1949; the figure was 63% in 1962.

The technological lead of U.S. *chemical producers* in petrochemicals was eroded as oil companies and engineering design firms diffused the technology internationally (see Section IIIB). The breakup of the cartels after World War II made technology very mobile, and the "follower" countries benefited greatly from it. Technology for a variety of important products – from the basic petrochemical inputs such as ethylene to newer materials such as polyethylene, polypropylene, and polyester – became more widely available. Furthermore, the oil and natural gas endowments of the United States also did not prove to be an overwhelming source of comparative advantage after the war. The discovery of the Middle East oil deposits, and the political guarantees provided by the United States regarding their availability, promoted the growth of the world market for crude oil, enabling countries without oil deposits of their own to develop petrochemical industries nonetheless. Government regulation of oil imports in the United States also played an important part. Since the late 1930s, the oil industry had been regulated by the government. Among other things, production of individual companies was regulated to prop up the domestic price of oil. After World War II, the regulations were extended to restrict imports of oil. The net effect, according to Chapman (1991, p. 188), was that the crude oil acquisition costs for U.S. refineries was 60–80% higher than the landed costs in Western Europe through the late 1950s and 1960s. The differential sharply narrowed in the 1970s as a result of the oil shock which raised the world prices of oil. But while the differential lasted, it served to reduce the advantage that its natural resource endowment had provided to the United States. However, one should point out that many U.S. firms had access to another cheap source of light hydrocarbons (such

[13] This growth took place alongside a rapid growth in the more efficient type of coke ovens (Tarr, 1994). In other words, in the initial period at least, coal tar based and petroleum and natural gas based feedstocks were used for somewhat different types of products. Over time, techniques such as catalytic reforming for producing aromatic organic compounds from petroleum fractions were developed. Together with the abundant reserves of oil and gas, the raw material basis of the chemical industry changed from coal to oil.

as ethane, propane, and butane), namely, natural gas. On the whole, the mineral wealth of the United States was instrumental in the country's developing an early technological and commercial lead in the newly emerging petrochemical sector.

Eventually, U.S. dominance was partially undercut by its very success, and by the end of the 1960s, European countries and Japan had succeeded in closing much of the gap. Since the 1960s, relative shares in world output have largely remained constant, with the exception of a small decline in the share of the United States and a rise in the share of Japan (Table 6.2). The oil shocks and the unsettled macroeconomic conditions of the 1970s slowed down the growth of the industry in all the developed nations. By 1980, Japan had overtaken Germany as the second largest chemical industry, accounting for 11% of the global output to Germany's 8%. More recent figures indicate that the aggregate Japanese chemical output may now be close to that of the United States. The rapid growth of the Japanese chemical industry was the result of massive domestic investments in the newly emerging fields of petrochemicals. The chemical industry was promoted through a variety of government policies, including preferential access to capital and imported technologies. Much of the new chemical capacity in Japan was based on technology licensed from abroad. The sources of demand for the Japanese chemical industry appear to have been largely domestic, rather than exports, although in recent years the Japanese chemical industry has become one of the leading exporters in the world.

Along with Japan, a number of other countries also attempted to develop their petrochemical sector. The rapid growth of chemical production in the non–Organization for Economic Cooperation and Development (OECD) countries is reflected in Table 6.3. As late as 1959, the United States, Japan, and Western Europe accounted for virtually all chemical exports. By 1993, their combined share was only 66%, with the rest coming from countries such as South Korea and Taiwan, Eastern European countries, and countries in the Middle East. Much of the capacity addition took place during the 1970s and especially the 1980s. Between 1970 and 1985, the installed ethylene capacity in the Arab world increased from 0 to 2.5 million tons per year, and installed methanol capacity by 2 million tons per year. In the 1980s, a cheaper dollar and declining growth opportunities in their home markets prompted European firms (and to a lesser extent, Japanese firms as well) to expand heavily into the U.S. market. The expansion, accomplished through direct investments as well as acquisitions and alliances, underlined both the globalization of the industry and the declining U.S. dominance.

The increase in industry capacity globally and the increase in the number of producers resulted in large excess capacity and falling profitability, especially after the oil shocks in the 1970s slowed economic growth. The longer-term prospects were not good either. The rising share of services in gross national product (GNP) at the expense of manufacturing meant falling demand multipliers for the chemical industries in the developed countries. As many products became "commodities," comparative advantage shifted in some cases to countries with growing demand, typically the more advanced developing countries such as Korea and Taiwan.

The Role of the Government. With a few notable exceptions, government policies during the interwar years had had only a modest effect on the development of the industry. Perhaps the single most important effect was indirect, by way of macroeconomic policies whereby the more traditional sectors of the industry were clearly hurt by the Depression. World War II changed the picture considerably. The United States government played a particularly important role in two critical areas – petroleum refining and synthetic rubber. Research into synthetic rubber in both Germany and the United States had begun well before World War II. During the military expansion in the 1930s, Hitler's government had put a very high priority on a substitute for natural rubber as a part of its drive toward self-sufficiency. At considerable expense, IG Farben, which had produced the first synthetic rubber during World War I, managed to develop a much better product based on copolymers of butadiene with styrene, and acrylonitrile, Buna-S, and Buna-N, respectively. In the United States, Du Pont had commercialized a high-performance but expensive rubber substitute, neoprene. Unlike in Germany, however, research in synthetic rubber was driven by commercial motives rather than political ones.

It was only during the war that the United States government took a more active part. It organized a cooperative program of research and development, involving the four major rubber companies and Standard Oil, with a number of major chemical companies also participating (see Morris, 1994; Howard, 1947). After Buna-S was chosen as the target, Dow was put in charge of the styrene production (although Monsanto, Union Carbide, and Koppers were also involved). A number of oil and chemical companies shared the production of butadiene. Rubber companies carried out the copolymerization and fabrication. The federal government invested approximately $700 million in the construction of plants, which private companies operated as government contractors. After the war, most of the government owned plants were sold to private firms, usually to those operating them during war, and usually on very favorable terms. The rubber program was a major success. Not only did rubber consumption rise substantially (from 800,000 long tons in 1941 to 900,000 long tons in 1945), no less than 85% of the total in 1945 was synthetic rubber compared with less than 0.5% in 1941.

In petroleum refining, the government played an indirect role, through its procurement policy. Between 1939 and 1945, operating capacity in refining increased by 29% (Chapman, 1991, p. 74). But more important was the effect on the composition of output. Hitherto, gasoline for motorcars had been the major output of the refining industry in the United States, produced through fractionation, and in the 1930s, by thermal cracking as well. Now, in addition to butadiene for synthetic rubber, the oil industry was asked to provide high-octane aviation fuel, as well as aromatic products such as toluene. To produce the required quantities of aviation fuel, as well as aromatics, new technologies such as catalytic cracking and alkylation (both vital to the production of high-octane fuel) and catalytic reforming (to produce aromatic compounds) had to be adopted. These techniques had been developed over the 1920s and 1930s but without the stimulus of the war would have diffused only slowly.

Entry and Competition, and Evolution of Industry Structure. In addition to direct subsidies and procurement, the government policies on the diffusion of technical information and expertise had a strong leveling effect. Cooperative research was actively encouraged. An important fallout of the rubber program was that after the war, a number of companies in the United States had both technological expertise and experience in synthetic rubber and therefore in synthetic polymers more generally. The heightened interfirm mobility of personnel led to the breakdown of many secrecy barriers. After the war, the government also compelled the licensing of some major product innovations.[14] Along with the entry of oil firms into chemicals and the wider availability of chemical process technology from specialized engineering firms (discussed later), the net effect was to reduce the technology gap between firms and increase the number of firms that were able to innovate in the future. Thus a number of firms were now capable of competing effectively with the established firms in virtually all sectors. These included the hitherto lesser known chemical companies, such as Dow and Monsanto, as well as oil and rubber firms. Organic chemicals, synthetic rubber, and especially plastics and resins saw widespread entry, and concentration in these sectors

[14] Du Pont was forced, albeit on attractive terms, to license nylon to Monsanto. Similarly, the ICI–Du Pont patents and processes agreement was terminated in 1952 as a part of a consent decree and the ICI polyethylene patent was licensed to a number of companies.

decreased substantially in the first two decades after the war. By 1967, concentration (measured as the share of the top four producers) was lower in organic chemicals than in inorganic chemicals such as alkalis or inorganic pigments (MCA, 1971).

Similar deconcentrating tendencies were less pronounced in Germany and Britain. The end of the war saw IG Farben redivided into the three major original constituent firms (Stokes, 1994). A number of well-known names such as Agfa, Knapsack, and Cassella remained parts of one of the big three. As a number of observers have noted, the big three German chemical firms did not aggressively compete with each other, having only limited overlap in their product portfolios. In Britain, by the end of the war, ICI had transformed itself partly into an R&D based company with product innovations (Perspex safety glass, polyethylene, polyester, acrylic, and a variety of pharmaceutical and plant disease control products like Gammaxene). Its transformation testifies to the power of large investments, an early start, and benefits that it and other follower companies derived from the impact of the two wars on the leading German companies. In Japan, the old *zaibatsu* groups had managed to catch up technically with the entrepreneurial *zaibatsu*, who had suffered more during the war. During the early phase of postwar Japanese development, a number of joint ventures, often involving firms from different groups, were formed to undertake the massive investments in petrochemical plants (Hikino, 1998).

The Oil Shocks and Industrial Restructuring. The first couple of decades after World War II were a period of strong growth in demand and output. Most established companies significantly diversified and expanded. A number of countries attempted to develop their domestic chemical industries and added to the number of producers. Oil companies and firms from related industries entered the industry as well. The established chemical companies faced competition from the oil companies, and from new entrants from other countries, with access to cheaper raw materials or capital (or weaker regulations). The oil shocks of the 1970s are widely acknowledged as the turning point in the industry, although some of the tendencies that the oil shocks exacerbated appear to have manifested themselves in the 1960s as well. The oil shocks sharply raised input costs for an industry that was now petroleum based. Perhaps equally importantly, the oil shocks of the 1970s were associated with a slowdown in overall economic growth in all the major developed economies. For an industry whose growth was closely tied up with manufacturing growth, the oil shocks meant a decline in demand precisely at a time when its costs were rising and when innovation opportunities were becoming rarer. The combination of increasing entry, slower demand growth, and diminishing opportunities for major product innovations on the scale of nylon or polyester forced a consolidation of industrial structure.

The responses of the established firms have varied, and although some companies attempted to integrate backward (e.g., Du Pont's purchase of an oil company, Conoco), most moved toward higher value added products, in which chemical companies may have a comparative advantage.[15] The first phase of restructuring took the form of rationalization of capacity, with older and less efficient capacity being phased out and only a part of it replaced by new capacity. In the United States the first phase of the restructuring appears to have been accomplished by the mid-1980s. The capacity reduction phase was followed by a restructuring in the corporate sector that appears to have reached its peak in the late 1980s.

The process of restructuring illuminates how, as a high-tech industry matures, the strategic importance of different types of investments, and along with it, the nature of corporate strategy and corporate governance, also change. The following aspects of restructuring are noteworthy in this respect. First, restructuring has been most marked in the basic and intermediate petrochemicals. A number of the traditional chemical companies in the United States, and to a lesser extent in Europe, are exiting from some of their commodity chemical businesses and moving downstream, focusing on businesses in which product differentiation based on quality and performance allows for higher margins. In their place, oil companies and other firms (such as Vista, Quantum, Cain, Sterling, and Huntsman) are stepping in. Many of the latter are new firms that have taken over the existing commodity chemicals businesses of other firms such as Conoco, Texaco, Monsanto, and USX. The general trend is toward a separation between the high value added, specialty chemicals and the larger-volume commodity chemicals. This suggests that many of the synergies that were characteristic of the industry are less important. In this context it is significant to note also that the restructuring is taking place at a time when major product innovation has dropped off and chemical firms are reducing R&D spending, focusing upon higher-value-added products and process innovation aimed at cheaper or environmentally more benign technologies.

The second major aspect of restructuring is that firms are narrowing their lines of business, reversing a long trend of diversification based on economies of scope. To some extent, these divestments are a correc-

[15] The discussion of industrial restructuring draws heavily upon Arora and Gambardella (1998).

tion of the earlier tendencies toward conglomeration and unrelated diversification of the 1960s. However, Arora and Gambardella (1998) conclude that restructuring has gone well beyond getting rid of the unrelated businesses. Through a series of divestitures, acquisitions, mergers, and alliances, firms are attempting to increase both the absolute size, as well as the market share, of their remaining businesses. At the moment it is not clear whether the search is for volume or for market share. In other words, the trends could be driven by some efficiency motives, such as the desire to spread fixed costs of process research, sales, and management over larger volumes (e.g., Cohen and Klepper, 1992). Alternatively, these trends could reflect an attempt to control price competition by exercising price leadership. The latter is a subtle point. With differentiated products, which are often branded, the key issue is not maintaining profit margins by restricted output. Rather, it is reducing the stringency of price competition from products that are perceived to be close substitutes. Consolidation can enable a firm to manage the interbrand competition more effectively, especially when faced with a large "competitive fringe" of producers. This appears to be an important motive behind the division swaps.

Although globalization has become something of a cant word, there is no doubt that chemical companies in the developed countries are becoming global in their outlook. The process of internationalization has been accelerated by the narrowing of business portfolios. In other words, firms are being driven to specialize more narrowly in accordance with comparative advantage (or core competence) in specific businesses. Liberalization of government controls over both international trade and international capital movements has doubtless played a very important role in this respect.

Fourth, restructuring has been driven by institutional innovations related to changes in the market for corporate governance and finance. The increasing importance of mutual funds and pension funds and the greater attention to "shareholder value" have been important forces behind the restructuring. The restructuring began in the United States and has taken place far more slowly in Europe, and even more slowly in Japan (Hikino, 1998). The social welfare implications of the restructuring are unclear, and the debate has been closely tied up with the broader debate on the virtues and vices of the Anglo-Saxon system of finance, versus the bank based systems of Germany and Japan (Richards, 1998; Da Rin, 1998). Stock markets appear to disfavor diversified firms with portfolios that include both commodities and specialties. The reasons perhaps lie in the greater difficulties of managing such firms, as well as the greater difficulties in evaluating the performance of the management of a diversified company. At any rate, the stock market appears to believe this to be the case.[16]

III. Determinants of Comparative Advantage

A. Firm Level Advantages

Economies of Scale and Scope, Cumulativeness, and Path Dependence. The process of restructuring appears to be a reversal of a long-standing pattern of development of the firms in the chemical industry. As the industry evolved, firms attempted to exploit the economies of scale and scope that their technological base made possible. First, firms diversified into product markets that had strong synergies with their existing knowledge bases. Dyestuffs led to pharmaceuticals, while synthetic fibers and plastics shared a common scientific base of polymer chemistry. Second, many firms attempted to integrate along the value chains in their major product markets. The result was the development of large diversified chemical firms, which Chandler has written about extensively (e.g., Chandler, 1990) and which have been the focus of much of our attention in this chapter. But not all firms were willing to invest so aggressively and broadly. Many remained more focused and smaller (although many of them are rather large in absolute size) – in electrochemicals, catalysts, surfactants, fertilizers, paints and surface coatings, engineered plastics, food, fragrances and other fine chemicals, herbicides and pesticides, and pharmaceuticals. These firms have played an important role in the industry, and their importance is likely to increase in the future. Arora and Gambardella (1998) show that the distribution of the different types of firms is roughly similar across the different countries. The one major difference is that Japanese firms are largely domestic in their operations. This suggests one possible reason for the limited international recognition that so large a chemical industry as the Japanese industry has enjoyed – the large, all around chemical companies typically do not have a substantial presence in Europe or the United States.

Histories of individual firms show the existence of dynamic sequences, whereby investments in one product provided capabilities and incentives for investments in other products that had not yet been discovered. The dependence on retained earnings for further investments further

[16] The breakup of ICI is a case in point. In 1992, before the demerger, ICI's sales were about $21 billion, and market capitalization was about $13 billion. By 1995, while sales increased by less than 10% to about $23 billion, its market capitalization *doubled* to about $26 billion. By contrast, in 1992 Bayer had sales of $26 billion and a market capitalization of about $11 billion. The corresponding figures for 1995 are $31 billion and $18.5 billion.

amplified these tendencies. Indeed, in the list of the top 50 chemical firms in Table 6.6 all the firms (with the exception of Huntsman) were founded before World War II, and many were founded before World War I. This testifies to the importance of cumulative advantages at the level of the firm. For instance, Du Pont acquired extensive experience with nitrocellulose as a result of its explosives business. When cellulosic polymer

Table 6.6. *Top 50 Chemical Producers, 1995*

Rank 1995	Rank 1994		Total sales 1995 $ millions	Chemical sales 1995 $ millions	Chemical sales percent of total sales
1	2	BASF (Germany)	$ 32,258	$ 22,030	68%
2	1	Hoechst (Germany)	36,409	21,716	60
3	5	Dow Chemical (U.S.)	20,200	19,234	95
4	4	Bayer (Germany)	31,107	18,798	60
5	3	DuPont (U.S.)	42,163	18,433	44
6	7	Shell (U.K./Netherlands)	150,669	15,375	10
7	6	ICI (U.K.)	16,210	13,048	80
8	11	Exxon (U.S.)	121,804	11,737	10
9	9	Elf Aquitaine (France)	41,729	11,119	27
10	-	Formosa Plastics (Taiwan)	10,784	10,784	100
11	8	Ciba (Switzerland)	17,504	10,741	61
12	13	Mitsubishi Chemical (Japan)	11,588	9,908	86
13	19	Sumitomo Chemical (Japan)	10,120	9,796	97
14	12	Rhone-Poulenc (France)	16,988	9,268	55
15	15	ENI (Italy)	34,556	8,553	25
16	21	Toray Industries (Japan)	10,008	8,164	82
17	14	Veba (Germany)	50,241	7,643	15
18	17	Monsanto (U.S.)	8,963	7,251	81
19	10	Asahi Chemical (Japan)	12,866	6,834	7
20	16	Akzo Nobel (Netherlands)	13,382	6,772	51
21	18	General Electric (U.S.)	69,768	6,628	10
22	24	Norsk Hydro (Norway)	12,586	6,404	51
23	22	British Petroleum (U.K.)	79,242	6,333	8
24	38	SABIC (Saudi Arabia)	6,299	6,299	100
25	36	Mobil (U.S.)	75,061	6,155	8
26	23	Solvay (Belgium)	9,273	6,153	66
27	20	Henkel (Germany)	9,907	6,088	61
28	26	DSM (Netherlands)	6,117	5,945	97
29	25	Union Carbide (U.S.)	5,888	5,888	100
30	31	Amoco (U.S.)	31,071	5,655	18
31	33	Air Liquide (France)	6,449	5,423	84
32	28	Occidental Petroleum (U.S.)	10,692	5,410	51
33	32	Dainippon Ink & Chemicals (Japan)	5,071	5,071	100
34	35	Eastman Chemical (U.S.)	5,040	5,040	100
35	30	BOC (U.K.)	5,923	4,987	84
36	29	Roche (Switzerland)	12,450	4,631	37
37	37	Unilever (U.K./Netherlands)	49,638	4,479	9
38	34	Showa Denko (Japan)	4,359	4,359	100
39	42	Total (France)	27,212	4,340	16
40	46	Huntsman (U.S.)	4,300	4,300	100

Table 6.6. *(cont.)*

Rank 1995	Rank 1994		Total sales 1995 $ millions	Chemical sales 1995 $ millions	Chemical sales percent of total sales
41	45	Arco Chemical (U.S.)	4,282	4,282	100
42	39	Zeneca (U.K.)	7,732	4,229	55
43	40	Mitsui Toatsu Chemicals (Japan)	4,146	4,146	100
44	43	Rohm and Haas (U.S.)	3,884	3,884	100
45	41	Sandoz (Switzerland)	12,891	3,815	30
46	50	Chevron (U.S.)	37,208	3,758	10
47	47	Allied Signal (U.S.)	14,336	3,713	26
48	48	W. R. Grace (U.S.)	3,666	3,666	100
49	27	Degussa (Germany)	9,673	3,612	37
50	-	Ashland (U.S.)	12,161	3,551	29

Note: Ranking based on chemical sales only to facilitate comparison with C&EN's Top 100. Excluded where possible are formulated products such as pharmaceuticals and cosmetics, and specialty equipment, energy, and other nonchemical operations.
Source: Chemical and Engineering News, July 22, 1996, p. 30.

based products, such as cellophane, lacquers, and rayon, appeared, it enjoyed a competitive advantage. Du Pont's experience with rayon and with dyestuffs had beneficial spillovers when it commercialized synthetic fibers. Du Pont's "polymer institute" reflects perhaps a clear awareness of the common knowledge base underlying the innovations the firm was commercializing in hitherto diverse markets such as synthetic fibers, synthetic rubber, and plastics (Hounshell and Smith, 1988). Similarly, BASF acquired significant competencies in high-temperature and pressure synthesis as a result of its commercialization of Haber's nitrogen fixation process. These competencies later focused it toward coal hydrogenation and oil-from-coal technologies based on the Bergius and Fischer-Tropsch processes. ICI's investments in ammonia inclined it toward high-temperature and high-pressure reactions, which later bore fruit in somewhat unanticipated ways in the form of high-pressure polyethylene. Degussa's experience in dealing with gold and other precious metals led it into the production of catalysts, which often use precious metals, and into cyanides, which were used in the processing of gold ores. Similarly, Dow's early experience with halogens (chlorine and bromine) led it into organic compounds containing halogens, such as polyvinyl chloride (PVC), and halogen based pesticides and insecticides. Today these are important parts of Dow's product lines.

Events far back in the history explain a great deal of structure of firms even today. The German dyestuffs firms, especially Bayer and Hoechst,

Table 6.7. *The Changing Sales Structure of IG Farben and Its Successors (BASF, Bayer, and Hoechst)*

Product Area	Proportion, in percent, of Sales Volume				
	1913	1929	1943	1974	1989
Dyestuff, paints	63	28	11	14	13
Chemicals	26	18	25	19	17
Pharmaceuticals	6	5	9	9	13
Agricultural Chemicals (including Nitrogen)	-	29	3	12	9
Fibers	3	7	6	4	8
Plastics	-	4	7	8	8
Rubber	-	-	4	20	19
Mineral Oil	-	-	9	3	2
Metals	-	1	8	1	1
Miscl	2	7	7	6	6
Sales (Billions DM)	0.6	1.5	3.2	59	137
Domestic	25	47	85	40	25
Abroad	75	53	15	60	75
Employees (thousands)	40	110	187	459	476

Source: Extracted from Teltschik (1992).

soon moved into pharmaceuticals, which shared a common scientific base with dyestuffs. But inorganic and other heavy chemicals were largely left to other companies such as Dynamit and Deutch Solvay. These technological lines of separation were reinforced by cartels and internal market sharing agreements along the lines of separation. The big three German companies are possibly the most diversified chemical companies in the world. In addition to a wide variety of chemicals, they are also major players in the pharmaceutical market, as shown in Table 6.7. By contrast, U.S. chemical companies lacked the organic chemistry base, and it was companies in fine chemicals and apothecaries, often with German links, that developed into pharmaceutical companies. A number of U.S. chemical companies, tempted by the high profitability of the pharmaceutical industry, did attempt to enter the industry in the 1970s and 1980s, but with decidedly less success than had been hoped for.[17] A similar story is true of British companies, except that ICI did have some background in

[17] German chemical companies appear to have gone down a dramatically different track. Witness BASF's acquisition of Boots ($2 billion); Knoll, Hoechst's acquisition of the generic drug maker Copley; and more recently, Marion-Merrill Dow ($7.5 billion), and Bayer's acquisition of Kodak's over the counter (OTC) drug business ($1 billion).

dyestuffs and therefore was more successful in developing a life-sciences business (pesticides as well as pharmaceuticals).[18] Both the United States and Britain, however, have fairly large, specialized pharmaceutical firms, such as Merck and Lilly in the United States, and Glaxo and Beecham in Britain.

The Japanese case is different and bears the imprint of its late industrialization. The availability of imported technology and the general backward state of the chemical industry itself enabled users – firms in downstream sectors – to play a more prominent role in the chemical industry. Although firms from downstream sectors are not unknown in the chemical industries in other regions (e.g., General Electric in plastics) the technological weakness of the chemical firms in Japan and the *keiretsu* group structure increased the relative importance of companies from user industries. For instance, synthetic fiber production, particularly of rayon, is dominated by textile producers, such as Kanebo, Teijin, Toyo Rayon, and Shinko Rayon. (By contrast, the synthetic fiber producers in the West are chemical firms like Du Pont or Hoechst.) Similarly, nitrogenous fertilizer companies in Japan integrated backward into chemicals (Molony, 1990, pp. 35–36). After World War II, many of the downstream user firms further integrated into petrochemicals, largely for internal use. Thus, Showa Denko, originally in fertilizers, diversified into various polyolefins; Daicel produced acetic acid and other derivatives to be used in its cellulose business; textile companies like Toray, Teijin, and Kanebo made similar moves (Spitz, 1988, pp. 375–384; Aftalion, 1989, p. 205).

Many petrochemical producers were themselves part of a larger group of companies (*keiretsu*) which included firms operating in downstream sectors such as electronics and automobiles. Chemical companies belonging to a group sold a substantial fraction of their output to downstream companies in the same group, rather than in the open market. Import protection provided incentives for domestic firms to diversify into the production of a wide range of products and each industrial group attempted some measure of self-sufficiency. The *keiretsu* structure therefore exacerbated the tendency, caused by import protection, toward production at scales that were too small to be economic. The influence exercised by the users is likely to have contributed to the high degree of product customization that exists in Japan. For instance, the number of grades of plastic resins is said to be an order of magnitude larger than in Europe or the United States, and Japanese automobile companies are

[18] In ICI's case, these investments took place much earlier, around the 1940s. However, more recently it too appears to have decided that synergies between its chemical and life sciences businesses are limited and the two businesses have been separated into ICI and Zeneca.

credited (or blamed) for inducing at high degree of product differentiation. Thus, although international technology trade and other factors have made some features of the Japanese industry more similar to those of other countries (e.g., the wide use of petrochemical technologies after World War II), important differences remain. Many of the special features of today's Japanese chemical industry, such as smaller scales of production, excess diversification, and excessive number of producers, appear to be a legacy of the conditions that characterized its early development (see Arora and Gambardella, 1998, for further details).

Initial investments and decisions conditioned the future choices made by firms in important ways and made for an important degree of path dependence in the trajectories followed by different firms. At the level of the industry the evidence of path dependence is much weaker. World wars, major technological discontinuities, and entry and exit have meant that no simple story of path dependence *at the industry level* based on technological cumulativeness is tenable. Path dependence at that level has to be seen as arising primarily from certain strategic interactions, whereby the initial patterns of specialization tend to get perpetuated. The Japanese case shows clearly that institutions and history can create path dependence; however, the rapidity with which petrochemicals replaced coal based chemicals, even in countries with as long a tradition and strength in coal chemistry as Germany, testifies to the power of international markets and historical events to shake industry loose of the grip of the past.

Research and Commercialization Capabilities. Technology and innovations have been important parts of the development of the chemical industry. Moreover, innovation in the industry has depended heavily on progress in science: organic chemistry, polymer chemistry, chemical engineering, and catalysis, to name only a few.[19] Therefore, many observers have looked to the role played by universities and research institutes to understand the dynamics of comparative advantage. For instance, a key to the rise of the German synthetic dyestuffs firms was the synthetic dyes that emerged from their in-house R&D laboratories in the 1870s and thereafter. Germany led other nations in organic chemistry and German firms were able to call upon distinguished and able German chemistry professors and their students. By contrast, it is said, British universities

[19] This relationship has not been one-sided, and many innovations continued to rely upon careful, systematic trial and error search activities. The Haber-Bosch process for synthetic ammonia was one of the most significant technological breakthroughs of the 20th century. But while reaction conditions were guided by theoretical considerations, the search for the right catalyst and equipment was still very much an empiricist process.

remained oblivious to the needs of the chemical industry. In other words, one has a simple causal story in which German universities produce larger supplies of trained and skilled organic chemists, as well as new knowledge, and in turn, this induces a more intensive use of organic chemists (and organic chemistry) in German firms.

There is much that is true in such a story, but a careful reading of the historical evidence casts considerable doubt on any simple supply side explanation. Organic chemistry in German universities was well established by the 1840s, and Germany was the leader in this field at the time. However, the scientific community was international even at that time, and communication of research findings was quite quick.[20] A number of distinguished German chemists worked in Britain, and many got industrial experience with British firms. For instance, Hoffman taught for many years in London and was Perkin's professor. Heinrich Caro (later research director at BASF) and Martius (later prominent at AGFA) trained at Robertson, Dale. After Perkin's initial discovery, a number of coal tar based synthetic dyes were discovered by researchers in Britain, France, Switzerland, and Germany in rapid succession in the 1860s. Perkin's path-breaking discovery is said to have been made obsolete in less than a decade, and possibly in as short a time as four years (see Travis, 1993; Haber, 1958).

Not just scientists, but entrepreneurs and skilled workers were mobile as well. For instance, Levinstein and Mond both migrated to Britain in the mid 19th century, and Leo Baekeland and Eugene Houdry to the United States in the beginning of the 20th century. A number of skilled French workers moved to Basel in Switzerland in the 1870s in the aftermath of the Fuchsine affair. Licensing and other technology transfer was not uncommon – Solvay, Nobel, and others had international licensing cartels or groups with financial interpenetration.[21] Therefore, even in the 1860s, the diffusion of knowledge and the production of dyestuffs across international boundaries were rapid. Further evidence against a simplistic supply side interpretation is provided by Haber, who notes that chemists enjoyed much higher prestige and salaries in German firms. By contrast, limited though the supply of trained English chemists may have been, the demand for their services appears to have been even more meager. Haber (1958, p. 188) notes that in 1897, about 4,000 chemists

[20] For instance, A. von Hoffman testified at a patent infringement trial in France in the 1860s, while living in England.

[21] The dynamite and explosives industry in the 1850s was dominated by the Nobel group, which is best seen as a network of companies linked through interlocking directorships and equity stakes. Similarly, the Solvays maintained close, equity based relationships with their licensers for the Solvay ammonia soda process, which was first commercialized in the 1860s.

were employed in industry in Germany. In Britain, far fewer trained chemists were employed. However, Haber also points out that the average annual starting salary in a German chemical firm for a university trained scientist was 2,400 marks, rising to about 4,000 marks in a few years, with additional bonuses and generous pensions. Although some chemists in Britain could get equivalent salaries, for the most part, they were paid less, with starting salaries closer to $100 (2,000 marks) per annum. This suggests that the problem was as much in the demand for chemists as it was in the supply.[22]

Put differently, inherent differences in *access* to scientific and technological knowledge cannot be the entire story, or even the most important part. This is not to suggest that a strong university base responsive to the needs of the industry is unimportant. Rather, it is to point to the important complementarity that is often missed. It appears that the importance of a strong university base lay as much in how it affected the willingness of management to invest in research as in the supply of trained researchers. What appears to distinguish the German firms from their British competitors is the willingness of the German firms to invest in the commercialization of science based innovations.[23] Simply put, German entrepreneurs grasped that science and technology could be strategic weapons of competition, no less than access to markets, raw materials, or capital. In turn, this willingness arose because German managers were trained and skillful chemists and enjoyed relationships of mutual respect with leading university professors.

In other words, German strengths in organic chemistry, in order to be translated into commercial success, required that managements of firms be trained in chemistry, if not skilled chemists themselves, as some leading German managers were. At the very least it required that managers be willing to invest in in-house capabilities, so as to be able to use the trained chemists whom the universities were educating. Thus, even though Perkin and Graebe and Lieberman (BASF) patented Alizarin at the same time in 1869, within five years, the German company was producing twice as much as Perkin's firm, despite the Franco–Prussian War

[22] It might be argued that this might be simply a reflection of the quality (of the training) of the chemists. One would still have expected British firms to seek out better trained chemists, possibly from overseas, and offer premia for experienced chemists, as Du Pont and Monsanto did in the interwar years. One would also have expected British students to seek admission to German and Swiss universities, much as American students would in the early part of the 20th century.

[23] Although there were exceptional British firms, such as those headed by Perkin, and by Levinstein, it was not till Brunner, Mond, and its descendent, ICI, that British firms were willing to make substantial investments in in-house R&D capabilities. Reader's account of ICI suggests that the initial investments were due to Mond's insistence (Reader, 1970).

and despite the larger British textile industry.[24] The example also points to the superior German commercialization capabilities. German firms made coordinated investments in large-scale production capabilities, in systematic research, and in marketing and technical sales. Within a couple of decades of being founded, BASF, Bayer, and Hoechst had subsidiaries in France and Russia (Haber, 1958, vol. I, p. 114). As Chandler has stressed, these companies made large, irreversible investments in production facilities, producing a large number of related products and integrating backward into the production of the inorganic intermediates and integrating forward into the marketing and sales. Although success at the level of the firm may not always translate into success at the level of national industry, in the case of organic dyestuffs, the correspondence is close because three firms accounted for 80% of the German output of dyes (which, at its peak, was about 80% of the world output).

Haber also points out that the Germans developed technical marketing and sales organizations in the 1870s and 1880s (1958, vol. I, p. 174). These were invaluable in training customers in the use of dyes. In turn, long-standing customers trained chemists from their suppliers. The attention to customers is even more remarkable since many of these customers were presumably in foreign countries. Haber discusses the attention German chemical firms paid to customers:

> Many works had their own dye-houses complete with all the necessary equipment. Dyers were invited to spend some weeks or even longer in the technical application departments to familiarise themselves with the latest colours and techniques. This practice became particularly valuable with the introduction of synthetic indigo and other fast vat dyes, because they presented many novel application problems. The elaborate technical service was supplemented by skillful marketing practices such as the preparation of splendid and costly pattern books, the care taken with labelling in foreign languages, the networks of selling companies dealing with many hundreds of agents, and, not least, careful market research. (vol. II, pp. 123–124)

Very similar observations can be made about U.S. firms at a later date. Hounshell and Smith (1988) describe in rich detail the commercialization capabilities of Du Pont: the comprehensive relationships with textile firms and the detailed knowledge of textile operations – pinning, weaving, and dyeing – that played a critical role in the success of prod-

[24] The latter aspect has received insufficient attention. Michael Porter's work has highlighted the importance of a domestic user industry that is competitive on a world scale. The German dyestuff industry overcame not only the putative disadvantage of being a follower, but also that of its primary rival's having access to a larger and more advanced domestic user industry.

ucts such as nylon, spandex fibers, and polyester. By contrast, British firms in the late 19th century appeared to lack these capabilities and appeared to have been unable or unwilling to invest in their development. The point is not to single out one or another type of investment. Rather, it is to emphasize that a number of related investments, in research, production, and marketing, as well as management, appear to have been needed for commercial success.

The failure of British firms in science based industries in the 1850s and 1860s has been remarked upon by a number of authors. There is much less consensus on the reasons for this failure. Some authors have looked for the reasons in the broader social and political context. These explanations point to the class structure in Britain and its social institutions, which are alleged to have siphoned off the best talents into the bureaucracy, law, finance, and the clergy. Related arguments focus on the distractions of running a worldwide empire. The dominance of the landed gentry in the social and political life of the country is also said to have contributed to this failure.

Another set of explanations hinge on the interrelationship between the conditions of capital supply and the nature of entrepreneurship. German firms were far more willing to invest on a larger scale and invest larger amounts in "sunk" assets such as a trained sales force, scientists, and overseas plants. By contrast, British firms were more cautious, sinking in much smaller amounts. There has been a great deal of discussion about the differences in the stock market based financial institutions of Britain and the United States, on the one hand, and the bank finance based institutions in Germany and Japan on the other. However, for the most part, companies in both countries invested out of retained earnings and only infrequently looked to the financial markets. Although the two types of systems do have significant implications for corporate governance, the implications for ultimate economic success are less clear.[25] Moreover, in recent times, with the increasing globalization of capital markets, it appears that the two systems are beginning to converge.

[25] On the basis of the rapid growth of the German chemical companies in the 1860s and 1870s, perhaps a more promising line of inquiry is to look at the conditions of capital supply for new firms. Whereas in Britain "rediscounting of bills" was a major source of such finance, in Germany financing appears to have had a greater component of relational finance. The British system was anonymous and arm's-length; the German system implied greater involvement of the lender and hence also favored greater "sunk" investments of the type that appear to have been important for commercial success in "high-tech" industries such as synthetic dyestuffs. This argument is more fully developed by Da Rin (1998). One should point out that no necessary causality is implied – rather, both the type of financial system and the system of management and entrepreneurship are codetermined in an evolutionary process.

B. Industry Level Determinants of Comparative Advantage

Complementarities Among Resource Endowments, Technology, and Market Size. The dependence of commercial success upon a number of coordinated fronts is a theme that plays well at the level of the industry as well: The historical record points to the crucial interplay among natural resource endowments, size of market, capital, and technology. It is important to appreciate both the multiplicity of the sources of comparative advantage and the mutual complementarities.

For instance, the chemical industry is raw material dependent and the terms on which raw materials are made available can often be crucial.[26] The U.S. industry has enjoyed a comparative advantage based upon natural resources (Rosenberg, 1972; Nelson and Wright, 1992; Arora and Rosenberg, 1998). From the early years of its history, the U.S. industry had a relatively large proportion of products based on minerals, on products derived from the destruction of wood, and on products such as naval stores. In the early 20th century, other natural resource based sectors, such as those based on chlorine and on cheap electrical power (such as carbide and ammonia), became important. Starting in the 1920s and 1930s, U.S. industry exploited abundant reserves of cheap natural gas and petroleum, laying the foundation for the petrochemical industry.

Although the intimate linkage between the oil and petroleum industries may seem natural, it was in reality a human creation, fashioned in the United States. The point to note is that the convergence was not just that the by-products of the oil refining industry were used as feedstocks by the chemical industry. The feedstock link has been crucial, and a number of authors have correctly pointed to it. But there are many other, more subtle and no less important linkages as well. As already noted, chemical techniques of catalysis, hydrogenation, and the like, were finding application in the oil industry, which had hitherto relied upon straight distillation but now required such techniques to produce higher-octane fuels, as well as to convert heavier oil fractions into more valuable gasoline range hydrocarbons.

Not only did oil refining become very much a chemical process, chemical production too benefited from advances made in the design and

[26] In some instances, government policies can have major (possibly unintended) impacts. For instance, in Japan, the tax on naphtha to subsidize heating oil is said to have had a significant adverse impact on the international competitiveness of the Japanese petrochemical industry.

engineering of refineries. Oil refining has always been extremely capital intensive and, therefore, put a premium on large-scale production. Moreover, since opportunities for product differentiation in gasoline and similar products were more limited than in chemical products such as dyestuffs, the payoffs to cost reduction and hence to process innovation were greater than in traditional chemicals. It is therefore not surprising that the oil refining sector played a major role in the development of chemical engineering – the science and practice of developing and operating large-scale, continuous flow chemical processes. Such knowledge proved to have much broader applications in the chemical industry as well. The transformation of the chemical industry as it existed in 1920 to the petrochemical industry as it matured after World War II was in large measure the achievement of the chemical engineering profession.

Chemical engineering was a distinctly American achievement and testifies to the unique nature of the university–industry interface in the United States.[27] The United States had adopted the 19th century German model of the university as an institution of higher research. MIT pioneered the rise of chemical engineering as a discipline in the 1920s, and in the course of the 20th century, a number of American universities introduced it in the curriculum. Beginning with the concept of unit processes, chemical engineering was an attempt to abstract the essential and common features of chemical processes for a wide variety of products. The systematic isolation, categorization, and analysis of the basic processes (unit processes and later unit operations) common to all chemical industries had three important implications. An engineer trained in terms of unit operations could mix and match these operations as necessary in order to produce a wide variety of distinct final products. Not only was such an engineer more flexible, he could also transfer techniques and methods from one type of industry to another. Put somewhat differently, he was not tied to any particular final product. This separation laid the basis for the rise of firms specializing in the design of chemical plants, a process that we discuss later.

Second, such abstraction made possible the accumulation and refining of methodological tools. These tools provided the basis of problem solving activities connected with the design of chemical plants. The awareness that there were a limited number of similar operations common to many industries served to identify research priorities and therefore to point to a disciplinary research agenda. This was not possi-

[27] See Landau and Rosenberg (1992) for a discussion of the role of MIT in the development of chemical engineering as a discipline.

ble as long as technologists remained lost in the particularities of innumerable specific products. Moreover, such abstraction had great pedagogical value; it provided the basis for a curriculum that could be taught. This did not happen immediately. Rather, the establishment of a curriculum of marketable skills had to await more extensive interaction with industry.

The large size of the market had introduced American firms, at an early stage, to the problems involved in large-scale production of basic products, such as chlorine, caustic soda, soda ash, and sulfuric acid. This ability to deal with a large volume of output, and eventually to do so with continuous process technology was to become a central feature of the chemical industry in the 20th century. Sulfuric acid provides a compelling illustration of this ability to design for production on a large scale. General Chemical Company invented a process for the large-scale production of sulfuric acid (the "contact" process) that had previously been commercialized by BASF.[28] A patent infringement suit by BASF against General Chemical was settled out of court by an exchange of patents and other agreements, giving each firm access to the other's process technology. Nevertheless, after officials from BASF visited and inspected General Chemical's facilities, they were so impressed by the efficiency of the large scale of plants that they placed a large order for the design and construction of four plants that General Chemical was to install at Ludwigshaven. Haynes (1947, vol. I, pp. 265–266), who describes this episode, pointedly notes that each unit was for 20,000 tons, *four times* the size of the largest existing BASF facility. General Chemical's accomplishment is even more remarkable because BASF was renowned for its engineering and development prowess, as evidenced later in the development of the Haber-Bosch process. General Chemical later received a similar order from Bayer that was to play an important role in supplying the German munitions industry in World War I.

This focus on large-scale production had additional future benefits when it turned out that the new petrochemical technologies had strong plant level economies of scale, with capital costs rising by less than two-thirds of the scale of output. Since "scaling up" output was not a simple matter and involved considerable learning, U.S. firms, which got a head start, enjoyed an advantage once petrochemicals became the dominant feedstock after the Second World War. The lead in know-how about

[28] In 1899 General Chemical (later merged into Allied Chemicals) tried to secure the American rights from BASF. In the face of very stringent licensing fees ($1 million lump sum and 25% royalty on value of output) General Chemicals decided to commercialize a domestically developed version of the process.

large-scale production technologies is significant because the U.S. industry did not have an initial advantage in terms of a lead in the basic science. Germany probably led the United States and other countries even in polymer chemistry; methyl rubber was used in Germany during World War I. Griesham Elektron had synthesized PVC (Paul Klatte) as early as 1912 before polymerization was well understood, but it was Union Carbide and Dow which really made the process innovations that made PVC a large-volume plastic. Polystyrene was a German invention, but US Rubber (Uniroyal) and Dow were able to commercialize it successfully later in the 1930s. Somewhat later (around 1938–1939), Germans demonstrated that they did not lag long in synthetic fibers, as IG Farben (Paul Schlack) quickly found a way of producing nylon that did not infringe Du Pont's patent. However, Du Pont clearly was more successful at commercializing the innovation. The superior commercialization capabilities of U.S. companies are also evident in polyester and polyethylene. Both these innovations originated in Britain in the years just before World War II, but Du Pont, Union Carbide, and Dow proved to be very capable "fast seconds" after the war.

The U.S. rise to dominance testifies to the importance of a constellation of favorable factors: abundant raw materials, large and growing markets, and technological change in chemicals and related sectors. The rise of petrochemicals owes a great deal to technological progress in refining (thermal and catalytic cracking, reforming, alkylation, amortization, design of new equipment, and optimization of processes). In turn, the latter owes much to the demand pull from the automobile sector, the demand for higher-octane gasoline, and the availability of cheap and abundant stocks of petroleum and natural gas. Thus, not only did refining and petrochemicals have beneficial technological spillovers, a compulsive sequence of innovations was triggered. Chemical firms looked for alternatives to coal based feedstocks (acetylene, benzene); oil companies looked to apply chemical techniques to increase the proportion of more valuable low- and medium-range hydrocarbon products such as ethylene and propylene.

It is instructive to compare Japan and the United States in this respect. In the 19th century, both depended upon imported technology, and the industry consisted of small firms operating with rather simple technologies. Nonetheless, the United States was richer and was much better off in terms of the development of manufacturing technologies and capabilities: The American system of manufactures was already in place. By contrast, the Japanese economy was in many ways "preindustrial" and as a consequence, the Japanese chemical industry could not grow in a symbiotic relationship with other industries such as steel, automobiles, and refining.[29]

Extent of Market, and Division of Labor.[30] The effects of large markets are not felt at the level of the firm alone. In some instances, industry level effects may be equally, if not more, significant. The rapid growth of the petrochemical industry also laid the groundwork for the rise of a division of labor that had a major impact on the diffusion of technology and know-how, and hence, on the patterns of comparative advantage. This division of labor involved a new type of specialized firm – the specialized process design and engineering contractors, hereafter the SEFs (see Landau and Rosenberg, 1992). In addition to supplying proprietary processes, a number of other SEFs also acted as licensers on behalf of chemical firms and provided design and engineering know-how. These firms played a crucial role in the development of new and improved processes, as well as their diffusion.

As one might expect, given the comparative emphasis on large-scale production, the United States enjoyed an early lead in chemical engineering of plants, handling the higher temperatures and pressures, and in selling such services, even though the German firms pioneered the commercialization of such processes. The first SEFs were formed in the early part of this century, and their clients were typically oil companies. However, SEFs also started operating in some bulk chemicals such as sulfuric acid and ammonia. The Chemical Construction Corporation built sulfuric acid and other plants, while the Chemical Engineering Corporation targeted synthetic ammonia and methanol processes, both attaining some success in project exports to Europe as well.[31] Later, most SEFs would operate in designing large-scale plants for refineries and petrochemical building blocks. Prominent among the early SEFs are companies such as Kellogg, Badger, Stone and Webster, and of course, UOP.

Initially, the chief market for the SEFs were firms in the United States,

[29] Many of the coke ovens in Germany and Britain were associated with steel plants. The coke ovens provided the basic raw materials for much of the organic industry prior to the rise of petrochemicals. Even after a decade of rapid growth, in 1929, Japan produced 1.3 million tons of steel. The corresponding figures for other countries are United States, 52.3, Britain, 9.8, and Germany, 16.2 tons.

[30] This section draws heavily upon Arora and Gambardella (1998).

[31] "These engineering enterprises created a unique phase of Cyanamid's business. The building of chemical plants, chiefly sulfuric acid, synthetic ammonia, and nitric acid operations, on a 'turnkey' basis, that is, delivered in running order, soon grew into a profitable, world wide enterprise" (Haynes, 1947, vol. IV, p. 46).

who could contract out some of the design and engineering services. Apart from oil companies, established chemical firms were less eager to outsource such functions, in part because of a tradition of secrecy, and in part because of the tendency of the chemical processes to be more complex and chemical plants smaller than was the case in refining. Established chemical companies were especially reluctant to buy technology from SEFs or to enter into alliances with them to develop new technology. But World War II, with its leveling effect, changed this as well. Landau (1966, p. 4), writing two decades after the end of the war, noted that the "the partial breakdown of secrecy barriers in the chemical industry is increasing . . . the trend toward more licensing of processes." The rise of synthetic polymers united what had been a number of disparate markets such as fibers, plastics, rubber, and films. The result was that the number of potential entrants increased, thereby increasing the demand for the services of SEFs. American SEFs also took advantage of the dislocation in Europe after World War II to combine their superior know-how in chemical process design with proprietary technologies, to offer technology packages to customers in Europe and the United States.[32]

European and Japanese firms (and later, firms in the Middle East and East Asia) benefited greatly from the technology transfer by the SEFs. Freeman (1968, p. 30) noted that for the period 1960–1966 nearly three-quarters of the major new plants were "engineered, procured, and constructed by specialist plant contractors." This figure is confirmed by a more recent study, which finds that for the period 1970–1990, over three-fourths of the petrochemical plants built all over the world were "engineered" by SEFs (Arora and Gambardella, 1998). By providing technology licenses to firms the world over, SEFs played a major role in the diffusion of chemical, especially petrochemical, technologies.[33] As independent developers of technology, SEFs were similar in some respects to today's biotech companies, often partnering with a number of chemical firms in developing new technologies.[34] By supplying technology and know-how for a wide variety of chemical processes the SEFs

[32] The technology transfers were not all from the United States to Europe. Spitz (1988) points out that many European chemical firms, particularly technology rich but cash poor German firms, were willing to license their technologies for revenue in the 1950s. For much of this period, however, Japan remained a net importer of technology.

[33] Freeman showed that for the period 1960–1966, SEFs as a group accounted for about 30% of all licenses (for processes), this percentage is consistent with the findings reported by Arora and Gambardella (1998).

[34] For instance, Badger used its fluidized bed catalytic process to develop processes for phthalic anhydride with Sherwin Williams, ethylene dichloride with BF Goodrich, and acrylonitrile with Standerd of Ohio. UOP similarly had a number of strategic partnerships: with Dow (Udex – benzene extraction), Shell (sulfonale – benzene extraction), Ashland

Table 6.8a. *Producers, Capacities, and Concentration Ratios for Selected Petrochemicals in the United States, 1957, 1964, 1972, and 1990*

	Ethylene	Polyethylene	Ethylene Oxide	Ethylene Dichloride	Styrene
1957					
Producers	16	13	7	8	8
1964					
Producers	20	17	10	10	9
Capacity	4.9	1.2	0.80	0.90	1.0
Concentration ratio	52.1	47.8	70.5	42.1	70.3
1972					
Producers	25	21	13	11	12
Capacity	9.8	3.7	1.9	4.7	2.6
Concentration ratio	40.5	40.8	72.0	60.8	54.1
1990					
Producers	22	16	12	11	8
Capacity	18.4	10.3	3.3	8.4	4.0
Concentration ratio	30.8	37.9	54.2	57.5	52.1

Note: Polyethylene includes LDPE and HDPE. Capacity is measured in millions of tons. Concentration ratio is measured as the share of the largest three producers, expressed as a percentage.
Source: Chapman (1991, Table 5.2, p. 104).

had a major impact on industry structure, both in the United States and abroad. A number of firms entered the industry, especially in petrochemicals, shown in Tables 6.8a and 6.8b. Often, these were not "new" firms, but rather firms that had operated in other sectors of the chemical industry and wished to exploit some real or perceived competitive advantage. These firms typically entered on the basis of licensed rather than proprietary technology.[35] The SEFs had an equally important indi-

oil (Hydeal – dealkylation of toluene), Toray (Tatoray – disproportionation of toluene and C4 to benzene and xylene), BP (Cyclar – reforming of LPG into aromatics). Scientific Design, an innovative SEF, followed a different strategy, developing technology without recourse to joint research.

[35] In a study of 39 commodity chemicals in the United States in a period from the mid-1950s to the mid-1970s, Lieberman (1989) found that controlling for demand conditions, experience accumulated by incumbents did not act to deter new entry. Given the importance of learning by doing, this suggests that entrants had access to other sources of know-how, most likely from SEFs. This interpretation is further supported by Lieberman's

Table 6.8b. *Producers, Capacities, and Concentration Ratios for Selected Petrochemicals in Western Europe, 1955, 1964, 1973, and 1990*

	Ethylene	Polyethylene	Ethylene Oxide	Styrene
1955				
Producers	13	N/A	N/A	N/A
Capacity	0.2	N/A	N/A	N/A
Concentration ratio	52.7	N/A	N/A	N/A
1964				
Producers	25	23	15	10
Capacity	2.0	0.8	0.3	0.5
Concentration ratio	27.6	40.3	33.6	57.7
1973				
Producers	38	40	16	15
Capacity	11.6	5.2	1.4	>2.8
Concentration ratio	24.3	18.7	41.5	40.2
1990				
Producers	29	26	10	12
Capacity	16.0	9.3	1.7	4.0
Concentration ratio	25.9	27.2	41.4	47.6

Note: Polyethylene includes LDPE and HDPE. Capacity is measured in millions of tons. Concentration ratio is measured as the share of the largest three producers, expressed as a percentage.
Source: Chapman (1991, Table 5.3, p. 105).

rect impact – by competing as technology suppliers, they induced chemical firms to license their technologies as well (Arora, 1997). ICI licensed its ammonia, polyethylene, and polyester technology. Union Carbide openly licensed its Unipol process for polyethylene, as did Montedison. Amoco, Shell, Mobil, and Arco are among the other prominent licensers of proprietary technologies.

findings that entry into concentrated markets, which were also marked by low rates of patenting by nonproducers (both foreign firms and SEFs), usually required that the entrant develop its own technology. By contrast, less concentrated markets were associated with high rates of patenting by nonproducers and high rates of licensing to entrants. In a related study (of a subset of 24 chemicals) Lieberman (1987) found that high rates of patenting by nonproducers were also associated with faster rates of decline in prices.

Thus, a major consequence of SEFs was, paradoxically enough, to reduce the strategic importance of process technology, in essence, by creating and supplying a market for it. With a large number of potential licensees, and the possibility of competing innovation, it became very difficult to gain long-term advantage from a single innovation. Only by continual improvements and innovation could a company hope to derive a long-term advantage, and in some cases, even that was not sufficient.[36] In addition to inducing entry and creating, in effect, competition on a global scale, the development of a market in technology licenses brought to the fore the importance of other factors influencing competitive success – raw materials, capital, proximity to market, and other idiosyncratic factors such as severity of environmental regulation and macroeconomic instability.

SEFs provide a vivid illustration of economies of market scale – economies of specialization – that operate at the level of the industry, rather than of the plant or the individual firm. The growth of SEFs was directly linked to the rapid growth of a large, relatively homogeneous market provided by firms wishing to enter into petrochemicals, and by the emergence of the discipline of chemical engineering that unified these markets (at least from the viewpoint of the production processes). As demand growth has faltered since the oil shocks and the rate of investment has fallen, the SEF sector has itself shrunk and consolidated. SEFs have drastically reduced R&D expenditures and a number have left the industry or been acquired by others. The important point is that although initially the benefits of the division of labor between chemical producers and SEFs accrued to U.S. chemical firms, over time these benefits became available to chemical producers in other countries as well. Put differently, the very factors that underpin the U.S. success were also responsible for enabling other countries to catch up.

Diversity and the Extent of the Market. Another aspect of the economies of scale at the level of the industry has also received less attention thus far. The U.S. market allowed a greater number of firms to specialize, pursue different strategies, and acquire different sets of expertise, without having to incur penalties of suboptimal scale. By contrast, in Britain and Germany a few companies dominated a large number of product markets. Although the latter were, and are, successful companies, it is only to be expected that they would miss important opportu-

[36] Spitz (1988) describes how a number of companies entered into vinyl chloride and PVC based on new technologies. However, since a number of new technologies became available, few firms managed to get sustained profits, unless they enjoyed some other advantage such as a cheap source of raw materials.

nities. Often, other firms in the industry in these countries were unable or unwilling to pursue these opportunities, in part because of numerous market sharing arrangements with larger firms.[37]

In the United States, by contrast, the large market afforded the luxury of a greater number of "experiments." U.S. firms followed a variety of strategies. Du Pont adopted a strategy of product innovation based on in-house research, and a product line with a common technological base. Allied Chemicals, which was about the same size as Du Pont in the 1920s, adopted a very different strategy of large-scale production of ammonia, dyestuffs, and inorganics. Unlike Du Pont, Allied chose what seemed at the time a financially prudent strategy to contemporary observers such as Haynes. Allied limited its investments in research and development and gave the individual business division great autonomy provided they met strict financial goals. With the benefit of hindsight it is clear that Allied's was not a very good long-term strategy at a time when technological opportunities were abundant and when the technology was marked by widespread synergies and spillovers across different product lines.[38] However, the U.S. industry as a whole did not have to pay a big price for Allied's relative failure, because other firms were willing and able to try a different strategy. Similarly, in the 1920s, new companies such as Union Carbide and Dow were experimenting with the use of oil and natural gas based feedstocks, even as Standard Oil tried to obtain the technologies for coal hydrogenation and gasification. By contrast, Britain lacked this luxury in that it lacked firms, apart from ICI, with the requisite size and ability to try different options.

IV. Summary and Conclusions

The Multifaceted Nature of Comparative Advantage. The growth of the chemical industry, as an intermediate goods sector, has depended on overall GDP growth, and countries that grow more rapidly have also

[37] In Britain, the industry around the time of World War I was about one-fourth the size of the German industry and dominated by alkali and inorganic firms. Apart from Brunner, Mond, Nobel, and UAC, there were only a couple of significant dyestuffs firms (Read Holliday, and Levinstein). Lever stayed in consumer products, Courtaulds in textiles, BOC in industrial gases, and Distillers in molasses and by-products. Convention and fear of strategic responses backed by explicit agreements prevented them from entering each other's businesses. Other sectors of the chemical industry were similarly dominated by a single chemical industry or at best a few large chemical industries.

[38] An alternative, though less plausible, explanation is that Allied Chemicals, realizing that it lacked the technological competencies to exploit the newly emerging technologies, acted in the best interests of its shareholders by, in essence, liquidating itself by paying out high dividends.

tended to have more rapidly growing chemicals sectors. Historically, there have been more specific complementarities with other sectors, such as automobiles, and oil refining. The chemical industry is intensive in natural resources, energy, and capital. It is also a science based industry, in which innovation and technological change play an important role. The historical evidence points first and foremost to the multifaceted nature of comparative advantage. For instance, in the United States, although initially the raw material endowment was crucial to the industry's growth, over time the size of the market and the technological advances, in both products and processes, came to be very important. The U.S. experience also underscores the complementarities among market size, resource endowment, and technology. The combined effect of a large market, abundant mineral resources, and technological change – exemplified for instance in the rise of petrochemical based synthetic polymers – was much greater than simply the sum of the individual parts.

By the same token, no single source of advantage appears to have lasted for very long. The development of new, global markets has seen to that. Alternative sources of raw materials, or synthetic substitutes, were developed when raw materials became a major bottleneck. The shortage of Chilean nitrates led first to the cyanamid process, and then to the famous Haber-Bosch process for nitrogen fixation. The U.S. endowments of oil and natural gas, although they played a crucial role in getting the petrochemical industry off the ground, did not prove to be a source of overwhelming advantage, as others sought and developed the vast oil and gas deposits in the Middle East.[39] Mobility of personnel, wars, and other historical accidents have also proved to be disruptive of long-lived leadership by individual countries.

Economies of Scale: Firm Versus Industry. Commercial leadership at the level of the firm has often lasted for long periods, when the firm has made the required investments in technology, production, and marketing – in research and commercialization of innovation. Successful commercialization requires close attention to user needs. In addition to knowledge based economies of scale and scope, investments in establishing effective links with users, akin to a "sunk" cost, are an important source of increasing returns at the level of the firm. Thus, early mover advantage has been an important component of firm success in the chemical indus-

[39] U.S. oil and gas deposits did, however, provide certain U.S. firms with a first mover advantage. Individually and collectively, U.S. firms accumulated experience with oil and natural gas based feedstocks and with process technologies to exploit these feedstocks. The United States remains to this day a leader in petrochemical technologies (Arora and Gambardella, 1997).

try. However, the benefits of initial technological leads may be short-lived if rivals have been willing to make the necessary investments to acquire and adapt.

The chemical industry (e.g., SEFs) shows that increasing returns at the level of the industry, not just the firm, are important. From an analytical point of view, the significance of the SEFs lies in how one thinks of learning. The teachings of the Boston Consulting Group on learning by doing and experience curves focused attention on the accumulation of learning at the level of the firm. The SEFs are the institutional embodiment of learning at the level of the industry. Put differently, the learning and experience, occasioned by the growth in output of the chemical industry, that accumulated in an SEF were put at the disposal of the entire industry.

Role of Government Policy. Very few government policies have been shown to have been successful in the sense of having had long-lasting effects on the success of the national industries. Nearly every country attempted trade and industrial policies to promote domestic chemical industries. Although one could argue about individual cases, these policies have had only limited success. The creation of ICI is arguably a counterexample, as an apparently failing set of chemical firms were transformed into a fairly innovative and progressive firm. There is some truth to this characterization, but even here one must note that ICI had among its constituents two successful companies – Nobel and Brunner, Mond, of which the latter was also technologically progressive. The growth of Japanese petrochemicals immediately after the war was nothing short of spectacular and presumably the Japanese government, especially MITI, had a hand in that. The primary source of growth, however, was a combination of imported technology and domestic investment. Technology was supplied by SEFs and others and Japanese firms proved to be superb users, as Japanese firms had been in other sectors as well. The large rates of investment are also well understood and well documented, and related to the high rates of saving and the industrial group structure in the Japanese economy. Moreover, this combination appears to have been less successful in the 1980s and 1990s.

Public support of research universities has been perhaps the only policy with some measure of success. As the rise of chemical engineering in the United States shows, what is crucial, although much harder to achieve in practice, is a way of linking universities with industry which makes universities responsive to the needs of industry while preserving the autonomy of universities. However, it would be a mistake to see universities solely as producers of new knowledge or trained researchers, although these functions are undoubtedly important. A first-rate university system may be important in rather subtle ways as well. As the history of synthetic dyestuffs shows, the willingness of firms to invest in promising but risky new technologies depends on their ability to understand the new technologies. Close links with leading researchers in the field, as well as the close involvement of researchers in the technological activities of firms, seem to be essential for firms to be willing to make such investments.

Although specific industry oriented policy successes are not common, there are a host of broader economywide policies that have affected the competitive position of national industries. Policies affecting labor markets, environmental regulation, and the like, have direct impacts on an industry such as chemicals, and undoubtedly the success of the U.S. and German industries is due to favorable overall economic and political environments as well. Dangerous as it is to predict the future, we can be certain that all the lessons of the past will not carry over unchanged to the future.

References

Aftalion, F. 1989, *History of the International Chemical Industry*, University of Pennsylvania Press, Philadelphia.

Arora, A., and Gambardella, A, 1998, "The Chemical Industry: Evolution of Industry Structure," in Arora, Landau, and Rosenberg (eds.), *Chemicals and Long Run Economic Growth*, Wiley, New York.

Arora, A., and Rosenberg, N., 1998, "Chemicals: A U.S. Success Story," in Arora, Landau, and Rosenberg (eds.), *Chemicals and Long Run Economic Growth*, Wiley, New York.

Arora, A., and Gambardella, A., 1997, "Domestic markets and international competitiveness," *Strategic Management Journal*, Winter, Special Issue.

Arora, A., 1997, "Patent, Licensing and Market Structure in the Chemical Industry," *Research Policy*, Vol. 26, pp. 391–403.

Bernheim, D., and Whinston, M., 1990, "Multimarket Contact and Collusive Behavior," *Rand Journal of Economics*, Vol. 21(1), pp. 1–26.

Cantwell, John, 1995, "The Evolution of European Industrial Technology in the Interwar Period," in Caron, Francois, Erker, Paul, and Fischer, Wolfram (eds.), *Innovations in the European Economy Between the Wars*, Walter de Gruyter, Berlin.

Chapman, K., 1991, *The International Petrochemical Industry*, Basil Blackwell, Oxford.

Chandler, A.D., 1990, *Scale and Scope*, Harvard University Press, Cambridge. Mass.

Chemical Facts and Figures, 1940, Manufacturing Chemists Association, Washington, D.C.

Chemical Manufacturers' Association (CMA), 1994, *U.S. Chemical Industry Statistical Handbook*, Washington, D.C.

Cohen, W.M., and Klepper, S., 1992, "The Anatomy of Firm R&D distributions," *American Economic Review*, Vol. 82, No. 4, pp. 773–799.

Da Rin, M., 1998, "Finance in the Chemical Industry," in Arora, Landau, and Rosenberg (eds.), *Chemicals and Long Run Economic Growth*, Wiley, New York.

David, P.A., and Wright, G., 1991, "Resource Abundance and American Economic Leadership," CEPR publication number 267, Stanford University.

Eichengreen, B., 1998, "Monetary, Fiscal, and Trade Policies in the Development of the Chemical Industry," in Arora, Landau, and Rosenberg (eds.), *Chemicals and Long Run Economic Growth*, Wiley, New York.

Freeman, 1968, "Chemical Process Plant: Innovation and the World Market," NIER, Vol. 45, August, 29–51.

Haber, L.F., 1958, *The Chemical Industry During the Nineteenth Century*, Oxford University Press Oxford.

Haber, L.F., 1971, *The Chemical Industry, 1900–1930*, Clarendon Press, Oxford.

Hikino, T. et al., 1998, "The Japanese Puzzle: The Development of the Japanese Chemical Industry," in Arora, Landau, and Rosenberg (eds.), *Chemicals and Long Run Economic Growth*, Wiley, New York.

Harada, T., 1995, "The Japanese Chemical Industry: The Paradox of Technology Transfer," unpublished working paper, Department of Economics, Stanford University.

Hardie, D.W.F., and Pratt, J., 1966, *A History of the Modern British Chemical Industry*, Oxford, Pergamon Press.

Haynes, W., 1947, *American Chemical Industry*, Vol. 1–6, D. Van Nostrand Company, New York.

Hounshell, D., 1995, "Strategies of Growth and Innovation in the Decentralized Du Pont Company," in Caron, Francois, Erker, Paul, and Fischer, Wolfram (eds.), *Innovations in the European Economy Between the Wars*, Walter de Gruyter, Berlin.

Hounshell, D., and Smith, J.K., 1988, *Science and Strategy: Du Pont R&D, 1902–80*, Cambridge University Press, Cambridge.

Landau, R., 1966, *The Chemical Plant: From Process Selection to Commercial Operation*, Reinhold Publishing, New York.

Landau, R., 1997, "Education, Moving from Chemistry to Chemical Engineering and Beyond," *Chemical Engineering Progress*, January, Vol. 52, p. 65.

Landau, R., 1998, "The Process of Innovation in the Chemical Industry," in Arora, Landau, and Rosenbay (eds.), *Chemicals and Long Run Economic Growth*, Wiley, New York.

Landau, R., and Rosenberg, N., 1992, "Successful Commercialization in the Chemical Process Industries," in Rosenberg, Landau, and Mowery (eds.), *Technology and the Wealth of Nations*, Stanford University Press, Stanford, Calif.

Landes, D.S., 1969, *The Unbound Prometheus*, Cambridge University Press, New York.

Lane, S., 1993, "Corporate Restructuring in the Chemical Industry," in Margaret Blair (ed.), *The Deal Decade: What Takeovers and Leveraged Buyouts Mean for Coporate Governance*, Brookings Institution, Washington, D.C.

Lieberman, M., 1987, "Patents, Learning by Doing, and Market Structure in the Chemical Industry," *International Journal of International Organization*, No. 5, pp. 257–276.

Lieberman, M., 1989, "The Learning Curve, Technological Barriers to Entry, Competitive Survival in the Chemical Processing Industries," *Strategic Management Journal*, No. 10, pp. 257–276.

Manufacturing Chemists Association, 1971, *Chemical Statistics Handbook*, 7th ed., Washington D.C.

Marsch, U., 1994, "Strategies for Success," *History and Technology*, Vol. 12, No. 13, p. 77.

Moloney, B., 1990, *Technology and Investment: The Prewar Japanese Chemical Industry*, Harvard University Press, Cambridge, Mass.

Morris, P.J.T., 1994, "Synthetic Rubber: Autarky and War," in Mossman and Morris (eds.), *The Development of Plastics*, Royal Society of Chemistry, Cambridge.

Mowery, D., 1981, *The Emergence and Growth of Industrial Research in American Manufacturing, 1899–1946*, Ph.D. dissertation, Stanford University.

Murmann, P., and Landau, R., 1995, Dynamic Comparative Advantage in the Chemical Industry: Britain and Germany, unpublished manuscript, CEPR, Stanford University.

Murmann, P., and Landau, R., 1998, "Changing Fortunes: Britain Versus Germany," in Arora, Landau, and Rosenberg (eds.), *Chemicals and Long Run Economic Growth*, Wiley, New York.

Rosenberg, N., 1972, *Technology and American Economic Growth*, Harper & Row, New York.

Rosenberg, N., 1998, "Technological Change in Chemicals: The Role of University-Industry Relations," in Arora, Landau, and Rosenberg (eds.), *Chemicals and Long Run Economic Growth*, Wiley, New York.

Nelson, R.R., 1995, "Recent Evolutionary Theorizing About the Firm," *Journal of Economic Literature*, No. 1, pp. 48–90.

Nelson, R.R., and Wright, G., 1992, "The Rise and Fall of American Technological Leadership: The Postwar Era in Historical Perspective," *Journal of Economic Literature*, December, pp. 1931–1964.

Reader, W., 1970, *Imperial Chemical Industries: A History*, Vol. I, Oxford University Press, London.

Reddaway, W.B., 1958, "The Chemical Industry," in D. Burns (ed.), *The Structure of the British Industry*, Vol. I, Cambridge University Press, Cambridge.

Richards, A., 1998, "Connecting Performance and Competitiveness with Finance:

A Study of the Chemical Industry," in Arora, Landau, and Rosenberg (eds.), *Chemicals and Long Run Economic Growth*, Wiley, New York.

Spitz, P.M., 1988, *Petrochemicals: The Rise of an Industry*, Wiley, New York.

Steen, K., 1995, "Confiscated Commerce: American Importers of German Synthetic Organic Chemicals, 1914–1929," *History and Technology*, Vol. 12, pp. 261–284.

Stokes, R.G., 1994, *Opting for Oil*, Cambridge University Press, Cambridge.

Sutton, J., 1991, *Sunk Costs and Market Structure*, MIT Press, Cambridge, Mass.

Tarr, J.A., 1994, "Searching for a 'Sink' for an Industrial Waste: Iron-Making Fuels and the Environment," *Environmental History Review*, Vol. 18, No. 1, pp. 9–34.

Teltschik, W., 1992, *Geschichte der Devtscher Grosschemie: Entwicklung und Einfluss in Staat und Gessellschaft*, VCtt Publishers, Weinheim, Germany.

Travis, A.S., 1993, *The Rainbow Makers: The Origins of the Synthetic Dyestuffs Industry in Western Europe*, Lehigh University Press, Bethlehem, Penn.

Trescott, M.M., 1981, *The Rise of the American Electrochemical Industry, 1880–1910*, Greenwood Press, Westport, Conn.

Wright, G., 1990, "The Origins of American Industrial Success, 1879–1940," *American Economic Review*, Vol. 80, No. 4, pp. 651–668.

CHAPTER 7

The Pharmaceutical Industry and the Revolution in Molecular Biology: Interactions Among Scientific, Institutional, and Organizational Change

REBECCA HENDERSON, LUIGI ORSENIGO, AND GARY P. PISANO

I. Introduction

The last 25 years have seen a revolution in the biological sciences that has had several dramatic effects on the global pharmaceutical industry.[1] These effects raise a number of fascinating questions about patterns of industrial evolution and about the interaction of scientific, organizational, and institutional changes. Although a cursory analysis might suggest that the revolution in molecular biology can be interpreted simply as a classic "Schumpeterian" event, in which the early days of the industry were characterized by high rates of entry and incumbents were gradually supplanted by a new breed of innovators, it has several features that make it quite distinctive from the "traditional" model.

First, whereas the traditional model is derived largely from the study of radical shifts in *engineering* knowledge (Abernathy and Utterback, 1978; Tushman and Anderson, 1986), the revolution in molecular biology represented a shift in the *scientific* knowledge base of an industry. Second, despite the sweeping nature of the molecular revolution, incumbent pharmaceuticals companies have *not* been swept away by new entrants. Third, and relatedly, the relationships between incumbents and entrants has entailed not only competition, but also cooperation and the establishment of complex interactions between firms. Finally, and perhaps most importantly, the revolution did not create a monolithic new paradigm of technical development, but instead created two quite

The authors would like to express their appreciation to the project participants and to Louis Galambos, Richard Nelson, Dick Rosenbloom, David Mowery, Anita McGahan, and Sidney Winter in particular for their helpful comments and suggestions on earlier drafts. The usual disclaimers apply.

[1] This revolution includes the dramatic advances in genetics and genetic engineering that popularly go by the name of "biotechnology," as well as important advances in peptide chemistry and in molecular and cell biology. For the purposes of this chapter we define these advances collectively as the "molecular biology revolution."

distinct trajectories of development that have only recently been combined: the use of biotechnology as a tool for the *production* of proteins whose therapeutic properties were already well understood, and the use of biotechnology as a tool in the *search* for entirely new therapies.

The revolution in molecular biology is also intriguing because despite the fact that it is global in nature, and despite the fact that scientific advances are normally thought of as creating a "free good," or as being instantaneously available throughout the world, the revolution is producing quite different changes in industry structure across different regions of the world. In the United States, it has spawned both the emergence of radically new actors – the new specialized biotechnology start-ups – as well as the gradual creation of biotechnology programs within established firms. In Europe, responses have differed dramatically from country to country. Despite a strong research tradition in molecular biology, in general Europe has not witnessed the creation of a specialized biotechnology sector. Several of the leading Swiss and British incumbent firms have attempted to build strong biotechnology capabilities through a combination of internal development and an aggressive program of external acquisition, but the French, German, and Italian firms have been much slower to adopt the new techniques. In Japan, where historically the pharmaceutical industry has been rather less innovative than its Western rivals, most substantial investments in biotechnology have been made by firms with historical strengths in fermentation based industries, and the large pharmaceutical companies have been particularly slow to embrace the new technology.

The case of the molecular biology revolution thus lends itself to a study of the detailed mechanisms of industrial transformation at the firm and industry levels and of the interaction and coevolution of scientific knowledge, on the one hand, and organizational capabilities, industry structure, and institutional context on the other. In this chapter we focus particularly on regional differences in the impact of biotechnology on pharmaceutical industry structure and the nature of competition, and thus hope to gain insight into the role of specific features of the "national systems of innovation" in shaping firm capabilities and the diffusion of new technology (Nelson, 1992).

Section II discusses briefly the structure of the pharmaceutical industry before the advent of the molecular biology revolution, focusing particularly on early patterns of competition, the variety of institutional structures across the world within which innovation was conducted, and the nature of pharmaceutical demand. Section III provides some background on the history and scope of the molecular biology revolution and examines its impact on the process of drug research and development, focusing particularly on its impact on the organizational capabilities fundamental to effective pharmaceutical R&D. Section IV describes the evolution of the structure of the pharmaceutical industry following the molecular revolution across the regions of the developed world. Section V speculates as to the ways in which institutional context has shaped the development of competence and the adoption of the new technologies across firms. Section VI concludes the chapter with implications for our broader understanding of the coevolution of science, national systems of innovation, organizational capabilities, and patterns of competition.

II. Historical Background: The Pharmaceutical Industry Before the Molecular Biology Revolution

The history of the pharmaceutical industry can be usefully divided into three major epochs. The first, corresponding roughly to the period 1850–1945, was one in which little new drug development occurred, and in which the minimal research that was conducted was based on relatively primitive methods. The large-scale development of penicillin during World War II marked the emergence of the second period of the industry's evolution, which we date somewhat arbitrarily as running from 1945 to roughly 1990. This period was characterized by the institution of formalized in-house R&D programs and relatively rapid rates of new drug introduction. During the early part of the period the industry relied largely on so-called random screening as a method for finding new drugs, but in the seventies the industry began a transition to "guided" drug discovery or "drug development by design," a research methodology that drew heavily on advances in molecular biochemistry, pharmacology, and enzymology. The third epoch of the industry, and the one constituting the main focus of this chapter, has its roots in the seventies but did not come to full flower until quite recently as the use of the tools of genetic engineering in the production and discovery of new drugs has come to be more widely dispersed.

In this section, we briefly review the first two of these periods. Understanding the evolution of the industry during these earlier periods is important since they played a critical role in molding not only the industrial and institutional structure of the industry, but also the organizational capabilities of individual firms that continue to influence the industry today. Indeed, we shall argue that the impact of biotechnology on industry structure cannot be understood without an appreciation of the fact that the techniques of guided drug discovery did not diffuse uniformly, and that this variation in diffusion was critically important in shaping incumbent firms' response to the revolution in molecular biology.

A. Early History

By almost any measure pharmaceuticals is a classic "high-technology" or "science-based" industry.[2] Yet drugs are as old as antiquity. For example, the Ebers Papyrus lists 811 prescriptions used in Egypt in 550 B.C. Eighteenth-century France and Germany had pharmacies where pharmacists working in well-equipped laboratories produced therapeutic ingredients of known identity and purity on a small scale. Mass production of drugs dates back to 1813, when J. B. Trommsdof opened the first specialized pharmaceutical plant in Germany. However, during the first half of the 19th century, there were virtually no standardized medicines for treating specific conditions. A patient instead would be given a customized prescription which would be formulated at the local pharmacy by hand.

The birth of the modern pharmaceutical industry can be traced to the mid-19th century with the emergence of the synthetic dye industry in German and Switzerland. At that time, Switzerland and Germany were the leading centers of the synthetic dye industry (this was due in part to the strength of German universities in organic chemistry, and in part to the fact that Basel was close to the leading silk and textile regions of Germany and France). During the 1880s, the medicinal effects (such as antiception) of dyestuffs and other organic chemicals were discovered. It was thus initially Swiss and German chemical companies such as Ciba, Sandoz, Bayer, and Hoechst, leveraging their technical competencies in organic chemistry and dyestuffs, who began to manufacture drugs (usually based on synthetic dies) later in 19th century. For example, salicytic acid (aspirin) was first produced in 1883 by the German company Bayer.

In the United States and the United Kingdom, mass production of pharmaceuticals also began in the later part of the 19th century. However, the pattern of development in the English-speaking world was quite different from that of Germany and Switzerland. Whereas Swiss and German pharmaceutical activities tended to emerge within larger chemical producing enterprises, the United States and United Kingdom witnessed the birth of specialized pharmaceutical producers such as Wyeth (later American Home Products), Eli Lilly, Pfizer, Warner-

[2] Including R&D intensity, innovative output, and use of new scientific concepts.

Lambert, and Burroughs-Wellcome. Up until World War I German companies dominated the industry, producing approximately 80% of the world's pharmaceutical output.

In the early years the pharmaceutical industry was not tightly linked to formal science. Until the 1930s, when sulfonamide was discovered, drug companies undertook little formal research. Most new drugs were based on existing organic chemicals or were derived from natural sources (e.g., herbs) and little formal testing was done to ensure either safety or efficacy. Harold Clymer, who joined SmithKline in 1939, noted:

> [Y]ou can judge the magnitude of [SmithKline's] R&D at that time by the fact I was told I would have to consider the position temporary since they had already hired two people within the previous year for their laboratory and were not sure that the business would warrant the continued expenditure. (Clymer, 1975)

World War II and wartime needs for antibiotics marked the drug industry's transition to an R&D intensive business. Penicillin and its antibiotic properties were discovered by Alexander Fleming in 1928; however, throughout the 1930s, it was produced only in laboratory-scale quantities and was used almost exclusively for experimental purposes. With the outbreak of World War II, the U.S. government organized a massive research and production effort that focused on commercial production techniques and chemical structure analysis. More than 20 companies, several universities, and the Department of Agriculture took part. Pfizer, which had production experience in fermentation, developed a deep-tank fermentation process for producing large quantities of penicillin. This system led to major gains in productivity and, more important, laid out an architecture for the process and created a framework in which future improvements could took place.

The commercialization of penicillin marked a watershed in the industry's development. Partially as a result of the technical experience and organizational capabilities accumulated through the intense wartime effort to develop penicillin, as well as the recognition that drug development could be highly profitable, pharmaceutical companies embarked on a period of massive investment in R&D and built large-scale internal R&D capabilities. At the same time there was a very significant shift in the institutional structure surrounding the industry. Whereas before the war public support for health related research had been quite modest, after the war it boomed to unprecedented levels, helping to set the stage for a period of great prosperity.

B. Patterns of Competition and Industrial Organization: 1950–1990

The period from 1950 to 1990 was a golden age for the pharmaceutical industry, as the industry in general, and particularly the major U.S. players – firms such as Merck, Eli Lilly, Bristol-Myers, and Pfizer – grew rapidly and profitably. R&D spending literally exploded and with this came a steady flow of new drugs. Drug innovation was a highly profitable activity during most of this period. Statman (1983), for example, estimated that accounting rates of return on new drugs introduced between 1954 and 1978 averaged 20.9% (compared to a cost of capital of 10.7%). Between 1982 and 1992, firms in the industry grew at an average annual rate of 18%. During the early 1980s, double-digit rates of growth in earnings and return on equity were the norm for most pharmaceutical companies and the industry as a whole ranked among the most profitable in the United States.[3]

A number of structural factors supported the industry's high average level of innovation and economic performance. One was the sheer magnitude of both the research opportunities and the unmet needs. In the early postwar years, there were many physical ailments and diseases for which no drugs existed. In every major therapeutic category – from painkillers and antiinflammatories to cardiovascular and central nervous system products – pharmaceutical companies faced an almost completely open field (before the discovery of penicillin, very few drugs effectively *cured* diseases).

Faced with such a "target rich" environment but very little detailed knowledge of the biological underpinnings of specific diseases, pharmaceutical companies invented an approach to research now referred to as "random screening." Under this approach, natural and chemically derived compounds are randomly screened in test tube experiments and laboratory animals for potential therapeutic activity. Pharmaceutical companies maintained enormous "libraries" of chemical compounds and added to their collections by searching for new compounds in places such as swamps, streams, and soil samples. Thousands, if not tens of thousands, of compounds might be subjected to multiple screens before researchers honed in on a promising substance. Serendipity played a key role since in general the "mechanism of action" of most drugs – the specific biochemical and molecular pathways that were responsible for their thera-

[3] Note that these figures are based on accounting rates of return. Figures that are recalculated to take account of the fact that the industry spends heavily on advertising and research suggest that rates of return were actually somewhat lower than the accounting figures would suggest (Myers and Howe, 1997).

peutic effect – were not well understood. Researchers were generally forced to rely on the use of animal models as screens. For example, researchers injected compounds into hypertensive rats or dogs to explore the degree to which they reduced blood pressure. Under this regime it was not uncommon for companies to discover a drug to treat one disease while searching for a treatment for another.

Although random screening may seem inefficient, it worked extremely well for many years and continues to be widely employed. Several hundred chemical entities were introduced in the 1950s and 1960s and several important classes of drug were discovered in this way, including a number of important diuretics, all of the early vasodilators, and a number of centrally acting agents including reserpine and guanethidine.

Beginning in the early seventies, the industry also began to benefit more directly from the explosion in public funding for health related research that followed the war. Publicly funded research had been important to the industry's health since the war, but it was probably most important as a source of knowledge about the cause of disease. From the middle seventies on, however, substantial advances in physiology, pharmacology, enzymology, and cell biology – the vast majority stemming from publicly funded research – led to enormous progress in the ability to understand the mechanism of action of some existing drugs and the biochemical and molecular roots of many diseases. This new knowledge made it possible to design significantly more sophisticated screens. By 1972, for example, the structure of the renin angiotensive cascade, one of the systems within the body responsible for the regulation of blood pressure, had been clarified by the work of Laragh and his collaborators (Laragh et al., 1972), and by 1975 several companies had drawn on this research in designing screens for hypertensive drugs (Henderson and Cockburn, 1994). These firms could replace ranks of hypertensive rats with precisely defined chemical reactions. In the place of the request "Find me something that will lower blood pressure in rats" pharmacologists could make the request "Find me something that inhibits the action of the angiotensin-2 converting enzyme."

In turn the more sensitive screens made it possible to screen a wider range of compounds. Prior to the late seventies, for example, it was difficult to screen the natural products of fermentation (a potent source of new antibiotics) in whole animal models. The compounds were available in such small quantities, or triggered such complex mixtures of reactions in living animals, that it was difficult to evaluate their effectiveness. The use of enzyme systems as screens made it much easier to screen these kinds of compounds. It also triggered a "virtuous cycle" in that the availability of drugs whose mechanisms of action was well known made possible significant advances in the medical understanding of the natural history of a number of key diseases, advances which in turn opened up new targets and opportunities for drug therapy (see Gambardella, 1995, and Henderson, 1994, for a fuller discussion of this transition, and Maxwell and Eckhardt, 1990, for a fuller discussion of the role of the public sector in making it possible).

These techniques were *not* uniformly adopted across the industry. For any particular firm, the shift in the technology of drug research from random screening to one of "guided" discovery or "drug discovery by design" was critically dependent on the ability to take advantage of publicly generated knowledge (Gambardella, 1995; Cockburn and Henderson, 1996) and of economies of scope within the firm (Henderson and Cockburn, 1996). Smaller firms, those farther from the centers of public research, and those that were most successful with the older techniques of rational drug discovery appear to have been much slower to adopt the new techniques than their rivals (Henderson and Cockburn, 1994; Gambardella, 1995; Cockburn et al., 1997). There was also significant geographical variation in adoption. Whereas the larger firms in the United States, the United Kingdom, and Switzerland were among the pioneers of the new technology, other European and Japanese firms appear to have been slow in responding to the opportunities afforded by the new science. These differences had significant implications for the industry's later response to the revolution in molecular biology.

As is well known to both practitioners and scholars of innovation, new products do not ensure profits, and the dramatic success of the industry's research efforts need not, in themselves, have generated supranormal returns. Rents from innovation can be competed away unless "isolating mechanisms" (Lippman and Rumelt, 1982) are in place to inhibit imitators and new entrants. For most of the postwar period, pharmaceutical companies (particularly those operating in the United States) had a number of isolating mechanisms working in their favor. Several of these mechanisms, including the strength of intellectual property protection and the nature of the regulatory regime for pharmaceutical products, were institutional in origin and differed significantly across national boundaries. We discuss these types of mechanisms in more detail later. However, it is important to note that the organizational capabilities developed by the larger pharmaceutical firms may also have acted as isolating mechanisms. Consider, for example, the process of random screening itself. As an organizational process, random screening was anything but random. Over time, early entrants into the pharmaceutical industry developed highly disciplined processes for carrying out mass screening programs. Because random screening capabilities were based on internal organizational processes and tacit skills, they were difficult for potential entrants to imitate and thus became a source of first-mover advantage. In addition, in the case of random screening, spillovers of knowledge between firms were relatively small since when firms essentially rely on the law of large numbers, there is little to be learned from the competition. These advantages, combined with the presence of scale economies in pharmaceutical research, may help to explain the dearth of new entry prior to the mid-1970s. Until that time, only one company – Syntex, the developer of the oral contraceptive – succeeded in entering the industry. Indeed, many of the leading firms during this period – companies like Roche, Ciba, Hoechst, Merck, Pfizer, and Lilly – had their origins in the "pre-R&D" era of the industry.

The advent of guided drug discovery appears only to have increased the advantages of incumbency. Although it increased the importance of publicly generated knowledge and thus reduced the importance of firm scale, it also appears to have increased returns to scope (Henderson and Cockburn, 1996). Moreover, under both regimes, the organizational capabilities developed to manage the process of drug development and delivery – competencies in the management of large-scale clinical trials, the process of gaining regulatory approval, and marketing and distribution – also appear to have acted as powerful barriers to entry into the industry.

However, significant differences in the competitive and innovative performance at the country level suggest that institutional factors have also played a critical role in generating isolating mechanisms. Although global in nature, the postwar pharmaceutical industry has been dominated by companies from the United States, Switzerland, Germany, and the United Kingdom. French and Italian firms have not played major international roles, and although Japan is the second largest pharmaceutical market in the world and is dominated by local firms (largely for regulatory reasons), Japanese firms have to date been consciously absent from the global industry. Only Takeda, for instance, ranks among the top 20 pharmaceutical firms in the world, and until relatively recently the innovative performance of Japanese pharmaceutical firms has been weak relative to that of their U.S. and European competitors.

We next turn to a discussion of the institutional forces that have shaped the industry. We argue that one of the central factors underlying U.S. success in pharmaceuticals has been a combination of institutional factors that provided powerful inducements to innovation.

C. Institutional Environments

From its inception, the evolution of the pharmaceutical industry has been tightly linked to the structure of national institutions. The pharmaceutical industry emerged in Switzerland and Germany, in part, because of strong university research and training in the relevant scientific areas. German universities in the 19th century were leaders in organic chemistry and Basel, the center of the Swiss pharmaceutical industry, was the home of the country's oldest university, long a center for medicinal and chemical study. In the United States the government's massive wartime investment in the development of penicillin, as we discussed, profoundly altered the evolution of American industry. In the postwar era, the institutional arrangements surrounding the public support of basic research, intellectual property protection, procedures for product testing and approval, and pricing and reimbursement policies have all strongly influenced both the process of innovation directly and the economic returns (and thus incentives) for undertaking such innovation. We now turn to a brief review of these four key areas.

Public Support for Health Related Research. Nearly every government in the developed world supports publicly funded health related research, but there are very significant differences across countries in both the level of support offered and the ways in which it is spent. In the United States, public spending on health related research took off after the Second World War and is now the second largest item in the federal research budget after defense. (Table 7.1 compares public spending on health care and other fields across a selection of OECD countries.) Despite the fact that the rate of increase in spending has slowed in recent years, federal spending is still roughly equivalent to the research budget of the entire U.S. pharmaceutical industry. Most of this funding is administered through the National Institutes of Health (NIH), although a significant fraction goes to universities. Detailed breakdowns of the nature of this funding are difficult to obtain; one can find divisions by therapeutic class, or disease target, but it is difficult to know how much of this research is oriented toward basic science and how much toward more applied work. The NIH certainly supports both kinds of research. Nevertheless there is consensus that a significant fraction of the support does go toward basic or fundamental science that is widely disseminated through publication in the refereed literature. Both qualitative and quantitative evidence suggests that this spending has had a significant effect on the productivity of those large U.S. firms that were able to take advantage of it (Maxwell and Eckhardt, 1990; Ward and Dranove, 1995;

Table 7.1. *Breakdown of National Expenditures on Academic and Related Research by Main Field, 1987*[a]

	Expenditure (1987 M$)						
	UK	FRG	France	Neth.	US	Japan	Average[b]
Engineering	436 15.6%	505 12.5%	359 11.2%	112 11.7%	1,966 13.2%	809 21.6%	14.3%
Physical sciences	565 20.2%	1,015 25.1%	955 29.7%	208 21.7%	2,325 15.6%	543 14.5%	21.2%
Life sciences	**864** **30.9%**	**1,483** **36.7%**	**1,116** **34.7%**	**313** **32.7%**	**7,285** **48.9%**	**1,261** **33.7%**	**36.3%**
Social sciences	187 6.7%	210 5.2%	146 4.6%	99 10.4%	754 5.1%	145 3.9%	6.0%
Arts & humanities	184 6.6%	251 6.2%	218 6.8%	83 8.6%	411 2.8%	358 9.6%	6.8%
Other	562 20.1%	573 14.2%	418 13.0%	143 14.9%	2,163 14.5%	620 16.6%	15.6%
Total	2,798	4,037	3,212	958	14,904	3,736	

[a] Expenditure data are based on OECD "purchasing power parities" for 1987, calculated in early 1989.
[b] This represents an unweighted average for the six countries (i.e., national figures have not been weighted to take into account the differing size of countries).
Source: Irvine et al. (1990, p. 219).

Cockburn and Henderson, 1996) and that it has played a major role in the emergence of the new biotechnology based firms in the United States (Zucker et al., 1998).

Public funding of biomedical research also increased dramatically in Europe in the postwar period, although the United Kingdom spent considerably less than Germany or France, and total spending did not approach American levels (Table 7.1). Moreover, the institutional structure of biomedical research evolved quite differently in continental Europe than in the United States and the United Kingdom.

In the United Kingdom biomedical research is conducted mainly in the medical schools. The Department of Health and the Department for

Education and Science – particularly through the Medical Research Council (MRC) – have been the main funding agencies. Over the last decade private foundations such as the Wellcome Trust have also emerged as major sources. The MRC funds intramural and especially (approximately two-thirds of the total) extramural research at universities, a much larger proportion than in France.

In France, in contrast, biomedical research is largely performed by CNRS and especially INSERM, which was founded in 1964 to strengthen basic research in the field. In Germany the main actors in biomedical research are the Deutsche Forschungsgemeinschaft (DFG) and the Max Planck Gesellschaft (MP). DFG funds extramural research; MPG receives funds from the federal and state governments for conducting essentially intramural research. After 1972 the newly founded Ministry of Science and Technology (BMFT) emerged as a major actor, sparking sometimes bitter conflict with the other agencies and with universities, particularly with the so-called big science centers which carry out independent research in a limited number of fields.

In addition to these differences in funding, institutional factors in continental Europe also came into play. These not only constrained scientific output, but generally led to science which was far less integrated with medical practice. First, in continental Europe within the medical profession, science does not confer the same status that it does within the Anglo-Saxon countries. Traditionally the medical profession in continental Europe has had less scientific preparation than is typical in either the United Kingdom or the United States. Medical training and practice have focused less on scientific methods per se than on the ability to use the results of research. Moreover, Ph.D.'s in the relevant scientific disciplines have been far less professionally oriented than in the United States or England (Ben-David, 1977; Braun, 1994). Partly as a consequence, within universities medically oriented research has tended to have a marginal role as compared to patient care, especially as compared to that in the United States. Historically the incentives to engage in patient care at the expense of research have been very high: France or Germany has only recently implemented a full-time system designed to free clinicians from their financial ties to patient-related activities. The organizational structure of medical schools has been such as to reinforce this effect. In continental Europe medical schools and hospitals are part of a single organizational entity, whereas in the United States and the United Kingdom they are autonomous actors, which periodically negotiate as to the character of their association. In principle, the European system should have a number of advantages with respect to research and teaching. In practice, the European system has tended to have negative consequences for research as patient care has tended to absorb the largest fraction of time and financial resources. In these systems, resources are not always targeted to specific activities, and given the difficulty of quantifying their cost, even when a fraction of the subsidies provided by the government are supposed to be used for purposes of research and teaching, patient care easily makes inroads into these supposedly "protected" resources (Braun, 1994).

In the United States and the United Kingdom, in contrast, medical schools are usually independent of hospital administrations. This status allows them to give clear priority to their intrinsic goals of research and teaching and often they are able to establish agreements with several different hospitals at the same time.

The weakness of the research function within hospitals in continental Europe is one of the reasons that the decision was made to concentrate biomedical research in national laboratories rather than in medical schools as happened in the United States and the United Kingdom. However, it has often been suggested that the separation of the research from daily medical practice had a negative effect on its quality and especially on the rate at which it diffused into the medical community.

Intellectual Property Protection. In many industries, successful new products quickly attract imitators. But rapid imitation of new drugs is difficult in pharmaceuticals for a number of reasons. One of these is that pharmaceuticals has historically been one of the few industries where patents provide solid protection against imitation. Because small variants in a molecule's structure can drastically alter its pharmacological properties, potential imitators often find it hard to work around the patent. Although another firm might undertake research in the same therapeutic class as an innovator, the probability of its finding another compound with the same therapeutic properties that did not infringe on the original patent could be quite small.[4] However, the scope and efficacy of patent protection has varied significantly across countries.

Both the United States and the majority of the European countries have provided relatively strong patent protection in pharmaceuticals. In contrast, in Japan and in Italy, until (respectively) 1976 and 1978, patent law did not offer protection for pharmaceutical *products*: only *process* technologies could be patented. As a result, Japanese and Italian firms tended to avoid product R&D and to concentrate instead on finding novel processes for making existing molecules.

[4] This is not always the case. The history of the discovery of the angiotensin converting enzyme (ACE) inhibitors provides some notable exceptions.

Procedures for Product Approval. Pharmaceuticals are regulated products. Procedures for approval have a profound impact on both the cost of innovating and firms' ability to sustain market positions once their products have been approved. As in the case of patents, there are substantial differences in product approval processes across countries.

Since the early 1960s most countries have steadily increased the stringency of their approval processes. However, it was the United States, with the Kefauver–Harris Amendment Act in 1962, and the United Kingdom, with the Medicine Act in 1971, that took by far the most stringent stance among industrialized countries, followed by the Netherlands, Switzerland, and the Scandinavian countries. Germany and especially France, Japan, and Italy have historically been much less demanding.

In the United States, the 1962 amendments were passed after the thalidomide disaster. They introduced a proof-of-efficacy requirement for approval of new drugs and established regulatory controls over the clinical (human) testing of new drug candidates. Specifically, the amendments required firms to provide substantial evidence of a new drug's efficacy based on "adequate and well controlled trials." As a result, after 1962 the the U.S. Food and Drug Administration (FDA) shifted from a role as essentially an evaluator of evidence and research findings at the end of the R&D process to an active participant in the process itself (Grabowski and Vernon, 1983).

The effects of the amendments on innovative activities and market structure have been the subject of considerable debate (see, for instance, Chien, 1979; Peltzman, 1974). They certainly led to large increases in the resources necessary to obtain approval of a new drug application (NDA), and they probably caused sharp increases in both R&D costs and the gestation times for new chemical entities (NCEs), along with large declines in the annual rate of NCE introduction for the industry and a lag in the introduction of significant new drug therapies in the United States when compared to Germany and the United Kingdom. However, the creation of a stringent drug approval process in the United States may have also helped create an isolating mechanism for innovative rents. Although the process of development and approval increased costs, it significantly increased barriers to imitation, even after patents expired. Until the Waxman–Hatch Act was passed in the United States in 1984, generic versions of drugs that had gone off patent still had to undergo extensive human clinical trials before they could be sold in the U.S. market, so that it might be years before a generic version appeared even once a key patent had expired. In 1980, generics held only 2% of the U.S. drug market.

The institutional environment surrounding drug approval in the

United Kingdom was quite similar to that in the United States. Regulation of product safety began in 1964 and from the very beginning relied heavily on formal academic medicine, in particular on well-controlled clinical trials, to demonstrate the safety and efficacy of new drugs. Extensive documentation and high academic standards were required of all submissions. The Committee on Safety of Drugs (CSD) (since 1971 the Committee on Safety of Medicines [CSM]) comprised independent academic experts, voluntarily organized and supported by the industry. The system was based on a strong cooperative attitude between the CSD/CSM, industry and academe, and effectively imposed very high standards on the industry (Davies, 1967; Wardell, 1978; Hancher, 1990; Thomas, 1994). As in the United States after 1962, the introduction of a tougher regulatory environment in the United Kingdom was followed by a sharp fall in the number of new drugs launched into Britain and a shakeout of the industry. A number of smaller, weaker firms exited the market and the proportion of minor local products launched into the British market shrank significantly. The strongest British firms gradually reoriented their R&D activities toward the development of more ambitious, global products (Thomas, 1994).

Japan represented a very different case from either the United States or the United Kingdom. In Japan, prior to 1967 any drug approved for use in another country could be sold without going through additional clinical trials or regulatory approval. As soon as the drug was listed in an accepted official pharmacopoeia, it could be sold in Japan (Reich, 1990). At the same time non-Japanese firms were prohibited from applying for drug approval. Thus Japanese firms were simultaneously protected from foreign competition and given strong incentives to license products that had been approved overseas. Under this regime the primary technology strategy for Japanese pharmaceutical companies became the identification of promising foreign products to license-in (Reich, 1990).

The Structure of the Health Care System and Systems of Reimbursement. Perhaps the biggest difference in institutional environments across countries was in the structure of the various health care systems. In the United States, pharmaceutical companies' rents from product innovation were further protected by the fragmented structure of health care markets and by the consequent low bargaining power of buyers. Moreover, unlike in most European countries (with the exception of Germany and the Netherlands) and Japan, drug prices in the United States are unregulated by government intervention. Until the mid-1980s the overwhelming majority of drugs were marketed directly to physicians, who largely made the key purchasing decisions by deciding which drug to prescribe.

The ultimate customers – patients – had little bargaining power, even in those instances in which multiple drugs were available for the same condition. Because insurance companies generally did not cover prescription drugs (in 1960, only 4% of prescription drug expenditures were funded by third-party payers), they did not provide a major source of pricing leverage. Pharmaceutical companies were afforded a relatively high degree of pricing flexibility. This pricing flexibility, in turn, contributed to the profitability of investments in drug R&D.

Drug prices were also relatively high in other countries that did not have strong government intervention in prices, such as Germany and the Netherlands. In the United Kingdom, price regulation was framed as voluntary cooperation between the pharmaceutical industry and the Ministry of Health. This scheme left companies to set their own prices, but a global profit margin with each firm was negotiated which was designed to assure each of them an appropriate return on capital investment, including research. The allowed rate of return was negotiated directly and was set higher for export oriented firms. In general, this scheme tended to favor both British and foreign R&D intensive companies which operated directly in the United Kingdom. Conversely, it tended to penalize weak, imitative firms as well as those foreign competitors (primarily the Germans) trying to enter the British market without direct innovative effort in loco (Burstall, 1985; Thomas, 1994).

In Japan, the Ministry of Health and Welfare set the prices of all drugs, using suggestions from the manufacturer based on the drug's efficacy and the prices of comparable products. Once fixed, however, the price was not allowed to change over the life of the drug (Mitchell et al., 1995). Thus, whereas in many competitive contexts prices began to fall as a product matured, this was not the case in Japan. Given that manufacturing costs often fall with cumulative experience, old drugs thus probably offered the highest profit margins to many Japanese companies, further curtailing the incentive to introduce new drugs. Moreover, generally high prices in the domestic market provided Japanese pharmaceutical companies with ample profits and little incentive to expand overseas.

III. The Revolution in the Biological Sciences and Changing Competence in Pharmaceutical Research and Development

The revolution in genetics and molecular biology that began more than 40 years ago with Watson and Crick's discovery of the double helix struc-

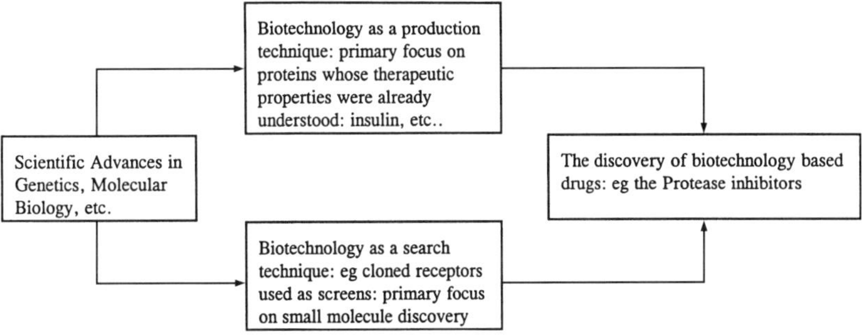

Figure 7.1

ture of deoxyribonucleic acid (DNA) and that continued with Cohen and Boyer's discovery of the techniques of genetic engineering has had an enormous impact on the nature of pharmaceutical research and development and on the organizational capabilities required to introduce new drugs.[5] As we discuss later, application of these advances initially followed two relatively distinct technical trajectories (see Fig. 7.1). One trajectory was rooted in the use of genetic engineering as a process technology to manufacture proteins *whose existing therapeutic qualities were already quite well understood* in large enough quantities to permit their development as therapeutic agents. The second trajectory used advances in genetics and molecular biology as tools to enhance the productivity of the discovery of conventional "small molecule" synthetic chemical drugs.

More recently, as the industry has gained experience with the new technologies, these two trajectories have converged. Contemporary efforts in biotechnology are largely focused on the search for large molecular weight drugs that must be produced using the tools of genetic engineering but whose therapeutic properties are not, as yet, fully understood. Understanding the distinction between these two trajectories is of critical importance to building an understanding of the history of the industry since the two require quite different organizational competencies and had quite different implications for industry structure and for the nature of competition across the world. Whereas in some regions – particularly the United States – the ability to manufacture proteins in quantity triggered an explosion of entry into the industry and a proliferation of new firms, the use of genetics as a tool for small molecule discovery appears to have reinforced the dominance of the large, global

[5] Biotechnology has also had far ranging impacts on a number of other fields, including diagnostics and agriculture. For the purposes of this chapter we limit ourselves to considering its impact on human therapeutics.

pharmaceutical firms at the expense of smaller regional players. As a first step toward understanding these outcomes and the ways in which they were shaped by both local competition and institutional structures, we focus on the organizational capabilities required to exploit biotechnology as a process technology and then turn to its use as a research tool.

A. Biotechnology as a Process Technology

Historically, most drugs have been derived from natural sources or synthesized through organic chemical methods. Although traditional production methods (including chemical synthesis and fermentation) allowed the development of a wide range of new chemical entities and many antibiotics, they were not suitable for the production of most proteins. Proteins, or molecules composed of long interlocking chains of amino acids, are simply too large and complex to synthesize feasibly through traditional synthetic chemical methods. Those proteins that were used as therapeutic agents – notably insulin – were extracted from natural sources or produced through traditional fermentation methods. However, since traditional fermentation processes – which were used to produce many antibiotics – could only utilize naturally occurring strains of bacteria, yeast, or fungi, they were not capable of producing the vast majority of proteins. Cohen and Boyer's key contribution was the invention of a method for manipulating the genetic characteristics of a cell so that it could be induced to produce a specific protein. This invention made it possible for the first time to produce a wide range of proteins synthetically and thus opened up an entirely new domain of search for new drugs – the vast store of proteins that the body uses to carry out a wide range of biological functions.

Since the human body produces approximately 500,000 different proteins, the great majority of whose functions are not well understood, in principle Cohen and Boyer's discovery thus opened up an enormous new arena for research. However, the first firms to exploit the new technology chose to focus on proteins such as insulin, human growth hormone, tPA, and factor VIII – proteins for which scientists had a relatively clear understanding of the biological processes in which they were involved and of their probable therapeutic effect. This knowledge greatly simplified both the process of research for the first biotechnology-based drugs and the process of gaining regulatory approval. It also made it much easier to market the drugs since their effects were well known and a preliminary patient population was already in place.

Thus for those firms choosing to exploit this route, the organizational capabilities that have been most critical to success have been those of manufacturing and process development: learning to use the new rDNA techniques as a process to produce natural or modified human proteins. The development of this competence created significant challenges for nearly all of the established pharmaceutical firms since it required both the creation of an enormous body of new knowledge and a fundamental shift in the ways in which manufacturing process development was managed inside the firm.

The manufacture of small molecular weight drugs is essentially a problem in *chemical* process R&D. It draws primarily on chemistry and chemical engineering, disciplines which have existed in academia and industry since the 18th century and in which there is a long history of basic scientific research. As a result much of the relevant theoretical knowledge has been codified in scientific journals and textbooks, and in searching for and selecting alternative chemical processes for the development of small molecular weight drugs, the pharmaceutical firm has at its disposal a wealth of scientific laws, principles, and models which describe the structure of relationships among different variables (e.g., pressure, volume, temperature). Thus process research chemists approaching the manufacture of a small molecular weight drug can often begin their work by deriving alternative feasible synthetic routes from theory.

The characteristics of the knowledge base underlying successful biotechnology process development are quite different. Recall that the major discovery underlying the field was only made in 1973, so that in comparison to small molecular weight drugs, biotechnology is in its infancy. Moreover, although there has been extensive basic scientific research in molecular biology, cell biology, biochemistry, protein chemistry, and other relevant scientific disciplines, most of this work has been geared toward the problems of product "discovery" or to the identification of potentially important proteins, rather than to their manufacture. There has been very little basic research conducted on the problems of engineering larger-scale biotechnology processes. Thus process developers in biotechnology have little theory to guide them in the development of new manufacturing processes.

Perhaps just as importantly, there is a long history of practical experience with chemical processes whereas process developers in biotechnology have almost no practical experience to draw on. The chemical industry emerged in the 18th century, and chemical synthesis has been used to produce pharmaceuticals since the late 1800s. Through this experience a large body of heuristics has evolved, which is widely used to guide process selection, scaleup, and plant design. Most pharmaceutical firms have also developed standard operating procedures for production activities such as quality assurance, process control, production scheduling, changeovers, and maintenance. Experience with these routines provides concrete starting points for development and guidance about what types of process techniques are feasible within an actual production environment.

In contrast, some observers were initially skeptical that recombinantly engineered processes could be scaled-up at all. The first biotechnology-based pharmaceutical to be manufactured at commercial scale, recombinant insulin, was approved by regulatory authorities in 1982. Since that time, only about 25 biotechnology-based therapeutics have been approved for marketing. When a company develops and scales up a specific new biotechnology process, it is not only likely that it represents the company's first attempt – it is probably also the first time *anyone* has attempted the process.

These differences imply that an organization developing a process for a protein molecule needs not only new technological or scientific capabilities, but also different organizational capabilities than those required for the development of a manufacturing process for a new small molecular weight compound. As described in Pisano (1996), biotechnology process development requires the capability to "learn by doing" in the actual production environment since it is virtually impossible to "learn before doing" in the laboratory. In contrast, small molecule pharmaceutical process development requires the capability to exploit the rich theoretical and empirical knowledge base of chemistry through laboratory research or what Pisano (1996) refers to as "learning before doing."

B. Biotechnology as a Research Tool

The new techniques of genetic engineering have also had a significant impact on the organizational competencies required to be a successful player in the pharmaceutical industry through their impact on the competencies required to discover "conventional," small molecular weight drugs. However, although the adoption of biotechnology as a process technology was unambiguously competence destroying for incumbent pharmaceutical firms, adoption of biotechnology as a search tool was only competence destroying for those firms who had not made the transition from "random" to "guided" drug discovery. For those firms that had made the transition, the tools of genetic engineering were initially employed as another source of "screens" with which to search for new drugs. For example, the techniques of genetic engineering allow researchers to clone target receptors, so that firms can screen against a "pure" target rather than against, for example, a pulverized solution of rat's brains that probably contains the receptor. They can also allow for the breeding of rats or mice that have been genetically altered to make them particularly sensitive to interference with a particular enzymatic pathway. Firms choosing to use biotechnology-based research tools thus had to strengthen their scientific capabilities. Nevertheless, the use of biotechnology as a research tool proved to be less destructive of existing research competences than the use of biotechnology for drug production, provided that the firm had already made the transition to guided or "science-driven" drug discovery. Firms that had not adopted this new approach to drug discovery found the biotechnology challenge to be forbidding.

The transition from random to guided drug discovery required the development of both a large body of new knowledge and substantially new organizational capabilities in drug research. So-called random drug discovery drew on two core disciplines: medicinal chemistry and pharmacology. Successful firms employed battalions of skilled synthetic chemists and pharmacologists, who managed smoothly running large-scale screening operations. Although a working knowledge of current biomedical research might prove useful as a source of ideas as to possible compounds to test or as a source of suggestions for alternative screens, by and large it was not critical to employ researchers at the leading edge of their field or to sustain a tight connection to the publicly funded research community, and firms differed greatly in the degree to which they invested in advanced biomedical research.

The ability to take advantage of the techniques of guided search, in contrast, required a very substantial extension of the range of scientific skills employed by the firm; a scientific work force that was tightly connected to the larger scientific community and an organizational structure that supported a rich and rapid exchange of scientific knowledge across the firm (Gambardella, 1995; Henderson and Cockburn, 1994). The new techniques also significantly increased returns to the scope of the research effort (Henderson and Cockburn, 1996).

Managing the transition from random to guided drug discovery was thus not a straightforward matter. In general, the larger organizations who had indulged a "taste" for science under the old regime were at a considerable advantage in adopting the new techniques and smaller firms, firms that had been particularly successful with the older regime, and firms that were much less connected to the publicly funded research community were much slower to follow their lead (Gambardella, 1995; Cockburn et al., 1998).

These differences were critical in shaping responses to the use of biotechnology as a research tool since for those firms that had made the transition to guided drug discovery, the adoption of the tools of genetic engineering to provide an additional resource in the search for small molecule drugs was a fairly natural extension of the existing competence base. Molecular geneticists could be hired to provide an additional scientific discipline among many, and the screens that they provided could be easily accommodated within the existing procedures by which research was conducted. Thus the larger, more scientifically sophisticated firms were at an enormous advantage in employing biotechnology as a research tool in the search for small molecule drugs (Zucker and Darby, 1996; 1997), and this advantage shaped national responses to the biotechnology revolution. It continues to shape responses as the two trajectories have begun to converge.

C. The Discovery of Biotechnology-based Drugs

More recently the pursuit of biotechnology has come to require new competencies in drug research because it has fundamentally shifted both the domain and the methods of search for new therapeutic agents. Whereas in the traditional synthetic chemical world researchers search among the entire universe of small molecules, biotechnology research focuses on the more than 500,000 proteins present in the human body. This search requires quite different technical and organizational capabilities since it calls for firms to develop deep understanding of the role of particular proteins in causing disease.

As we outlined, early entrants into biotechnology sidestepped the need to develop these new competencies through a focus on proteins that either were already in use as drugs (insulin, human growth hormone, factor VIII) or whose functions were relatively well understood but that had not historically been available in large enough quantities to support commercial development (e.g., tissue plasminogen activase [tPA], erythropoetin [EPO]). The majority of the biotechnology-based proteins that have been approved for marketing to date were all developed this way, and they all emerged without the firms' concerned needing to develop new research competencies.

The larger firms who adopted biotechnology as a search tool sidestepped the need to develop significantly new competencies through their use of the technology as a source of screens. Their initial focus remained on the discovery of small molecular weight drugs, so that their historic competencies in small molecule search and synthesis were not initially challenged.[6]

[6] In our view the new techniques of combinatorial chemistry and rapid throughput screening had a similar impact in that they were largely competence enhancing rather than competence destroying. For a slightly different view of the impact of biotechnology on the competence of established pharmaceutical firms see Zucker and Darby (1997).

As these avenues have become exhausted, two new strategies have emerged. The first explores the therapeutic properties of a known protein. The case of beta interferon is an example of this type of "protein in search of a use" strategy in action. Almost every organization involved in the early days of the biotechnology industry pursued the development of beta interferon. Initially there was optimism that it would be an effective cancer treatment, but preliminary development along these lines proved frustrating and it was subsequently explored as a treatment for a wide range of diseases. To date its only formally approved use is as a treatment for multiple sclerosis, a therapeutic indication that was never mentioned in the early discussions of the drug. This search strategy thus mirrors in an intriguing way the "random" approach to conventional drug research discussed earlier, although it explores the effects of large molecules in humans rather than the effects of small molecules in animals or in chemical screens.

A second strategy has been to focus on a specific disease or condition and to attempt to find a protein that might have therapeutic effects. Here detailed knowledge of the biological characteristics of specific diseases is an essential foundation for an effective search. For example, researchers working in cancer, Acquired Immunodeficiency Syndrome (AIDS), and autoimmune diseases have focused on trying to discover the proteins responsible for modulating the human immune system. Since this type of knowledge is fundamental to the guided or science based approach to drug discovery that has been adopted by the leading pharmaceutical companies in pursuit of new small molecular weight drugs, it is a strategy that draws heavily on the competencies of established firms. However, since its focus is on large molecules as therapeutic agents, it also requires the process development capabilities that have typically been developed by the new entrants to the industry.

Both strategies also draw on organizational competencies in clinical development, marketing, distribution, and the process of gaining regulatory approval more typically associated with the larger established pharmaceutical companies since they both result in the discovery of "novel" agents, or agents whose therapeutic properties are not completely understood.

IV. Patterns of Industry Evolution

Thus the techniques of molecular biology had dramatic implications both for the discovery of new drugs, on the one hand, and for the ways in which they were manufactured, on the other. "Biotechnology," in the

Table 7.2. *Patent Applications at the European Patent Office, 1978–1993*

	World Patent Shares (%) 1978-1993	No. Firms 1978-1986	No. Firms 1987-1993
USA	36.5	213	303
Japan	19.5	108	185
UK	5.9	39	64
Germany	12.0	45	58
France	6.0	37	52
CH	4.2	11	19

popular sense, has provided an important additional source of new drugs, but, as discussed, it is by no means the only way in which these techniques have changed the industry. Each trajectory – biotechnology-based proteins and the use of genetics as a tool in the search for conventional drugs – has been associated with different organizational regimes and patterns of industry evolution across countries.

Tables 7.2 and 7.3 present some summary data that provide a preliminary view of some of these differences. Table 7.2 shows the number of firms active in biotechnology across the world for the periods 1978–1986 and 1987–1993, as defined by their actively patenting at the European patenting office. Although the United States clearly hosts the majority of firms, notice that the Japanese are also very highly represented. Table 7.3 illustrates the dramatic differences in institutional forms visible across the world that we have discussed. Newly founded firms are far more impor-

Table 7.3. *Activity in Genetic Engineering by Type of Institution*

	% Patents by institution, European patent office data		
	NBFs	Established corporations	Universities & other research insitutions
		1978-1986	
USA	43.2	34.5	22.3
Japan	0.00	87.7	12.3
Germany	0.01	81.8	17.7
UK	27.3	49.1	23.6
France	18.7	21.5	59.8
Switzerland	0.00	92.9	7.1
Netherlands	12.7	56.4	30.9
Denmark	0.00	93.5	6.5
Italy	0.00	95.7	4.3
		1987-1993	
USA	40.4	38.1	20.7
Japan	3.1	86.9	10.0
Germany	3.0	80.0	17.0
UK	23.7	44.7	31.6
France	16.7	35.0	48.3
Switzerland	4.7	89.0	6.3
Netherlands	20.0	62.5	17.5
Denmark	5.7	92.5	1.9

tant in the United States and the United Kingdom than they are elsewhere, whereas the public sector plays a disproportionately important role in France. New firms (NBFs) play a negligible role in the industry in Japan, Switzerland, and Germany. We do not have the comprehensive data that would allow us to match trajectory to institution type, but we believe that the vast majority of the NBFs initially pursued the first trajectory, or a focus on biotechnology as a process technology, and the established firms – with the important exception of the Japanese firms entering the industry from fermentation related fields – largely pursued the second trajectory, or a focus on the use of biotechnology as a research tool in the search for small molecule drugs. Newly founded firms were initially far more successful than the established firms in bringing new biological entities to market, for example. Zucker and Darby present an analysis of 21 new biological entities approved for the U.S. market by 1994: 7 were discovered by small independent firms, 12 by small firms that were subsequently acquired, and only 2 by established pharmaceutical firms acting "in their own right" (Zucker and Darby, 1996).

More recently, as the two trajectories have merged, there has been an explosion of intracompany agreements, the majority between the NBFs and the larger, established firms. Many companies that were initially slow to respond to the opportunities offered by the new science have attempted to "catch up" through joint research agreements or the outright purchase of promising new firms. For example, out of 95 biotechnology drugs that entered clinical trials in the United States between 1980 and 1988, 15 were developed solely by pharmaceutical firms, 36 were developed solely by biotechnology firms, and 44 were developed jointly by pharmaceutical and biotechnology firms (Bienz-Tadmore et al., 1992).

We next explore these geographical differences in more detail as prelude to our discussion in Section V of the degree to which they can be explained by differences in the institutional structure surrounding the industry across the different regions of the world.

A. The United States

In the United States, the use of biotechnology as a process technology was the motive force behind the first large-scale entry into the pharmaceutical industry since the early post–World War II period. The first new biotechnology start-up, Genentech, was founded in 1976 by Herbert Boyer (one of the scientists who developed the recombinant DNA technique) and Robert Swanson, a venture capitalist. Genentech constituted the model for most of the new firms. They were primarily university spin-offs and they were usually formed through collaboration between scientists and professional managers, backed by venture capital. Their specific skills resided in the knowledge of the new techniques and in the research capabilities in that area. Their aim consisted in applying the new scientific discoveries to commercial drug development.[7] Genentech was quickly followed by a large number of new entrants (Ryan et al., 1994). Entry rates soared in 1980 and remained at a very high level at least until 1985. By the beginning of 1992, there were 48 publicly traded biotechnology companies specialized in pharmaceuticals and health care and several times this number still privately held.

The first biotechnology product, human insulin, was approved in 1982, and between 1982 and 1992, 16 biotechnology drugs were approved for the U.S. market. As is the case for small molecular weight drugs, the distribution of sales of biotechnology products is highly skewed. Three products were major commercial successes: insulin (Genentech and Eli Lilly), tPA (Genentech in 1987), and erythropoietin (Amgen and Ortho in 1989). By 1991 there were over 100 biotechnology drugs in clinical development and 21 biotechnology drugs with applications submitted to the FDA (Grabowski and Vernon, 1994): this was roughly one-third of all drugs in clinical trials (Bienz-Tadmore et al., 1992). Sales of biotechnology-derived therapeutic drugs and vaccines had reached $2 billion, and two new biotechnology firms, Genentech and Amgen, have entered the club of the top eight major pharmaceutical innovators (Grabowski and Vernon, 1994).

Established pharmaceuticals initially played a less direct role in this application of biotechnology, at least in the United States. Zucker and Darby show that of all the firms in their sample (U.S. firms with "affiliated" or "linked" "stars") taking out worldwide genetic-sequence patents between 1980 and 1990, 81% were dedicated biotechnology firms (Zucker and Darby, 1996). Most of the major companies invested in biotechnology R&D through collaborative arrangements, R&D contracts, and joint ventures with the new biotechnology start-ups (Arora and Gambardella, 1990; Pisano, 1991; Barbanfi et al., 1998). As we outlined, the application of molecular biology to the development of protein-based drugs required a completely different set of competencies in both drug discovery and process development. Incumbents were thus poorly positioned to exploit the technical opportunities afforded by the new trajectory through in-house research or manufacturing. However, because the competencies required for clinical development, regulatory approval, and marketing were essentially the same for biotechnology and traditional synthetic drugs, incumbents were sought out as partners who

[7] In principle, these techniques could have a wide range of applications, including in agriculture, chemicals, or food. However, the majority of the new firms focused on pharmaceuticals, particularly on diagnostics, and the use of monoclonal antibodies and therapeutics.

could help commercialize the fruits of the new firms' R&D. Thus, during the 1970s and 1980s, a market for know-how emerged in biotechnology with the start-up firms positioned as upstream suppliers of technology and R&D services and established firms positioned as downstream buyers who could provide capital as well as access to complementary assets (Pisano and Mang, 1993).

With the notable exception of Eli Lilly, in the United States the more established firms moved slowly to exploit the techniques of genetic engineering as a *production* tool. In general they began to acquire the technology through processes of collaboration – both with small biotechnology firms and directly with university laboratories – and then moved gradually to a process of outright acquisition either through the acquisition of small firms or through a process of internal group building. As of this writing a few of the larger pharmaceutical firms – including, most prominently, Merck, Hoffman La Roche, and Eli Lilly – have quite sophisticated "biotechnology" capabilities in-house, but the large firms have yet to emerge as major players in the large molecular weight drug market in their own right (Zucker and Darby, 1996).

In retrospect it is clear that in the early days of the new technology the new firms filled two crucial roles. On the one hand, they acted as "middlemen" in the transfer of technology between universities – which lacked the capability to develop or market the new technology – and established pharmaceutical firms that lacked technical expertise in the new realm of genetic engineering but that had the downstream capabilities needed for commercialization (Orsenigo, 1995). On the other, the new firms also made a major contribution in responding to the *systemic* or *architectural* implications of biotechnology. The pursuit of large molecular weight compounds as drugs not only required new competencies in both research and process development, but also altered the relationship between these. Historically, process development and research had been managed as highly separate activities. Since genetic engineering is, at its roots, a process technology, it inherently involves a far higher degree of *integration* between research and process development, on the one hand, and manufacturing activities on the other. Thus one of the critical institutional roles played by the small U.S. start-ups was to develop an entirely new set of "architectural" competencies that enabled them to act as effective integrators across research, manufacturing, and process development.

Whereas the use of genetics as a source of large molecular weight drugs was pioneered, at least in the United States, by newly founded firms, this was not the case with the use of genetic technology as a tool for the discovery of traditional, or small molecular weight drugs. This technology was pioneered largely by established firms – although there was enormous variation across firms in the speed with which the new techniques were adopted.

For those firms that were already heavily investing in fundamental research and in which participation in the broader scientific community was already recognized to be of value, the new knowledge presented itself as a natural extension of existing work. They might have been exploring the mechanisms of hypertension, for example: knowledge of the genetic bases of this mechanism was a fairly easily accommodated "competence," and in general these firms moved quite quickly to adopt the new techniques (Gambardella, 1995; Zucker and Darby, 1997). Within the United States, for example, firms such as Merck, Pfizer, and SmithKline-Beecham made the transition relatively straightforwardly.

Those firms that had been more firmly oriented toward the techniques of random drug design, however, found the transition much more difficult. It was often hard to recruit scientists of adequate caliber if the firm had no history of publication or of investment in basic science, and once they were recruited it proved to be difficult to create the communication patterns that the new techniques required. The new techniques probably also significantly increased returns to scope. As drug research came to rely increasingly on the insights of modern molecular biology, discoveries in one field often had implications for work in other areas, and firms that had the size and scope to capitalize on these opportunities for cross-fertilization – and the organizational mechanisms in place to take advantage of these opportunities – reaped significant rewards. Thus one of the major impacts of the revolution in molecular biology has been to drive a wedge between those firms that have been able to absorb the new science into their research efforts and those that are still struggling to make the transition (Zucker and Darby, 1997).

B. Europe and Japan

The exploitation of genetics as a tool to produce proteins as drugs in Europe and Japan lagged considerably behind that in the United States and proceeded along different lines. The most striking difference, of course, is the virtual absence of the phenomenon of the specialized biotechnology start-ups in Europe and Japan, with the partial exception of the United Kingdom and other isolated cases, notably in France (Genetica and afterward Transgene), at least until the second half of the 1980s.

This difference is particularly striking given that in most European countries, and in Japan, governments (at various levels: the European

Commission [EC], national, and local governments) have devised a variety of measures to foster industry–university collaboration and the development of venture capital to favor the birth of new biotechnology ventures. To date the results of these policies have not been particularly impressive, although the increase in the rate of formation of new biotechnology based firms in the 1990s may reflect the fact that these policies are now beginning to have an impact. Ernst and Young (1994) suggests that there are now approximately 380 biotechnology companies in Europe. Britain is the European country with the largest number of NBFs, followed by France, Germany, and the Netherlands (Escourrou, 1992; SERD, 1996). Recent data, moreover, suggest a dramatic increase of NBFs in Germany, with different sources estimating their number in the 400–500 range or as more than 600 (Coombs, 1995).

However, very few of these companies resemble the American prototype. Many of the new European firms are not involved in drug research or development but are instead either intermediaries commercializing products developed elsewhere or active in diagnostics, in the agricultural sector (especially in the Netherlands), or in the provision of instrumentation and/or reagents (Merit, 1996). Moreover, some of these companies (especially the most significant ones, like Celltech and Transgene) have been founded through the direct support and involvement of both governments and large pharmaceutical companies rather than through the venture capital market.

The contribution of this new breed of companies to the development of European biotechnology remains to be seen. They already seem to be suffering from the disadvantages of entering the market relatively late. Only the earliest entrants are significant innovators, and some of the most successful have already been acquired (or predict that they will be acquired shortly) by U.S. companies, like many of their American counterparts.

In the absence of extensive new firm founding, most of the innovation in biotechnology in mainland Europe has occurred within established firms. In France there has been significant entry, largely from firms diversifying into biotechnology and from other research institutions, while in Germany there has been almost no entry at all. Thus in mainland Europe a few firms account for a large proportion of biotechnology patents, and innovation in biotechnology rests essentially on the activities of a relatively small and stable group of large established companies. However, whereas the majority of the established American firms adopted the techniques of genetic engineering as a manufacturing tool primarily through acquisition and collaboration with the small American start-ups, the European firms showed considerable variation in the methods through which they acquired the technology.

The British (Glaxo, Wellcome, and to a lesser extent ICI) and the Swiss companies (particularly Hoffman La Roche, Ciba Geigy, and Sandoz) moved earlier and above all more decisively in the direction pioneered by the large U.S. firms in collaborating with or acquiring American start-ups. Firms in the rest of Europe tended to focus primarily on the establishment of a network of alliances with local research institutes, although it is worth emphasizing that German companies lagged somewhat behind. Hoechst signed a 10-year agreement with Massachusetts General Hospital as early as 1981, but Bayer did not enter seriously until 1985. In general the Germans made little progress in the field and they are not now considered to be among the leaders in European biotechnology. In some countries (e.g., Italy), the scientific community took the lead in the attempt to promote the commercial development of genetic engineering, through the establishment of linkages and collaboration with the pharmaceutical industry. The biggest European innovators are a research institution, Institut Pasteur, and two companies that have not been traditional players in the pharmaceutical industry: Gist-Brocades and Novo Nordisk.

In Japan, entry in biotechnology was pioneered by the large food and chemical companies with strong capabilities in process technologies (e.g., fermentation), like Takeda, Kyowa Hakko, Ajinomoto, and Suntory. Although these firms have strong competencies in process development, they generally lack capabilities in basic drug research. During the 1980s there was concern among some U.S. observers that biotechnology would be the next industry in which Japanese firms achieved dominance, but to date this has not occurred and there has been only limited entry into the pharmaceutical industry via biotechnology.

Within Europe the large British and Swiss firms – Glaxo, Wellcome, and Hoffman La Roche, for example – were also able to adopt the technology. Those firms that had smaller research organizations, that were more local in scope, or that were more oriented toward the exploitation of well-established research trajectories – in short, those firms that had not adopted the techniques of "rational" or "guided" drug discovery – have found the transition more difficult (Henderson and Cockburn, 1994; Gambardella, 1995). Although data speaking directly to this issue are difficult to obtain, it appears that many of the smaller American companies, and almost all of the established French, Italian, German, and Japanese companies have been slow to adopt the tools of biotechnology as an integral part of their drug research efforts.

V. National Systems of Innovation and the Evolution of the Pharmaceutical Industry: How Did Institutions Matter?

This brief description of the impact of the revolution in molecular biology on the pharmaceutical industry highlights the diversity of responses across the world and suggests that there are a number of "stylized facts" to be explored in examining the relationship between "national systems of innovation" and the evolution of the industry. *First, why was it the case that the use of molecular biology as a production tool was pioneered in the United States by small, newly founded firms; in Japan by firms diversifying into the industry from other fields; and in Europe largely by established pharmaceutical firms?* Why did new entrants play a much smaller role in the European context? *Second, did national systems of innovation play a role in shaping the diffusion of the use of molecular biology as a research tool?* This technology was in almost every case pioneered by established pharmaceutical firms, yet its rate of adoption varied widely across the world. *Last*, what can the answers to these questions tell us about the central question addressed by this book: that of the degree to which competitive advantage in this industry was shaped by firm versus national characteristics?

A. The Evolution of "Biotechnology"

The question of why the phenomenon of the small, independently funded biotechnology "start-up" was initially an American one is an old and much discussed issue. One of the reasons that it cannot be answered definitively is that the answer is to a large degree overdetermined. As the discussion of Section III suggested, the use of molecular biology as a production technology was a competence destroying innovation for the vast majority of the established pharmaceutical firms. In the United States a combination of factors made it possible for small, newly founded firms to take advantage of the opportunity this created. These factors included a favorable financial climate; strong intellectual property protection; a scientific and medical establishment that could supplement the necessarily limited competencies of small, newly founded firms; a regulatory climate that did not restrict genetic experimentation; and, perhaps most importantly, a combination of a very strong local scientific base and academic norms that permitted the rapid translation of academic results into competitive enterprises. In Europe (although to a lesser extent in the United Kingdom) and in Japan many of these factors were not in place, and it was left to larger firms to exploit the new technology.

A Strong Local Scientific Base and Academic Norms That Permitted the Rapid Translation of Academic Results into Competitive Enterprises. The majority of the American biotechnology start-ups were tightly linked to university departments, and the very strong state of American academic molecular biology clearly played an important role in facilitating the wave of start-ups that characterized the eighties (Zucker et al., 1998). The strength of the local science base may also be responsible, within Europe, for the relative British advantage and the relative German and French delay. Similarly the weakness of Japanese industry may partially reflect the weakness of Japanese science. There seems to be little question as to the superiority of the American and British scientific systems in the field of molecular biology, and it is tempting to suggest that the strength of the local science base provides an easy explanation for regional differences in the speed with which molecular biology was exploited as a tool for the production of large molecular weight drugs.

Although this explanation might seem unsatisfying to the degree that academic science is rapidly published and thus, in principle, rapidly available across the world, the American lead appears to have been particularly important because in the early years of the industry the exploitation of "biotechnology" required the mastery of a considerable body of tacit knowledge that could not be easily acquired from the literature (Zucker et al., 1998; Pisano, 1996).

The transmission of this kind of tacit knowledge was probably facilitated by geographic proximity (Jaffe et al., 1993). In the case of biotechnology, however, several authors have suggested that the U.S. start-ups were not simply the result of geographic proximity (Zucker et al., 1998). These authors have suggested that the flexibility of the American academic system, the high mobility characteristic of the scientific labor market, and, in general, the social, institutional, and legal context that made it relatively straightforward for leading academic scientists to become deeply involved with commercial firms were also major factors in the health of the new industry.

The willingness to exploit the results of academic research commercially also distinguishes the U.S. environment from that of either Europe or Japan. This willingness has been strengthened since the late 1970s and the passage of the Bayh–Dole Act, and the resulting role of universities as seedbeds of entrepreneurship has probably also been extremely important in the takeoff of the biotechnology industry.

In contrast, links between the academy and industry – particularly the ability freely to exchange personnel – appear to have been much weaker in Europe and Japan. Indeed, the efforts of several European governments were targeted precisely toward the strengthening of industry–university collaboration, and it has been argued that the rigidities of the research system of continental Europe and the large role played in France and Germany by the public, nonacademic institutions have significantly hindered the development of biotechnology in those countries.

The importance of these kinds of factors, as distinct from the strength of the science base per se, as being absolutely critical to the wave of new entry in biotechnology that occurred in America in the early eighties is given further credibility by the rate at which the use of molecular biology diffused across the world.

Access to Capital. It is commonly believed that lack of venture capital restricted the start-up activity of biotechnology firms outside the United States. Clearly, venture capital – which is to some extent a largely American institution – played an enormous role in fueling the growth of the new biotechnology based firms. However, at least in Europe, there appear to have been many other sources of funds (usually through government programs) available to prospective start-ups. In addition, the results of several surveys suggest that financial constraints did not constitute a significant obstacle to the founding of new biotechnology firms in Europe (Ernst and Young, 1994; Merit, 1996). In addition, although venture capital played a critical role in the founding of U.S. biotechnology firms, collaborations between the new firms and the larger, more established firms provided a potentially even more important source of capital. This raises the question, Why couldn't prospective European or Japanese biotechnology start-ups turn to established pharmaceutical firms as a source of capital? Though we can only speculate, a plausible answer revolves around the evolution of the market for know-how. The way the market for know-how in biotechnology evolved created many opportunities for European and Japanese companies to collaborate with U.S. biotechnology firms. Although some United States–based NBFs such as Amgen, Biogen, Chiron, Genentech, and Genzyme pursued a strategy of vertical integration from research through marketing in the U.S. market, most firms' strategies emphasized licensing product rights outside the United States to foreign partners. Thus to an even greater extent than many established U.S. pharmaceutical firms, European and Japanese firms were well positioned as partners for U.S. NBFs. Given the plethora of U.S. NBFs in search of capital, European and Japanese firms interested in commercializing biotechnology had little incentive to invest in local biotechnology firms. Even in the absence of other institutional barriers to entrepreneurial ventures, start-ups in Europe or Japan might have been crowded out by the large number of United States–based firms eagers to trade non-U.S. marketing rights for capital.

Intellectual Property Rights. In Section II we discussed the degree to which strong patent protection (or the lack of it, in the case of Italy and Japan) has shaped the industry's history. The establishment of clearly defined property rights also played a major role in making possible the explosion of new firm foundings in the United States, since the new firms, by definition, had few complementary assets that would have enabled them to appropriate returns from the new science in the absence of strong patent rights (Teece, 1986).

In the early years of "biotechnology" considerable confusion surrounded the conditions under which patents could be obtained. In the first place, research in genetic engineering was on the borderline between basic and applied science. Much of it was conducted in universities or was otherwise publicly funded, and the degree to which it was appropriate to patent the results of such research became almost immediately the subject of bitter debate. Millstein and Kohler's groundbreaking discovery – hybridoma technology – was never patented, whereas Stanford University filed a patent for Boyer and Cohen's process in 1974. Boyer and Cohen renounced their own rights to the patent but nevertheless were strongly criticized for having being instrumental in patenting what was considered to be a basic technology. Similarly a growing tension emerged between publishing research results versus patenting them. Whereas the norms of the scientific community and the search for professional recognition had long stressed rapid publication, patent laws prohibited the granting of a patent to an already published discovery (Merton, 1973; Kenney, 1986; Etzkowitz, 1996). In the second place the law surrounding the possibility of patenting life formats and procedures relating to the modification of life-forms was not defined. This issue involved a variety of problems, but it essentially boiled down first to the question of whether living things could be patented at all and second to the scope of the claims that could be granted to such a patent (Merges and Nelson, 1994).

These hurdles were gradually overcome. In 1980 Congress passed the Patent and Trademark Amendments of 1980 (Public Law 96-517), also known as the Bayh–Dole Act, which gave universities (and other nonprofit institutions, as well as small businesses) the right to retain the property rights to inventions deriving from federally funded research.

The 1984 passage of Public Law 98-620 expanded the rights of universities further, by removing certain restrictions contained in Bayh–Dole regarding the kinds of inventions that universities could own, and the right of universities to assign their property rights to other parties. In 1980, the U.S. Supreme Court ruled in favor of granting patent protection to living things (*Diamond* v. *Chakrabarty*), by granting a patent to a scientist working for General Electric who had induced genetic modifications on a *Pseudomonas* bacterium that enhanced its ability to break down oil, and in the same year the second reformulation of the Cohen and Boyer patent for the rDNA process was approved. In the subsequent years, a number of patents were granted establishing the right for very broad claims (Merges and Nelson, 1994). Finally, a one-year grace period was introduced for filing a patent after the publication of the invention.

It is often stressed (see, for instance, Ernst and Young, 1994) that the lack of adequate patent protection was a major obstacle to the development of the biotechnology industry in Europe. First, the grace period introduced in the United States is not available: any discovery that has been published is not patentable. Second, the interpretation has prevailed that naturally occurring entities, whether cloned or uncloned, cannot be patented. As a consequence, the scope for broad claims on patents is greatly reduced and usually process rather than product patents are granted. In 1994 the European Parliament *rejected* a draft directive that attempted to strengthen the protection offered to biotechnology.

Although it is clear that stronger intellectual property protection is not unambiguously advantageous, as the controversy surrounding the NIH's decision to seek patents for human gene sequences clearly illustrated, our suspicion is that at least in the early days of the industry the United States reaped an advantage from its relatively stronger regime. (For more on this difficult and complex subject see Merges and Nelson, 1994.)

A Regulatory Climate That Did Not Restrict Genetic Experimentation. Although public opposition to genetic engineering was a significant phenomenon in the United States in the earliest years of the industry (Kenney, 1986) it has quickly became less important and in general the regulatory climate in the United States has been a favorable one. In contrast, opposition to genetic engineering research by the "Green" parties is often quoted as an important factor hindering the development of biotechnology, especially in Germany and in other Northern European countries, and public opposition to biotechnology is said to have been a factor behind the decision of some companies to establish research laboratories in the United States.

B. The Use of Molecular Biology as a Research Tool

Explaining variations in the rate of adoption of molecular biology as a research tool across the regions of the world is, in contrast, rather more difficult. In general the techniques were adopted first by the large, globally oriented U.S., British, and Swiss firms. Adoption by the other European firms, and by the Japanese, appears to have been a much slower process. At first glance the relative strength of the local science base and the degree to which university research was connected to the industrial community appear to be as important an explanation here as it was in understanding the case of the diffusion of "biotechnology." American and U.K. science was arguably rather more advanced than either Japanese or mainland European: hence the slow diffusion of the new techniques to Japanese and mainland European pharmaceutical firms. Unfortunately this explanation is made much less plausible by the Swiss case. The Swiss companies established strong connections with the U.S. scientific system, suggesting that geographic proximity played a much less important role in the diffusion of molecular biology as a research tool.

A second possible explanation is that diffusion was shaped by the relative size and structure of the various national pharmaceutical industries. Henderson and Cockburn (1996) have shown that between 1960 and 1990 there were significant returns to size in pharmaceutical research, and that post 1975 these returns have come primarily from the exploitation of economies of scope. They interpret this as suggesting that the effective adoption of the techniques of guided search and rational drug design placed a premium on the ability to integrate knowledge within the firm and thus that the larger, more experienced firms may have been at a significant advantage in the exploitation of the new techniques. To the degree that those firms that had already adopted the techniques of "rational" drug discovery were at a significant advantage in adopting molecular biology as a research tool, as we have argued, the preexistence of a strong pharmaceutical national industry, with some large internationalized companies, may thus have been a fundamental prerequisite for the rapid adoption of molecular biology as a tool for product screening and design. The U.S. pharmaceutical industry has traditionally been internationally oriented and – at least from the early 1980s – open to international competition in the domestic market. But in many European countries (particularly in Italy and to a lesser extent in

France), the pharmaceutical industry was highly fragmented into relatively small companies engaged essentially in the marketing of licensed products and – as far as R&D is concerned – in the development of minor products for the domestic markets.

Notice, however, that although size or global reach may have been a necessary condition, the failure of the largest German and Japanese firms to adopt these techniques suggests that it was not sufficient. The largest Japanese and German firms were arguably quite as international and quite as large as the Swiss.

The most plausible explanation is that institutional variables – particularly the stringency of the regulatory environment and the nature of the patent regime – were also important. As mentioned in Section II, there is now widespread recognition that the introduction of the Kefauver–Harris Amendments had a significant impact in inducing a deep transformation of the U.S. pharmaceutical industry, particularly through raising the cost and complexity of R&D. Partly as a result many U.S. firms were forced to upgrade their scientific capability.

Similarly, as discussed in Section II, the two European countries whose leading firms did move more rapidly to adopt the new techniques – Britain and Switzerland – appear to have actively encouraged a "harsher" competitive environment. The British system encouraged the entry of highly skilled foreign pharmaceutical firms, especially the American and the Swiss, and a stringent regulatory environment also facilitated a more rapid trend toward the adoption by British companies of institutional practices typical of the American and Swiss companies: in particular, product strategies based on high-priced patented molecules, strong linkages with universities, and aggressive marketing strategies focused on local doctors. The resulting change in the competitive environment in the home market induced British firms to pursue strategies aiming less to the fragmentation of innovative efforts into numerous minor products than to the concentration on a few important products that could diffuse widely into the global market. By the 1970s, the ensuing transformations of British firms had led to their increasing expansion into the world markets.

Lacy Glenn Thomas has suggested that the slowness with which the vast majority of the European firms (British and Swiss excluded) adopted the techniques of guided drug discovery reflected much weaker competitive pressures in their domestic markets (Thomas, 1994). The Japanese experience also looks in many respects like that pursued in Europe outside Switzerland and the United Kingdom. In Japan legal and regulatory policies combined to frame a very "soft" competitive environment that appears to have seriously slowed the adoption of modern techniques by the Japanese pharmaceutical industry. As a result of the combination of patent laws, the policies surrounding drug licensing, and the drug reimbursement regime, Japanese pharmaceutical firms had little incentive to develop world-class product development capabilities, and in general they concentrated on finding novel processes for making existing foreign or domestically originated molecules (Mitchell et al., 1995; Reich, 1990). Moreover, Japanese firms were protected from foreign competition and simultaneously had strong incentives to license products that had been approved overseas. Under this regime the predominant technology strategy for Japanese pharmaceutical companies became the identification of promising foreign products to license-in (Reich, 1990).

Mitchell, Roehl, and Slattery (1995) have noted that some of these institutional factors are beginning to change, and that these changes are starting to have effects on the R&D strategies and capabilities of some (but not all) firms participating in the Japanese pharmaceutical sector. After 1967, foreign-originated products required clinical testing in Japan in order to be approved for sale. After 1976, drug products could be patented. After 1981, the ministry changed its pricing policy such that prices for established drugs are reviewed periodically and compared against those of newer drugs. Together these factors have combined to increase the incentives for original research. Recent evidence suggests that the share of new chemical entities approved in the United States that originate from Japan has increased substantially in recent years – from 4% in the 1970s to around 25% in 1988 (Mitchell et al., 1995) – despite the fact that perhaps because they lack a history of strong internal R&D, it is taking time for Japanese pharmaceutical companies to match world-class research capabilities.

Strong domestic competition, the existence of appropriate incentive mechanisms toward aggressive R&D strategies, and integration into the world markets thus certainly appear to be important explanatory variables in an analysis of variations in the diffusion of the new technologies in drug screening and design across *regions*. Notice, however, that they appear to tell us little about variations in diffusion across *firms*.

Most of the firms that rapidly adopted the new techniques were large multinational or global companies, with a strong presence, at least as research is concerned, in the United States and generally on the international markets. Zucker and Darby present some evidence that size alone is a reasonable predictor of adoption, at least in the United States (Zucker and Darby, 1996). As we have suggested, we suspect that this correlation reflects the fact that adoption is highly correlated with the degree to which firms have made the transition to guided drug discovery. By and large these were larger firms that had early developed a "taste" for science and that were able to build and sustain tight links to the public research community (Gambardella, 1995; Cockburn and Henderson, 1996; Zucker and Darby, 1997). Here institutional factors appear to have been a necessary but not sufficient condition: to the extent that the adoption of the new techniques involved also the successful adoption of particular, academiclike, forms of organization of research within companies (Henderson, 1994), and this process was in turn influenced by the proximity and availability of first-rate scientific research in universities, it was much easier for American (and to a lesser extent British) firms to adopt them.

From this perspective, it is tempting to suggest that the origin of the American advantage in the use of biotechnology as a research tool, as well as a process technique, lies in the comparatively closer integration between industry and the academic community, as compared to that in other countries. One might also speculate that this was – at least to some extent – the result of the strongly scientific base of the American medical culture and – relatedly – of the adoption of tight scientific procedures in clinical trials. Through this mechanism, American companies might have to develop earlier and stronger relationships with the biomedical community and with molecular biologists in particular. Segregation of the research system from both medical practice and close contact with commercial firms (as in France and possibly in Germany) has been highlighted as a major factor hindering the transition to molecular biology in these two countries (see, for instance, Thomas, 1994).

VI. Conclusion

The processes by which advances in basic science influence commercial R&D play a critical role in the prosperity of modern economies. The case of the revolution in molecular biology and its impact on the pharmaceutical industry provides an intriguing window into how these processes work, and how they both shape and are shaped by institutional forces. In the case of "biotechnology," or the use of molecular biology as a production technique, advances in basic science made several of the core competencies of existing firms – particularly those related to process development and manufacturing – obsolete. In the United States, institutional flexibility on a wide range of dimensions led to the formation of specialized biotechnology firms which could provide these competencies and bridge the gap between basic university research, on the one hand, and clinical development of drugs, on the other. Thus the NBFs were, in many ways, an institutional response to the technical opportunities created by new scientific know-how.

The case of biotechnology as a research tool presents a different but complementary picture. This trajectory was born within the confines of established pharmaceutical firms, and institutional factors appear to have played a "necessary" rather than "sufficient" role in its diffusion. The use of biotechnology as a research tool was adopted by pharmaceutical firms as a way to use molecular biology to enhance the value and productivity of their existing assets and competencies and was in this sense "competence enhancing." But it was only competence enhancing for *some* pharmaceutical firms – those that were already oriented toward "high science" research and that were already firmly embedded in the global scientific community. Thus this case is one of existing institutional arrangements and structures shaping, rather than creating, the path of technical change. Forces facilitating institutional flexibility and responsiveness played a less prominent role in this domain. This may help to explain why U.S. firms have been joined by both Swiss and British firms as leaders in the application of molecular biology to small molecule discovery.

What conclusions can be drawn as to the role of national systems of innovation? Different systems of innovation may be better suited to promoting different types of innovation. Since competence destroying technical change generally requires the emergence of new organizations, new organizational forms, and new institutional arrangements, it may tend to flourish in locations which support institutional flexibility and variety. This appears to have been the case in biotechnology. In contrast, relative performance across countries in the adoption of rational drug design, a competence enhancing trajectory developed by incumbents, varied more with the strength of existing institutional arrangements such as the strength of links between universities and other factors favoring incumbents' access to the new technology. Clearly, a better understanding of the processes by which basic scientific advances influence commercial R&D activities, and how these processes work in different environments, would seem to be a potentially fruitful research trajectory in its own right.

References

Abernathy, W.J., and J. Utterback (1978) "Patterns of Industrial Innovation," *Technology Review*, June–July, pp. 40–47.

Arora, A., and A. Gambardella (1990) "Complementarity and External Linkage:

The Strategies of the Large Firms in Biotechnology," *Journal of Industrial Economics*, Vol. 37 (4), pp. 361–379.

Barbanti, P., A. Gambardella, and L. Orsenigo (1998) "The Evolution of the Forms of Organization of Innovative Activities in Biotechnology," *Biotechnology/International Journal of Technology Management.*

Ben-David, J. (1977) *Centers of Learning: Britain, France, Germany and the United States*, McGraw-Hill, New York.

Bienz-Tadmore, Brigitta, Patricia A. Decerbo, Gilead Tadmore, and Louis Lasagna (1992, 1992) "Biopharmaceuticals and Conventional Drugs: Clinical Success Rates, "*Bio/Technology*, Vol. 10, pp. 521–525.

Braun, D. (1994) *Structure and Dynamics of Health Research and Public Funding: An International Institutional Comparison*, Kluwer Academic Publishers, Amsterdam, The Netherlands.

Burstall, M.L. (1985) *The Community's Pharmaceutical Industry*, Commission of the European Communities, Brussels.

Chien, R.I. (1979) *Issues in Pharmaceutical Economics*, Lexington Books, Lexington, Mass.

Clymer, H.A. (1975) "The Economic and Regulatory Climate: U.S. and Overseas Trends," in R.B. Helms (ed.), *Drug Development and Marketing*, American Enterprise Institute, Washington, D.C.

Cockburn, Iain, and Rebecca Henderson (1996) "Public-Private Interaction in Pharmaceutical Research," in *Proceedings of the National Academy of Sciences* 93/23 (November 12, 1996), pp. 12725–12730.

Cockburn, Iain, Rebecca Henderson, and Scott Stern (1997) "Fixed Effects and the Diffusion of Organizational Practice in Pharmaceutical Research," MIT Mimeo.

Cockburn, lain, Rebecca Henderson, and Scott Stern (1998) "Balancing Research and Production: Internal Capital Markets and Promotion Policies as Incentive Instruments," MIT Mimeo.

Coombs, Aston (1996) *The European Biotechnology Yearbook*, EBUS, Netherlands.

Davies, W. (1967) *The Pharmaceutical Industry: A Personal Study*, Pergamon Press, Oxford.

Ernst and Young (1994) "Biotechnology in Europe," *Ernst & Young Annual Report*, London.

Ernst and Young (1995) "European Biotech 95: Gathering Momentum, *Ernst & Young Annual Report*, London.

Escourrou, N. (1992) "Les Sociétés de Biotechnologie Européennes: Un Reseau Très Imbriqué," *Biofutur*, July–August, pp. 40–42.

Etzkowitz, Henry (1996) "Conflict of Interest and Commitment in Academic Science in the United States," *Minerva*, Vol. 34(3), pp. 326–360.

Gambardella, A. (1995) *Science and Innovation in the US Pharmaceutical Industry*, Cambridge University Press, Cambridge.

Grabowski, H. and J. Vernon (1994) "Innovation and Structural Change in

Pharmaceuticals and Biotechnology,"*Industrial and Corporate Change*, Vol. 3(2), pp. 435–450.

Grabowski, H. and J. Vernon (1983) *The Regulation of Pharmaceuticals*, American Enterprise Institute for Public Policy Research, Washington, D.C., and London.

Hancher, L. (1990) *Regulating for Competition: Government, Law and the Pharmaceutical Industry in the United Kingdom and France*, Oxford University Press, Oxford.

Henderson, Rebecca (1994) "The Evolution of Integrative Competence: Innovation in Cardiovascular Drug Discovery," *Industrial and Corporate Change*, Vol. 3(3), pp. 607–630.

Henderson, Rebecca and Iain Cockburn (1994) "Measuring Competence? Exploring Firm Effects in Pharmaceutical Research," *Strategic Management Journal*, Vol. 15, Winter special issue, pp. 63–84.

Henderson, Rebecca and Iain Cockburn (1996) "Scale, Scope and Spillovers: The Determinants of Research Productivity in Drug Discovery," *Rand Journal of Economics*, Vol. 27(1), pp. 32–59.

Irvine, J., B. Martin, and P. Isard (1990) "Investing in the Future: An International Comparison of Government Funding of Academic and Related Research," *Edward Elgar*, p. 219.

Jaffe, Adam B., Manuel Trajtenberg, and Rebecca Henderson (1993) "Geographic Localization of Knowledge Spillovers as Evidenced by Patent Citations," *Quarterly Journal of Economics*, August 1993, pp. 578–598.

Kenney, M. (1986) *Biotechnology: The Industry-University Complex*, Cornell University Press, Ithaca, N.Y.

Laragh, J.H. et al. (1972) "Renin, Angiotensin and Aldosterone System in Pathogenesis and Management of Hypertensive Vascular Disease," *American Journal of Medicine*, Vol. 52, pp. 644–652.

Lippman, S.A. and R.P. Rumelt (1982) "Uncertain Imitability: An Analysis of Interfirm Differences in Efficiency Under Competition," *The Bell Journal of Economics*, Vol. 13(2), pp. 418–438.

Maxwell, Robert A. and Shohreh B. Eckhardt (1990) *Drug Discovery: A Case Book and Analysis*, Humana Press, Clifton, N.J.

Merges, R. and R.R. Nelson (1994) "On Limiting or Encouraging Rivalry in Technical Progress: The Effect of Patent Scope Decisions," *Journal of Economic Behavior and Organization*, Vol. 25, pp. 1–24.

MERIT (1996) "The Organization of Innovative Activities in the European Biotechnology Industry and Its Implications for Future Competitiveness, Report for the European Commission," Maastricht.

Merton, D. (1973) in N.W. Starer (ed.), *The Sociology of Science: Theoretical and Empirical Investigation*, University of Chicago Press, Chicago.

Mitchell, W., T. Roehl, and R.J. Slattery (1995) "Influences on R&D Growth Among Japanese Pharmaceutical Firms, 1975–1990," *Journal of High Technology Management Research*, Vol. 6(1), pp. 17–31.

Myers, Stewart and Christopher Howe (1997) "A Life Cycle Financial Model of Pharmaceutical R&D," MIT Program on the Pharmaceutical Industry, Working Paper #41-97.

Nelson, R.R. (ed). (1992) *National Systems of Innovation*, Oxford University Press, Oxford.

Orsenigo, Luigi (1995) *The Emergence of Biotechnology*, Pinter Publishers, London.

Peltzman, Sam (1974) *Regulation of Pharmaceutical Innovation: The 1962 Amendments*. Washington American Enterprise Institute for Pubic Policy, Washington, D.C.

Pisano, G. (1991) "The Governance of Innovation: Vertical Integration and Collaborative Arrangements in the Biotechnology Industry," *Research Policy*, Vol. 20, pp. 237–249.

Pisano, G. (1996) *The Development Factory: Unlocking the Potential of Process Innovation*, Harvard Business School Press, Boston.

Pisano, Gary and Paul Y. Mang (1993) "Collaborative Product Development and the Market for Know-How: Strategies and Structures in the Biotechnology Industry," in R. Rosenbloom and R. Burgelmon (eds.), *Research on Technological Innovation, Management and Policy*, Vol. 5, JAI Press, Greenwich, Conn.

Reich, Michael (1990) "Why Japanese Don't Export More Pharmaceuticals: Health Policy as Industrial Policy," *California Management Review*, Winter, pp. 124–150.

Ryan, A., J. Freenan, and R. Hybels (1994) "Biotechnology Firms," in G. Carroll and M. Hannan (eds.), *Organizations in Industry Strategy, Structure, and Selection*, Oxford University Press, New York.

SERD (1996) "The Role of SMEs in Technology Creation and Diffusion: Implications for European Competitiveness in Biotechnology, Report for the European Commission," Maastricht.

Statman, Meir (1983) *Competition in the Pharmaceutical Industry: The Declining Profitability of Drug Innovation*, American Enterprise Institute, Washington, D.C.

Teece, D.J. (1986) "Profiting from Technological Innovation: Implications for Integration, Collaboration, Licensing and Public Policy," *Research Policy*, Vol. 15(6), pp. 185–219.

Thomas, L.G., III (1994) "Implicit Industrial Policy: The Triumph of Britain and the Failure of France in Global Pharmaceuticals," *Industrial and Corporate Change*, Vol. 3(2), pp. 451–489.

Tushman, M.L. and Anderson, P. (1986) "Technological Discontinuities and Organizational Environments," *Administrative Science Quarterly*, Vol. 31, pp. 439–465.

Ward, Michael and David Dranove (1995) "The Vertical Chain of R&D in the Pharmaceutical Industry," *Economic Inquiry*, Vol. 33, pp. 1–18.

Wardell, W. (1978) *Controlling the Use of Therapeutic Drugs: An International Comparison*, American Enterprise Institute, Washington, D.C.

Zucker, G. Lynne, and Michael R. Darby (1996) "Costly Information in Firm Transformation, Exit, or Persistent Failure," *American Behavioral Scientist*, Vol. 39, pp. 959–974.

Zucker, G. Lynne, and Michael R. Darby (1997) "Present at the Revolution: Transformation of Technical Identity for a Large Incumbent Pharmaceutical Firm After the Biotechnological Breakthrough," *Research Policy*, Vol. 26(4, 5), pp. 429–447.

Zucker, Lynne, Michael Darby, and Marilynn Brewer (1997) "Intellectual Human Capital and the Birth of U.S. Biotechnology Enterprises," *American Economic Review*, June, Vol. 87(3).

CHAPTER 8

Diagnostic Devices: An Analysis of Comparative Advantages

ANNETINE C. GELIJNS AND NATHAN ROSENBERG

I. Introduction

One of the most spectacular fields of medical device innovation since the end of the Second World War has been the field of diagnostics. Here we have seen the successive introduction of a wide range of sophisticated diagnostic devices, such as computed tomography (CT) scanners, magnetic resonance imaging (MRI) machines, and fiber-optic endoscopes. These devices have undoubtedly transformed modern medical practice, but have also resulted in significant changes in the industrial organization of the diagnostic medical devices sector. Unlike the rest of the medical device industry, which consists of a large number of small firms, the medical imaging sector is one that is dominated by a handful of very large firms. In the world imaging industry, technological breakthroughs, such as the CT scanner and MRI machine, were not introduced by established producers of X rays, but rather by a new breed of innovators. Yet, first-mover advantages do not seem to have been very significant and, as we will see, these new entrants failed to sustain themselves over time. In fact, established American and European X-ray companies have remained leaders in the imaging industry, with Japanese firms starting to play a more prominent role in the international arena only in recent years. In the endoscopy area, there appears to be a well-defined international division of labor, with the Europeans holding the world market in rigid endoscopes (also known as laparoscopes), the Americans being especially strong in disposable microsurgical instruments (i.e., "throwaways") introduced through the channel of the endoscope, and the Japanese dominating the flexible endoscopy market.

The authors would like to thank Richard Nelson, David Mowery, Ruud van Geuns, Ewoud Meijerink, Jan Kees van Soest, Rinus Gelijns, Samuel O. Thier, and Richard Rosenbloom for their insightful comments. The authors gratefully acknowledge the analysis of endoscope patent data by Xuesong Tong. This research has been supported by the Robert Wood Johnson's Health Policy Scholars Program and the Canadian Institute for Advanced Research.

The central purpose of this chapter is to examine the factors affecting leadership in diagnostic devices, and national or regional differences in such leadership, over time. The diagnostic device industry can be divided into five categories: (1) imaging devices that are noninvasive, such as X rays, CT scanners, MRIs, nuclear scans, and ultrasound; (2) imaging devices that are invasive, such as angiography and cardiac catheterization; (3) direct visualization technologies, such as endoscopes, that do not leave permanent images, but are invasive; (4) electrical devices, such as electrocardiograms and electromyograms; and, in recent years, (5) "enhancing" technologies, such as picture archiving and communication systems, which are highly software dependent. Among this wide range of technologies, we decided to focus on key technologies in two sectors: the noninvasive imaging industry and the industry that manufactures endoscopes. The starting point of our analysis is X rays and the rigid endoscope, both of which first emerged at the turn of the century. X rays, and their later offspring, have been characterized by high fixed capital outlays, whereas the rigid endoscope, and its successors, have not been so characterized. The high capital intensity of imaging devices has resulted in elaborate planning and budgetary constraints in the national organization of health care that have significantly affected the market for these devices. In this chapter, we will examine the extent to which success in the marketplace has been due to the technological and commercial competencies of the participating firms, on the one hand, or the ways in which national policies have shaped the overall market for these products, on the other.

In addressing these issues, it is obviously necessary to examine the underlying supply-side factors, which relate to a country's or region's science base and technological infrastructure, as well as demand-side factors, which relate to the size and operation of national markets. On the supply side, the modern research university and national research institutes, such as the Max Planck Gesellschaft in Germany and the Karolinska in Sweden, are key institutions within a country's innovation system. In medical devices, one has to take into account the extent to which the prospect for success of firms is related to the strength of the scientific, technological, and industrial base in nonmedical sectors of the economy, as well as the knowledge base in medicine itself. A major reason for this emphasis is that the industry has been invigorated many times in the past half century by the absorption of new technological capabilities that had their origin entirely outside the normal boundaries of this industry. If one were to look only at the most important contributions to diagnostic technology, for example, one would find that the CT scanner drew heavily on advances in computers and mathematics, ultrasound had its origins in submarine warfare, and MRI originated in the work of experimental physicists exploring the behavioral properties of the nucleus of the atom. Thus, medical device innovation has been outward-looking by nature, and medical device firms exploit research and new technological capabilities that have been developed by physics departments, engineering schools, the military, the electronics industry, and a range of firms manufacturing essential, specialized materials, such as high-quality glass for fiber optics or inert materials for prosthetic devices.

At the same time, medical device innovation is inherently interdisciplinary by nature, and advances in engineering and the physical sciences need to be integrated with those in medicine. Academic medical centers, and the public support of biomedical research, provide a critical infrastructure for medical device innovation in this respect. Departments in academic medical centers are built around medical specialties. The emergence of medical specialties, in turn, has been closely connected to the invention and employment of new medical devices. The invention of the X-ray machine, for example, spawned the specialty of radiology. Similarly, the development of coronary angioplasty had much to do with the emergence of the interventional cardiologist. But, of course, this formulation is excessively static, because the considerable expertise of medical specialists, particularly those in academic medicine, has also become an essential input in the development of new or improved instruments. These specialists conduct basic biomedical research, mostly in the test tube or animal models, and study the basic mechanisms of physiological processes and disease in humans. In addition, medical specialists are now heavily involved in the development of prototype medical devices. They are indispensable in testing the benefits and risks of new devices for a particular clinical indication. Moreover, they have been the driving force in expanding the indications of use for particular medical devices, and more generally, in determining their appropriate place within the clinical armamentarium. Consequently, close relationships with both universities and academic medical centers are, as we shall see, a critical factor in the successful performance of medical device firms.

It is also necessary to consider the extent to which the evolution of the diagnostic device industry is influenced by the size of markets, and the various ways in which those markets are regulated. This includes protectionist measures, often of a nontariff sort. International differences in markets may reflect differences in the size and wealth of the population, their demographic makeup, and variations in disease prevalence among nations. At the same time, the size of the market depends on the decisions of physicians and hospital administrators, who adopt technology and who may usefully be thought of as agents acting on behalf of their patients. The activities within these hospitals are powerfully shaped by the number of physicians and their breakdown into various specialties, as well as the regulatory constraints and financial incentives that prevail.

The observation that the ultimate users of this technology are a highly educated group of professional specialists is of considerable significance in examining the determinants of commercial success in the realm of medical diagnostics. In selling new or improved technologies to these buyers, diagnostic imaging firms and their sales representatives need to possess a considerable sophistication in the specific uses to which their products will eventually be put. Indeed, such sophistication is essential at the earlier stage when new diagnostic capabilities are first conceptualized and designed, as well as at a later stage, when feedback concerning performance characteristics (including deficiencies) of new technologies is likely to be critical to ultimate commercial success. Thus, the producer–user interface is exceptionally important in this industry, and the success of individual firms is strongly driven by their own technological capabilities and their ability to address the specific needs of the medical sector with these capabilities.

In the next sections of the chapter, we will first focus on the evolution of X rays, CT scanners, and MRI machines, and the various capabilities of the participating firms, including marketing skills as well as technological competencies. The endoscopy industry will be examined in a similar manner. Subsequently, we will address the issue of the extent to which the success of firms in these industries is determined by features of the national innovation system: the strength of the science base, the role of intellectual property protection, and the structure of the health care system, particularly the hospital infrastructure, the patterns of medical specialization, and the financial policies and regulatory mechanisms that affect the diffusion of diagnostic devices. This exploration raises questions concerning the appropriateness of the concept of a "national innovation system," at least insofar as the term "system" suggests prior planning of a systematic nature, rather than an evolutionary process with many historically contingent elements. It may, for example, be difficult to explain technological developments of the past half century in medical devices without considering the huge advances in microelectronics that resulted from the pressure cooker circumstances of the Second World War.

II. The Imaging Industry

A. X Rays

The X-ray device, which for the first time could penetrate clothing and skin and provide noninvasive images of bones (an important asset in Victorian times), emerged in Germany. Wilhelm Roentgen, a professor of physics at the University of Wurzberg, had no professional connection with medicine when he made his great, serendipitous discovery in late 1895. While using vacuum tubes fitted with positive and negative electrodes to investigate the properties of mineral salts, Roentgen discovered that particle streams, later called cathode rays, produced fluorescence. His January 1896 article, Uber eine Neue Art von Strahlen, which included a picture of the bones in his wife's hand, took the professional world and lay public by storm (Blume, 1992). As the devices (induction coils, cathode-ray tubes, photographic plates) required for generating X rays were readily available, it quickly became widely used by physicists, physicians, and engineers (Kevles, 1997). Within months, academic investigators began to improve image sharpness and reduce imaging time, and, within a year, the first commercial devices were marketed.

Early Entrants. The first industrial firms to produce X-ray equipment in 1896 included Siemens AG from Germany and General Electric (GE), both existing electrical equipment manufacturers.[1] As Roentgen was not interested in patenting the device, other firms were readily able to enter the field. In the United Kingdom, three firms, all established manufacturers of scientific instruments and microscopes, started manufacturing X-ray equipment (Tunnicliffe, 1973). In the United States, eight firms began manufacturing Roentgen tubes by the end of 1896 (Blume, 1992). In Japan, the first firm, Shimadzu Corporation, entered the X-ray field in 1911, followed soon after by Toshiba (Mitchell, 1988). Many of the first X-ray manufacturers of a century ago continue to be major players in the diagnostic imaging industry today, a century later.

The First World War had a major impact on the X-ray industry, since

[1] The technical performance of the early X-ray tubes remained somewhat "cranky" in the early years, encountering reliability problems in the form of unexpected failures and delivery of insufficient radiation (Wise, 1985). GE's assessment of the market, furthermore, was that it was likely to be modest in size, and it withdrew from the production of tubes in 1911. In the next few years, however, it continued to perform development work on the more sophisticated Coolidge tube, and by 1914 GE's Research Laboratory was employing a physician to acquaint the members of the medical profession with the advantages of this tube (Wise, 1985).

it brought in its wake a great increase in the number of X-ray procedures that needed to be performed. For GE this meant a contract to deliver to the military a large number of portable X-ray machines that incorporated the Coolidge tube. At the same time, it warranted continued development work on X-ray apparatus. Shortly after the war, GE decided to become a full-line supplier of X-ray machines and purchased Victor X-Ray Company, at the time the largest American manufacturer of X-ray equipment (Wise, 1985). GE's eminence in this line of products has been continuous since this period. Another American firm, Picker, later to be one of the major firms in this industry, was established in 1915 and began producing X-ray tubes. The Dutch electronics company Philips diversified from its incandescent-lamp business into X rays, when Dutch physicians could not get their "roentgen lamps" repaired in Germany during the war (Kramer and Borden, 1986).

In the 1920s and 1930s, the number of firms in the industry grew rapidly. According to Blume, the emergence of a specialized user group, radiologists, was an important development in influencing the structure of demand for X-ray apparatus (Blume, 1992). In the earlier years, the industry was confronted with a heterogeneous customer base, in which X rays were the purview of no particular clinical specialty. This changed with the emergence of radiology as a distinct new clinical discipline. In Britain, for example, the British Association for the Advancement of Radiology and Physiology was established in 1917 (Blume, 1992). X-ray equipment became centered within the hospital in the radiology department, and radiologists came to play a crucial role in developing new prototype equipment, evaluating its clinical potential, and providing feedback concerning its limitations to manufacturing firms. The convergence of interests of radiologists and industrial firms resulted in years of ongoing incremental innovation. During these years, firms also established their distribution networks, including sales forces that interacted with radiologists and hospital administrators and after-sales services networks.

The X-Ray Industry in the Early Post–World War II Years. The Second World War brought about a fundamental transformation of the medical device industry, including imaging devices. Wartime research stimulated many advances in science and engineering, such as microwaves, radar, ultrasound, and new materials. These were to prove to be of great benefit to the development of diagnostic devices and had much to do with the postwar growth of the industry. In the period after the Second World War, this field was pushed forward under the leadership of AT&T's Bell Laboratories; it culminated in the development of the transistor in December 1947. Enormous emphasis was placed upon improving the performance of the transistor, leading eventually to the integrated circuit in 1960 and the microprocessor in 1971.

In the United States, the large size of the military, and their needs, played a major role in shaping the further development of microelectronic technologies. The demands of the military provided a powerful impulse involving the transistor, integrated circuits, microwaves, and the computer in detecting incoming missiles, on the one hand, and guiding such missiles to their destinations, on the other. Thus, a variety of electronic capabilities became available for uses in other industrial contexts, including the diagnostic device industry. It must be emphasized that these electronic capabilities grew as a result not only of extensive R&D spending, but also of the enormous demands for military procurement. It is not clear to us what was the contribution in Western European countries of meeting the demands of their military sectors, although procurement was typically tied to the industrial base of a number of separate countries, each of which, however, was small by comparison with that of the United States. In the first half of the postwar period, Japanese electronics received only very minimal stimulation from the needs of its small military sector. On the other hand, as we shall see, they developed considerable skills in maintaining a very high degree of standardization, precision, and quality control across a range of consumer durable products, such as automobiles, transistorized radios, and cameras.

During the same period, the aggregate market for medical devices was expanding rapidly in most Organization for Economic Cooperation and Development (OECD) countries, stimulated in part by rapid growth in the hospital sector, the increase in the number of physicians, and the great expansion of medical insurance coverage. Whereas European nations traditionally provided universal access to health care for their citizens (a practice going as far back as Bismarck's Germany), Japan amended its National Health Insurance Law in 1958, to provide universal coverage for all Japanese. Moreover, with the establishment of Medicare and Medicaid in the mid-1960s, medical insurance coverage of the American population became much more comprehensive. The combination of increasing coverage with the proliferation of generous benefit plans fueled the demand for medical services, and, in turn, the growth of the (diagnostic) device industry itself.

After the 1950s, the X-ray industry became stabilized, but not the technology itself. The development of the image amplifier and the integration of X rays with electrooptical technologies, such as television, allowed significant reductions in the dosage of radiation and improvements in spatial separation. These developments became the basis for coronary angiography, which uses X rays to visualize coronary arteries, and the use of X rays in the operating room. Westinghouse developed and introduced the image amplifier in the United States. Philips was the first European firm to introduce the image amplifier, and as a result of this development and in combination with its core competence in television, became a prominent supplier of coronary angiography equipment. This new technology also allowed Philips to strengthen its market share in X-ray technology, including the U.S. market. In comparison with U.S. firms, both Philips and Siemens, which had relatively small national markets, had an aggressive export philosophy.

In 1958, there were 16 firms selling X-ray equipment for a $40 million U.S. market (Mitchell, 1988). With few exceptions, the X-ray markets were dominated by a few large firms that produced a wide range of electrical products, in addition to X-ray machines. The American firms at that time, GE and Picker X-Ray, and the European companies, Philips and Siemens, were the leading suppliers, holding 70–75% of the U.S. market (Mitchell, 1988). During the first half of this century, and in the years following World War II, the smaller Japanese industry remained predominantly focused on its internal market; X-ray equipment was controlled by three firms: Toshiba, Hitachi, and Shimadzu. The European market was dominated by European firms, particularly Philips, Siemens, and the French Compagnie Générale Radiologique (CGR). Immediately after the Second World War, these firms had built production facilities in the major European nations and as such had developed long-standing relationships with hospitals. By comparison, American firms were less export-oriented and were at a competitive disadvantage because the European market, with its many countries, was more difficult to access for foreign firms.

Later Improvements in X Rays. For more than half of the twentieth century, X rays were *the* diagnostic imaging industry. In the course of the 1970s and 1980s, however, rapid technological changes in microelectronics and minicomputers made possible dramatic improvements in diagnostic capabilities. Whereas, in 1972, X rays accounted for $245 million of a $285 million U.S. market (nuclear medicine accounted for $32 million and ultrasound for $3 million), in 1987 the U.S. market had grown to $2.32 billion, with X rays having stabilized at $1 billion (all figures in 1987 dollars). In real terms, using a capital equipment price deflator, this amounted to an annual growth rate of 8% over a period of

Table 8.1. *The U.S. Market for Diagnostic Imaging Technologies (Current $ Millions)*

Year	X-Ray	CT	Ultrasound	Nuclear Medicine	MRI	Total
1972	245	-	3	32	-	280
1973	276	5	8	42	-	331
1974	311	27	20	56	-	414
1975	350	82	50	75	-	557
1976	393	170	75	85	-	723
1977	440	208	82	100	-	830
1978	492	122	90	117	-	821
1979	550	141	99	137	-	927
1980	625	190	113	157	-	1,085
1981	725	328	171	134	-	1,358
1982	949	404	229	164	9	1,755
1983	934	543	237	152	50	1,916
1984	1,050	350	280	145	120	1,935
1985	1,025	304	313	149	337	2,128
1986	1,000	300	340	152	458	2,250
1987*	1,000	280	375	155	510	2,320

* Estimates.
Source: Trajtenberg (1990).

15 years (Trajtenberg, 1990). In a decade and a half the industry was transformed by a wave of new imaging modalities, most notably CT scanners and MRI (see Table 8.1).

At the same time, the introduction of the CT scanner encouraged an increased level of innovation in the old technology: X rays. The same technological capabilities (i.e., microelectronics and digitalization) that led to the CT scanner were employed to develop a wide range of improvements in X rays, particularly digital subtraction angiography. The introduction of digital vascular imaging, for example, provided information about the vascular system without the need for catheterization. An important next step was the development of picture archiving and communication systems (PACS), which replace X ray film with medical images on computer screens and, as such, allow digital transmission of diagnostic information from the radiology suite to the operating room (OR), the bedside, or other clinical facilities. In 1996, Philips and Siemens were the leading manufacturers, with a worldwide market share in X rays of 20% each, whereas GE had a 12%, Toshiba an 11%, and Shimadzu a 5% share, respectively.[2]

B. The CT Scanner

The world of conventional X rays was fundamentally changed by the introduction of the computed tomography (CT) scanner, an invention that joined X-ray technology to the remarkable computational capabilities of the digital computer. CT scanning relies on X rays but uses mathematical techniques and computer technology to produce images from which one can derive three-dimensional information; compared to X rays, it reduces radiation exposure and the images are more sensitive to density variations in the body. In addition to its remarkable diagnostic capabilities, it is, like X rays, noninvasive. European radiologists developed the concept and techniques of tomography, in which both the x-ray source and film are moved perpendicular to the patient (Roessner et al., 1997). In 1961, neurologist Oldendorf from the University of California at Los Angeles (UCLA) developed and patented a tomographic device that would provide cross-sectional images of the head, but he was unable to secure funding for its further development (Trajtenberg, 1990). Subsequently, Alan Cormack, a nuclear physicist at Tufts University, conducted critical experiments measuring the amount of X-ray energy that was absorbed by the body and used this information to calculate linear absorption coefficients (Mitchell, 1988). Surprisingly, however, their work did not generate much interest in the medical world, and it is interesting to note that in Britain, where the CT, which combined a tomographic device with the computer, was developed, the government supplied financial support to the development of the technology at a critical juncture in time.

EMI and the Introduction of the CT Scanner. It was Electrical and Musical Industries Ltd. (EMI), a total outsider to the established X-ray industry, that would bring the first CT device to market in 1973. EMI was formed in 1931. Its core business had been in recording, broadcasting, and home entertainment equipment (such as televisions), but after the Second World War the firm, which was long recognized for the quality

[2] In 1996, GE, Siemens, and Philips were the leading manufacturers in the U.S. X-ray market, with about 20% market share each. In Europe, Philips and Siemens were the market leaders in 1996, with GE a somewhat distant third. In Asia, Toshiba, Siemens, Shimadzu, Philips, and Hitachi were the main suppliers.

of its research in both basic and applied fields, decided to diversify into civilian and defense-related electronics. Godfrey Hounsfield, an engineer who worked at the central research laboratory of EMI on issues of pattern recognition and computer storage techniques, and who later shared the Nobel Prize with Cormack, conceived and patented a CT scanner. EMI's management decided to invest in its development and turned to the British Department of Health and Human Services (DHHS) to help organize and finance collaborations with the medical profession.[3]

At the 1972 meeting of the Radiological Society of North America, Ambrose, a leading neuroradiologist, and Hounsfield presented their clinical results, which were received extremely enthusiastically (Blume, 1992). Subsequently, their papers were published in the *British Journal of Radiology*, and requests for the CT scanner came streaming in. Three CT scanners (supported by DHHS) were placed in the United Kingdom. As European nations generally have more tightly controlled budgetary systems and well-established planning laws for the distribution of advanced medical technology, both of which sharply constrain the size of the market, the firm decided to focus its marketing efforts on the large U.S. market, which at the time was relatively unconstrained by budgetary limitations. In fact, the United States accounted for half of the world market for imaging technologies in the 1970s (Trajtenberg, 1990). The first commercial scanner was installed in the Mayo Clinic in 1973, followed soon after by Massachusetts General Hospital (MGH).

Increasing Competition. By mid-1975, EMI had installed over 120 scanners, it had orders for 416 more by the end of that year, and it held about 40% of the U.S. market (Trajtenberg, 1990; Blume, 1992). At the time, EMI also had a dominant position in the European market, and EMI's CT scanner was first introduced in Japan by the established X-ray manufacturer Toshiba, acting as EMI's distributor (Yoshikawa et al., 1993). However, competition was on the rise from different kinds of industrial firms: start-up firms, firms that wanted to diversify into medical diagnos-

[3] EMI's management had originally conceived of the CT scanner as a mass screening device for, among other things, breast cancer. In their discussions with DHHS, however, the government pushed the company into brain imaging because of the need for less invasive and less risky procedures in this area. In 1969, DHHS officials visited the EMI facilities and, sufficiently impressed, decided to co-finance the further development of a CT prototype. DHHS arranged collaboration between Hounsfield and Ambrose, a leading neuroradiologist at Atkinson Morley's Hospital (Blume, 1992). In 1971, DHHS decided to purchase one prototype and finance the manufacture of four more.

tics (especially pharmaceutical firms such as Pfizer, Syntex, and Searle), and established X-ray manufacturers.[4]

During this time, two major types of technological development occurred: the introduction of the whole-body scanner and the generation of new operating methods, which reduced imaging time. Robert Ledley, a professor of physiology, biophysics, and radiology at Georgetown University Medical School, set out to develop a device that would scan the whole body (not only the head) and be relatively inexpensive. He developed a prototype, patented it, and established a company, Digital Information Systems, to bring it to market. The pharmaceutical firm Pfizer, which was conducting clinical trials with one of their drugs at Georgetown University, heard about the device and, wanting to diversify into medical devices, decided to license it. Pfizer introduced its scanner into clinical practice in 1975.

At the same time, major improvements were made in image construction time, and thereby in image quality, as a result of the introduction of new operating methods. First-generation scanners took around 5 minutes to produce an image. Second-generation scanners, introduced by Technicare and Syntex, brought image construction times down to 18–20 seconds. Third-generation scanners brought these numbers down further to between 5 and 10 seconds and were introduced by Artronix, a nuclear computer manufacturer, in 1975. GE quickly introduced their third-generation technology, as did Varian, Searle, and Siemens – and imaging times decreased further to under 5 seconds (Mitchell, 1988). Fourth-generation scanners emerged with the support of the National Cancer Institute (NCI) of the National Institutes of Health (NIH). In view of the CT scanner's potential for the early diagnosis of cancer, NCI awarded a contract to the small aerospace company American Science and Engineering (AS&E) to develop a CT scanner in collaboration with investigators from Columbia-Presbyterian Medical Center and Bell Labs. AS&E could rely on its core competence in electronic and airport-x-ray equipment to introduce the first fourth-generation scanner in 1976; it also generated images in less than 5 seconds (Mitchell, 1988).

[4] Encouraged by the clinical successes of the CT scanner and the rapidly growing market, imaging industry incumbents expanded into the CT business. Ohio Nuclear worked with scientists in Cleveland to develop a whole-body scanner. Their scanner was introduced in June 1975, and Ohio Nuclear became a subsidiary of Technicare, a nuclear camera supplier. Siemens introduced its CT scanner to the European market in 1975. GE entered into an exclusive agreement with Neuroscan, a Californian start-up, in late 1975 to market its head scanner and began production of a body scanner of its own design in 1976. Philips introduced its body scanner in 1977, at the same time as Picker. Varian and Searle, both active in the ultrasound imaging area, expanded their activities into CT scanning.

Thus, following EMI's introduction of its CT scanner, the mid-1970s was a time of very rapid development: this imaging subfield was populated by up to 20 firms in the mid-1970s; technical improvements were extremely rapid, fueled by a flow of information drawn from clinical experience to manufacturers; and there was major uncertainty about whether third- or fourth-generation scanners would become the dominant design (Trajtenberg, 1990).

Shakeout of the Industry. After the mid-1970s, the U.S. market for CT scanners changed fundamentally. Certificate-of-need (CON) laws, introduced by state governments to plan the distribution of CT scanners, were intended to limit their diffusion in the United States. At the same time, many companies had entered the CT field, and keeping up with the rapid technical improvements required high R&D investments. As a result of both constraints on purchasing and the growth of competition within the field, EMI's sales and profits collapsed by 1978 and the company merged with Thorn in 1979. A year later, EMI Medical International was sold to GE and EMI Medical U.S. to Omnimedical, a nuclear and ultrasonic imaging company, which had bought Neuroscan's assets in 1978. At the same time, AS&E licensed its system to Pfizer, which subsequently sold its imaging business to Elscint in 1981. Elscint, an Israeli nuclear imaging manufacturer, had entered the CT field in 1978. Whereas Thompson-CGR, a French X-ray manufacturer entered the U.S. market in 1979, most firms exited the CT field.[5]

In 1981, GE held 60% of the U.S. market (Mitchell, 1988). Several factors appear to account for GE's high market share. First, GE, a company with huge financial resources to commit to R&D, acquired the CT operations of several competitors. Second, by combining in-house and external technologies, it created a technologically more advanced product. Third, through its well-established radiology services and sales network, it was at a significant advantage in establishing its third-generation design as the dominant design (Mitchell, 1988). GE, and the other firms that survived the CT scan shakeout, had had considerable earlier experience in the conventional X-ray market. This was not only relevant to their ability to generate rapid performance improvements; it was also crucial to their superior marketing skills in dealing with the customer base, which was essentially the same as the customers for X-ray machines, i.e., radiologists. Thus, there were considerable "spillovers" from their established competences with an older technology. But the

[5] Searle had sold out to EMI, and Syntex shut down and sold licenses to Varian and GE (Varian then sold its division to GE). Artronix filed for bankruptcy in 1979. Picker was purchased by RCA, and then in 1981 was sold to the British firm GEC (Mitchell, 1988).

Table 8.2. *Distribution of Installed CT Scanners by Selected Country, 1979 and 1990*

Country	Total 1979	Scanners per million population 1979	Scanner per million population 1990
United States	1,254	5.7	26.17
(West) Germany	150	2.7	11.89
Canada	38	1.7	7.14
Sweden	14	1.7	10.51
Netherlands	20[a]	1.4	7.36
United Kingdom	57	1.0	4.35
France	30[b]	0.6	7.26

[a] The Netherlands planned to install 30 head scanners and 8 body scanners.
[b] In France, an additional 21 scanners were authorized in July 1979.
Source: 1979 data: Banta (1984); OTA (1995). 1990 data: Lazaro (1995).

spillovers were not exclusively technological in nature. As Trajtenberg has observed, such firms "could therefore take advantage of scale economies in marketing, servicing, and already established reputations" (Trajtenberg, 1990). And, of course, GE's advantages in these respects were powerfully reinforced by the fact that the United States during the 1970s accounted for one-half of the world imaging market. In the early 1980s, although the CT market grew again, several more firms exited the field.[6] GE remained the leading manufacturer, with 35% U.S. market share in 1986, but other X-ray companies, such as Picker, Philips, and Siemens, closed in. In 1996, GE still held about 35% of the North American market, followed by Siemens (27%), Picker (18%), Toshiba (9%), and Philips (4%).

In Europe, CT scanners disseminated more slowly than in the United States, and European nations generally exhibited a much lower level of adoption of these devices. Table 8.2 depicts the distribution of installed scanners in several countries in 1979 and 1990. The whole-body units were more expensive than head units ($400,000 to $600,000 vs. $250,000

[6] Omnimedical had competed with other firms by focusing on mobile CT scanners, a successful strategy for several years. However, in 1983, the mobile CT market shifted to ambulatory facilities and, consequently, Omnimedical had to leave this declining product market. Then Technicare, a subsidiary of Johnson & Johnson, having lost important market position as a result of technical difficulties with its third-generation scanner, left the field and J&J sold its Technicare division to GE. Thomson-CGR also sold its imaging assets to GE.

to $400,000). Yet they could also visualize abdominal organs, and these devices quickly dominated the European, as well as the American, market. By the end of 1990, the total number of installed CT scanners in European nations was 2,780 compared to 6,760 in the United States (Lazaro and Fitch, 1995). An important factor accounting for these differences is the heavier reliance on budgetary controls (either at the hospital, regional, or national level) and planning laws for high-tech clinical interventions in European nations. In addition, differences in specialization patterns may account for some of the variation. In 1979, the United Kingdom, for example, had only half the number of radiologists per capita of the United States (Aron and Schwartz, 1984). The European CT market currently is dominated by GE and the two European firms, Siemens and Philips.[7]

After some initial delays, the diffusion of CT scanners in Japan was very rapid, and by 1990 Japan had more CT scanners installed than the United States, with only half the population. The CT scanner was added to the government's fee schedule soon after the first CT was installed in 1975. The reimbursement rate for CT scanning was set low ($48) in 1978 and had not changed by 1992. Japanese physicians, who also have a strong diagnostic culture, may have responded to the low reimbursement rate by increasing the number of procedures, and in 1987 utilization rates per capita were three times higher than those in the United States (Yoshikawa et al., 1993). By comparison to the U.S. system, the Japanese health care system has many more hospitals, especially smaller hospitals. These hospitals were limited in their capital outlays and able to purchase only the less expensive head scanners (as contrasted to the U.S. demand for body scanners). Between 1976 and 1979, Toshiba, Hitachi, and Shimadzu began to manufacture their own devices. During these years, these companies focused mainly on their domestic market and on the production of head scanners for this market. Competition among the medical equipment divisions of major Japanese electronics corporations pushed prices further below those prevailing in the United States, further increasing the market. According to Yoshikawa (1993), the price of an average CT scanner in Japan fell from about $700,000 in 1976 to about $200,000 for head scanners and about $400,000 for body scanners in 1980.

In the early 1980s, Japanese manufacturers began to focus on body scanners, and the Japanese market share of foreign firms fell significantly

[7] In France, the dominance of French industry was encouraged by government intervention: planning laws were deliberately used to limit the diffusion of CT scanners until the French industry was able to produce its own (Office of Technology Assessment [OTA], 1995). However, the preliminary professional judgment in France was that patients suffered while waiting.

Table 8.3. *Cumulative Number of CT Scanners in Japan*

	1982			1988			1992		
	Head	**Body**	**Total**	**Head**	**Body**	**Total**	**Head**	**Body**	**Total**
Total	1,009	677	1,686	1,513	4,583	6,096	1,538	8,098	9,636
Japanese-made	872	313	1,185	1,403	4,072	5,475	1,514	6,085	2,037
Foreign-made	137	364	501	110	511	621	24	2,013	2,037
Foreign share%	13.6	53.8	29.7	7.3	11.1	10.2	1.6	24.9	21.2
Head/Body Scanners-%Ratio									
Total	59.8	40.2	100	4.8	75.2	100	16.0	84.0	100
Japanese-made	73.6	26.4	100	25.6	74.4	100	19.9	80.1	100
Foreign made	27.3	72.7	100	17.7	82.3	100	1.2	98.8	100

Source: Sentan Inyokiki Databook (1992) Shin Iryo.

(see Table 8.3). By 1992, the market share of foreign firms in Japan was increasing again, but Toshiba still held 40% of the market. During the 1980s, Japanese firms began focusing on entering the U.S. and European markets, particularly by offering lower-priced CT scanners. Currently, Toshiba holds 36%, GE 32%, Siemens 10%, Shimadzu 8%, and Hitachi 7% of the Asian market.

Thus, the CT scanner began its product life in the United Kingdom, where EMI, a firm with no previous experience in medical technology, played a pioneering role. But, within the course of a few years (i.e., by the end of the 1970s) EMI had exited the industry and subsequent product improvement was largely concentrated in the United States, whose residents accounted for more than 50% of all CT patents (Trajtenberg, 1990). After the shakeout, the U.S. and European firms that came to dominate the CT scanner market were, overwhelmingly, firms that had also played prominent roles in the market for conventional X-ray machines. Especially prominent were such huge multinational firms as GE, Siemens, and Toshiba. In recent years, there has been more of a shift in manufacturing locus to Japan (Mitchell, 1988). Consider, for example, GE. GE had decided to sell CT systems in Japan in 1976 using Yokagawa Electric Works (YEW) as a distributor. In 1982, GE and YEW set up a joint venture, Yokagawa Medical Systems (YMS), to manufacture medium-priced CT systems. YMS now produces all but GE's top-end CT systems. Similarly, Picker has set up a joint venture with Toray Industries and Fuji Electric Co. Hitachi now manufactures most of Philips's systems that are sold with Philips's brand name in the U.S. market.

C. Magnetic Resonance Imaging

As Table 8.1 has shown, the first MRI machines were introduced into the U.S. market in 1982, and within three years their sales value exceeded that of the CT scanner, which was already, by then, a mature technology. MRI has advantages over CT and X rays in several areas, although it did not supplant these modalities. In contrast to CT, MRI employs radio waves and magnetic fields instead of ionizing radiation. MRI provides excellent tissue contrast without the need for the injection of contrast agents, which are potentially toxic (OTA, 1984). It is the preferred means for soft tissue visualization, such as visualization of the brain stem and spinal cord, because bone does not interfere with nuclear magnetic resonance (NMR) signals. Moreover, as it examines chemical and physical properties of cells, it provides a new means for the early detection of disease (Steinberg et al., 1987).

MRI traces its origins to the research of university physicists. I. I. Rabi of Columbia University confirmed the existence of the phenomenon of nuclear magnetic resonance in 1938 (and also coined the term). In 1946, E. M. Purcell at Harvard demonstrated the existence of NMR in solids and F. Bloch at Stanford established its existence in liquids (all these individuals were to receive the Nobel Prize). In the 1950s and 1960s, NMR spectroscopy became a major tool of chemical research, in which it was used to identify the chemical composition of materials. In the late 1960s and early 1970s, the instrumentation was strengthened by huge improvements in two complementary technologies: (1) the introduction of more powerful superconducting magnets, which was accomplished by Oxford Instruments and Bruker Instruments and (2) improvements in computing power that made possible the introduction of Fourier transform methods into NMR spectroscopy. The role of university research, in both the United States and the United Kingdom, remained central throughout the early stages in the development of this new technology.

The first MRIs were developed as a result of a convergence of research activities of both physics departments and academic medical centers in the United States and the United Kingdom. Prominent participants in the process were the following: (1) Raymond Damadian, a physician and assistant professor of biophysics at Downstate Medical Center of

New York, published a paper in *Science* (Tumor Detection by Nuclear Magnetic Resonance) in 1971 that created enormous academic interest in using magnetic resonance in medicine (Damadian, 1971); (2) Paul Lauterbur at SUNY Stony Brook achieved the first NMR image of two tubes in water in 1973;[8] (3) another academician whose professional competence straddled disciplinary lines was John Mallard, a professor of medical physics at the University of Aberdeen, who also saw the connection between these scanning modalities and the field of oncology; and (4) Raymond Andrew of the Nottingham University physics department applied some of his wartime radar experience to radio frequency spectroscopy. The first human image, using an enlarged NMR spectrometer, was accomplished in Nottingham in 1977 (Blume, 1992).

In the next five years, the basic technology having been proved, further research was taken up by private industry. European firms played a prominent role as early entrants in the R&D process (OTA, 1984). EMI, at the height of its CT business, began development work on MRI in 1976, with support from DHHS. EMI was followed a year later by the Dutch electronics giant and imaging incumbent Philips, as well as the German firm Bruker Instruments. Philips entered early as it wanted to avoid the mistake it made in the CT field, where Philips had been a late entrant. Moreover, in the MRI area, Philips could draw on its previous experience of manufacturing NMR spectrometers for research labs. Similarly Bruker Instruments, although not a medical imaging company, could draw on its experience in NMR spectroscopy. In 1978, the German imaging firm Siemens entered into the development of MRI. The first U.S. company, Fonar, was a single-product start-up firm that drew heavily on Damadian's work at the Downstate Medical Center of New York. Fonar was responsible, in 1980, for the first commercial placement of an MRI instrument outside the company's plant. Technicare, involved in imaging and surgical instruments, and a subsidiary of Johnson & Johnson, entered in 1979, at the same time as the French imaging firm, CGR, a subsidiary of the electronics firm Thompson-Brandt. GE was relatively late and only decided to become involved in MRI in 1980.

In addition to establishing internal R&D programs, there were several other modes of entry into the MRI market. Some firms entered this imaging subfield, or strengthened their position in it, by acquiring tech-

[8] Damadian received a patent in February 1974, "Apparatus and Method for Detecting Cancer in Tissue." Lauterbur, by contrast, was unsuccessful in obtaining a patent (Roessner, 1997). Recently, in the summer of 1997, the courts supported Damadian's patent suit against GE and ordered GE to pay Fonar \$128.7 million. Fonar had also sued Hitachi, J&J, Philips, and Siemens for patent infringement, and each of these firms settled out of court for undisclosed sums of money.

nology from other firms (OTA, 1984). Diasonics, an ultrasound imaging firm, bought all the rights to the technology developed by Pfizer under an agreement with UCSF's Radiological Imaging Laboratory. Picker, which was acquired by the British imaging firm GEC, then bought all MRI technology from EMI in 1981. Another mode of entry was the creation of small single-product firms that were university spin-offs. In addition to Fonar, at least three such firms were established: M&D Technology, founded in 1982, drew heavily on Mallard's work at the University of Aberdeen; Nalorac Cryogenics originated from the research at the University of Nottingham; and OMR Technology was closely affiliated with UCLA.

In the early 1980s, MRIs were placed in academic medical centers of numerous European countries and the United States. In terms of early clinical placements, Technicare, Diasonics, Siemens, Fonar, Philips, and Bruker were leaders[9] (OTA, 1984). Numerous incremental improvements were achieved in the hardware, a process in which feedbacks to manufacturers from these early medical users of the technology were especially important – the powerful magnets, for example, turned out to play havoc with other electronic equipment in hospitals, requiring extensive, and expensive, modification of the adjacent portions of the hospital's plant. At least equally important, however, before a stable design paradigm could be achieved, were modifications in software, i.e., the method of spatial encoding.

MRI did not employ the same algorithms as the CT scanner. However, the conceptualization of the fundamental problem – converting a massive flow of numerical data into clinically meaningful visual dimensions – was common to both diagnostic devices. Skills that were acquired in formulating algorithms for the CT scanner provided competences that were of great competitive advantage in the development of algorithms for the subsequent introduction of MRI. That is to say, there were substantial intertemporal spillovers. Alternatively expressed, new entrants into MRI, with no prior experience with CT scanners, were likely to find themselves at a serious technological disadvantage.

The economic importance of improvements in imaging algorithms can hardly be overstated. Until the early 1990s, the slow, standard imaging algorithm in MRI was hugely problematical. Examination time to construct an image was about 2 minutes, and a full-body scan required 30 to 60 minutes; the difficulty this imposed on the patient, who could not remain absolutely still for such periods of time, led to substantial image

[9] Diasonics, Technicare, and Picker International were the first firms to obtain FDA approval in 1984.

degradation; and scans over an extended period involved insuperable difficulties in the imaging of moving organs (heart, lungs, intestines).

There were, of course, compelling reasons for improving these imaging algorithms. Since MRI represents a very high fixed cost and low marginal cost technology, economic efficiency and therefore profitability of use depended on the achievement of faster imaging times. Thus, the recent development and commercialization of a number of algorithms for "ultrafast scanning" – which can create an image in less than one-tenth of a second, and a full body scan in five minutes – have constituted a major breakthrough for MRI. The ability of firms to persuade potential buyers of such a high fixed cost technology of their reliability in delivering such follow-on improvements in the software elements of the MRI system has been a critical factor in determining commercial success.

By 1990, there was a significant difference in the number of MRI units in the United States (2,080) and European nations (744; Lazaro and Fitch, 1995). The worldwide market share of firms in 1996 was 28% for GE, 24% for Siemens, 17% for Philips, 8% for Toshiba, 7% for Hitachi, and 17% for other firms. In 1997, Siemens accounted for 27%, GE accounted for 22%, Philips for 11%, Hitachi for 12%, Picker for 10%, and Hitachi for 10% of sales (as measured by the number of units sold); together these firms accounted for 92% of annual MRI sales in the North American market.

Japan was among the earliest users of MRI in the early 1980s. As early as 1981 Asahi, a large chemical firm that was interested in diversifying into the diagnostic imaging market, was financing Mallard's research group, in exchange for which Asahi was permitted to send its scientists to Aberdeen to learn about the technology. A critical issue in the diffusion of MRI in Japan was its addition to the fee schedule in 1985. The pattern of adoption in Japan, as is the case with respect to other diagnostic technologies, occurred first in large hospitals, especially academic medical centers, and then gradually diffused to other smaller hospitals, of which Japan has a much larger number than the United States.

Over a three-year period, from 1989 to 1992, the Japanese MRI market tripled (see Table 8.4). In this process the Japanese firms dominated, initially Hitachi, who produced smaller and cheaper devices (i.e., less powerful magnets), which made it possible for smaller hospitals to purchase them. GE, operating in Japan in a joint venture with Yokagawa, dominated the middle- and high-tesla MRIs, whereas Siemens's sales were segmented at the extreme upper and lower ends of the market (Philips and Picker held very small market shares). Among the three major Japanese firms, there was a well-defined specialization with respect to the size of the MRI devices. Hitachi dominated the lower-tesla end of

Table 8.4. *Cumulative MRI Market Share of the Major Firms in Japan*

Year	Total	Siemens	Shimazdu	Toshiba	Hitachi	GE/Yokogawa
1989	473	67	72	121	107	61
1990	746	89	116	182	180	126
1991	1,048	108	165	276	263	183
1992	1,286	132	190	324	328	254
1992						
Sales	238	24	25	48	65	71
%	100	10	10.5	20	27.3	29.8

Source: Sentan Iryokiki Databook (1992) Shin Iryo.

MRIs, Toshiba was especially prominent in the middle-tesla range, and Shimadzu was strongly focused on the high end. Toshiba strengthened its position at the lower end of the MRI market by purchasing the MRI division of the U.S. firm Diasonics. In 1996, GE was the leader in the Asian market, followed by Siemens, Toshiba, Philips, and Hitachi.

The position of Japanese firms in the American market has recently involved the attempt of Japanese electronic firms to introduce models that deliver the performance features of larger American models but that are smaller, more compact, and cheaper. It seems to be the expectation of the Japanese firms that their products will prove to be increasingly attractive in the American market as that market attempts to accommodate itself to the pressures of cost containment. It is interesting to note that the attempt to enter the American market with cheaper and more compact products represents a repetition of Japan's earlier successes in the U.S. market with respect to automobiles, semiconductors, and other consumer products. Thus, the American market has come to be dominated by the large multiproduct electronic firms, including firms from each of the three regions under discussion.

There have been several distinctive features to the short industrial history of MRI. First, as suggested, the rate of innovative activity and resulting performance improvement have been very high over the period 1985 to 1993, during which time the installed base rose from 395 units to 3,382 units in the United States. Second, the "table stakes" for remaining competitive in this market segment are very large in terms of required R&D spending. Firms in this segment have invested about 12% of sales in R&D, a rate substantially higher than that of the rest of the medical device industry. At the same time, university research played a major role in expanding the range of uses of the new technology, and in testing for safety and efficacy in clinical trials, functions that were essential to the many upgrades thrown up by the rapid rate of technological change. Third, first-mover advantages do not seem to have been of decisive significance, and small firms, especially numerous start-up firms, have failed to sustain themselves through the eventual shakeout period. Smaller firms, such as Fonar, Elscint, and Diasonics, which played prominent roles in the early years of MRI, eventually lost their earlier prominence. Fourth, after the shakeout in this segment, the American and European markets were dominated by a small number of large multinational companies that were already dominant in other imaging markets.

Fifth, broadly speaking, the firms that came to dominate the MRI market were the same as those that dominated the CT scan market. This does not appear to be an accident, since there are significant economies of scope for firms competing in both markets, especially when dealing with the same group of purchasers: radiologists. Firms such as GE, Siemens, and Toshiba, that had dominated CT scanning by 1980, had acquired a number of core competences in that segment that also conferred competitive advantages on them in the MRI market. Most obvious, although not necessarily most important, are the technical competences. The requirements of MRI with respect to data gathering and data processing bear close similarities to those of CT scanning. Moreover, a firm like Philips, which was not such a strong performer in the CT market but has high-level capabilities in physics research, could draw strength from its experience in NMR spectroscopy. Perhaps more important are reputation effects for firms with diversified product lines, as was characteristic of the firms that were successful in the MRI segment. Reputation is especially important in the health care industry, especially for firms offering a range of imaging devices. A firm that was successful in the CT and X-ray markets would necessarily have established a network of contacts with the same decision makers – radiologists and radiology departments – who made purchasing decisions with respect to MRI equipment. Of course, the essential point about reputations is that they have to be established, and periodically reconfirmed, by experience.[10]

The dynamics of the competitive process in a new market segment would favor a firm that, in an older segment, had already demonstrated the technical sophistication of its products, the quality and reliability of

[10] Trajtenberg has well expressed the converse point: "Information on the experience of individuals with medical equipment flows rapidly and widely within the medical community. Thus, abusing the firm's reputation in one market at one time is very likely to affect badly the performance of the firm in other markets and over a long period of time. In plain

its service and support networks, and the ability to provide upgrades to its customers, especially in an industry with a high degree of technological obsolescence.

III. The Endoscopy Industry

Endoscopes, like X-ray machines, have a lengthy history. Cystoscopy – which involves using a rigid endoscope to look into the urethra and which in essence created the specialty of urology – became a fairly well-established procedure around the turn of the century. At this time, efforts to develop and manufacture such scopes were concentrated in Germany, a concentration that was presumabiy closely linked to their preeminent physics departments and German technical skills in the design and manufacture of instrumentation generally, and optical instruments in particular. In the mid-1940s, two German endoscope manufacturers, Karl Storz and Richard Wolf, were established; they were to become the leading manufacturers in rigid endoscopes. On flexible scopes, a different picture emerged.

A. Flexible Scopes

In gastroenterology, a rigid instrument could provide only limited opportunity for informatic inspection of certain organs, such as the digestive tract, and several versions of a semiflexible gastroscope were developed in Germany. During World War II, with German instruments no longer available, U.S. firms, such as the Cameron Surgical Company and the Eder Instrument Company, introduced modifications of the semiflexible gastroscope for the American market.

But the difficulties and limitations in gastroscopy before the advent of fiber optics are hard to exaggerate. At best, the semiflexible endoscope afforded the examiner fleeting and partial visual impressions of only portions of the stomach, inside the gut of a (presumably) very uncomfortable and apprehensive patient. The innovation that was responsible for the transformation in flexible endoscopy that began in the 1950s was the emergence of fiber optics.

The Fiber-Optic Era. Flexible gastrointestinal (GI) endoscopy had its origins in the early 1950s, when physics research focused on the possi-

words, a hospital that finds a CT scanner to be inferior to its expected quality, having formed its expectations – inter alia – on the basis of price, is not likely to purchase x-ray machines, or intensive care units, or perhaps even pharmaceuticals from the same manufacturer" (1990, p. 147).

bility of transmitting images along an aligned bundle of flexible glass fibers. The findings of van Heel in Holland and Hopkins and his student, Kapany, in the department of physics at the Imperial College in London were simultaneously reported in *Nature* (1954). These papers laid down the principles of coherent image transmission. It is important to observe that the work of these academics was made possible at this particular time because of major industrial improvements in the manufacture of glass that had the effect of reducing the loss of light in transmission.

Upon reading the *Nature* articles, Hirschowitz, a young academic gastroenterologist at the University of Michigan, formed an interdisciplinary research team with Peters, an optical physicist, and Curtiss, an undergraduate student, to develop a workable fiber-optic instrument for visualizing the upper GI tract.[11] After resolving numerous problems, Hirschowitz tested the first functional gastroscope on himself in February 1957. Significantly, in view of the great impact it was to have in just a few years, the fiberscope generated little interest at first, even at the annual meeting of the American Gastroscopic Society. Nor was there much initial enthusiasm among instrument manufacturers. Eventually American Cystoscope Makers, Inc. (ACMI), which had tried unsuccessfully to make usable fiber-optic bundles, undertook to manufacture fiberscopes, under license, but only if Curtiss, Peters, and Hirschowitz agreed to act as consultants to get the glass-fiber making off the ground with ACMI engineering staff.

The instrument went through a succession of improvements in four or five months until the so-called Mark V, the model T of fiber-optic endoscopy, was introduced in 1961. Firms other than ACMI attempted to develop and manufacture flexible endoscopes. The American entrants, such as the Eder Instrument Company, that were actively involved in the production of semiflexible gastroscopes, were unable to make the discontinuous leap to a world of fiber optics and were driven out of the industry. American Optical Company did introduce a flexible endoscope, but a long patent infringement suit, eventually won by ACMI, developed between ACMI and American Optical (AO). Whereas ACMI had filed

[11] Peters, Curtiss, and Hirschowitz confronted numerous obstacles. The fiber glass available at that time was inadequate and there was as yet no available apparatus for the purpose of forming the fiber bundles. Fortunately, through Hirschowitz's connection with colleagues at the Corning Corporation, they were given access to a supply of optical glass rods, and they then put together an apparatus for aligning fiber. A number of problems remained to be solved, the most serious of which centered on "cross-talk" – i.e., when fibers come into contact, light jumps from one fiber to another, leading to loss in image transmission. Eventually, by December 1956 Curtiss found a solution by coating fibers with glass of a lower refractive index.

about a dozen patents in the United States and Europe, it had not filed any patents in Japan. This is surprising in view of the fact that gastrointestinal problems had long constituted a major health concern in that country and that the Japanese were already launched on a trajectory that would eventually lead to their global dominance in optoelectronics. During the 1960s, AO licensed the technology to Olympus and Machida, who were already producing semirigid endoscopes. This action was to have large implications for the competitive position of American firms.

Japan and the Transition to Videoendoscopy. The remarkable success of Japanese firms in the world GI endoscopy market can be partially explained by major variations in disease prevalence: Japanese death rates from gastric cancer are nearly seven times higher than those in the United States. This had already early on focused the attention of the Japanese profession and medical device firms on finding improved methods for the early diagnosis of such cancer.

As early as 1950, a physician at Tokyo Branch Hospital, Dr. Tatsumo Uji, and a group of engineers from a then-small company that made cameras, the Olympus Optical Company, introduced a prototype gastrocamera into clinical use. This camera was widely used in Japan but received only minor attention in America, presumably because of its severe limitations.[12] In 1966 there were 10,000 gastrocameras in use in Japan and, in that year alone it was employed as a diagnostic tool on 516,000 patients (Morrissey, 1983). In any case, the gastrocamera was overtaken by the improvements in fiber-optic technology. After the ACMI fiberscope had been developed the Japanese quickly built one themselves in 1961. Then, combining their established camera skills with the new fiberscope, they built a prototype device, a gastrocamera fiberscope, "that combined the virtues of Hirschowitz's fiberscope with Uji's gastrocamera" (Morrissey, 1983). Thus, Japan's prior diagnostic successes with miniaturization of cameras, in particular the case of the gastrocamera, provided them not only with a high receptivity to the fiberscope, but also with the technical capability of attaching it to a camera.

A period of intense competition between ACMI and various Japanese firms ensued, continuing into the 1970s, a period of very rapid growth in

[12] The camera was attached to the tip of the endoscope. The operator could inspect the contents of the patient's stomach only after the film had been developed. Moreover, swallowing a camera, even a miniaturized one, remained a distinctly unwieldy and unpleasant experience.

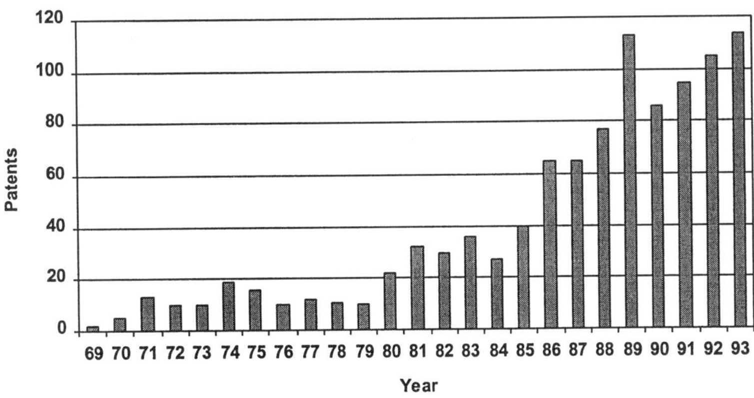

Figure 8.1. Total Endoscope Patents Granted by USPTO

endoscopy use, during which (1971) the Japanese introduced the first fiberscope built especially for the export market (Morrissey, 1983). During this period a stream of incremental improvements as well as occasional radical improvements were introduced. The use of cameras, in conjunction with endoscopes, was followed by experimentation with various lightweight movie cameras, and then with add-on television cameras. These advances were succeeded by a revolutionary change that was embodied in a prototype colonoscope, first introduced by the U.S. firm Welch Allyn in 1983. In this prototype the optical fiber bundle was replaced by a charge couple device (CCD), a kind of microprocessor chip, that was placed at the distal end of the endoscope. This chip has the capability of converting the intensity and color of light into a digitalized signal that is electronically transmitted to a video processor for display on a television monitor. In effect, it married the earlier optical innovation with the potential of computer hardware and software, resulting in today's medical optoelectronics. The ensuing integrated videoendoscopy system, apart from offering vastly superior images, also meant a significant reduction in manufacturing costs, since microprocessor chips are far less expensive to produce than optical fiber bundles. The CCD was invented by Boyle and Smith in 1969 and – as these academicians had not filed a patent – it was available to all manufacturers. Following the introduction of Welch Allyn's colonoscope and gastroscope, the German firm Storz, and Japanese manufacturers such as Fujinon, Pentax, and Olympus, introduced their versions of integrated videoendoscopes.

As the endoscope patent data show (Fig. 8.1), the period of the second half of the 1980s and early 1990s, following the introduction of the CCD, was one of a more than doubling of endoscope patenting. What the data on total patents granted also show, however, is the dominance of Japanese firms and, especially, the overwhelming dominance of a single Japanese firm: Olympus, which holds no fewer than 630 endoscope patents (Fig. 8.2). The patent data show that Olympus was a full order of magnitude ahead of its four closest rivals, all of which were Japanese, and Olympus's post-CCD patents make frequent references to Welch Allyn's prior invention. In fact, Olympus alone has 18 patents based upon Welch Allyn's patent 4491865. The first non-Japanese firm in the patent ranking is Richard Wolf, a German manufacturer.

In terms of market share, Olympus in 1991 held over 75% of the world market for flexible endoscopes. Olympus was followed by Circon/ACMI, with 9% market share, focusing particularly on the genitourinary tract (in which both flexible and rigid endoscopes are employed). ACMI was acquired in 1986 by Circon, a market leader (50% market share) in medical video cameras. Other suppliers include Wolf, Pentax, and Storz (BBI, 1991).

How is one to account for the spectacular success of Olympus in the GI endoscopy market? Our patent data, which are not available for the period before 1969, indicate that the Japanese firms made most of the device improvements since the early 1970s, and that these were primarily incremental modifications of the original device. Although it is impossible to adjudicate with any pretense of precision among the possible factors accounting for Japanese success, several points are obviously relevant. On the demand side, the high incidence of gastric cancer powerfully focused national attention in Japan on improved techniques of early diagnosis in the upper GI tract. This is reflected in mass screening programs that were initiated in 1961 (Kasumi et al., 1993). A related index of national concern is that when the first World Congress of Gastrointestinal Endoscopy was held in 1966 the Japanese Endoscopic Society, founded in 1958, already had more than 3,000 members, whereas its American counterpart, the American Society for Gastrointestinal Endoscopy, had a mere 263 members. These characteristics led to far greater diffusion of GI endoscopes in Japan than in the United States.

On the supply side, possibly the most persuasive explanation is that, when the endoscope came upon the scene in the 1960s, the prior trajectory of technological developments found the potential Japanese players especially well positioned to exploit these new opportunities. The endoscope drew upon technological capabilities in which the Japanese firms had already distinguished themselves: the design and manufacture of

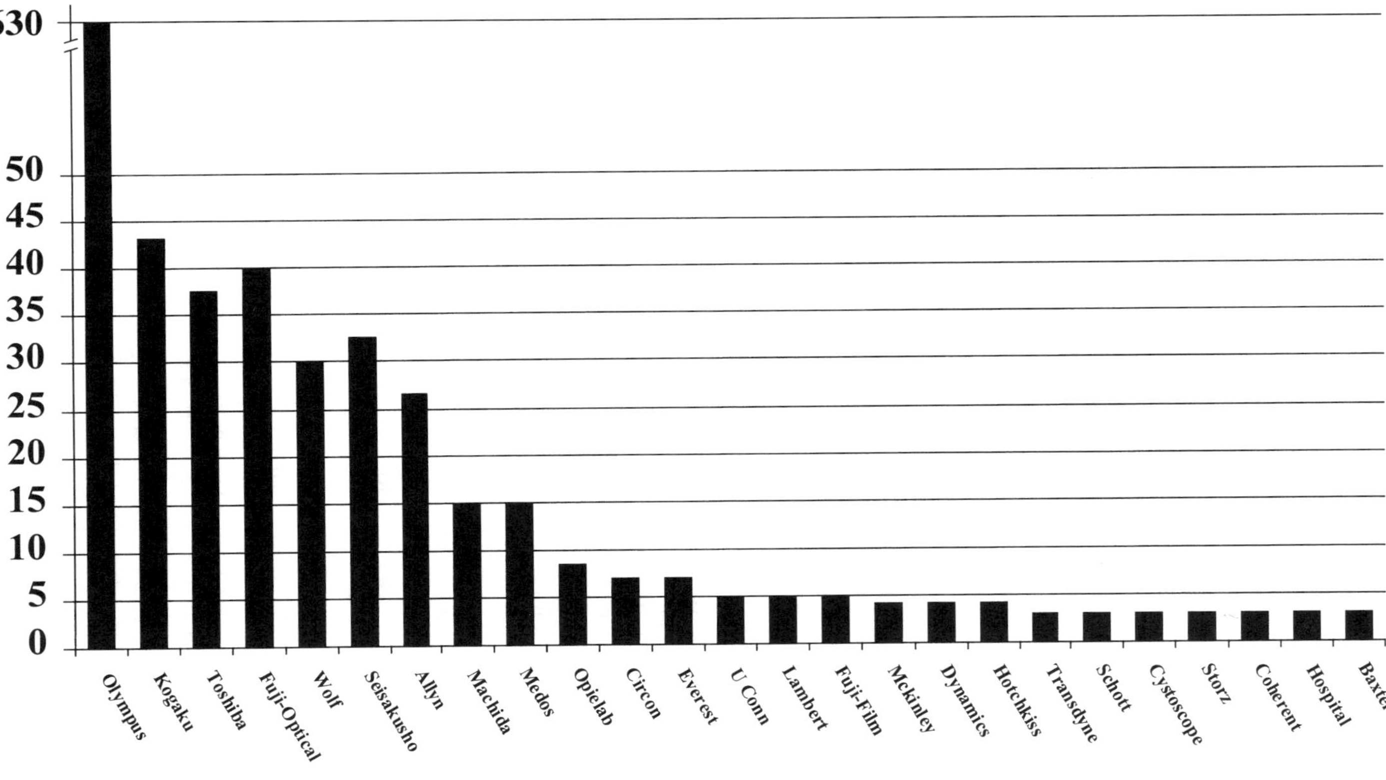

Figure 8.2. USPTO Endoscope Patents by Firm, 1969–93

cameras and outstanding skills in the process of miniaturization.[13] Moreover, the introduction of the CCD in 1983 drastically changed the nature of the market. Optical fibers could now be replaced with a CCD and a direct link to the videoendoscope, which made possible the continuous display of a high-resolution image on a television monitor. This development gave Japan a further comparative advantage in that it could exploit its already-established skills in television transmission and display.

B. Rigid Scopes and Microsurgical Instrumentation

Laparoscopes. Following the emergence of cystoscopy around the turn of the century, other specialties began to experiment with rigid scopes as well. In internal medicine, laparoscopes were inserted through a small incision to visualize the upper abdominal organs, and in the mid-1940s the first attempts were made by the French gynecologist surgeon Palmer to transfer this instrument into gynecology. Two newly established endoscope manufacturers, the German optics companies Richard Wolf and Karl Storz, were able to enter the laparoscopy market by creating alliances with Palmer and several leading German academic gynecologists, particularly Kurt Semm at the University of Kiel.

The adoption of these gynecological procedures was very limited in the 1960s, mainly as a result of significant technical and clinical limitations. A gynecological version of the fiber-optic endoscope, which provided improved illumination (but not image transmission), was developed by Palmer in conjunction with the Wolf firm, and Storz introduced its "cold-light" endoscope a few years later in 1960. A major improvement in optics was the development of the rod-lens system by the British optical physicist Hopkins, which was introduced by Storz in 1966. With improved devices, gynecologists expanded to more complex surgical procedures, such as the evaluation of treated pelvic malignancies and the treatment of infertility. This expansion – in turn – led to demands for still more sophisticated instruments.

Our analysis indicates that the competitive success of a particular firm often hinges on forging close relationships with medical specialists in

[13] One medical authority on the endoscope, writing before the widespread adoption of the CCD, makes the curious observation that "the esthetics of the view through the Japanese fiberscopes turned out to be a strong selling point" (Morrissey, 1983). But he makes the statement in a context in which it is clear that the Japanese technique for manufacturing the finest possible fiber bundles resulted in a far higher degree of resolution than that achieved by competing foreign products, surely a consideration that, from a medical point of view, is more than merely aesthetic.

academic medical centers. In gynecology, for example, Storz collaborated successfully with Semm at the University of Kiel to develop a wide range of therapeutic instruments that could be moved through the surgical channel of the endoscope. These instruments played a vital role in the development and further popularization of gynecological laparoscopy. Through Storz's ability to create close collaborations with Semm and his colleagues, this firm became the leading manufacturer in laparoscopes – holding 40% of the world market and 30% of the market in rigid endoscopes in 1990. Storz was followed by another German firm, Wolf, which held nearly 18% of the laparoscopy and 25% of the rigid endoscopy market. ACMI, which was diverting its energy to competing with Japanese firms in the gastroenterological area, dropped out of the gynecological field in the 1970s. By the 1990s, Circon/ACMI still was among the top five companies in the rigid endoscope field, as are Olympus and the U.S. firm Cabot.

Microsurgical Instrumentation. Despite the extensive use of endoscopes and laparoscopes by gastroenterologists and gynecologists, the general surgeon did not adopt these tools until the late 1980s. What were the reasons for this time lag? Whereas this interval may be partially explained by the fact that more complex surgical procedures had to await the introduction of complementary technologies, such as videoendoscopy, this alone does not appear to provide a satisfactory explanation. The delay in transfer appears to be intimately linked to issues surrounding the definition and the boundaries of clinical specialties.

Internal medicine and its subspecialties, such as gastroenterology, have traditionally borne primary responsibility for diagnostic activities, and endoscopic tools were part and parcel of the culture and training of these specialties. By contrast, recent generations of surgeons had little training in endoscopic procedures. Moreover, and probably more importantly, laparoscopy, which in effect requires one to operate outside the patient's body, was in many ways contrary to the culture of surgery. In abdominal surgery, for example, the leading paradigm was to make large incisions that allowed surgeons to visualize and palpate the abdomen.

In the 1990s, however, the attitudes of surgeons underwent dramatic change, as is probably most significantly illustrated in gallstone surgery, which was the first major surgical procedure to be transformed into a laparoscopic one. In fact, in the United States more than half of all 33,000 general surgeons acquired the necessary skills within 18 months, a breathtakingly rapid adoption of a new medical procedure by any historical standard. By comparison, the initial adoption of laparoscopic cholecystectomy was slower in Europe (the first laparoscopic cholecystectomy was performed in France in 1990), and much less pronounced in Japan.

As the laparoscope was similar to that used in gynecology, leading manufacturers of laparoscopes, such as Storz and Wolf, early on saw a major new opportunity and quickly capitalized on their technologies and reputations. These manufacturers initially focused on the U.S. market. Clinical innovators realized that applying surgical sutures through an endoscope was difficult and particularly time-consuming and would discourage a major part of the surgical profession from adopting the technique. The surgical innovators Reddick and Olsen worked together with U.S. Surgical, an existing wound closure company that more than 20 years ago developed a stapling device, to adapt this device for use through an endoscope. This achievement facilitated the application of laparoscopic cholecystectomy tremendously, and in the early 1990s U.S. Surgical became the dominant firm in the field of disposable microsurgical instrumentation. U.S. Surgical's leading position, however, is currently being contested by Johnson & Johnson's newly formed Ethicon Endo-Surgery division (Ethicon was the leading sutures manufacturer, making more than 80% of all sutures in the United States). Interestingly, European manufacturers lead in the reusable market, a division of labor that is presumably connected to differences in the nature of European and U.S. health care systems.

IV. The Role of National Innovation Systems

Our study of the diagnostic device industry has pointed to important regional differences in industry performance. As far as the imaging industry is concerned, the leading firms of the 1990s were very similar to those of the late 1950s. The top five firms include the European firms Siemens and Philips, the American company General Electric, and the Japanese firms Toshiba and Hitachi. Whereas the dominant players have not changed much over the past four decades, recently there has been an important shift in manufacturing locus of imaging devices to Japan. At the same time, the Japanese have not been at all prominent in the early stages of imaging devices.

As far as endoscopes are concerned, one can discern distinct patterns of regional specialization. European manufacturers, for instance, dominate the rigid endoscope and laparoscope market and the reusable microsurgical instrumentation market, whereas U.S. firms lead in the disposable microsurgical instrumentation market. Flexible endoscopy, by contrast, presents a very different industrial picture. First American firms and then Japanese firms experienced great success in world markets.

As mentioned earlier, the innovation that was responsible for the transformation in flexible endoscopy was the emergence of fiber optics. The initial research breakthroughs that led to fiber optics occurred in Europe, but the first workable instruments were developed in the United States, and most of the subsequent successful commercialization of the new technologies was achieved in Japan.

In the rest of this section, we will examine the extent to which success resides in features of national innovation systems, particularly the strength of the local science base, intellectual property protection, and those characteristics of the health care system that are key in determining the national market.

A. The Strength of the Local Science Base

Universities played important and multifaceted roles in the evolution of medical imaging devices and endoscopes. A common denominator in the early days of all of these technologies is that basic advances in physics were an important source of new diagnostic capabilities. These advances were typically generated in departments of physics at universities in Europe and the United States. This is true all the way from Roentgen, a German professor of physics, to the U.S. and U.K. physics departments involved in research on nuclear magnetic resonance phenomena. The tradition of university research in the realm of physics and chemistry has persisted much longer in Europe than in the United States, as is reflected in the allocation of national research budgets. European nations, such as the United Kingdom, Germany, France, and the Netherlands, invest relatively more of their total research budgets (i.e., 24.2%) in the physical sciences than the United States (i.e., 15.6% [Irvine, 1990]).

Thus, in contrast to pharmaceuticals, academic medical centers (AMCs) are typically not the dominant source of basic scientific and technological knowledge underlying medical device innovation (the "R" of R&D). Nevertheless, they do play a critical role in the development of new medical devices (the "D" of R&D). Although the first CT scanner was built at EMI, the first whole-body scanner was constructed at Georgetown University Medical School and important incremental advances were generated at other academic medical schools. Moreover, both physics departments and medical schools were heavily involved in the development of the first prototype MRI. In the case of endoscopy, the academic/medical trio at the University of Michigan medical school not only solved a critical technological problem with respect to the new device – the cladding of the glass fiber – and developed the first prototype, but were also instrumental in teaching the industrial firm how to solve some complicated manufacturing problems – the making of the fiber-optic bundles. This is, to say the least, a drastic departure from what might be regarded as the "normal" division of labor between academia and private industry.

These advances have been transferred to industry by various routes. A common practice in the imaging industry was to use academic researchers as consultants or to hire these researchers, sometimes after firms had sponsored their research. It is reported that several American firms, including Technicare, Picker International, and GE, added to their relevant technical competences by "aggressively" recruiting a number of people who had played prominent roles in earlier British research. Such personnel movements were particularly important in overcoming the late American entry into MRI. The transatlantic movements of Richard Edelstein are illuminating, if not necessarily representative. Edelstein was a key figure in GE's emergence as a major player in MRI. He was a Harvard physics Ph.D. who took a postdoctoral degree at the University of Glasgow after finishing his graduate work, apparently because he could not find suitable employment in the United States. Edelstein spent more than six years in postdoctoral positions at the Universities of Glasgow and Aberdeen, where some of the key physics research in NMR imaging was being conducted. He was recruited by GE in 1980, when he joined their corporate laboratory in Schenectady, and he was a central figure in the firm's rapid entry into MRI (Roessner et al., 1997). Another pathway can be found in licensing practices. Pfizer, for instance, licensed Georgetown's whole-body scanner, whereas Syntex, Varian, and GE all entered the CT field by licensing important technical improvements from Stanford University (Mitchell, 1988).

But, in addition, academic medical centers played a primary role, well past the prototype stage, that was a major determinant of commercial success. Improvements in product design turned in large measure upon extended clinical testing that required close collaborative relationships, sometimes with several major medical schools and their teaching hospitals. The clinical data generated by such testing not only fed back to alterations in product design by the manufacturing firm; they also laid the basis for obtaining FDA premarketing approval, and thereby widespread market access. Of course, the development process does not end with the more widespread introduction of a new product into practice. Their eventual uses turn upon an extensive improvement process that may vastly expand their practical application. Users, often clinicians in academic medical centers, provide the necessary feedback concerning the shortcomings of a device and expand its application to new clinical indications of use as well. In the case of GI endoscopy, for instance, academicians expanded the use of fiber-optic endoscopes from the upper GI tract to other gastroenterological sites, such as the esophagus, duodenum, and colon. In imaging, new applications of MRI during surgery or within cardiovascular medicine are emerging only recently.

Whereas academic medical centers in the United States and Europe played a critical role in the evolution of these industries, their counterparts in Japan appear to have been less important in this respect. Why would this be the case? At first glance, academic medical centers in the United States, Japan, and European nations have the same three-pronged mission: (1) they train physicians and biomedical researchers, and, thereby, shape the distribution of skills and specialties, and in no small measure define role models and prestige hierarchies of enduring influence to graduates; (2) they conduct a whole range of biomedical research activities; and (3) they provide advanced specialty and tertiary care, and as such are early adopters of "the latest" in technology. Yet, academic medicine in these three regions exhibits interesting differences in the following respects: (1) the amount of resources that go into the life sciences, (2) the organization of the biomedical research enterprise, and (3) the entrepreneurial nature of AMCs, and the ease with which university–industry interactions take place.

In the United States, academic medical centers, and basic biomedical research in particular, have been major beneficiaries of postwar science policy, including, especially, massive amounts of government spending for biomedical research. As compared to other OECD countries, the United States spends the largest amount of its overall research budget in the life sciences, and the NIH (with an annual budget now approaching $15 billion) is by far the largest single biomedical research funding agency in the world. Nearly 80% of its extramural monies are spent in AMCs, providing strong support for their research enterprise. At the same time that biomedical research spending increased significantly in the postwar years, health insurance coverage expanded and third-party payment systems insulated patients and physicians from the financial implications of their medical care decisions, creating a large demand for advanced medical technology. These financial incentives encouraged the spectacular growth of American academic medicine. Between 1960 and 1992, the average medical school budget in the United States expanded in real terms nearly 10-fold (see Table 8.5). The basic science faculty increased from 4,023 to 15,579, whereas clinical faculty increased, far more rapidly, from 7,201 to 65,913. It is particularly these clinical specialists who are involved in the clinical testing and modification of diagnostic devices.

American AMCs, and their parent universities, have had long-

Table 8.5. *Growth of U.S. Academic Medicine, 1960–1992* (1992 $)

	1960	1970	1980	1992
Support from NIH (millions of $)	1,320	3,028	5,419	8,407
Average Medical School Budget (millions of $)	24.1	64.6	91.9	200.4
Full-time Medical School Faculty (no.)				
Basic	4,023	8,283	12,816	15,579
Clinical	7,201	19,256	37,716	65,913
Matriculated				
Medical Students (no.)	30,288	40,487	65,189	66,142

Source: Adapted from Iglehart (1994).

standing relationships with industry. In recent years, the number and diversity of these relationships with industry appear to be increasing. These relationships include consulting arrangements, research contracts and collaborative agreements, technology licenses, and spin-off firms based upon university-originated research. The passage of the Bayh–Dole Act in 1980 significantly increased the incentive for universities to patent and license the results of university research. Partly as a result of Bayh–Dole, there has been a growth in university patenting, from 57 patents per billion dollars of research spending in the mid-1970s to 96 in 1995. The medical school is a major locus of inventive activity, with patents especially concentrated in biotechnology and medical devices. In general, American AMCs distinguish themselves through their entrepreneurial nature and the ease and frequency of interactions with industrial firms; that is less the case in Europe.

Although in Europe there has also been a significant growth in the public financing of biomedical research, Europeans tend to spend much less of their overall research budget in the life sciences. Also, most Northern European countries regulate the training of physicians and medical specialists, affecting the size of clinical programs. Moreover, in Europe, the biomedical research enterprise has been organized differently. Whereas Western European nations have academic medical centers with the same three-pronged mission as American ones, in some European nations a significant portion of the basic biomedical research enterprise is located in specialized research institutes, such as INSERM in France and the Max Planck Institutes in Germany. As a result, basic bench scientists and clinical scientists live in less close proximity, and that separation may impede mutual learning and collaborative efforts, particularly regarding the development of new technologies.

In what ways do industrial firms draw upon European universities, and particularly AMCs, and what can we say about the ease and frequency of university–industry relationships? As mentioned, European universities have maintained their strong presence in the physical sciences, and – in accordance with their traditional role – have made major contributions to the knowledge base in these areas. Industrial firms clearly have drawn upon these contributions. At the same time, Northern European nations, such as Sweden, the Netherlands, and the United Kingdom, have strong clinical research traditions, especially in the conduct of clinical trials. Device firms, thus, have conducted many of their clinical trials in these countries, which have established a reputation of rigorous clinical evaluative research with the U.S. FDA. Although we have cited several cases in which academic faculty (e.g., Semm in Germany) have been involved in the development of prototype devices, our impression is that European academic faculty are less entrepreneurial in this respect and that the connections with industry are less intimate and interactive in this area than in the United States. Parenthetically, it is not clear whether what appears to be entrepreneurial weakness may really be a reflection of a regulatory environment that renders entrepreneurship much more difficult. This is probably one of the reasons that imaging firms, such as Siemens and Philips have collaborative programs not only with German and Dutch AMCs, but also with numerous U.S. AMCs (OTA, 1984).

By contrast to that in the United States and Europe, the Japanese AMC is much more geared toward providing primary health care and educating primary care physicians. Japanese academic medical centers have about 30% of the U.S. rate of inpatient admissions, despite their larger average numbers of beds, and perform many fewer surgical or other clinical invasive procedures. In general, one can observe that the scale of American teaching hospitals, whether in terms of revenues generated, proportion of staff (physicians and nurses) and services supplied, or number of patients admitted, is far greater than that of Japanese teaching hospitals (Holt et al., 1992). Of course, it is not only a matter of scale, but of housing these highly specialized research activities that are so characteristic of the American scene, and which are less prominent in Japanese AMCs.

B. Intellectual Property Rights

By comparison with that of pharmaceuticals, the value of patent protection in diagnostic device development is far less evident. In the device area, it is probably easier to invent "around" a patent by developing another technique for achieving a given purpose. For example, a variety of operating methods were developed in CT scanning to bring down image construction time. At the same time, the decision by ACMI not to take out any patents on fiber-optic endoscopy in Japan allowed easy entry of Japanese firms, such as Olympus, and ultimately had major negative effects on the market position of ACMI. Olympus subsequently fortified its world market position with extensive patenting. Moreover, it is not clear that Olympus's strength in these markets has depended heavily on property rights as opposed to its strong technological and marketing skills. Moreover, the proprietary rights of small firms have often been ignored. The Damadian Fonar story is relevant here. GE, as mentioned earlier, was ordered to compensate Damadian in the amount of $128 million, and the other major players settled out of court for undisclosed sums. But by the time those rights were reasserted by the courts, the small innovative firm had long since been left behind.

C. Health Care System Characteristics

Several key characteristics of health care systems determine the ultimate market for diagnostic devices. Among these are the number of physicians and the patterns of specialization, as well as the hospital infrastructure, of a country. Of special importance are also the regulatory and payment policies that affect the adoption decisions of physicians and hospital administrators.

Patterns of Medical Specialization and Hospital Infrastructure. The diffusion, as well as the development, of medical diagnostic devices are heavily shaped by the size of the physician pool in a country and their degree of specialization. The United States, Western Europe, and Japan differ significantly in the number of physicians per population as well as specialization patterns. The ratio of physicians to population ranges from 1.4 per 1,000 in the United Kingdom, to 1.7 in Japan, 2.3 in the United States, and 2.7 and 3.1 per 1,000 in France and Germany, respectively. But, although the United States does not have the highest ratio of physicians per capita, it is by far the most highly specialized of all OECD countries. In most European nations, about 40% of doctors are trained as specialists. In the United States, the number of specialists now exceeds 65% of the total. If comparing patterns of specialization, the United States especially has many more surgical specialists per capita than

European nations, and far more than Japan. This was a factor in the very rapid diffusion of laparoscopic cholecystectomy and allowed American microsurgical instrumentation firms, such as U.S. Surgical and Ethicon, to access a larger pool of surgeons for feedback on the performance characteristics of their instrumentation. This is also the reason why European laparoscope manufacturers, such as Storz and Wolf, initially focused on the U.S. market. A similar story can be told about imaging devices. Although the United States does not have many more hospital beds, on a per capita basis, than European nations, American hospital administrators – important decision makers in the adoption of high-cost imaging devices – are much more unfettered by regulatory and budgetary constraints than their European counterparts. Moreover, U.S. hospitals operate in a competitive market, where having the latest in technology confers an important competitive advantage. There are also more radiologists per capita than in many European countries, one of the reasons why EMI first presented its results at the American Radiological Association's meeting.

The Japanese health care system, however, has been heavily influenced by Chinese medicine and exhibits a strong focus on holistic and noninvasive medicine.[14] In Japan, by contrast to the United States, nearly all physicians are generalists (either family practitioners or "specialized" in internal medicine), who provide primary care. One very prominent specialty, partly as a result of the high incidence of gastric cancer, is gastroenterology. These specialists, as shown, have played an important role in the postintroduction improvement process of endoscopic devices, and Olympus has benefited from close and ready access. More generally, one would expect that Japanese physicians would focus heavily on diagnosing disease and treating disease conditions with pharmaceuticals, whereas in nations where there is a higher degree of specialization one would find a heavier reliance on surgical and other interventional clinical procedures. In fact, the average number of surgical procedures in Japan is less than one-fourth of that of the United States, 22/1,000 persons vs. 91/1,000 persons (Ishikawa and Kaihara, 1993). The Japanese industry is heavily focused in the area of diagnostic devices, as well as in pharmaceuticals. As far as therapeutic devices are concerned, Japan con-

[14] This is most clearly evident in what was a long-standing taboo on organ transplantation. This taboo was reinforced by the Japanese legal definition of death until the fall of 1997, according to which a patient is not considered to be dead as long as the heart continues to beat. Since the heart and liver are rendered useless once the heart has stopped, this definition of death essentially precluded heart and liver transplantation. The Japanese Diet in October 1997 passed a law allowing for organ transplantation, which did not define death, but relegated such responsibility to the Ministry of Health and Welfare.

tinues to have to rely on imports for four major categories of cardiovascular devices: pacemakers, heart valves, defibrillators, and coronary angioplasty systems. By comparison, the U.S. and European device industries are more diversified. In addition to manufacturing diagnostic devices, the latter countries manufacture highly specialized precision instruments for surgical and other invasive procedures.

In comparison to the United States, Japan has many more small hospitals. These hospitals were interested in adopting the lower-priced CT head scanners and lower-tesla MRI devices, and thereby provided Japanese firms with an easily accessible home market when they were establishing themselves in the newer imaging modalities.

Health Care Financing and Regulatory Policies. The largest single market for diagnostic medical devices is the United States, although for several subsectors of diagnostic devices, such as CT scanners or GI endoscopes, Japan comes close. Traditionally, the United States has not relied heavily on planning and regulatory mechanisms to limit or distribute the supply of health care resources, allowing the unhindered diffusion of advanced medical technologies. These regulatory mechanisms focus generally on capital-intensive equipment, such as imaging devices. Moreover, the dominance of retrospective hospital reimbursement until the 1980s and fee-for-service physician payment systems, bolstered by permissive third-party insurance schemes, provided strong economic incentives for hospitals to adopt the latest in medical technology. It is therefore not surprising that CT scanners disseminated rapidly and widely in the United States. The MRI, however, came onto the health care scene a decade after the CT, at a time of increased concern about escalating health care costs. At that time, the health care financing and regulatory environment had changed dramatically as compared to a decade earlier. The retrospective hospital reimbursement system had been succeeded by a prospective payment system for Medicare enrollees and certificate-of-need regulations had come to play a more prominent role. Also, in 1976 the Device Amendments to the Food and Drug Law were introduced, requiring a manufacturer to show safety and efficacy before being able to gain marketing approval. In the case of diagnostic devices, however, these requirements were more lenient than in the case of therapeutic devices (i.e., manufacturers only had to demonstrate safety). Moreover, newer versions of laparoscopes and endoscopes were "grandfathered" in under so-called 510K provisions, because these devices had been on the market before the 1976 device regulation came into effect. Despite the more constrained environment, as well as the high price tag of MRIs (somewhere between $1 and $2 million), these devices were adopted at an amazingly rapid rate in the late 1980s. In fact, the United States has 8.1 MRIs per million population, almost four times the mean of OECD nations (Lazaro and Fitch, 1995).

On the other side of the Atlantic we observe diffusion patterns of capital-intensive equipment that are much lower. Why is this the case? Europeans depend much more heavily on public planning and regulatory tools to provide, limit, or distribute the supply of health care resources (i.e., hospital facilities, advanced medical technologies, and medical personnel). Moreover, Europeans rely strongly on publicly determined global budgets for hospitals and legally binding fee schedules for those providers who are compensated on a fee-for-service basis. These budgetary caps have provided a framework that forces explicit choices among technologies. In the United Kingdom, for instance, decisions on capital spending occur at the regional level. That is, National Health Service administrators may have to decide whether to buy an MRI for one major center or to purchase fluoroscopic radiographs for, say, seven district hospitals. These financing and regulatory policies, as mentioned, have resulted in a much lower level of diffusion per million population in European nations and have forced companies such as EMI to focus initially on the American market.

The diffusion of diagnostic devices in Japan was extremely rapid. This can be partially explained by certain religious and cultural traditions as well as by the organization of the Japanese health care system. As in European nations, the Japanese social insurance–based system provides universal access; employees are covered by private insurance, and other citizens are covered by public insurance. Hospitals and clinics are paid on a fee-for-service basis. However, the fee schedules for each office visit, procedure, drug, and device are determined by the Japanese Ministry of Health (Vogt et al., 1996). These fee schedules have provided Japanese doctors with strong financial incentives to employ the most advanced available diagnostic technology. Moreover, in contrast to those in European nations, hospitals are subject to very little regulation regarding their capital expenditures and no planning laws exist for the distribution of high-technology interventions, further encouraging the very high rate of diffusion of imaging devices in Japan. They lead the world, by far, in the diffusion of CT scanners (Japan had almost five times the OECD mean) and were second, after the United States, with regard to MRI diffusion. In the case of endoscopy, of course, the high incidence of gastric cancer has powerfully focused national attention in Japan on improved techniques of early diagnosis in the GI tract. This is reflected in mass screening programs that were initiated in 1961, which further encouraged the diffusion of endoscopic procedures.

V. Determinants of Success: National Innovation Systems or Firm-Specific Capabilities?

If we examine the patterns of international leadership in the diagnostic device industry, explanatory variables can be found both in particular features of national innovation systems, as well as in firm-specific capabilities and strategies. In examining the conditions determining success, however, it is of critical importance to make a distinction between those conditions determining success in making the *initial innovation*, and those determining *eventual commercial* success.

In the pioneering stages of diagnostic technologies, universities and academic medical centers have played an exceedingly prominent role. In the years after the Second World War, the United States developed an outstanding research capability when the federal government became the major patron of scientific research. The NIH controlled the world's largest biomedical research budget, and the great bulk of it came to be concentrated in AMCs, which, in turn, became the focal point for clinical as well as basic biomedical research. As this chapter reveals, American AMCs have also been very active in the development of prototype technologies. The European countries have maintained a major commitment to the physical sciences, and Northern European countries particularly have derived considerable strength in diagnostics from their AMCs. The United Kingdom, for instance, which can draw on a strong tradition in physics research in its universities and great capabilities at the clinical evaluative research level, has been at the forefront of generating new imaging devices. By comparison, university-based research in Japan is much weaker and their academic medical centers are primarily focused on primary care medicine. As a result, they have not, with one important exception, had the scope or strength of activity in subspecialized medicine, and in related research areas, to initiate major new diagnostic technologies.

In addition to universities, small firms, which were an important transfer mechanism between universities and industry, have played an important role in advancing new products, even though they have not usually survived commercial shakedown. There is evidence that start-up firms in Britain, and Europe more generally, had great difficulty in finding private financial support for new products, whereas, in the United States, entry into the medical device industry was powerfully strengthened by a uniquely American institutional innovation: the venture capital industry.

However, the capabilities that are most relevant when new technologies mature and become more stabilized are very different from the skills and kinds of creativity associated with innovative activities at the earlier pioneering stages of innovation. The United Kingdom, for instance, remains eminently successful in early university-research stages of imaging technologies, but loses control as technologies mature, and as costly manufacturing and marketing skills have to be mobilized to meet the needs of large competitive markets, with technologies experiencing rapid performance improvements. These preconditions for commercial success appear to have smothered the smaller entrants in the end.

The story of the diagnostic imaging industry supports the proposition that, in this sector, first-mover advantages have not been of primary importance to eventual success in the marketplace when new technologies possess certain significant commonalities with earlier ones. Although the large multinationals were often late entrants, they quickly traversed the ground already covered by the smaller, pioneering early entrants and asserted their R&D capabilities and other commercial advantages to assume dominant positions. Similarly, in endoscopy first-mover advantages do not appear to have been so important. For example, Japan, at one time or another, drew upon relevant capabilities in photography, electronics, miniaturization, and videotechnology in achieving its domination of the flexible endoscopy market. Germany, on the other hand, failed to make the transition from endoscopic technologies based upon optical lenses to drastically different endoscopes based on fiber optics. However, they remain the world leader in rigid endoscopes that draw upon their traditional skills in lensmaking. Where path dependence is a significant factor, established firms may have superior capabilities in exploiting new technologies because of their greater skills in manufacturing, but perhaps even more important, in marketing and modifying the technology in response to the experience, and articulation of needs, of the specialized final users.

Japan, which has not, on the whole, been a major contributor to the introduction of new technologies, has come to play a vastly more prominent role later on in their life cycle. Japan's great manufacturing skills in consumer electronics are well documented. As the dynamics of technological change in medical imaging generated a shift toward a more intensive utilization of electronic capabilities, there has been a clear drift favoring Japan's role in imaging. This has manifested itself in two particular ways. Large multinationals have entered into joint arrangements, such as Philips with Hitachi and GE with Yokagama, thus exploiting Japanese manufacturing capabilities. Second, as new diagnostic products have come to incorporate more electronics, all the large Japanese electronics giants established their own medical subsidiaries. Furthermore, many Japanese manufacturing products are reported to have succeeded in U.S. markets because their firms have paid particularly great attention to the needs of the ultimate users. This appears to be the case in medical diagnostics, in which products have had to be "finetuned" to the needs of specific categories of users. This shows up especially well in the way they have catered to the needs of hospitals of different sizes. Indeed, as we have seen, this pattern has extended to the point where industrial electronics firms have concentrated their attention on diagnostic products of different sizes for different size hospitals. Moreover, Japanese endoscopic firms have an excellent reputation for providing rapid, high-quality after-sales service through the world markets where large numbers of their endoscopes have been sold. They are said to excel in the speed with which repairs are accomplished and in provision of temporary replacements while original equipment undergoes repair.

A critical issue arises, then, within the context of this chapter: how relevant is the concept of national boundaries, and how difficult is it to cross these boundaries? Sweeping generalizations are inappropriate. An initial, but partial answer in diagnostic technologies is that national boundaries do not seem to offer major impediments to the transmission of the findings of basic research. Both European nations and the United States currently have strong bases in physics research. The knowledge of the scientific advances that result from these investments in research appears to transfer across national boundaries, among this group of countries, quite readily. Even a hundred years ago, firms in Britain and the United States were manufacturing X-ray machines within months of the announcement of Roentgen's stunning discovery of X rays. Similarly, the development of the fiber-optic endoscope proceeded all the way to the working prototype stage almost immediately after a gastroenterologist at the University of Michigan medical school read the 1954 articles in *Nature*, by European scientists, concerning the potential of image transmission with fiber optics. (Hopkins and Kapany, 1954; van Heel, 1954).

Furthermore, it seems appropriate to speak in terms of a distinctive Anglo-American research community, in the sense that scientists and engineers have moved more readily across the national boundaries of these two countries, both within the university world and within private industry, as well as from academe into industry. The ease and frequency of such movements have been central features of technological change in medical diagnostics technology over the past 30 years or so. This Anglo-American research community has produced results that redounded primarily to the benefit of the American participants in the medical diagnostics sector. Britain, on the whole, has failed to gain great commercial benefit from distinguished scientific and innovative contributions to the CT scanner and MRI.

The answer to the question about the crossing of national boundaries needs to be qualified if we consider the transmission of findings of clinical R&D. Much of the relevant interchange during the clinical development process occurs between firms and AMCs. A central point here is that AMCs have become international institutions. That is to say, the big multinationals can now "tap into" these centers quite readily, and national boundaries do not seem to constitute major barriers for them. European multinationals, for example, for many years have had extensive linkages with American AMCs. The OTA report on MRI devices shows that Philips had connections with such AMCs as Columbia-Presbyterian and Siemens with AMCs such as Washington University (OTA, 1984). Japanese multinationals, by contrast, do not seem to have much of this. But this is consistent with our conclusion that Japanese firms, at least so far, have not made a mark at the innovation level; rather, they have come to play a significant role when the product has matured, at which point they have entered and exploited their much-vaunted manufacturing skills.

At the same time, the interface with private industry is best conducted under conditions of close personal interaction between technical and medical specialists when dealing with such issues as developing new imaging prototypes and deciding how next to proceed. At a yet later stage, AMCs have played a critical role – perhaps the critical role – in clinical testing. These tests are of decisive importance as the final hurdle that needs to be surmounted before entry into the marketplace can occur. Here proximity matters, because clinical testing is likely to lead to all sorts of related feedbacks to industrial firms, feedbacks based upon clinical findings and upon the need to modify the technology to suit the requirements of different medical specialties. But medical specialists are unlikely to understand the technical constraints, or the costs, associated with modification, and extensive discussion is commonly necessary in evaluating the various trade-offs that these different constraints generate. Once again, proximity may not be absolutely essential, but it is likely to make this interaction quicker and more thorough. Thus, the question is not whether national boundaries can be crossed. Of course they can be crossed. But it is also frequently more costly, more difficult, and, not least important, more time-consuming to cross these boundaries, and speed in product modification and redesign has been an essential ingredient in commercial success in medical imaging.

A final question is whether national markets matter. The answer is that they do matter if a technology is in the early stages of its evolution. EMI, in the case of CT scanning, had to focus on the U.S. market, whereas GE had the advantage of a large home market. The high presence of gastric cancer and the consequent large number of gastroenterologists in Japan conferred significant benefits on Olympus in improving flexible endoscopy. Once the product has matured, however, small domestic markets do not appear to have been a great impediment, as the case of Philips amply demonstrates, because access to other European markets and to North America has become increasingly open. Imaging technology has not been a story of markets being reserved for the home firm, although national firms are all market leaders in their own region. Japan's frequent practice of limiting access to her markets until her own producers came "up to speed" applied to imaging technologies as well, although no explicit protectionist measures were enforced. The hospital infrastructure of Japan, for example, allowed Japanese firms to exploit a niche market (e.g., head scanners, lower-tesla MRIs) until Japanese firms were ready to compete internationally.

In conclusion, we have argued that firm-specific capabilities have been very important in establishing eventual commercial success. The same few firms have dominated the imaging sector for a long time. They have transferred skills from one product to the next in a sequence: X rays, CT scanners, MRI. Also in rigid endoscopy, the European firms have dominated the market for a long time, and Japanese firms have dominated GI endoscopy by drawing upon their skills in miniaturization and photography. Generally speaking, Japan has not been a major innovator. Indeed, it is at least possible that Japan would have been more successful as an innovator in medical imaging technologies had it been in closer touch, at an earlier date, with the relevant research centers in Europe and the United States. If we consider the questions of innovative success for diagnostic devices at the global level, characteristics of national innovation systems become more important.

References

Aaron, H.J., and W.B. Schwartz, *The Painful Prescription: Rationing Hospital Care*. Brookings Institution, Washington, D.C., 1984.

Banta, D.H., "Embracing or Rejecting Innovations: Clinical Diffusion of Health Care Technology." In S.J. Reiser, and M. Anbar (eds.), *Machine at the Bedside*. Cambridge University Press, Cambridge, 1984.

Biomedical Business International, U.S. Market for Products in Laparoscopic/Endoscopic Surgery. Santa Ana, Calif., 1991.

Blume, S.S., *Insight and Industry: On the Dynamics of Technological Change in Medicine.* MIT Press, Cambridge, Mass., 1992.

Damadian, R., "Tumor Detection by Nuclear Magnetic Resonance." *Science* 1971;171:1151.

Gelijns, A.C., *Innovation in Clinical Practice: The Dynamics of Medical Technology Development*. National Academy Press, Washington, D.C., 1991.

Gelijns, A.C., and N. Rosenberg, "From the Scalpel to the Scope: Endoscopic Innovations in Gastroenterology, Gynecology, and Surgery." In A.C. Gelijns, and N. Rosenberg (eds.), *Medical Innovation at the Crossroads.* Volume V. *Sources of Medical Technology: Universities and Industry*. National Academy Press, Washington, D.C., 1995.

Holt, M., K.B. Ishikawa, S. Kaihara, A. Yoshikawa et al., *Medical Ivory Towers and the High Cost of Health Care*. Stanford University, Stanford, Calif, 1992–93.

Hopkins, H.H., and N.S. Kapany, "A Flexible Fiberscope, Using Static Scanning." *Nature* 1954;17:39–41.

Iglehart, J.K., "Rapid Changes for Academic Medical Centers." *N Engl J Med* 1994;331(20):1391–1395.

Ishikawa, K.B., and S. Kaihara, "Medical Education in Japan." In D.I. Okimoto, and A. Yoshikawa (eds.), *Japan's Health System: Efficiency and Effectiveness in Universal Care*. Faulkner & Gray, Inc., New York, 1993.

Kasumi, W., A. Kashmi, and K.B. Ishikawa, "The Spread of Gastrointestinal Endoscopy in Japan and the U.S." *International Journal of Technology Assessment in Health Care* 1993;9(3):416–425.

Kevles, B.H., *Naked to the Bone: Medical Imaging in the Twentieth Century*. Rutgers University Press, New Brunswick, N.J., 1997.

Kramer, C., and P.J.M. Borden, "Medical Systems in the Last Half Century." *Philips Technical Review* 1986;42:352–358.

Lazaro, P., and K. Fitch, "The Distribution of 'Big Ticket' Medical Technologies in OECD Countries." *International Journal of Technology Assessment in Health Care* 1995 Summer;11(3):552–570.

Mitchell, W., Dynamic Commercialization: An Organizational Economic Analysis of Innovation in the Medical Imaging Industry. Doctoral dissertation, University of California at Berkeley, 1988.

Morrissey, J.F., "Gastrointestinal Endoscopy: Twenty Years of Progress." *Gastrointestinal Endoscopy* 1983;29:53–56.

Office of Technology Assessment (OTA), *Policy Implications of the Computed Tomography (CT) Scanner*. Congress of the United States, Washington, D.C., 1978.

Office of Technology Assessment (OTA), *The Emergence of NMR Imaging Technology: A Clinical, Industrial and Policy Analysis*. Congress of the United States, Washington, D.C., 1983.

Office of Technology Assessment (OTA), *Federal Policies and the Medical Devices Industry*. Congress of the United States, Washington, D.C., 1984.

Office of Technology Assessment (OTA), *Health Care Technology and Its Assessment in Eight Countries*. Congress of the United States, Washington, D.C., 1995.

Roessner, D., B. Bozeman, I. Feller, C. Hill, and N. Newman, "Magnetic Resonance Imaging." The Role of NSF's Support of Engineering in Enabling Technological Innovation. Prepared for the National Science Foundation, SRI International, Arlington, Va., January 1997.

Sentan Inyokiki Databook (1992) Shin Iryo. In D.I. Okimoto and A. Yoshikawa (eds.), *Japan's Health System: Efficiency and Effectiveness in Universal Care*. Faulkner & Gray, Inc., New York, 1993.

Steinberg, E.P., J.E. Sisk, and K.E. Locke, "The Diffusion of Magnetic Resonance Imagers in the United States and Worldwide." *International Journal of Technology Assessment in Health Care* 1987;3:531–543.

Teece, D., "Profiting from Technological Innovation." *Research Policy* 1986, pp. 285–305.

Trajtenberg, M., *Economic Analysis of Product Innovation: The Case of CT Scanners*. Harvard University Press, Cambridge, Mass., 1990.

Tunnicliffe, E.J., "The British X-Ray Industry: A Brief Historical Survey." *British Journal of Radiology* 1973;43:861.

van Heel, A.C.S., "A New Method of Transporting Optical Images without Aberration." *Nature* 1954;17:39.

Vogt, W.B., I. Bhattacharya, S. Kupor, A. Yoshikawa, and T. Nakahara, "Technology and Staffing in Japanese University Hospitals: Government versus Private." *International Journal of Technology Assessment in Health Care* 1996 Winter;12(1):93–103.

Wilkerson Group, Forces Reshaping the Performance and Contribution of the U.S. Medical Device Industry. A report prepared for The Health Industry Manufacturers Association (HIMA). June 1995.

Wise, G., *Willis R. Whitney, General Electric, and the Origins of U.S. Industrial Research*. Columbia University Press, New York, 1985.

Yoshikawa, A., M. Holt, with K.B. Ishikawa, and W. Kasumi, "High Tech Fad: Medical Equipment Use in Japan." In D.I. Okimoto and A. Yoshikawa (eds.), *Japan's Health System: Effectiveness in Universal Care*. Faulkner & Gray, Inc., New York, 1993.

CHAPTER 9

Explaining Industrial Leadership

DAVID C. MOWERY AND
RICHARD R. NELSON

What explains the pattern of industrial leadership revealed in the seven case studies presented in this volume? Do early leaders generally maintain their dominance, or do they often falter? What factors influence change in the pattern of industrial leadership over long time periods? What lessons do these studies yield for public policy? This chapter summarizes and synthesizes the conclusions of our industry studies that bear on these questions.

Section I highlights the factors stressed by the chapter authors in explaining the pattern of industrial leadership in their industry. Section II considers the extent to which differences in the domestic supply of critical inputs and the national institutions that often lie behind these differences can explain the locus of leadership. In Section III, we discuss the importance of differences in the pattern of domestic demand as a factor explaining the national locus of leadership. Section IV considers the question, Where does industrial leadership reside: in the firms themselves, in regional or sectoral systems, or in nationwide factors? In Section V, we examine the dynamics of industry structure, considering the factors that influence change in the locus of leadership and change in industry structure over time. Finally, Section VI considers the implications of these conclusions for public policy.

I. Explanations for Industrial Leadership in These Seven Industries

In the Introduction, we presented summary histories of the shifting patterns of industrial leadership in seven industries. In this section, we summarize the explanations for these patterns set forth by the authors of each chapter.

Mazzoleni's discussion of machine tools in Chapter 5 emphasizes the differences among the United States, Western Europe, and Japan in domestic demand for machine tools as a key factor in this industry's changing pattern of industrial leadership. American manufacturing firms adopted mass production techniques in the late 19th and early 20th centuries, well before their widespread diffusion within Western

Europe and Japan. The widespread use of mass production methods created a large domestic market for machine tools designed for such applications that was dominated by U.S. firms. After World War II, the emergence of numerical control opened up several new possibilities for machine tool design. The difference between the profiles of domestic demand for machine tools in the U.S. and Japanese markets led Japanese machine tool producers to design and sell low-cost CNC machine tools. This market segment has turned out to be very large, and Japanese firms continue to dominate it. Japanese machine tool firms also benefited from the establishment of a standard for electronic controllers by FANUC, the dominant global designer and supplier of these components.

Arora, Landau, and Rosenberg in Chapter 6 focus on different causal factors to explain the shifting locus of industrial leadership in the chemical products industry. German universities' research strength, together with the ability to sell their products abroad, lay behind the dominance by German firms of this "high-technology" manufacturing industry from the 1870s through the early 1920s. The authors also emphasize the farsighted strategies of the German firms themselves, which (among other investments) pioneered in the development of in-house R&D facilities to take advantage of the new scientific opportunities. During the 1920s, U.S. firms began to develop petrochemical-based products and processes, aided by the abundance of cheap domestic petroleum and rapid growth in the American market for organic chemical products. The rise of U.S. firms also relied on the important contributions by U.S. universities to the development of these petroleum-based manufacturing technologies.

The postwar erosion of U.S. and European firms' leadership in some segments of the chemicals industry was at least partly due to the rise of specialized engineering firms that diffused process technologies throughout the world economy. In some respects, the postwar evolution of this industry, like others in this collection, is consistent with the pattern outlined in the Vernon (1966)–Posner (1961) product cycle model of international competition and investment. As the technology became more routinized, it diffused more widely, and U.S. and European firms lost competitive advantage in "commodity" products to countries with lower labor costs.

The dominant position of German and Swiss firms in early 20th-century pharmaceuticals rested on the same factors that underpinned German and Swiss competitive strength in dyestuffs – close links between corporate and university research, as well as an abundant supply of skilled scientists and production personnel. The rise to leadership of

American pharmaceutical firms after World War II benefited from massive U.S. postwar government investments – through the National Institutes of Health – in biomedical research that enabled U.S. firms to exploit the new scientific basis for pharmaceuticals development that resulted from the revolutionary breakthroughs of the 1930s.

These factors also enabled U.S. firms to exploit advances in biotechnology quickly for pharmaceutical applications. Subsequently, U.S. leadership in pharmaceutical biotechnology relied to an even greater extent on close links between U.S. firms and university research, as well as an abundant supply of venture capital for the formation of new biotechnology firms. Throughout the postwar period, U.S. pharmaceuticals firms have also benefited from their large, price-insensitive domestic market for drugs.

The modern medical devices industry began with the entry by diversified German and U.S. electrical equipment producers into the development and production of medical devices (especially imaging equipment) in the early 20th century. As was true of pharmaceuticals, the influence of regulatory controls, along with demanding requirements for national and global marketing and product support networks, enabled these early entrants to maintain dominance, although other firms frequently were the first to design and try to market new products. The strength of their national university systems in physics and medical research also contributed to the leadership of German and U.S. medical device firms. The post-1945 entry into endoscopy and imaging by Japanese optics and camera firms drew on their close interaction with domestic users and their ability to apply their optical competences to this new area.

Industrial leadership in semiconductors, computers, and software reflects a common set of influences. U.S. firms were among the first entrants into all three industries and benefited from the procurement and R&D programs of the Department of Defense. Defense-funded university research and training proved especially important in expanding a domestic pool of skilled scientists and engineers for these industries that was substantially larger than that available to firms in Japan or Western Europe. The large domestic market for commercial mainframe computers in the United States aided the growth of firms in both semiconductors and computer hardware. The large U.S. domestic market of demanding and innovative users, along with a strong antitrust policy, contributed to the emergence of independent U.S. software firms. The sophisticated venture capital industry in the United States provided financing for new firms in the computer hardware industry and in semiconductors.

In two of these three industries, we observe periods during which U.S. dominance was challenged. The rise of Japanese memory chip production and the subsequent growth of South Korean output of these components appear to be consistent with the Vernon–Posner product cycle theory. U.S. competitive advantage has declined in these "commodity" products, and more recent entrants from South Korea have challenged Japanese dominance. In the personal computer industry, Taiwan and other Asian industrializing economies (e.g., Singapore) have entered the production of systems and critical peripherals (e.g., disk drives). This too appears broadly consistent with the product cycle models.

II. Factor Endowments, Institutions, and Industrial Leadership

In the Introduction we noted the long-standing inclination among economists to try to explain the locus of comparative advantage in terms of differential access to critical inputs. To what extent do our authors' explanation for industrial leadership emphasize differences in the domestic supply of critical inputs? What aspects of these differences in supply conditions were most influential?

Differences in the availability of natural resources seldom played an important role. The original location of the German chemicals industry along the Rhine was influenced by proximity to domestic coal deposits, but prior to 1914, German firms imported much of their feedstock coal from the United Kingdom. During the 1920s and 1930s, abundant deposits of petroleum encouraged American chemical and petroleum firms to develop manufacturing technologies and products that relied on petroleum as a feedstock. But U.S. firms' innovative efforts in this direction were motivated in large part by the large size of the American market, which increased the profitability of continuous-flow production technologies that relied on petroleum. In addition, the U.S. natural resource endowment should be understood as partly endogenous – exploitation of the large domestic petroleum deposits relied on advances in exploration and production technologies.

On the other hand, international differences in the availability of high-level skilled labor have mattered in virtually all of our industries. In particular, an abundant domestic supply of scientists and engineers contributed to the entry and growth of German and U.S. firms in chemicals and pharmaceuticals, to U.S. firms' leadership in computer software and computer hardware, and to the emergence of new U.S. firms in pharmaceutical biotechnology.[1] In some cases, such as machine tools, the development of a domestic pool of skilled labor resulted from the growth of the machine tool industry itself and did not depend on supporting institutions external to the industry.[2] But in most of the other industries for which scientific and engineering talent have proved to be essential, domestic university systems have played an important training role.

Differences in the domestic availability of capital also contributed to international differences in the pace and structure of growth of such industries as semiconductors, computer hardware, and pharmaceutical biotechnology. Increased international integration of the domestic capital markets of the industrial economies since 1970 has not removed the strong influence of purely national elements within domestic capital markets.

For example, the rapid growth of the Japanese semiconductor industry during the early 1980s contrasted with the difficulties experienced by American semiconductors companies during the same period and reflected U.S.–Japanese differences in the sources and costs of investment capital for this industry. The size and strength of the venture capital market in the postwar United States, and its relative weakness in the other industrial economies considered here, were important in several of our industry histories. Venture capital facilitated the entry by new U.S. firms into semiconductors, computer hardware, software, and pharmaceutical biotechnology, among other industries, leading to the development of industry structures in the United States that contrast with those observed elsewhere. And in several of these industries, the firms supported by venture capital became industrial leaders, albeit not always enduring leaders.

Behind these important differences across nations in the availability of highly skilled and specialized labor and venture capital were important institutional differences. National university systems are important factors in our seven industry histories. The importance of university-based research and training varies among our industries, but the strength or weakness of national universities was identified as a key influence on the locus of industrial leadership in virtually all of them. We focus here on university research.

[1] As we noted earlier, the growing presence of South Korean and Taiwanese firms in the semiconductor and personal-computer industries during the 1980s and 1990s may reflect a decline in the importance of advanced-degree holders, relative to middle-skill labor (e.g., bachelor's-degree holders), consistent with the product-cycle model.

[2] Indeed, the failure of U.S. universities to develop a more effective research and training base for the postwar U.S. machine tools industry may have contributed to this industry's decline.

We have noted the key role played by German universities in enabling German firms to take the lead in the new dyestuffs industry. Somewhat later American university research paved the way for American firms to take the lead in petrochemicals technology by creating the new field of chemical engineering. University research in the United States and Europe has been a source of strength for national firms in medical diagnostics, and in pharmaceuticals, particularly in the age of biotechnology.[3]

Academic researchers in Great Britain and the United States were directly involved in the development of electronic computers in the immediate aftermath of World War II. After this early involvement, however, the contributions of university research to computer hardware development lay more in the area of basic research and in the training of a large supply of skilled engineers and scientists. This role was fulfilled most effectively by U.S. universities, with the aid of generous public funding for defense-related research. In computer software, U.S. universities remain important sources of technology and fundamental research, in addition to training of computer scientists. In all of these areas, the strength of American university research has been an important reason for the leadership of American firms. The university systems of most Western European economies and Japan have proved less responsive to the research and training needs of these industries, and we believe that the weaker links with unversities have had significant consequences for the performance of their high-technology firms.

The U.S. venture capital market, which is largely a postwar development, was another American institution that in several of these industries lent advantage to American firms. In turn, venture capital rested on the strong U.S. market for public offerings of new and young firms. During the 1970s and 1980s, the expanding "market for corporate control" in the United States appears to have enforced greater flexibility and responsiveness by U.S. firms to changes in market demand or technological opportunities.[4] During the 1980s in particular, U.S. financial markets forced rapid restructuring in relatively mature industries, such as chemicals.

[3] Interestingly, however, domestic university research has proved to be of little importance in the development of the internationally competitive Japanese medical diagnostic device industry.

[4] The disciplinary function of the equities markets does not operate flawlessly. The U.S. equities markets of the 1960s arguably overvalued the "synergies" created by conglomerate mergers (Shleifer and Vishny, 1991; Ravenscraft and Scherer, 1987), and other scholars (e.g., Chandler, 1990; Dertouzos et al., 1989) have argued that the U.S. system of corporatc governance tends to penalize long-term investments.

III. The Role of Domestic Market Demand in Industrial Leadership

The key role of users and international differences in the profile of domestic demand are central to understanding the evolution of many of these industries. Although leading German chemical products firms catered largely to foreign markets from the early years of the industry's development, this case appears to be an exception. More generally, domestic markets tend to dominate the sales of firms in the early development of most of these industries.

Three of our industries found their early markets in military and space applications. The U.S. Department of Defense supported the early growth of American firms in computers, semiconductors, and software, by demanding technologically sophisticated products. By contrast, in our two medical products industries the high profitability of the American market was associated with relatively few explicit government controls on health care costs, which facilitated the rapid adoption of new products. In contrast, new products often faced tight constraints in the highly regulated markets in most Western European nations.

Although the character of domestic demand has been an important shaping factor in most of our industries, exploiting their domestic market required that firms innovate. And their technological innovations, in turn, have had major effects on the growth and structure of demand. Continuous declines in price/performance ratios for semiconductor and computer technologies, for example, have led to their diffusion into a steadily expanding array of commercial applications, customers, and market segments that differ from one another. The progressive opening of new markets for computer hardware in turn created opportunities for entry by new U.S. firms that challenged the dominance of established firms. The rapid growth of new segments of demand within the U.S. domestic computer market, along with the inability of hardware producers to meet demand for software for these new segments, created opportunities for entry by new independent software firms.[5] The growth of new segments of the computer hardware industry in the United States also proved indispensable to the rapid development of the microprocessor segment of the U.S. semiconductor industry, which transformed the financial and competitive outlook for the U.S. industry during 1985–1997.

The importance of the "intranational" user–producer interactions that

[5] A similar pattern in the evolution of the computer storage-disk industry has been discussed by Christensen and Rosenbloom (1994).

seem to pervade these industries has important implications. Even in a world where markets are global, large domestic markets provide an invaluable "springboard" for firms seeking to enter new industries or seize new technological opportunities. Where fixed costs, such as product R&D outlays, are high and production and marketing activities involve economies of scale, strong first-mover advantages may accrue to firms in the country where the market opened first.

We do not mean to downplay the strength and significance of transnational technology and product flows, which in some cases reduce the significance of purely national user–producer links. The strength of British textile firms did not prevent German chemicals firms from dominating the British market for textile dyestuffs. The development by Japanese firms of new medical diagnostic instruments that relied on U.S.-developed optical fiber technologies is a case in which the flows of key enabling technologies spanned the Pacific. The adoption and improvement by German chemicals firms of U.S.-developed manufacturing processes after World War II provide another example of the international flow of technology within an industry. And the refinement and application by Japanese firms of computer controllers to low-cost machine tools relied on technologies originally developed by U.S. electronics firms.

Nonetheless, the national upstream–downstream links were very strong in most of our case studies. Policies that ignore the existence or importance of these links may lead to unanticipated troubles.

IV. The Locus of Industrial Leadership: Firms, Sectors, or the Nation-State?

Our introductory chapter pointed out that some theories of industrial leadership locate the key causal factors in features of the national environment; other theories emphasize the capabilities developed by the firms themselves, and still others focus on regional or sectoral systems as the source of leadership. What light do these industry studies shed on theories of the locus of industrial leadership? Our discussion begins by considering industries in which the locus of leadership at both the firm and national levels has been remarkably stable for a lengthy period. We then examine cases in which the locus has changed and consider whether these changes involved shifts in the identity of the leading firms, in the nationality of these leading firms, or in both.

The chemicals industry is one of extraordinarily enduring firm-level competitive advantage. Virtually all of today's leading firms were established many years ago; such companies as BASF, Hoechst, Bayer, and

DuPont all trace their roots well into the 19th century. Similarly, the pharmaceuticals firms that have mastered the challenge of a new "technological paradigm" have been in existence for substantially more than 75 years, dominating the pharmaceuticals industry for much of this period.

In these industries, it is clear that much of what makes for industrial leadership is located substantially in the firms themselves. Leading firms fit Alfred Chandler's analysis (1990) of the sources of industrial leadership, and strong first-mover advantages have been important and durable. The firms have built and solidified competitive advantage through their own investments and learning in an imperfectly competitive environment that resembles that discussed by the Schumpeter of *Capitalism, Socialism, and Democracy* (1950).

But leading firms in these industries have also benefited from their national institutional and policy environments. In particular, as we stressed, German chemical firms were strengthened by the high quality of the German university system, and the rise of the American chemicals industry was associated with the growing strength of American universities. Similar national factors supported the growth of firms in the other industries we group here, where both firm and national level leadership has been long-lived.

In other cases, e.g., computer software, medical devices, and computer hardware, we observe higher rates of turnover among "dominant firms," but the shifting collection of dominant firms is composed mainly of those headquartered in the United States. The Chandler–Schumpeter model of particular firms that achieve and sustain dominance over long periods does not fit these industries. Rather, such industries as the U.S. software or semiconductor industries fit the model described in the earlier Schumpeter of *The Theory of Economic Development* (1934). The relative stability of industrial leadership at the national level in industries marked by considerable turnover among the leading firms suggests that the factors behind leadership in these industries reside at the level of the nation-state (e.g., domestic factor supply and demand conditions, university systems, or industrial finance) and are relatively durable.

In machine tools, firms from a single nation have dominated different segments at various points in time, but in recent years at least, neither the firm-level nor the national locus of industrial leadership has endured. German and U.S. dominance during the 1950s and 1960s was challenged (and largely overturned) in all but the most specialized segments of the industry by firms from Japan and Taiwan. These changes in leadership are related to differences in national markets and changes in these markets over time.

The picture of the locus of industrial leadership that emerges from our industry studies thus is complex. Nevertheless, we think three broad conclusions can be drawn from these histories. First, the issue is not whether it is firms themselves, or the broader national environment in which they reside, that produces industrial leadership. Both the environment, and what firms make of that environment, matter. Second, although many comparative analyses assume that the institutional environment of firms is determined largely by forces beyond the reach of firms, in fact, firms often exert significant influence on industry-level supporting institutions and policies. Third, to a considerable extent, the sources of industrial leadership reside in structures intermediate between nations and firms. We refer to these as "sectoral support systems."

Interaction. The complex interaction between the performance of firms and the nature of the institutional environment within which they operate is readily apparent in the chemical products and pharmaceuticals industries. German firms were supported by strong German university research and training of organic chemists, but these firms also invented the industrial research and development laboratory and pioneered in providing technical consulting services for their customers. In pharmaceuticals, the support provided by the National Institutes of Health for research and training in the biomedical sciences created considerable opportunities for American-based firms. Nevertheless, these firms displayed considerable skill in exploiting such opportunities.

The same symbiosis between industry support policies and the response of business firms occurs in the computer and semiconductor industries. During the early 1950s, the U.S. Department of Defense provided the primary market for computer hardware. DoD also organized and funded many of the early critical design and development projects through which American computer firms developed their technical skills. Nevertheless, although U.S. firms' dominance of the worldwide commercial mainframe computer industry might have been impossible without these defense procurement and R&D programs, that dominance was not inevitable. Some U.S. firms, such as IBM, "bet the company" and expanded into commercial markets during the 1950s, while others either did not or did so more gradually, eventually ceding dominance in mainframes to IBM. In semiconductors, a large early market reserved for American firms once again was provided largely by the DoD, which also supported industry R&D to develop designs for military applications. But the major technological achievements of the 1950s were in most cases accomplished by companies using their own funds and following avenues very different from those the DoD was funding.

Industry Influences on Supporting Institutions. As we noted, firms located in a particular nation often gain an early advantage in a new industry because the nation's institutions provide them with a more supportive environment than that faced by firms in other countries. However, as an industry develops, the firms themselves may play a powerful role in molding their institutional environment.

Thus, although German chemicals firms had little direct role in the strength of their domestic universities in teaching and research in organic chemistry, once this industry began to develop, German firms provided considerable political support for German government funding of university training and research in chemistry. Indeed their subsequent dissatisfaction with the increasing inflexibility and lack of responsiveness of German universities to industrial research needs contributed to industrial lobbying for government endorsement of the formation of the industrially funded Kaiser Wilhelm Gesellschaft for chemical research in 1910 (see Beyerchen, 1988). U.S. pharmaceutical companies long have supported growth in the NIH budget for biomedical research and training. The mature U.S. semiconductor industry lobbied federal agencies during the 1980s for R&D subsidies to SEMATECH and trade agreements to improve their access to the Japanese market.

National firms also influence their regulatory environment. U.S. biotechnology firms have been involved in the formulation of policies on intellectual property rights and federal funding of university research. The evolution during the 1980s of American intellectual property rights law and practice for software was shaped to a considerable degree by the interests of the American packaged software companies.

Sectoral Innovation Systems. One lesson that can be drawn from many of the industry studies is the importance of national institutions that are highly specific to particular sectors and of sectoral systems more generally. Although they are embedded in and supported by broader national institutions, in many cases the key sectoral ones have a structure and a life of their own.

Thus, German university strength in organic chemistry was, to some extent, a natural consequence of the broad strength of the 19th-century German university system in the natural sciences. But once the German dyestuffs industry began to grow, academic chemistry in Germany had its own particular sources of support, and the links between German universities and German companies in chemistry had their own particular structure, molded by the key professors and their students who had gone out into industry. University–industry research and training linkages in the U.S. pharmaceutical biotechnology and medical device industries have relied for decades on funding from the National Institutes of Health and operate primarily through academic medical centers that combine clinical and fundamental research activities. In turn, the U.S. pharmaceuticals industry supports growth in the NIH budget. This sectoral structure differs from the academic research and training infrastructure that supports the computer, semiconductor, and software industries, which have relied on funding from the U.S. Department of Defense and operates in large part through physical science departments and engineering schools within U.S. universities.

Similarly, the venture capital firms, or at least the key people within the firms, operating in semiconductors, computer hardware, and software are quite different from those focusing on pharmaceutical biotechnology. In each sector, the specialized venture capital firms are knit into the complex networks that link firms, universities, and professional societies.

In some cases sectoral innovation systems are concentrated in particular regions. Examples of regional industrial districts among the industries discussed in this volume include the contemporary biotechnology industry's concentration in the Seattle, San Francisco, San Diego, and Boston areas; the clustering of the leading German chemicals firms in the Rhineland in the late 19th century; and the concentrations of U.S. and German machine tool firms, respectively, in Milwaukee and the Connecticut River Valley, and southwestern Germany. A regional system, like a sectoral system more generally, may involve a collection of industries. The original "Silicon Valley" has grown from its origins in semiconductors to encompass computer hardware and software and biotechnology.

Despite the importance of these regional effects, however, the sectoral system appears to be a more meaningful analytic concept for understanding the sources of industrial leadership. The sectoral system may or may not be concentrated geographically but in any case typically involves an array of supporting institutions and an industry structure that are distinctive. The study of sectoral innovation systems and how they differ across industries, countries, and eras ought to be high on the research agenda of economists and other scholars interested in the sources of industrial leadership.

V. The Evolution of Industry Structure

Our introductory chapter described several different theories of the dynamics of industrial leadership. Here we consider what light these theories shed on the different patterns revealed in our seven industry studies.

Because the period covered in all of our industry histories is relatively long, and because most of these studies cover a wide range of products, theories of industry "life cycles" that focus on the evolution of individual product classes are of limited use.[6] Nevertheless, in some of our industries one does see the emergence of "dominant designs" for at least a portion of the period analyzed by these histories. The IBM 360 fulfilled such a role among mainframe computers for much of the 1960s and 1970s. But the dominance of the computer industry by IBM was ultimately eroded by the emergence of new segments of market demand, first in minicomputers in the late 1960s, then (of far greater significance) in desktop systems in the early 1980s. Since the early 1980s, the "Wintel" architecture for personal computers has been a dominant design, although its emergence is associated with high levels of entry by new firms, rather than declines in entry (as in the Abernathy-Utterback, 1978, and other theories). The limited relevance of "dominant design" theories reflects a broader characteristic of these industries' development. Virtually without exception, industrial evolution has involved the progressive opening of new segments of market demand, for which existing "dominant designs" were poorly suited.

Theories of industry evolution that emphasize dynamic increasing returns and durable first-mover advantages also have validity in some but not all of our industry histories. Modern-day dominant firms in the chemical products industry and in pharmaceuticals have retained leadership positions for more than three-quarters of a century. Outside the United States, long-established, diversified electrical equipment companies have played a durable continuing role in computers, machine tools, and semiconductors, and both U.S. and non-U.S. firms from these industries have been important in medical equipment.

Although some form of dynamic increasing returns or other first-mover advantages appear to be important in explaining such enduring leadership, the companies that have maintained leadership over a long period have not done so through their control of a dominant design or exploitation of scale economies. Instead, these long-term leaders have maintained their technological and nontechnological capabilities in the face of significant change in the underlying basic technologies. For these firms and industries, the concept of "dynamic capabilities" (Teece et al., 1997) has considerable descriptive power. But where changes in the underlying technologies were accompanied by

[6] The most prominent examples of these frameworks are the models developed by Abernathy and Utterback (1978) and Mueller and Tilton (1969).

significant changes in the structure of demand, incumbents have proved less successful.

Rather than well-behaved, relatively stable "product cycles" within industries or technologies, many of these industry histories may be best portrayed as a series of "punctuated equilibria," i.e., a series of discrete, dominant technologies, with the successor significantly different from the predecessor. In machine tools, the advent of numerical control was a major "punctuation." In chemical products the development of petroleum as the basic feedstock was such a punctuation. In pharmaceuticals, the discovery of antibiotics was a punctuation, and the advent of biotechnology an even more dramatic one. The invention and development of the integrated circuit, and later the microprocessor, clearly are technological punctuations in the history of the semiconductor industry. The new computer designs that these inventions permitted – the first, minicomputers, and the second, personal computers – also mark punctuations in the computer industry.

Some theories of industrial evolution argue that these sharp shifts in underlying technologies are competence-destroying in their effects on incumbent firms, and therefore result in the displacement of established industry leaders (Tushman and Anderson, 1986; Henderson and Clark, 1990). Does this pattern characterize our industry histories? Our studies provide mixed evidence on the importance of such competence destruction for long-run industry evolution. The development of petroleum-based chemicals process and product technologies was undertaken by both incumbent and new entrants within the U.S. chemicals industry during the 1920s and 1930s (a number of firms, including Standard Oil of New Jersey, entered the production of chemical products at this time). Moreover, European chemicals firms were able to purchase petroleum-based process technologies from specialized engineering firms and established U.S. firms and successfully switched their process technologies to exploit the new feedstock. A number of established U.S. and European producers of pharmaceuticals also have proved capable of maintaining their positions of dominance in the face of a dramatic technological threat in the form of biotechnology.

On the other hand, major shifts in the underlying technologies have caused considerable trouble for prevailing leaders when technological change has been accompanied by a change in the nature of the markets. The "destabilizing" effects associated with the emergence of new segments of market demand have been most significant when the nontechnological "complementary assets" of established firms have been of little use in the new markets. In chemicals, this dynamic has not been of great importance. In medical devices and pharmaceuticals, government regulation has enabled incumbent firms to develop broad complementary assets in the form of regulatory expertise that applies to a broad variety of products. The costs and expertise needed to manage medical-device and pharmaceutical regulation and marketing are so substantial that they have contributed to relatively low turnover among dominant firms in the face of radical technological advances.

But in the electronics complex, incumbent firms repeatedly have found that their marketing, manufacturing, and other capabilities were insufficient to maintain dominance in new segments of rapidly growing market demand. Similarly, the capabilities developed by U.S. machine tool firms to serve their "Detroit automation" and aerospace customers were not easily applied to the new markets in which Japanese firms proved successful during the 1970s and 1980s.

Another important characteristic of several of the industries analyzed in this volume is the complex development of vertical specialization. In electronics, for example, growth is associated with "dis-integration" and increased specialization over time by firms at different points on a vertical value chain. This tendency appears to have emerged first and to have advanced furthest in U.S. firms.

All three product groups studied in our chapters on electronics (computer hardware, computer software, and semiconductor components) were manufactured in the 1960s by integrated firms such as IBM or Digital Equipment, and both IBM and Digital Equipment maintained a presence in semiconductor components, software, and computer systems until at least 1997. Since then, however, the presence of these large, vertically integrated U.S. enterprises has been overshadowed by the entry of independent U.S. suppliers of components and software, and Digital Equipment was acquired in 1997 by Compaq Computer, a new firm that entered the computer industry in 1982 as a specialized producer of PCs.[7] The rise of biotechnology has produced similar tendencies toward higher levels of vertical specialization in the modern pharmaceuticals industry. A number of established producers of pharmaceuticals have formed "alliances" or contractual relationships with smaller biotechnology specialists for the discovery and development of new drugs.

[7] Indeed, there is significant evidence that component design and manufacture are being separated, as a large number of specialized "design firms" have entered the U.S. semiconductor industry. The design firms provide custom designs of components, which are produced in "foundry" facilities maintained by other firms.

These tendencies toward vertical specialization seem to be strongest in the United States. Major Japanese computer manufacturers, such as Hitachi, NEC, and Fujitsu, all produce electronic components and software, and large Western European electronics firms, such as Philips and Siemens, are also more highly vertically integrated than their U.S. competitors. Similarly, in Europe and Japan the traditional pharmaceuticals companies themselves have tried to diversify into biotechnology, and a specialized collection of biotech research firms has not developed there.

The chemicals industry has for much of the postwar period been characterized by an unusual pattern of vertical specialization, in which "specialized engineering firms" (SEFs) developed new process technologies and built facilities for the manufacture of commodity products by major firms in the United States, Western Europe, and Japan. SEFs also transferred process technologies to other firms, intensifying competitive pressure on the long-established U.S., European, and Japanese firms and forcing a far-reaching restructuring of the industry in the 1980s.

Many elements of the progressive extension of horizontal and vertical specialization that show up in some of our industry histories seem broadly consistent with Stigler's theory (1951). But the Stigler theory does not explain why leading U.S., German, and British chemicals firms have remained diversified and "Chandlerian" (Chandler, 1990). In some cases, such as electronics, entry by vertically specialized firms (independent software vendors, merchant semiconductor producers) seems to have forced some dis-integration of established firms, consistent with Stigler's theory and particularly the arguments of Langlois and Robertson (1995). But why this development should have proceeded further in the United States than in Europe and Japan requires much more analysis. In our earlier discussion we proposed that the U.S. venture capital system is an important part of the explanation, but this only pushes the question back a stage. Why has no comparable institution developed elsewhere?

The picture revealed by our seven industry studies of how technologies and industries evolve over time thus is a complex and variegated one. There is no single pattern that fits all industries. Similarly, the theories that attempt to explain or predict the dynamics of comparative advantage at a national level provide only limited illumination.

We have noted that the theory that posits durable first-mover advantage seems to fit some of our cases but not others. The Vernon–Posner product cycle theory of international trade, which posits a systematic shift in the locus of comparative advantage as an industry matures, also fits some cases but not others. Thus the theory seems to explain the growth of manufacture of standard components of desktop computers, such as monitors and circuit boards, in Taiwan during the 1980s; the growth of "commodity" chemicals production in industrializing nations during the 1970s and 1980s; and South Korean entry into DRAM manufacture in the 1980s and 1990s. In some but not all of these cases, shifts in the locus of production led to shifts in the locus of product development and R&D – such shifts occurred in DRAMs, for example, but not in chemicals. But in pharmaceuticals, medical diagnostics, and the most advanced, "design-intensive" microelectronic components, no such shift to low-wage countries has occurred, perhaps because user–producer interactions and advances in production architecture are both important and highly dynamic.

VI. Lessons and Implications for Public Policy

In the introductory chapter, we reminded our readers that the debate about industrial policies has been going on for over 200 years. In our view, the more recent exchanges have produced more heat than light, largely because neither side has grounded its case solidly in empirical assessment of the historical experience.

The contemporary proponents of active sectoral specific policies argue that governments can successfully promote the growth of industries and have done so for centuries. A modern wrinkle to the argument is that high-technology industries, most of which are characterized by high fixed costs and strong first-mover advantages, lend themselves to such policies. On the other side, opponents of active government policies to assist industries argue that governments almost never are effective overseers of industrial development, and that promotional policies can impose high costs on other industries and the taxpaying public. The evidence from our studies shows both sides of this argument to be partly right and partly wrong. More generally, the picture is much more complex, and subtle, than either side of the debate allows.

Policies that directly aim to encourage the development of an industry by protection and subsidy have a very mixed record. Such policies certainly have aided some industries (e.g., Japan's electronics industry) in catching up with technology leaders. However, for countries that already are at the technological frontier, targeted industrial policies are much riskier and generally less successful. And we think it important to recognize that successful policies generally have avoided public funding of specific commercial products or designs, instead confining themselves to promoting a broad sector or industry.

The economic support environment for industrial development is important. Adam Smith and his contemporary admirers certainly are right in arguing that an essential governmental role in stimulating industrial development involves investment in supporting infrastructure and a broader legal and institutional framework that results in productive investment and competition. Nevertheless, in many of the industries studied in this project, important elements of the government-provided infrastructure and supporting policies that gave strength to an industry were sector-specific.

Although we have made these points elsewhere, we think it sufficiently important, and apparently controversial, that we want to develop the argument further in this concluding section.

A. Lessons for Sectoral Policies

Many public policies and programs whose benefits, costs, and design typically are debated as if their influences were economywide, in fact have strong sector-specific elements and effects. Much R&D infrastructure is sector-specific, as is support for the training of engineers and scientists. Intellectual property rights regimes have technology-specific elements and effects; thus patent protection is more important in fine chemicals and pharmaceuticals than in most other industries (see, e.g., Levin et al., 1987). A number of regulatory policies are sector-specific by definition and design, as in the case of the FDA and the U.S. pharmaceuticals industry. Other policies, such as antitrust, are neither framed by nor targeted on specific sectors. Nevertheless, antitrust policy has had significant, sectorally specific effects, as our studies of the chemicals and computer industries reveal. The fact that policies bearing on industry are sectoral is inevitable in any society where policy develops in response to particular demands, problems, and challenges, and where the nature of the technologies, the demands, and the demanders varies across sectors. As we noted earlier, both the institutions and the policies that affect these sectors are to a considerable extent endogenous to their historical development.

The policies associated with the development of a strong industry vary significantly from sector to sector, in scope, in kind, and in impact. Our history of machine tools reveals only a few instances of sector-specific government policies that have had major impact. The rise of the American machine tool industry toward the middle of the 19th century undoubtedly was facilitated by the interest of the War Department in guns made with interchangeable parts; even in this case, however, the impact of this stimulus may have been minor relative to that of the overall rise of mass-production industry in the United States during the same period. The research support by the U.S. Air Force that brought into existence numerical control undoubtedly hastened the development of that technology. But in this case, the specific goals of this R&D program actually appear to have drawn American machine tool designers and manufacturers away from the development of tools that could support flexible manufacturing, where the big commercial market turned out to reside. There is little evidence that government support of university research and training, protection and subsidies, or particular regulations have had much influence on the evolution of industrial leadership in machine tools.

In contrast, there is little question that broadly targeted government policies have had an important impact on the evolution of chemical product technologies and the strength of national firms. But governments typically have not targeted specific technologies in chemicals, although for national security reasons the German and British governments sponsored the development of synthetic fuels during the interwar period, and the American government supported the development of synthetic rubber during World War II. Rather, the important government policies have been "upstream," particularly through the broad support of university research in the relevant fields. More recently, environmental regulations have had a significant influence.

Pharmaceuticals and medical diagnostic equipment both benefited during the postwar period from large-scale funding of biomedical research by government in the United States, Great Britain, and elsewhere in Western Europe. Public support for biomedical research during this period was far less significant in Japan, however, and limited public funding does not appear to have retarded the development of a vigorous Japanese medical devices industry.

Government regulation of pharmaceuticals and medical devices has been another important influence on the development of these industries. Interestingly, recent evidence suggests that stringent regulation of new pharmaceutical products' safety and efficacy in the United States and selected Western European nations is associated with stronger performance. In contrast, the weaker regulatory structure in Japan has supported imitative strategies among Japanese firms.

The computer industry, the semiconductor industry, and the software industry reveal even broader public sector involvement. In some cases, government involvement has helped national firms gain industrial leadership, and in other cases, this involvement has hindered national firms. As with pharmaceuticals and medical devices, government-supported upstream infrastructure, in the form of R&D and training, has been very important. Public R&D funding of university research also aided the creation of an ample supply of well-qualified electrical engineers, materials scientists, computer scientists, and sophisticated programmers, which has been an important factor in U.S. leadership in these industries.

Government procurement policies have a mixed track record in supporting the commercial performance of firms in these defense-related industries. In semiconductors and computer hardware, the large-scale procurement programs of the U.S. Department of Defense provided an important impetus to the growth of new and established firms during the first two decades of each industry's existence and strengthened the commercial competitiveness of firms in both industries.[8] But defense-related procurement in France and Great Britain proved to be a much less effective catalyst for industrial leadership in civilian markets for computers and semiconductors. And the high-precision demands of the military market for NC machine tools pulled American firms away from where the big civilian market developed.

The explanation for these differences appears to lie in the structure of these programs. Partly because of the greater size of the U.S. defense budget, U.S. procurement programs involved competition for R&D contracts and for purchases – Western European defense programs more frequently awarded contracts on a noncompetitive basis to a "national champion." Another critically important distinction in the structures of many U.S. and Western European defense procurement programs was the greater participation by young computer and semiconductor firms in U.S. R&D and procurement programs. The availability of defense contracts was a powerful magnet for the entry of new firms into both U.S. industries.

B. Generic Policy Principles

Thus far, we have stressed the differences among the government policies that were effective in our different industries. We conclude here by attempting to identify some common, generic characteristics of effective industrial policies. We focus on three broad areas: government R&D support, competition policy, and policy regarding intellectual property rights.

Public R&D funding has been an important source of technological advance and industrial leadership in most of these industries, but the structure of public R&D programs appears to be at least as important

[8] Since the computer software industry was a barely distinguishable part of the computer hardware industry during this early period, such procurement also indirectly benefited the development of the computer software industry.

as the size of their budgets. In general, our industry studies support the use of extramural R&D programs that are subject to competitive allocations among performers based on some assessment of merit, rather than reliance on public laboratories that are insulated from competition or peer review to perform such R&D. In most successful programs, the results of publicly funded R&D also have been widely diffused within an industry, whether through publication, R&D collaboration among firms, or some other mechanism.

We have emphasized the role of universities in research and training. Consistent with the principle we proposed, the structure of national university systems appears to be as important as the magnitude of government support in determining the contributions made to industrial development. Thus the decentralized structure of the U.S. university system and the associated strong interuniversity competition for students, faculty, and research resources contrast favorably with the more centralized Japanese and most Western European university systems. These factors have contributed to considerable institutional innovation within the U.S. university system, as the nascent academic disciplines of chemical engineering, molecular biology, materials science, and computer science (to name but a few) were given the legitimacy of departmental status relatively rapidly, with the aid of external funding from federal and industrial sources. American universities were far quicker than European and Japanese ones in making these changes.

If competition among universities and other research organizations is one hallmark of an effective sectoral innovation system, competition among firms in applying and commercializing technological advances is another. In most of our industries, the firms themselves spend far more on R&D than the government. Alternative approaches to the application and commercialization of new technologies, a process fraught with high levels of uncertainty, are more likely to be deployed, and selection among them is more likely to be effective, when competition among these firms (and, in many cases, between domestic and foreign firms) is more intense.

Perhaps for this reason, competition policy has played an important role in shaping the national locus of industrial leadership in several of the industries treated in this volume. Although it rarely receives extensive attention in discussions of technology and competitiveness, the relatively stringent postwar competition policy of the United States aided the growth of new industries. U.S. antitrust policy weakened the ability of incumbents in such industries as computers and semiconductors to control new technologies and markets. The U.S. computer software industry benefited as well from the restructuring of the U.S. telecommunications industry in the wake of the *U.S.* v. *AT&T* antitrust suit that was settled in 1982. In contrast, in Europe and Japan, where competition policy has been pursued much less aggressively, the development of new technologies has been left largely in the hands of established firms, and often these have moved very slowly.

A closely related area of government policy that has affected many of these industries relates to intellectual property rights. Although scholarly and policymaker opinion in the United States, at least, recently has shifted to favor strong intellectual property rights in technology-intensive industries, the history of these seven industries suggests that a more nuanced interpretation of the costs and benefits of stronger intellectual property rights is needed.

In the fields of chemical products and pharmaceuticals, intellectual property rights have tended to be strong since the turn of the 20th century, and this has enhanced the ability of firms to capture the returns to their R&D. However, these industries tend to be unusual in the extent to which they depend on intellectual property rights in order to profit from their innovations (see Levin et al., 1987).

In semiconductors, a combination of historical accident and U.S. government policy resulted in a relatively weak intellectual property rights environment for most of the first three decades of the U.S. industry's development. This environment was conducive to high levels of cross-licensing and entry by new firms, which contributed to rapid growth and innovation. Since the early 1980s, however, the role of formal intellectual property rights in semiconductors appears to have increased considerably – indeed, the "renaissance" of the U.S. industry, based as it is on microprocessors, has greatly increased the incentives for aggressive private enforcement of these rights, and litigation has grown rapidly. In computer hardware, U.S. antitrust policy also mandated liberal cross-licensing at an early stage in the development of the U.S. industry, reducing barriers to entry. In many areas of computer technology, firms can profit from a head start if they aggressively exploit it, and patents are of less importance to the profitability of inventions.

In computer software, intellectual property rights were of little consequence during the era of custom software. But the growth of mass markets for packaged computer software, rather than formal government policy, has greatly increased the importance of intellectual property rights in this industry. Although U.S. packaged software firms benefited from strong domestic and strengthened international enforcement of intellectual property rights during the 1980s and 1990s, the long-term effects of such strict enforcement on innovative performance remain uncertain.

The case for relatively narrow protection of intellectual property thus receives some support, in our view, from these industry studies. At a minimum, we believe that the burden of proof for stronger intellectual property rights should lie with the proponents of greater stringency. This burden of proof should be highest during the early stages of an industry's development.

In summary, two issues deserve emphasis. First, each one of our industry histories provides strong evidence regarding the major uncertainties involved in the evolution of any rapidly developing technologies. There will be winners and losers in the contest, but these are extraordinarily difficult to predict. Policies toward new technologies and the industries that seek to exploit them should favor greater diversity in the commercial "bets" that are placed on the development of such technologies. Second, government policies that involve placing large bets on particular paths of development or particular firms are likely to fail. One exception to this rule occurs when such public policies are used to catch up with a clear leader, whose characteristics can be evaluated and targeted. But even here, the leader that provided such a clear target may have been surpassed by another technology or firm by the time the chase is in full sway (as the fate of Japanese policies aimed to catch up with IBM amply witnesses). And if the objective is to achieve or maintain leadership, the only reasonable way to accomplish it is to encourage pluralism and competition.

But this does not mean that public policies should be minimal or passive. Government policies powerfully influence the vigor and fruitfulness of dynamic competition. Government research support policies can fuel it. Government regulatory policies may be needed to channel it so that what firms find profitable is also in the public interest. The earlier literature on national innovation systems (see Nelson, 1993) pointed out the complex and variegated institutional structures that are involved in economic growth fueled by technological progress. Our industry studies reaffirm that conclusion, sector by sector.

References

Abernathy, W. and Utterback, J. "Patterns of Industrial Innovation," *Technology Review*, 1978, pp. 41–47.

Beyerchen, A. "On the Stimulation of Excellence in Wilhelmian Science," in J.R. Dukes and J. Remak, eds., *Another Germany: A Reconsideration of the Imperial Era*, Boulder, CO, Westview Press, 1988.

Chandler, A. *Scale and Scope: The Dynamics of Industrial Capitalism*, Cambridge, MA, Harvard University Press, 1990.

Christensen, C. and Rosenbloom, R. "Technological Discontinuities, Organizational Capabilities, and Strategic Commitments," *Industrial and Corporate Change*, 1994, pp. 655–685.

Dertouzos, M., Lester, R., and Solow, R. *Made in America*, Cambridge, MA, The MIT Press, 1989.

Henderson, R. and Clark, N. "Architectural Innovation: The Reconfiguring of Existing Technologies and the Failure of Established Firms," *Administrative Sciences Quarterly*, 1990, pp. 9–30.

Langlois, R. and Robertson, P. *Firms, Markets, and Economic Change*, New York, Routledge, 1995.

Levin, R., Klevorick, A., Nelson, R., and Winter, S. "Appropriating the Returns to Industrial R and D," *Brookings Papers on Economic Activity*, 1987, pp. 783–820.

Mueller, D. and Tilton, J. "Research and Development as Barriers to Entry," *Canadian Journal of Economics*, 1969.

Nelson, R., ed. *National Innovation Systems*, New York, Oxford University Press, 1993.

Posner, M.V. "International Trade and Technical Change," *Oxford Economic Papers*, Oct. 1961.

Ravenscraft, D.J. and Scherer, F.M. *Mergers, Selloffs, and Economic Efficiency*, Washington, D.C., Brookings Institution, 1987.

Schumpeter, J. *Capitalism, Socialism, and Democracy*, Harper, New York, 1950.

Schumpeter, J. *The Theory of Economic Development*, Cambridge, MA, Harvard University Press, 1934 (first published in 1911).

Shleifer, A. and Vishny, R.W. "Takeovers in the '60s and '80s: Evidence and Implications," *Strategic Management Journal* 12, 1991, 51–59.

Stigler, G. "The Division of Labor Is Limited by the Extent of the Market," *Journal of Political Economy*, 1951, pp. 185–193.

Tushman, M. and Anderson, D. "Technological Discontinuities and Organizational Environments," *Administrative Sciences Quarterly*, 1986.

Vernon, R. "International Investment and International Trade in the Product Cycle," *Quarterly Journal of Economics*, 1966.

Index

1812